# THE CONDUCT OF PUBLIC INQUIRIES:
## LAW, POLICY, AND PRACTICE

# The Conduct *of* Public Inquiries

*law, policy, and practice*

ED RATUSHNY

IRWIN LAW

The Conduct of Public Inquiries: Law, Policy, and Practice


Published in 2009 by

Irwin Law Inc.
14 Duncan Street
Suite 206
Toronto, ON
M5H 3G8

www.irwinlaw.com

ISBN 978-1-55221-168-7

**Library and Archives Canada Cataloguing in Publication**

Ratushny, Ed, 1942–
The conduct of public inquiries : law, policy and practice / Ed Ratushny.

Includes bibliographical references and index.
ISBN 978-1-55221-168-7

1. Governmental investigations—Canada. I. Title.

KE4765.R38 2009 342.71'066 C2009-904913-9
KF5422.R38 2009

The publisher acknowledges the financial support of the Government of Canada through the Book Publishing Industry Development Program (BPIDP) for its publishing activities.

We acknowledge the assistance of the OMDC Book Fund, an initiative of Ontario Media Development Corporation.

Printed and bound in Canada.

1 2 3 4 5 13 12 11 10 09

# *Summary Table of Contents*

# Detailed Table of Contents

# Foreword

Edward Ratushny has written an excellent book on public inquiries. The writing is crisp and clear and the research has been done thoroughly and well. His experience as a lawyer, a professor of law, and counsel in numerous inquiries qualifies him as an expert in the field.

He has reviewed the reasons for public inquiries, why they are required, how they should be organized, conducted, and eventually written. He has set out guidelines and suggestions that will be of great value to all who have anything to do with public inquiries whether as commissioner, counsel to the commissioner, parties, intervenors, or witnesses.

He has referred to many inquiries of all kinds, from those that dealt with wrongful convictions to those that dealt with broad public issues. He has rightly given high praise to the conduct of some commissioners, particularly and appropriately, to Associate Justice Dennis O'Connor for his work in the Arar and Walkerton water inquiries. He has, as well, pointed out the faults and weaknesses apparent in other inquiries.

He has given very sound advice to all who undertake inquiries. His recommendations are invaluable as he proceeds through every step of the process from the terms of reference, and the recommended discussions pertaining to those terms, from the physical set up of the facilities for the hearing, through to the need for a restrained and dignified relationship between the media, the commissioner, counsel for the commission, and all who are employed by the commission.

Anyone who has anything to do with public inquiries should read this excellent book. All, from law students to law professors, lawyers, and judges, will benefit, from the insights it provides to the sound and excellent recommendations it makes.

Besides, as a bonus, it is a delight to read.

The Honourable Peter Cory C.C., C.D.

# *Preface*

My early professional career as a lawyer and law professor was heavily concentrated in the field of criminal procedure and evidence but I also taught constitutional and administrative law. Over the years, as my emphasis shifted from criminal procedure to administrative processes, procedure in administrative law also evolved, from a rather technical set of rules to a broad principle of procedural fairness. This enhanced the opportunity in the field of administrative law for creativity in adapting processes to address practical legal problems effectively, expeditiously, and fairly. Nowhere is that opportunity greater than when conducting commissions of inquiry because each one is so unique.

As an administrative law "generalist," I have had the privilege to be retained frequently as a consultant or counsel in diverse subject areas, particularly by public institutions. These assignments often involve "fact finding" or "investigations" or "inquiries" and have included inquiries into the conduct of independent tribunal members and superior court judges. They have also involved acting as an adjudicator or arbitrator in diverse administrative hearings.

I have acted in three formal royal commissions in three different capacities: as counsel to parties, as a commissioner, and as counsel to a commissioner. The first was as general counsel to the police commissioners, chief of police, and police force in the Colter Commission of Inquiry into the Niagara Regional Police Force in 1987. The second was as a commissioner inquiring into systemic racism in the Ontario criminal justice system in 1992. Finally, I had the great honour of acting as senior counsel to the late Right Honourable Antonio Lamer in his inquiry into three unrelated murder cases in Newfoundland in 2003. This was Chief Justice Lamer's last role in an illustrious legal and judicial career, and I know that, in the midst of his failing health at the time, he felt very proud of his final contribution to the administration of justice. I have thought of him often and fondly while writing this book.

It has been a challenging, yet enjoyable, mission to try to pull together the diverse information and experience of past commissions into a coherent exposition of how commissions of inquiry should be conducted. Their reports tell many unique, important, and interesting stories. There are occasional examples of abuse of power by commissioners, such as the inquiry by Ivan Rand into the conduct of Leo Landreville. But, generally, there is an impressive record of excellent reports by many dedicated commissioners and staff.

It was difficult to make "final" revisions to this book because of so many ongoing developments in this field. But these developments tend to be "illustrations" of the underlying principles rather than changes to them. This book is current to 1 July 2009, but I am confident that the basic concepts will be valid for many years to come.

I am grateful to many people who have made it easier to complete this book. Dean Bruce Feldthusen and my colleagues at the University of Ottawa's Faculty of Law supported the six-month sabbatical leave that allowed me to conduct the bulk of the planning and research and to start writing. My long-time assistant and dear friend, Fran Russo, was hard-working and meticulous in handling the word processing. Deepali Lugani was an industrious and valuable research assistant.

Two other law school colleagues and friends for decades were eager to help. Professor Jamie Benidickson read the entire manuscript and offered many incisive observations. Professor Brad Morse provided wise guidance in the complex area of Aboriginal issues which are raised in the final chapter.

The Foundation for Legal Research provided generous funding for this project and Chairman Justice John R.R. Jennings was especially helpful. Without their assistance, this book would not have been possible in such a timely manner. It was a great pleasure to have this book published by Irwin Law. My friend and colleague, Bill Kaplan, was enthusiastic from our first conversation. President Jeffrey Miller and Vice President Alisa Posesorski joined him in providing support and accommodation throughout.

Associate Chief Justice Dennis O'Connor was extremely generous in reading the entire first draft and providing valuable comments. His own role as a commissioner in the Walkerton and Arar inquiries provided important material for the content of this book through his approach, rulings, reports, and personal example. Quite apart from all of the advice in this book, the best way to ensure a successful commission of inquiry would be to appoint Dennis O'Connor as the commissioner.

The Honourable Peter Cory was magnanimous in agreeing immediately to provide the Foreword. In his typically diligent and industrious manner, he read the entire manuscript before doing so. He has written the two most important judgments of the Supreme Court of Canada related to commissions of inquiry arising out of the Krever and Westray Inquiries. He acted as commissioner in the valuable inquiry into the wrongful conviction of Thomas Sophonow. He demonstrated integrity and courage in standing up to the British government following his investigation into the role of British and Irish security forces in eight murders. Peter Cory is a shining model for every lawyer and judge, a great Canadian, and a wonderful friend.

Writing is sometimes described as a lonely pursuit but I was never lonely through the long days and months when writing this book. It was pleasant to do all of the writing in my home office, accompanied by pride and peace of mind at seeing our children, Kim and Dan, pursue their own legal careers with such success and enjoyment. I also was accompanied frequently by pleasant thoughts and memories of our son, Greg, who is never far away. Finally, I have been blessed daily, as I have been for decades, by the support and wisdom of my wonderful wife, Lynn.

# *Table of Authorizing Statutes*

| *Chosen Name* | *Formal Name* | *Website* |
|---|---|---|
| Inquiries Act | *Inquiries Act*, R.S.C. 1985, c. I-11 | www.canlii.org/en/ca/laws/stat/rsc-1985-c-i-11/latest/rsc-1985-c-i-11.html |
| Alberta Act | *Public Inquiries Act*, R.S.A. 2000, c. P-39 | www.canlii.org/en/ab/laws/stat/rsa-2000-c-p-39/latest/rsa-2000-c-p-39.html |
| British Columbia Act | *Public Inquiry Act*, S.B.C. 2007, c. 9 | www.canlii.org/en/bc/laws/stat/sbc-2007-c-9/latest/sbc-2007-c-9.html |
| Manitoba Act | *Manitoba Evidence Act*, (Part V) C.C.S.M. c. E150 | www.canlii.org/mb/laws/sta/e-150/20090324/part1.html |
| New Brunswick Act | *Inquiries Act*, R.S.N.B. 1973, c. I-11 | www.canlii.org/nb/laws/sta/i-11/20090324/whole.html<br>www.canlii.org/nb/laws/regu/1983r.167/20090324/whole.html<br>www.canlii.org/nb/laws/regu/1984r.96/20090324/whole.html |
| Newfoundland and Labrador Act | *Public Inquiries Act*, 2006, S.N.L. 2006, c. P-38.1 | www.canlii.org/nl/laws/sta/p-38.1/20090324/whole.html |
| Nova Scotia Act | *Public Inquiries Act*, R.S.N.S. 1989, c. 372 | www.gov.ns.ca/legislature/legc/statutes/pubinqur.htm<br>www.canlii.org/en/ns/laws/stat/rsns-1989-c-372/latest/rsns-1989-c-372.html |
| Ontario Act | *Public Inquiries Act*, R.S.O. 1990, c. P.41 | www.canlii.org/en/on/laws/stat/rso-1990-c-p41/latest/rso-1990-c-p41.html |

| *Chosen Name* | *Formal Name* | *Website* |
|---|---|---|
| Prince Edward Island Act | *Public Inquiries Act*, R.S.P.E.I. 1988, c. P-31 | www.canlii.org/pe/laws/sta/p-31/20090324/whole.html |
| Quebec Act | *An Act respecting Public Inquiry Commissions*, R.S.Q. c. C-37 | www.canlii.org/en/qc/laws/stat/rsq-c-c-37/latest/rsq-c-c-37.html |
| Saskatchewan Act | *Public Inquiries Act*, R.S.S. 1978, c. P-38 | www.canlii.org/en/sk/laws/stat/rss-1978-c-p-38/latest/rss-1978-c-p-38.html |
| Northwest Territories Act | *Public Inquiries Act*, R.S.N.W.T. 1988, c. P-14 | www.canlii.org/nt/laws/sta/p-14/20090324/whole.html |
| Nunavut Act | *Public Inquiries Act*, R.S.N.W.T. 1988, c. P-14 | www.canlii.org/nu/laws/sta/p-14/index.html |
| Yukon Act | *Public Inquiries Act*, R.S.Y. 2002, c. 177 | www.gov.yk.ca/legislation/acts/puin.pdf |

# Table of Past Commissions of Inquiry

| *Chosen Name* | *Formal Name* | *Reference to the Report* | *Website* |
|---|---|---|---|
| Abella Commission | The Royal Commission on Equality in Employment | Ottawa: Minister of Supply and Services, 1984 | Not available online |
| Aboriginal Peoples Commission | Report of the Royal Commission on Aboriginal People | Ottawa: The Commission, 1996 | www.ainc-inac.gc.ca/ap/rrc-eng.asp |
| Air India Inquiry | Commission of Inquiry into the Investigation of the Bombing of Air India Flight 182 | Ottawa: Minister of Public Works and Government Services, 2008 | www.majorcomm.ca |
| Arar Inquiry | Commission of Inquiry into the Actions of Canadian Officials in Relation to Maher Arar | Ottawa: Minister of Public Works and Government Services, 2006 | http://epe.lac-bac.gc.ca/100/206/301/pco-bcp/commissions/maher_arar/07-09-13/ www.ararcommission.ca/default.htm |
| Baird Commission | Royal Commission on New Reproductive Technologies | Ottawa: The Commission, 1993 | http://epe.lac-bac.gc.ca/100/200/301/pco-bcp/commissions-ef/baird1993 |
| Canadian Judicial Council | Canadian Judicial Council | | www.cjc-ccm.gc.ca |
| Cornwall Inquiry | The Cornwall Public Inquiry | Report not yet released | www.cornwallinquiry.ca |

| *Chosen Name* | *Formal Name* | *Reference to the Report* | *Website* |
|---|---|---|---|
| Driskell Inquiry | Commission of Inquiry into Certain Aspects of the Trial and Conviction of James Driskell | Winnipeg: The Commission, 2007 | www.driskellinquiry.ca |
| Gomery Inquiry | Commission of Inquiry into the Sponsorship Program and Advertising Activities | Ottawa: Minister of Public Works and Government Services, 2005<br>Ottawa: Minister of Public Works and Government Services, 2006 | Report Phase 1: Who is Responsible?: http://epe.lac-bac.gc.ca/100/206/301/pco-bcp/commissions/sponsorship-ef/06-03-06/www.gomery.ca/en/phase1report/index.asp<br>Report Phase 2: Restoring Accountability: http://epe.lac-bac.gc.ca/100/206/301/pco-bcp/commissions/sponsorship-ef/06-03-06/www.gomery.ca/en/phase2report/index.asp |
| Gordon Commission | Royal Commission on Canada's Economic Prospects | Ottawa: Queen's Printer, 1957 | Not available online |
| Goudge Inquiry | Inquiry into Pediatric Forensic Pathology in Ontario | Toronto: Ministry of the Attorney General | www.goudgeinquiry.ca |
| Grange Inquiry | Royal Commission of Inquiry into Certain Deaths at the Hospital for Sick Children and Related Matters | Toronto: Ontario Ministry of the Attorney General, 1984 | Not available online |
| Hall Commission | Royal Commission on Health Services | Ottawa: R. Duhamel, Queen's Printer, 1964: Volume I; 1965: Volume II | Not available online |

| *Chosen Name* | *Formal Name* | *Reference to the Report* | *Website* |
| --- | --- | --- | --- |
| Hall Commission #2 | Health Services Review (1979–80) | Ottawa: Department of National Health and Welfare, 1980 | Not available online<br>Report titled: Canada's National-Provincial Health Program for the 1980's: A Commitment for Renewal |
| Iacobucci Inquiry | Internal Inquiry into the Actions of Canadian Officials in Relation to Abdullah Almalki, Ahmad Abou-Elmaati and Muayyed Nureddin | Ottawa: The Inquiry, 2008 | www.iacobucciinquiry.ca |
| Ipperwash Inquiry | The Ipperwash Inquiry | Toronto: Ministry of the Attorney General, 2007 | www.ipperwashinquiry.ca |
| North Battleford Inquiry | North Battleford Water Inquiry | Regina: The Commission, 2002 | www.northbattlefordwaterinquiry.ca |
| Lamer Inquiry | The Lamer Commission of Inquiry pertaining to the Cases of Ronald Dalton, Gregory Parsons & Randy Druken | St. John's: Government of Newfoundland and Labrador, 2006 | www.justice.gov.nl.ca/just/lamer |
| Landreville Inquiry | Commission to Inquire into the Dealings of the Honourable Mr. Justice Leo A. Landreville with Northern Ontario Natural Gas Limited | Ottawa: Queen's Printer, 1966 | Not available online |

| *Chosen Name* | *Formal Name* | *Reference to the Report* | *Website* |
|---|---|---|---|
| Laurendeau-Dunton Commission | The Royal Commission on Bilingualism and Biculturalism | Ottawa: Queen's Printer, 1967 | Not available online<br>Unofficial Links: Laurendeau-Dunton, Forty Years Later: www.ocol-clo.gc.ca/html/speeches_discours_29032007_e.php<br>CBC coverage: http://archives.cbc.ca/politics/language_culture/topics/655 |
| Le Dain Commission | Commission of Inquiry into the Non-Medical Use of Drugs | Ottawa: Information Canada, 1972 | Unofficial link to the report: www.druglibrary.org/schaffer/library/studies/ledain/ldctoc.html |
| Lord Durham's Report | Report of Lord Durham on the Affairs of British North America | London: Spectator: 1839 | http://faculty.marianopolis.edu/c.belanger/quebechistory/docs/durham |
| Macdonald Commission | Royal Commission on the Economic Union and Development Prospects for Canada | Ottawa: The Commission, 1985 | http://epe.lac-bac.gc.ca/100/200/301/pco-bcp/commissions-ef/mcdonald1985-eng/mcdonald1985-eng.htm |
| Marshall Inquiry | Royal Commission on the Donald Marshall Jr. Prosecution | Halifax: The Commission, 1989 | Not available online |
| Massey-Levesque Commission | The Royal Commission on National Development in the Arts, Letters and Sciences | Ottawa: King's Printer, 1951 | www.collectionscanada.gc.ca/massey/h5-302-e.html |
| McDonald Inquiry | Commission of Inquiry concerning Certain Activities of the Royal Canadian Mounted Police | Ottawa: Minister of Supply and Service Canada | First Report: Security and Information (1979) http://epe.lac-bac.gc.ca/100/200/301/pco-bcp/commissions-ef/mcdonald1979-81-eng/mcdonald1979-81-eng.htm |

| *Chosen Name* | *Formal Name* | *Reference to the Report* | *Website* |
| --- | --- | --- | --- |
| McDonald Inquiry cont'd | | | Second Report: Freedom and Security under the Law (1981): http://epe.lac-bac.gc.ca/100/200/301/pco-bcp/commissions-ef/mcdonald1979-81-eng/mcdonald1979-81-eng.htm<br>Third Report: Certain R.C.M.P. Activities and the Question of Governmental Knowledge (1981): http://epe.lac-bac. |
| Milgaard Inquiry | Commission of Inquiry into the Wrongful Conviction of David Milgaard | Saskatoon: The Commission, 2008 | www.milgaardinquiry.ca |
| Morin Inquiry | Kaufman Commission on Proceedings involving Guy Paul Morin | Toronto: The Commission, 1998 | www.attorneygeneral.jus.gov.on.ca/english/about/pubs/morin/ |
| Mulroney-Schreiber Inquiry | Commission of Inquiry into Certain Allegations respecting Business and Financial Dealings between Karlheinz Schreiber and the Right Honourable Brian Mulroney | Report not yet released | www.oliphantcommission.ca |
| RCMP Public Complaints Commission | Commission for Public Complaints against the RCMP | | www.cpc-cpp.gc.ca |

| *Chosen Name* | *Formal Name* | *Reference to the Report* | *Website* |
|---|---|---|---|
| Romanow Commission | Commission on the Future of Health Care in Canada | Saskatoon: The Commission, 2002 | www.hc-sc.gc.ca/hcs-sss/hhr-rhs/strateg/romanow-eng.php |
| Rowell-Sirois Commission | Royal Commission on Dominion-Provincial Relations | Ottawa: J.O. Patenaude, Printer to the King, 1940 | Not available online |
| Somalia Inquiry | Commission of Inquiry into the Deployment of Canadian Forces to Somalia | Ottawa: The Commission, 1997 | www.dnd.ca/somalia/somaliae.htm |
| Sophonow Inquiry | The Inquiry regarding Thomas Sophonow | Winnipeg: Manitoba Justice, 2001 | www.gov.mb.ca/justice/publications/sophonow/index.html? |
| Stevens Inquiry | Commission of Inquiry into the Facts of Allegations of Conflict of Interest concerning the Honourable Sinclair M. Stevens | Ottawa: Minister of Supply and Services Canada, 1987 | Not available online |
| Stonechild Inquiry | Commission of Inquiry Into Matters relating to the Death of Neil Stonechild | Regina: The Commission, 2004 | www.stonchildinquiry.ca |
| Systemic Racism Commission | Commission on Systemic Racism in the Ontario Criminal Justice System | Toronto: The Commission, 1995 | Not available online |
| Taman Inquiry | Taman Inquiry into the Investigation and Prosecution of Derek Harvey-Zenk | Winnipeg: The Inquiry, 2008 | www.tamaninquiry.ca |

| *Chosen Name* | *Formal Name* | *Reference to the Report* | *Website* |
|---|---|---|---|
| Toronto Leasing Inquiry | Toronto Computer Leasing Inquiry/Toronto External Contracts Inquiry | Toronto: City of Toronto, 2005 | www.toronto.ca/inquiry/inquiry_site/index-home.html |
| Walkerton Inquiry | Walkerton Commission of Inquiry | Toronto: Ontario Ministry of the Attorney General, 2002 | www.attorneygeneral.jus.gov.on.ca/english/about/pubs/walkerton |
| Westray Inquiry | Commission of Inquiry into the Westray Mine Tragedy | Halifax: The Inquiry, 1987 | www.gov.ns.ca/lwd/pubs/westray |

*". . . launching a commission of inquiry is a risky process—a bit like sending a ship out to sea. You don't know where it will go, how long it will take, how much it will cost or what it will bring back. And trying to relocate a ship lost at sea and bring it back to port can be a costly experience (especially if the captain is not in a hurry to come home)."*

IPAC, *Commissions of Inquiry in Canada: Lessons Learned from Recent Experience*, Peter Larson Associates, Quoted at page 130

CHAPTER ONE

# Introduction

## A. RELATIONSHIP TO ADMINISTRATIVE LAW

At the first legal conference on public inquiries in Canada, one of the presenters commented: "The actual diversity of inquiries may pre-empt any systematic conceptualization of inquiry procedure . . . In the final analysis, the problem is that inquiries have different functions and goals and are created for numerous and diverse reasons."[1] But this is true, generally, of administrative law. There are literally thousands of administrative bodies operating in Canada today, described variously as "tribunals," "agencies," "boards," "commissions," and "committees," which were created for diverse reasons and which perform diverse functions. Some Crown corporations also have regulatory functions and occasionally public servants are given some independent decision-making powers.[2] They encompass subject areas such as the environment, energy, transportation, communications, labour, human rights, immigration and refugee status, the military, and many more.

---

1 Patrick Robardet, "Should We Abandon the Adversarial Model in Favour of the Inquisitorial Model in Commission of Inquiry?" in A.P. Pross, I. Christie, & J.A. Yogis, eds., *Commissions of Inquiry* (Toronto: Carswell, 1990) at 129–30.

2 Canadian Bar Association Task Force on the Independence of Federal Administrative Tribunals and Agencies in Canada, *The Independence of Federal Administrative Tribunals and Agencies in Canada* (Ottawa: Canadian Bar Association, 1990) at 4–5.

The roles and functions of such administrative bodies are at least as diverse as those of the commissions of inquiry that have been established in Canada. In fact, these commissions are simply one *genre* of administrative tribunals. Their most unique feature is that they are established for a specific purpose—to investigate and report—and then cease to exist once that purpose has been achieved. But, similar to all administrative bodies, they are legally bound by the statute under which they are created as well as by the principles of administrative law.

Unlike the author quoted above, and others, I do not view the diversity of commissions or any other administrative bodies as a "problem." To the contrary, that diversity is a great strength and is reflected in the flexibility of procedures authorized by administrative law. Such procedures are now expressed as conforming to a broad "principle" rather than as "rules." The principle is simply fairness. This permits administrative bodies to be flexible and creative in selecting procedures that will facilitate expeditious proceedings while still ensuring fair treatment to individuals who may be adversely affected by those proceedings.

Take this simple example of a procedure adopted by the National Energy Board, many decades ago, for conducting hearings involving complex technical and scientific evidence. The normal court and tribunal process at that time was to call each expert individually as a witness and have the evidence adduced orally, then to subject each witness to cross-examination following examination-in-chief. The board established a procedure whereby the testimony of each expert would be reduced to writing and distributed to all parties in advance of the hearing. The evidence would not have to be repeated orally. The experts would then be made available, often together as a "panel," for questioning by the parties. Such questioning did not require that each expert be fully questioned separately but allowed questioners to move from one to another in a flexible manner. This process was a great improvement over the previous practice by saving time, increasing accuracy, and facilitating the assessment of complex evidence.

The same approach is now used regularly at a variety of hearings including those of commissions of inquiry. Indeed, in the "policy" phases of inquiries where individual conduct is not in question, commissioners have utilized "seminars," "roundtables," and even "town hall meetings." The flexible administrative law principle of fairness requires that, when the hearings have greater potential to affect the rights, interests, and reputations of individuals, the procedural protections must also be greater. Where the purpose is entirely about policy and participation, there is no need to remain in the traditional hearing room.

This flexibility is reflected in A.W. MacKay's observation: "The balance between the rights of the individuals involved and the need for flexible procedures for articulating public policy must be struck anew in each particular case. Accepting that there are few universal rules for the operation of commissions of inquiry would go a long way . . . "[3] Denis Lemieux echoes this observation: "While courts, tribunals, legislative bodies and public authorities generally function within a framework of rules, there are relatively few rules applying to commissions of inquiry."[4] Another scholar, Bryan Schwartz, goes further: "At trials, strict rules of evidence exclude unreliable sources of information, such as hearsay, speculation, or opinion evidence by non-experts. At public inquiries, witnesses are relatively free to trash the reputation of others in front of a large television audience."[5] This is not an accurate description of how inquiries should be conducted. Before commissions of inquiry, the principle of fairness should address all of the concerns raised by these and other rules of evidence. In a properly conducted inquiry, witnesses should never be "relatively free to trash the reputation of others." While the practices adopted by these commissions are not subject to rigid "rules," they must be fair. Any abuse of witnesses or denial of other procedural protections must be attributed not to the inherent nature of commissions of inquiry but to how they are conducted.

And, in fact, there are many overarching rules that must be respected when conducting such inquiries. For example, there are the statutory requirements in the federal *Inquiries Act*[6] itself. There are constitutional constraints arising out of the federal-provincial distribution of powers, the *Canadian Charter of Rights and Freedoms*, and the *Canadian Bill of Rights*. Additional legal issues also arise, for example, from the laws re-

---

3 A. Wayne Mackay, "Mandates, Legal Foundations, Powers and Conduct of Commissions of Inquiry" in Pross, Christie, & and Yogis, eds., above note 1 at 47.

4 Denis Lemieux, "Securing Accountability through Commissions of Inquiry, Commentary" in Allan Manson & David Mullan, eds., *Commissions of Inquiry, Praise or Reappraise?* (Toronto: Irwin Law, 2003) at 150.

5 Bryan Schwartz, "Public Inquiries," in Manson & Mullan, eds., *ibid.* at 455.

6 R.S.C. 1985, c. I-11. There is comparable "framework" legislation in each of the provinces and territories, discussed in Chapter 7, Section B.

lated to privilege. There is a considerable body of judicial precedents specifically addressing the proper scope and conduct of commissions of inquiry. The mandatory requirement of the administrative law principle of fairness, itself, continues to evolve to meet new situations.

In addition to these legal requirements, there are many "practices" that have been adopted by past commissions. Some of them provide useful guidance for future commissions. Occasionally, they also reveal mistakes to be avoided. These have been selected here on an *ad hoc* basis since it has not been possible to conduct a comprehensive examination of all of the myriad reports and rulings of the many commissions established by both federal and provincial governments. But the ones identified should assist in the conduct of future inquiries.

## B. DEARTH OF LITERATURE

Numerous observations have been made about the dearth of literature on commissions of inquiry in Canada. For example: "Given how frequently they are commissioned, it is surprising how little has been written about public inquiries . . . . The lack of serious attention paid to inquiries may be a product of their diversity . . . . Grouping such different objectives and activities under a single category—namely, inquiries—is intrinsically difficult."[7] That said, a valuable contribution to the literature has been made by the publication of the proceedings of three conferences held at three Canadian law schools over the past two decades. The Dalhousie University Conference[8] was described by its hosts as exploring the conflict between "lawyers' values and policy makers' values." The publication of its proceedings consists of a series of chapters by different authors. A few involve analysis by academic writers while most relate personal experiences and opinions arising out of service as commissioners, commission counsel, administrators, or researchers. The University of New Brunswick Conference[9] tended to focus on the relationship of inquiries to the criminal process and the related rights of individuals.

---

7 Liora Salter, "The Two Contradictions in Public Inquiries" in Pross, Christie, & Yogis, eds., above note 1 at 173. See also Mackay, above note 3 at 30.

8 Published in Pross, Christie, & Yogis, eds., *ibid.*

9 Published in (1994) 43 U.N.B.L.J. 379–434.

The Queen's University Conference[10] covered a much broader range of issues and included international perspectives from England, Australia, and New Zealand. I refer frequently to the valuable information found in this conference's proceedings, though the publication is a series of only casually related articles.

Another helpful publication is *A Handbook on the Conduct of Public Inquiries in Canada*. This work was largely informed by the experience of the authors in relation to the Mackenzie Valley Pipeline Commission. The authors state in their Preface: "We have tended to concentrate on information-gathering and project type inquiries, as opposed to inquiries established to investigate suspected wrong-doing."[11] In contrast, it is the latter focus that is the emphasis of this book, although the starting point is usually "what went wrong" rather than "who is guilty of misconduct?" Also, most "investigative" commissions have a "systemic" or "policy" component as well.

In addition to these publications, the reports on public inquiries by the Canada, Ontario, and Alberta law reform commissions[12] contain useful background information, although they are focused on law reform. The remaining legal literature consists of a limited range of articles often restricted to a particular narrow theme rather than the intrinsic nature of public inquiries and the manner in which they should conduct their proceedings. I have been informed by all of these sources and cite them in the pages that follow. (Citations are not given where comments are repeated in a variety of publications and are accepted as general knowledge.)

In its final report on commissions of inquiry, the Canada Law Reform Commission made three recommendations. The first was to enact a new statute to replace the *Inquiries Act*. The third recommendation was that caution be exercised in granting powers of inquiry in other statutes.

---

10 Manson & Mullan, above note 4.

11 Russell J. Anthony & Alastair R. Lucas (Toronto: Butterworths, 1985) at v.

12 Law Reform Commission of Canada, *Administrative Law: Commissions of Inquiry*, Working Paper No. 17 (Ottawa: The Commission, 1977) and *Report on Advisory and Investigatory Commissions* (Ottawa: The Commission, 1979); Ontario Law Reform Commission, *Report on Public Inquiries* (Toronto: The Commission, 1992); Alberta Law Reform Institute, *Public Inquiries*, Issues Paper No. 3 (Edmonton: The Institute, 1991) and *Proposals for the Reform of the* Public Inquiries Act (Edmonton: The Institute, 1992).

Neither has been adopted. The second recommendation was "that a manual be prepared to provide guidelines for commissioners respecting administrative, legal and other matters."[13] The report refers to the commission's earlier Working Paper for an indication of what the contents of such a guide might be,[14] including:

- the law that governs commissions including the *Inquiries Act* and elaboration on its provisions and relevant judicial precedents;
- unofficial guidance culled from the experience of previous commissions as to how difficult situations might be handled, including procedures and precedents;
- suggestions as to the structures and "various stages" of an inquiry;
- advice about administration: finances, budget, staff, expediting translation, and publication; and
- the reporting of evidence (and findings).

No such manual has been produced either, but this book should at least fill that need.

To return to the first sentence of this chapter, my challenge has been to provide "a conceptualization of inquiry procedure" encompassing rather than being pre-empted by the broad diversity of public inquiries. I hope I have done so in a sufficiently comprehensive and integrated manner to contribute to a better understanding and working of this important Canadian legal institution.

## C. ORGANIZATION OF CHAPTERS

The next chapter commences with some historical background that traces the origins and development of commissions of inquiry in England. The purposes they fulfil are discussed and their role as an institution within the machinery of government is analyzed. Some assessment is made of their contributions. There is a brief overview of their legal nature, including their "jurisdiction" as established by the constitution, the statute and their diverse terms of reference. Inquiries authorized by other statutes and in other jurisdictions are mentioned together with

---

13 *Report on Advisory and Investigatory Commissions*, *ibid.* at 9–10.

14 *Administrative Law: Commissions of Inquiry*, Working Paper No. 17, above note 12 at 60–61.

proposals to amend the *Inquiries Act* and corresponding legislation in Ontario and Alberta.

Chapter 3 canvasses a few selected commissions in each of five broad categories. These are commissions that: (1) investigate events and related conduct; (2) provide public policy recommendations; (3) investigate the specific event of a wrongful criminal conviction; (4) involve the investigation of criminal conduct; and (5) carry out ongoing inquiries according to a more specific statutory mandate. This survey should give the reader an overview of how our commissions of inquiry have been deployed in the past. It will also demonstrate some interesting features of each and how some have been important "players" in events that helped to shape aspects of Canadian society. They provide a context for the analysis in subsequent chapters.

Chapter 4 focuses on the decision to establish a commission of inquiry. What is the basic problem that is of crucial concern? Are other institutional responses adequate, such as criminal investigation or the political forum, including legislative committees? Why does a commission of inquiry generate greater public confidence than alternative processes? What other *ad hoc* alternatives could be invoked? The importance of the content and scope of a commission's terms of reference is emphasized as well as the choice of commissioner (or panel of commissioners). The availability of sitting judges as commissioners has changed in recent years and raises perennial issues that are discussed.

Chapter 5 explores the role of a commissioner. Unlike the passive role of a judge in our adversarial trial system, the commissioner's responsibility is to "inquire" actively into the issues as well as to "manage" the business of a commission. At the same time, public confidence in the inquiry process demands that a commissioner maintain a stature of independence and impartiality. The implications of this responsibility are explored, with recent graphic examples of the pitfalls to be avoided.

Chapter 6 analyzes the role of legal counsel and, especially, counsel to the commissioner. The impartiality of the commissioner may be adversely affected if commission counsel assumes an adversarial role. Yet it may be essential that counsel be aggressive in cross-examining parties and other witnesses in order to test the reliability of their testimony. Suggestions are made as to how this dilemma may be resolved in a manner that enhances rather than detracts from the impartiality of a commissioner. The role of the counsel to parties with standing is also discussed.

Chapter 7 draws together the legal framework of commissions of inquiry. Legal issues are discussed throughout in the various contexts in which they arise. In this chapter, their underlying legal character is described: constitutional; statutory; subordinate legislation; common law; policy. The relationship of commissions of inquiry to "parallel" legal proceedings is assessed together with interim judicial review which may enforce their legal boundaries.

Chapter 8 addresses the "nitty gritty" of conducting hearings in a manner that is effective as well as fair. Specific rules of evidence are examined under the light of the principle of fairness. A wide range of practical legal problems are addressed, such as compelling testimony, contempt, privilege, bias, interim judicial review, *in camera* hearings, and publication bans.

Chapter 9 deals with the final report on findings arising out of those hearings, including findings of misconduct and the delicate line forbidding findings of criminal or civil liability. The nature of "misconduct" and the standard of proof to be applied are examined. The procedural requirements of providing "notice" and adequate opportunities to respond are analyzed. Findings of "cultural" or other systemic misconduct are explored together with the dangers of imposing "hindsight" on the assessment of conduct. This discussion of the final report and its recommendations includes conflicts between the government and commissioners as to what should be made public or withheld. Examples are provided of successful judicial review to declare findings of some reports to be invalid.

Chapter 10 focuses on commissions with a policy/advisory mandate that engages broader consultation, research, expert opinion, and public participation. Investigative commissions may also have a policy or "systemic" component that is normally addressed in a separate "phase" of its hearings but these are usually related to the problems identified in the investigative stage. This chapter culminates in a brief discussion of the important Aboriginal Peoples Commission and the book ends with an introduction to "truth and reconciliation" commissions in the light of recent Canadian experience.

The organization of these various chapters has tried to be "user-friendly" to readers. This has resulted in the same subjects recurring in different places, but to varying degrees and for different purposes. For example, it was not possible to talk about the "nature" of commissions of inquiry in Chapter 2 without at least an overview of their "legal" nature. This necessarily includes their statutory basis in the *Inquiries Act*. But more detailed analysis of the legislation and general legal framework is left for Chapter 7. Specific provisions of the legislation are introduced and discussed throughout under the specific headings to which they are most relevant. For example, section 13 of the Act is analyzed in greater detail in Chapter 9, in the context of findings of misconduct, because of the central importance of these findings to the final report. Similarly, the same commission of inquiry is often referred to in different chapters to illustrate issues related to the subject of each of those chapters.

But, generally, the first three chapters are an introduction to the world of commissions of inquiry, including a broad overview of the work of a considerable number of them. The next three chapters move to an analysis of when and how they are established and the roles of the commissioner, legal counsel, and the parties. The next three chapters address the general legal framework, practical problems in conducting hearings in a fair and expeditious manner, and then the process of making findings and reporting. The last chapter discusses the much broader approach of policy/advisory commissions.

## D. AUTHORIZING STATUTES AND PAST COMMISSIONS

The *Inquiries Act* provides the framework legislation for establishing commissions of inquiry at the federal level. There is comparable legislation in each province and territory, but the content and names of the statutes vary. Some are called the "public inquiries act," Quebec uses "public inquiries commissions," and in Manitoba the relevant provisions are contained in the *Manitoba Evidence Act*. Rather than repeatedly citing these authorizing statutes, the Canadian statute is referred to as the *Inquiries Act* and the others are simply referred to as the Alberta Act, the Quebec Act, the Yukon Act, and so on. The Table of Authorizing Statutes, at the front of this book, contains a list of all of these statutes with their chosen names, legal names, and legal citations.

In view of the voluminous references to specific commissions of inquiry, I have used popular names for them rather than their longer formal names. For example, the "Commission of Inquiry into the Sponsorship Program and Advertising Activities" is simply called the Gomery Inquiry. The "Commission of Inquiry into the Investigation of the Bombing of Air India Flight 182" is simply the Air India Inquiry. These are not documented in the footnotes either. Instead, the Table of Past Commissions of Inquiry, at the front of this book, contains a list of these commissions of inquiry, with the following information for each of them:

- the popular name chosen;
- the corresponding formal name;
- the documentary reference to the commission's report; and
- the address for the commission's website, if one exists.

Where websites do not exist, some reports are still otherwise available electronically and, if so, these references are also provided.

Where available, the commission websites are particularly helpful in containing much more than the final report. They may contain a list of the witnesses heard and the schedule of hearings, rules of procedure, rulings made by the commissioner, actual transcripts of evidence, written submissions of the parties, and more. The headings and subheadings of the reports often make it easy to go directly to the source for matters discussed in this book.

CHAPTER TWO

# *Nature and Purpose of Commissions of Inquiry*

## A. BACKGROUND

A commission of inquiry is here defined as a body created by a government under Part I of the *Inquiries Act*[1] or the corresponding provincial or territorial legislation. Its purpose is to make inquiries and report to the government its findings and any related recommendations. The subject of its inquiries and report are established by the government and described in its terms of reference. It has powers to carry out its inquiries by requiring persons to testify before the commission and to produce any relevant documents. It may only report and recommend. It cannot adjudicate disputes or determine rights.

However, in making its report and recommendations, a commission of inquiry may comment on the conduct of persons in a way that could adversely affect their reputations or other interests. When doing so, it is legally bound to treat such persons fairly. The legal principle of fairness establishes standards for such treatment. After a commission makes its report, it ceases to exist.

The first commissions of inquiry were royal commissions established by British monarchs to assist them in governing: "The source of royal

1 The comparable Acts in other jurisdictions are discussed in Chapter 7, Section B. Commissions established by a minister, as opposed to a government, are also discussed there.

commissions is to be found in the generally assumed right of the Crown to appoint officials to perform duties temporarily or permanently on behalf of the King."[2] Such duties could encompass judicial and administrative responsibilities as well as investigation. Thomas Lockwood describes the investigation that occurred between 1080 and 1086, and that resulted in the completion of the Domesday Book, as being the work of the first royal commissioners: "This awesome investigation resulted in the compilation of a mass of information respecting landholding, cultivation and population of the manors throughout England shortly after the Conquest."[3] Royal commissions became "an established feature of English administration" and represented the expanding jurisdiction of the king. As such, they were a target of efforts to curb the king's powers that began with the *Magna Carta* and continued with the subsequent rise of Parliament.

Parallel events were occurring in relation to the development of a criminal process to try criminal offences.[4] The earliest stages involved an "accusatory system" where a specific wrong had to be identified before a person could be found guilty. However, the Fourth Lateran Council, which abolished trial by ordeal in 1215, also established an inquisitorial process allowing the "judge" to compel any person to testify. At first, the requirement of an "accusation" was respected but judges began to receive accusations in secret and then to initiate inquisitions on their own "suspicions." This arbitrary power soon came to be used as a weapon of religious and political suppression. The consequences were particularly harsh when the vague offence of "heresy" was charged and the punishment involved execution by burning. The process allowed a person to be compelled to testify, cross-examined about his or her religious beliefs, and then told that these beliefs constituted heresy. A refusal to testify could, itself, be subject to punishment by the "rack."

These powers were adopted from the ecclesiastical courts by the hybrid Court of High Commission and then by the Court of Star Chamber, composed of the Privy Council sitting judicially together with the chief

---

2 Thomas J. Lockwood, "A History of Royal Commissions" (1967) 5 Osgoode Hall L.J. 172 at 179.

3 *Ibid.* at 180.

4 Ed Ratushny, *Self-Incrimination in the Canadian Criminal Process* (Toronto: Carswell, 1979) at 159–74.

justices of the common law courts. In 1641, after Parliament had gained supremacy, these courts were abolished. However, to this day, the term "Star Chamber" describes a process whereby individuals may be unfairly tarnished by some form of guilt through a process that is unfair. Such a process emerged again in the United States during the 1950s in the form of the hearings of the House Committee on Un-American Activities chaired by Senator Joe McCarthy: "The McCarthy hearings, as they came to be known, developed into a zealous 'witch-hunt' for present and past associations with communism, however tenuous those associations might have been. The process involved the pathetic spectacle of individuals who had committed no criminal offenses, being tarred in full public view, sometimes with serious consequences to their careers."[5] Although witnesses could refuse to testify under the Fifth Amendment of the US Constitution, to do so amounted to an admission of guilt in the public eye.

It has been said that "after the Revolution of 1688 the political centre of gravity moved from the Crown to Parliament; thus the legal base for Royal Commissions was removed and they fell into decay and insignificance for over one hundred years."[6] Yet, while "royal" commissions fell into disuse, legislative inquiries multiplied. Hundreds of select committees of Parliament were established to inquire into a wide range of subjects that might have been performed by royal commissions. But the Crown's right to appoint such commissions was never abolished and they were rediscovered by the government in the nineteenth century in the context of: limitations on the expertise of parliamentary committees; a public service that was only in its infancy; the consolidation of political power in the executive branch of government (the Cabinet); and the explosion of social legislation.

A number of British royal commissions during the nineteenth century pertained directly to Canada. Perhaps the most important of these was the appointment of Lord Durham as both governor and royal commissioner in 1840 following the rebellions in Upper and Lower Canada in 1837–38. His report led to the passage of the *Act of Union* which established a single province of Canada with equal representation from Upper and Lower Canada. Although it was insensitive to the rights and

---

5 *Ibid.* at 5–6.

6 Lockwood, above note 2 at 181.

aspirations of French Canadians, Lord Durham's report as a royal commissioner was an important step in the evolution of Canada as a nation. Following the *Act of Union*, the Parliament of Canada made frequent use of royal commissions in diverse subject areas which "laid the groundwork" for Confederation in 1867.[7]

The Law Reform Commission of Canada reported in 1979 that "there have been about 400 inquiries" established by the government (Cabinet) under section 2 of the *Inquiries Act* with respect to the "good government" or "public business" of Canada. In addition, there were "close to 1,500 departmental investigations" appointed by ministers under section 6 related to the business of their departments.[8] The Law Reform Commission of Ontario reported that, to 1984, 189 inquiries had reported in that province. All of these were appointed by the Cabinet since the Ontario Act does not provide for "departmental" inquiries.[9]

The Law Reform Commission of Canada emphasized the distinction between commissions that primarily advise and those that primarily investigate:

> Broadly speaking, commissions of inquiry are of two types. There are those that advise. They address themselves to a broad issue of policy and gather information relevant to that issue. And there are those that investigate. They address themselves primarily to the facts of a particular alleged problem, generally a problem associated with the functioning of government. Many inquiries both advise and investigate . . . . But almost every inquiry primarily either advises or investigates.[10]

This distinction is helpful for descriptive purposes but it is important to keep in mind that it describes different "functions" rather than "institutions." It is the same institution, established under the *Inquiries Act*, that may be given the function of investigating or of advising or some combination of both functions. A commission that primarily investigates may implicitly "advise" through fact finding that will suggest possible

---

7 *Ibid.* at 190.

8 Law Reform Commission of Canada, *Report on Advisory and Investigatory Commissions* (Ottawa: The Commission, 1979) at 1.

9 Law Reform Commission of Ontario, *Report on Public Inquiries* (Toronto: The Commission, 1992) at 7.

10 Law Reform Commission of Canada, *Administrative Law: Commissions of Inquiry*, Working Paper No. 17 (Ottawa: The Commission, 1977) at 13.

action to be taken. A commission that primarily advises must also establish the basis for its advice, perhaps through "social fact" investigation. Investigations into specific events may reveal "systemic" problems that invite a reconsideration of broader policies. Frequently, the terms of reference will specifically mandate commissions to conduct find-finding and to review related policies and to report on both.

Because these functions are different, commissions often will fulfil them by establishing separate stages or phases for each. Some of the distinguishing features of each may be identified. The policy/advisory function requires an assessment of the success of past practices and policies, in order to develop and identify alternatives or options for the future. This may involve extensive research including comparative approaches from other jurisdictions. It may involve obtaining the advice of experts or specialists in relevant disciplines. The commission is likely to engage in broad public consultation, as well as providing a "voice" for stakeholders or those with a special interest in the recommendations that might be made.

In contrast, the investigative function focuses on specific events and the related conduct of individuals. It essentially involves fact finding in relation to recent events that have generated great public concern. Since individual conduct may be assessed, procedural fairness must be respected. This may result in the proceedings becoming more "court-like," with pre-hearing disclosure of information to those affected, legal representation at the hearings, and the opportunity to cross-examine adverse witnesses.

The Law Reform Commission of Ontario observed that "general classification schemes for public inquiries abound." It provided a useful discussion of the various approaches to classification and a critique of the "advisory/investigative" dichotomy referred to above.[11] While some commissions may be described as entirely "policy/advisory," most "investigative" commissions exercise some combination of both functions. In the end, the value of any classification appears to depend on the purpose for classifying. In the next chapter, I have grouped inquiries into five broad categories simply as a helpful way to introduce the reader to how they have been deployed, generally, in the past and to provide a context for the analysis in subsequent chapters.

---

11 Above note 9 at 140–50.

## B. PURPOSE

The Law Reform Commission of Ontario identified the following six principal functions of commissions of inquiry:

> (a) they enable the government to secure information as a basis for developing or implementing policy; (b) they serve to educate the public or legislative branch; (c) they provide a means to sample public opinion; (d) they can be used to investigate the judicial or administrative (police, civil service, Crown corporations) branches; (e) they permit the public voicing of grievances; (f) they enable final action to be postponed.[12]

But it also recognized, as a practical matter, that the detached pursuit of optimal public policy is not their only purpose. They are also born of scandals and disasters. Justice Peter Cory elaborated:

> One of the primary functions of public inquiries is fact-finding. They are often convened, in the wake of public shock, horror, disillusionment, or scepticism, in order to uncover "the truth" .... In times of public questioning, stress and concern they provide the means for Canadian to be apprised of the conditions pertaining to a worrisome community problem and to be a part of the recommendations that are aimed at resolving the problem.[13]

Justice Cory then referred to the "social function" which commissions of inquiry may serve in our democratic society by quoting the following passage: "a commission has certain things to say to government but it also has an effect on perceptions, attitudes and behaviour .... There is much more than law and governmental action involved in the social response to a problem."[14]

This purpose transcends policy recommendations by serving an educative function and by transforming public opinion through a form of dialogue. However, when established in response to a catastrophe, scandal, or perceived injustice, the crucial function of a commission of inquiry

12 *Ibid.*

13 *Phillips v. Nova Scotia (Commission of Inquiry into the Westray Mine Tragedy)*, [1995] 2 S.C.R. 97 at para. 62 [*Phillips*].

14 *Ibid.* at para. 64, citing Gerald E. Le Dain, "The Role of the Public Inquiry in Our Constitutional System" in Jacob S. Ziegel, ed., *Law and Social Change* (Toronto: Osgoode Hall Law School, York University, 1973) at 85.

is "to restore public confidence not only in the institution or situation investigated but also in the process of government as a whole."[15]

This raises two related questions. What are the characteristics of commissions of inquiry that can instil such public confidence? Why are other institutions of government (courts, legislative committees, police, other specialized agencies) incapable of doing so?

Perhaps the most important feature of a commission of inquiry that inspires public confidence is its *independence*. The commissioner has no vested interest in the outcome and is expected to proceed objectively and "let the chips fall where they may." This is in contrast to an "internal investigation," which may be perceived by the public as having a motive of "protecting" the institution that is under suspicion by favouring personal associates. Often judges or retired judges are appointed to enhance the perceived status of independence, because of the guarantees of independence associated with judicial office.

A second feature is public confidence in the *effectiveness* of the commissioner to "get to the bottom" of the problem. In this respect, it occasionally becomes apparent that not every good judge is well suited to the role of commissioner. The ability to be effective arises not only from the commissioner's personal and professional qualifications but also from the nature of the assignment. A commissioner is able to set aside all other professional obligations and devote all available time and energy to the inquiry. Resources and staff are provided to create a team that can give its intense and undivided attention to the task at hand. This is a luxury that ministers and public officials simply cannot afford.

The public will also derive confidence from the *mandate* of the commission, which will be designed to address the very questions and issues that give rise to public concern. The public scrutiny of commissions through the media essentially precludes governments from attempting to direct a particular outcome by restricting the terms of reference. Indeed, they often give commissioners authority to pursue any additional avenues that they may consider relevant to their prescribed mandates.

A commissioner also has broad investigative *powers* to compel the testimony of witnesses and the production of documents. The commissioner is not a passive observer, as in a trial, but may "go where the evidence leads." There are no restrictions arising out of the law that is

15 *Ibid.* at para. 62.

to be applied or the pleadings of the parties. Indeed, there are no pleadings or parties as there are in civil litigation. Nor is there a "charge" or an "accused" as in criminal cases. The relevant issues may evolve as the inquiry progresses.

Another feature that enhances public confidence is the *transparency* of the proceedings. Most inquiries receive detailed coverage in the media, some are televised, and most now have websites with access to the hearings. The process of conducting open and public hearings is an important component in the process of restoring public confidence.

Other institutions have some of these features but not all of them. The courts have independence, the ability to be effective, and transparency but their mandate does not permit them to fulfil the role of a commissioner. They are restricted by the legal issues in the case and the pleadings of the parties or, in a criminal case, the charge. In our adversary system, judges play a passive role. It is the parties who frame the issues and present the evidence. Judges do not take the initiative to call witnesses. Nor do they explain to the public "what happened and why." They simply decide the issues placed before them.

Legislative committees can have broad mandates and conduct public hearings. However, they are not able to devote lengthy periods of time to such hearings or to probe with the intensity of a commission of inquiry. As well, their partisan nature raises questions about their potential independence and objectivity in the eyes of the public. Past experiences in the Landerville and Mulroney matters (discussed later) demonstrate the inadequacy of parliamentary committees in this respect.[16]

A criminal investigation is another possible avenue in some situations and such an investigation may well proceed parallel to a commission of inquiry. Yet criminal investigations may do little to address public concern because they are conducted in private. They also, ultimately, focus on specific individuals or corporations rather than providing a report to the public as to "what happened and why." Finally, they lack

16 Chapters 3, Section B(1) and 4, Section B(1). These cases both involved committees of the House of Commons. It is possible that discrete Senate committees could be designed and resourced in a manner to be more effective in conducting inquiries. Over the years, a number of individual senators have produced valuable reports on subjects such as poverty, the media, health, and national security and defence.

the power to compel testimony and the production of documents. This means that the results of their own findings must be tested in court.

In other words, a commission of inquiry is a unique institution serving special purposes in our political-legal system. As (then) Justice Antonio Lamer stated: "There is no doubt that commissions of inquiry at both the federal and provincial levels have played an important role in the *regular machinery of government* . . . [and] . . . in particular serve *to supplement* the activities of the mainstream institutions of government.[17] Justice Cory explained why commissions of inquiry are able to make a special contribution to the role of government: "As *ad hoc* bodies, commissions of inquiry are free of many of the institutional impediments which at times constrain the operation of the various branches of government. They are created as needed . . . ."[18] They have now become "an integral part of our democratic culture."[19]

The specific nature of commissions of inquiry within the machinery of government was analyzed in a ruling of the McDonald Inquiry concerning certain activities of the Royal Canadian Mounted Police (RCMP).[20] The appointment of such a commission is the creation of "an organism of the Executive branch of government." Even though it may hold hearings, it is not a branch of the judiciary but "fulfils Executive or administrative functions." This body is specifically created and designed (through its terms of reference) to examine some particular aspect of government (i.e., the executive): "The Executive branch, through its chosen Executive instrument, is examining itself."[21] Since it is entirely a creature of the executive's order in council, a commission's terms of reference may be changed or it may be completely abrogated, at any time, by another order in council. But to do so normally would invite adverse political consequences because of the public expectations aroused by the commission's creation.

The public expects that a commission will fulfil its role in accordance with the features described above: independently, effectively, according

---

17 *Starr v. Houlden*, [1990] 1 S.C.R. 1366 at 1410 [emphasis added] [*Starr*].

18 Above note 13 at para. 60.

19 *Canada (Attorney General) v. Canada (Commission of Inquiry on the Blood System in Canada—Krever Commission)*, [1997] F.C.J. No. 17 at para. 30 (C.A.), Decary J.A.

20 *Re Commission of Inquiry* (1979), 94 D.L.R. (3d) 365 at 370.

21 *Ibid.*

to its mandate, relying on its extraordinary investigative powers, and transparently. In this respect:

> a Commission of Inquiry is not a unit of the executive branch of government like other government departments and agencies. Short of direction by Order-in-Council, it cannot be directed by a Minister or even by the Cabinet to interpret its terms of reference in a particular manner, or to follow this procedural course or that. It is for the Commissioners to interpret the instrument that gave birth to the Commission.[22]

It is this feature of independence together with its specific authority and transparent operation that sets commissions apart from the remainder of the executive.

A commission of inquiry might best be described as a "residual institution" because it is invoked as a remaining alternative when other institutions or processes are inadequate. It restores public confidence through fact finding, analysis, and recommendations that bring reassurance and closure. It is a check on partisan or institutional politics but may also serve as a political tool to give the government some distance from problems through the delegation of immediate responsibility.[23]

## C. ASSESSMENT

It seems contradictory to describe commissions of inquiry as being both a "check on politics" and a "political tool" but both aspects are a reality. They are present with many commissions of inquiry to varying degrees and they may operate in tension or in harmony with each other. A government may wish to escape public criticism by shifting a problem to a commission of inquiry. But that might also serve the public well by contributing to a thoughtful, objective, and fact-based response to the subject of that criticism, as opposed to a reflexive political response.[24]

The government terminated the Somalia Inquiry at the very time when it was about to examine some of the higher levels of accountabil-

---

22 *Ibid.*

23 The term "residual institution" is taken from Kim Ratushny, unpublished J.S.D. Dissertation Proposal, Yale Law School, 1997.

24 See also John D. McCamus, "The Policy Inquiry: An Endangered Species?" in Allan Manson & David Mullan, eds., *Commissions of Inquiry: Praise or Reappraise?* (Toronto: Irwin Law, 2003) at 222.

ity in government. In a subsequent personal memoir, one of the commissioners wrote: "For a government with a strong majority to carelessly ignore the independence of a public inquiry, and for blatantly political purposes, is almost inconceivable. The media's slow and muted response is even more surprising."[25] He was even more disappointed by the lack of response from the Canadian public, attributing it, in part, to "exaggerated" government criticism about the expense and delay of the commission. He acknowledged that "Canadians are also tired of bad news. In this respect, Defence Minister Doug Young has read the public mood correctly."[26] The government appeared to suffer no adverse political consequences from terminating the Somalia Inquiry and won another majority in the ensuing general election. It is rare for a government to confront a commission of inquiry in such a blatant way but, no doubt with the assistance of public-opinion polls, it concluded that the daily "bad news" of the hearings would be more harmful politically than the consequences of termination.

The Law Reform Commission of Canada also acknowledged the potential political uses of commissions of inquiry:

> Finally, we recognize that commissions of inquiry may often be put to political use. It has been suggested, for example, that commissions may be established to stave off pressure, to postpone an awkward issue, to back up (hopefully) a government decision already made, or to make the man-on-the-street so sick of a particular issue that he will accept any resolution so long as the subject ceases to appear in the pages of his favorite newspaper. It is inevitable that this be the case.[27]

Justice Cory similarly noted that commissions of inquiry are vulnerable to public criticism in spite of their value:

> Cynics decry public inquiries as a means used by the government to postpone acting in circumstances which often call for speedy action. Yet, these inquiries can and do fulfil an important function in Canadian society . . . . Nonetheless, it cannot be forgotten that harsh and persuasive criticisms have been leveled against them. *Every inquiry created*

25 Peter Desbarats, *Somalia Cover-Up: A Commissioner's Journal* (Toronto: McClelland & Stewart, 1997) at 255.

26 *Ibid*. at 246.

27 Above note 10 at 20–21.

> *must proceed carefully in order to avoid complaints pertaining to excessive cost, lengthy delay, unduly rigid procedures or lack of focus.*[28]

The message is clear that criticisms may arise not because of the institution of commissions of inquiry but because of the manner in which particular inquiries are conducted. Conducting inquiries does not just mean holding hearings, although how that is done is very important. It also means managing the business of the inquiry. The nature of the mandate given to a commission may also influence its success.

One standard by which the success of commissions of inquiry may be measured is the extent to which their recommendations are implemented. The track record of commissions is greatly varied in this respect. Some random examples of the contributions of policy/advisory commissions to Canadian society include: public broadcasting; universal health care; policies on bilingualism, biculturalism, and multiculturalism; North American free trade; employment equity; and the creation of a number of independent administrative tribunals and agencies.

Provincial inquiries on wrongful convictions, in particular, have had a significant impact on our criminal justice system. It was not until 1990 that there was public acknowledgment, for the first time, that an innocent person had been convicted and imprisoned. The Nova Scotia commission reporting on the wrongful conviction of Donald Marshall, Jr. also found that racism played a role in that miscarriage of justice. Since then, a series of commissions in other provinces have reported on other wrongful convictions with findings of improper police and prosecutorial practices. These findings have led to systemic reforms and financial compensation for the victims.

But the adoption of a commission's recommendations is not the only measure of its value or success. In the wrongful-conviction commissions and the federal Maher Arar inquiry into his imprisonment in Syria, fact finding in itself was an important public contribution. The "shining of light into dark places" and exposing them publicly can have a significant impact on the future conduct of officials and public opinion, quite apart from any recommendations that are made or implemented.

Another important contribution of commissions lies in their hearings themselves. Speaking in the context of the Westray Mine disaster

---

28 Above note 13 at paras. 62 and 65 [emphasis added].

in Nova Scotia, Justice Cory said: "Open hearings function as a means of restoring the public confidence in the affected industry and in the regulations pertaining to it and their enforcement. As well, it can serve as a type of healing therapy for a community shocked and angered by a tragedy."[29] Both Commissioner Samuel Grange and legal authors have commented on the crucial importance of public hearings into the deaths of babies at Toronto's Sick Children's Hospital. The state's failure to solve the murders in question was a matter of intense public concern: "The Grange Inquiry was open, however, and one of the virtues in the exercise in openness was that the public became privy to the problems the state faced in trying to solve the mysterious deaths and could assess the efficacy of the state's actions."[30] The Walkerton Inquiry into the contamination of that small community's water supply also provides an excellent illustration of how a commission can contribute to the "healing therapy" referred to by Justice Cory. This commission is discussed in the next chapter, but, generally, it gained the confidence of the community not only through its report but also by the expeditious and sensitive manner in which it carried out its mandate.

Participation and process are also important for "policy/advisory" commissions that are focused almost entirely on public policy formulation. They involve a blend of some of the purposes listed at the start of the previous section. They also engage the "social function" described there, as public opinion is educated and in turn influences public policy formulation. The public process elevates the level of discussion by bringing together diverse views. In short, such commissions' value does not rest solely with the extent to which their recommendations are adopted.[31] Some illustrations of these commissions are given in the next chapter.

The institution of commissions of inquiry is an important component of our government. It is available to perform a "residual" role in a unique manner that is beyond the capacity of other governmental institutions.

---

29 *Ibid.* at para. 117.

30 Jamie Cameron, "Comment: The Constitutional Domestication of Our Courts . . ." in Philip Anisman & Allen M. Linden, eds., *The Media, the Courts and the Charter* (Toronto: Carswell, 1986) at 340–41. S.G.M. Grange, "How Should Lawyers and the Legal Profession Adapt?" (1990) 12 Dalhousie L.J. 151. (Both cited by Cory J. in *Phillips*.)

31 See, generally, J.G. Godsoe, Q.C., "Comment on Inquiry Management" in A.P. Pross, I. Christie, & J.A. Yogis, eds., *Commissions of Inquiry* (Toronto: Carswell, 1990) at 72–73.

Its success in specific situations depends both on the mandate commissions are given and the manner in which they are conducted.

## D. THE LEGAL NATURE

A variety of legal issues involving commissions of inquiry are discussed throughout this book and are tied together in Chapter 7. This section is merely an introduction to the legal nature of this institution.

A commission of inquiry is created under the authority of a statute, as are all (by definition) statutory tribunals. Whether described as a tribunal, board, agency, commission, or another name, each shares its origin as a "creature of statute." Such statutory bodies owe not only their existence but also their authority or "jurisdiction" to their statutes. Unlike most other statutory bodies, a commission of inquiry derives its jurisdiction not only directly from its statute but also, in a supplemental way, from its terms of reference. The *Inquiries Act* "delegates" to the government the power to define a commission's jurisdiction through an order in council. This enables the government to give each commission a different mandate tailored to the specific problem to be addressed. This elaboration on the powers granted by the Act has legal effect in specifying the jurisdiction of the commission.

Because a commission's jurisdiction is defined by law, it can be overruled by a court if it tries to act beyond its jurisdiction. In some circumstances, it also could be compelled to carry out the duties imposed by its jurisdiction if it fails to do so. This legal status also carries with it a "procedural" obligation. It must treat anyone affected by its process in accordance with the legal principle of fairness.

It is possible for a commission of inquiry to be established, without statutory authority, through the Crown prerogative (in effect, the discretion of Cabinet) to create a royal commission. Such a royal commission does not have the power to compel witnesses to testify or to produce documents.[32] The practice in Canada since Confederation has been to initiate the appointment of a commission by order in council under the *Inquiries Act* and then execute it by royal warrant under the Great Seal of Canada. As a result, commissions appointed under the *In-*

32 *Quebec (Attorney General) v. Canada (Attorney General)*, [1979] 1 S.C.R. 218 at 240, Pigeon J.

*quiries Act* are also described as royal commissions. Sometimes the term "judicial inquiry" is used, but this means only that the commissioner happens to be a judge.

I have chosen to use the term commission of inquiry or, occasionally, either commission or inquiry. In describing this body, the *Inquiries Act* uses the term "commissioner" rather than "commission" although, for example, the Ontario Act uses "commission." When referring to this body as an institution, the plural is often used because of the *ad hoc* and diverse nature of commissions of inquiry.

The name used to describe a particular commission of inquiry may be selected in a variety of ways. All recent federal inquires have been given a legal name by the order in council that creates it, such as "The Commission of Inquiry into the Sponsorship Program and Advertising Activities." But most acquire a more recognizable name through popular usage—in this case, the Gomery Commission or Gomery Inquiry. A commission may adopt its name by using it on its website, letterhead, other documents and as the title of its report. It is difficult to characterize precisely why different names are used but they all seem to involve some predominant aspect of the particular mandate or the profile of the commissioner. The "Walkerton Inquiry" and the "Cornwall Inquiry" seem to reflect the communities affected. The "Somalia Inquiry" reflects where the most significant events occurred and also the broader aspects of the military mission involved. The "Westray Inquiry" and the "Air India Inquiry" both reflect where tragic events occurred but also suggest the "operations" involved.

A commission may derive its name from the "victim" of events where one is clearly identifiable as the subject of the inquiry. This was the case for most of the wrongful-conviction inquiries such as Marshall, Morin, Sophonow, Milgaard, and Driskell. It was also the case in the "Arar Inquiry" into his detention, removal to Syria, imprisonment, and torture. Sometimes the first names of these victims are also used. Similarly, a commission may take the name of a particular official whose conduct is being investigated, such as the "Stevens Inquiry" into the potential conflict of interest of a Cabinet minister.

Often a commission will be named after a commissioner who is prominent, particularly where the subject matter is diverse. For example, the "Lamer Inquiry" was headed by a former Chief Justice of Canada but it also had three unconnected victims rather than one. The "Gomery Inquiry" was headed by a commissioner whose prominence tended to be influenced by his affection for media attention. In both the Walkerton and Arar inquiries, Commissioner Dennis O'Connor appeared deliberately to avoid a high personal public profile. In all of these examples, the term "inquiry" is frequently interchanged with "commission," which seems to be more common when the commissioner's name is used. It is also more common when describing policy/advisory commissions. The Table of Past Commissions of Inquiry at the front of this book identifies the popular names I have chosen for the commissions of inquiries discussed here.

Since commissions of inquiry may be appointed under both federal and provincial legislation, it follows that the jurisdiction of a commission is restricted by the constitutional authority of the appointing government. (They are also subject to other constitutional constraints.) For example, a provincial commission may not be used to investigate individual criminal conduct, because criminal law and procedure are the responsibility of the federal government under section 91(27) of the *Constitutional Act, 1867*. But a provincial government may establish a commission to inquire into public concerns about the criminal justice system of that province. Such an inquiry falls within provincial authority for the administration of justice under section 92(14) of the *Constitution Act, 1867*.

Concerns about potential constitutional challenges based on the federal-provincial distribution of powers may be addressed by "joint" appointments. For example, Mr. Justice Horace Krever was appointed on 27 October 1993 by the government of Canada to inquire into the safety of the blood system in Canada. On 10 and 15 December 1993 and 6 April 1994, the governments of Prince Edward Island, Ontario, and Saskatchewan, respectively, granted him a similar mandate under provincial legislation. An earlier precedent had been established when, in March 1982, the governments of Canada and Newfoundland established a joint commission into the collapse and sinking of the "Ocean Ranger" oil-drilling unit, with the loss of the entire eighty-four-man crew.[33]

33 See, generally, the discussion of the Ocean Ranger Commission by its secretary, David M. Grenville: "The Role of Commission Secretary" in Pross, Christie, & Yogis, eds., above note 31 at 51.

Another variation is a joint provincial commission whereby a number of provinces combine to establish an inquiry into the same issues but throughout their combined territorial jurisdictions. In December 1966 the provinces of Alberta, Saskatchewan, and Manitoba created such a commission "to inquire into the cause of price increases and the general cost of living in Saskatchewan, Manitoba and Alberta." The detailed terms of reference were adopted separately by all three provinces and they all appointed the same three commissioners, one from each province. The organization and operational challenges to such a joint venture may appear daunting but, as it turned out, were manageable.[34]

It is important to emphasize that commissions of inquiry have no authority to make decisions, apart from fact finding. They simply investigate and report. Their reports usually include recommendations but these recommendations are not binding and governments may simply choose to ignore them. Commissions may not make findings of criminal responsibility or civil liability. Provided they do not go that far, they may reach conclusions about whether the conduct of an individual was improper. They may not impose any sanctions for such improper conduct.

However, a finding of misconduct by a commission, in itself, may be a serious consequence for the individual affected. It could reflect badly on the individual's personal and professional reputation, with corresponding adverse consequences. The stature of commissioners and the other features discussed above mean that the public is likely to accept commission findings and opinions as authentic. That is why commissions must conduct their inquiries according to law and, particularly, the principle of fairness, even though they do not make legally binding decisions.

## E. OTHER INQUIRIES

The definition given to a commission of inquiry at the very beginning of this chapter was restricted to those created under Part I of the federal

34 Prairie Provinces Cost Study Commission (Canada), *Report of the Royal Commission on Consumer Problems and Inflation, Manitoba, Saskatchewan and Alberta* (Ottawa: Queen's Printer, 1968). The commission specifically noted the success of its executive secretary, W.T. Molloy, in managing "a myriad of procedural and practical problems" and the importance of liaison "with the relevant provincial authorities."

*Inquiries Act* or the corresponding provincial or territorial legislation. Part I gives very broad authorization to establish inquiries related to "the good government of Canada" or any part of its "public business." In contrast, Part II authorizes investigations into a government department and the duties carried out by its officials. These do not require the approval of Cabinet but may be appointed by the minister who is responsible for that department. Specific powers are granted for obtaining testimony and other evidence.

Many additional statutes establish administrative bodies that function on an ongoing basis and are granted specific powers to conduct inquiries in relation to the subject matter of their functions. Under the *Auditor General Act*,[35] the office is created and broad power is given under section 5 to the "auditor of the accounts of Canada" to

> make such examinations and inquires as he considers necessary to enable him to report as required by this Act.

Under section 13(1), the auditor general

> is entitled to free access at all convenient times to information that relates to the fulfilment of his or her responsibilities.

Section 13(4) authorizes the examination of persons under oath:

> and for the purpose of any such examination the Auditor General may exercise all of the powers of a commission under Part I of the *Inquiries Act*.

Thus, some powers are expressly given by the statute and others by incorporation of provisions of the *Inquiries Act*. The auditor general is an officer of Parliament and reports to the House of Commons rather than to the government.

The *Judges Act*[36] establishes the Canadian Judicial Council and authorizes it to conduct inquiries into whether a superior court judge should be removed from office. Section 63(4) provides that in making such inquiries, the council or an inquiry committee is "deemed to be a superior court" with power to compel testimony and other evidence. No reference is made to the *Inquiries Act*.

---

35 R.S.C. 1985, c. A-17.

36 R.S.C. 1985, c. J-1, ss. 59 and 63.

Under the *Explosives Act*,[37] the Canadian Transportation Accident Investigation and Safety Board may be directed to inquire into any accidental explosion and is given "all the powers and authority of a commissioner appointed under Part I of the *Inquiries Act*." Although the board is an ongoing body, created under another statute, for the purpose of conducting this type of inquiry, it is simply given all of the powers of a commission of inquiry under the *Inquiries Act*.

The RCMP Public Complaints Commission has authority to conduct hearings into complaints about RCMP officers. The *Royal Canadian Mounted Police Act* gives it specific powers to require "oral or written evidence" as well as the production of documents.[38]

There are many examples and variations of such powers of inquiry, scattered through both federal and provincial legislation. The Law Reform Commission of Canada identified "at least" forty-seven federal statutes that incorporate powers of inquiry from the *Inquiries Act*. They identified as well "at least" forty additional federal statutes that confer powers of inquiry without reference to the *Inquiries Act*.[39] In addition to comparable provisions at the provincial level, a province may also empower municipalities to authorize a judicial inquiry into matters of municipal concern. The Supreme Court of Canada recently reviewed this practice and commented:

> The power to authorize a judicial inquiry is an important safeguard of the public interest, and should not be diminished by a restrictive or overly technical interpretation of the legislative requirements for its exercise.[40]

The term "judicial inquiry" was used here simply because the relevant legislation in this case required that such inquiries be conducted by a judge.

Commissions of inquiry are also utilized in other parliamentary democracies.[41] For example, the Commonwealth of Australia establishes

---

37 R.S.C. 1985, c. E-17, s. 15(2).

38 R.S.C. 1985, c. R-10, s. 24.1(3)(a).

39 Above note 10 at 6.

40 *Consortium Developments (Clearwater) Ltd. v. Sarnia (City)*, [1998] 3 S.C.R. 3, Binnie J. delivering the judgment of the Court at para. 26. The legislative provision in this case was *Municipal Act*, R.S.O. 1990, c. M.45, s. 100.

41 Barry Winetrobe, "Inquiries after Scott: The Return of the Tribunal of Inquiry" [1997] Public Law 18 at 23.

them under the *Royal Commissions Act 1902* and each state also has authorizing legislation. In New Zealand, they are created under the *Commissions of Inquiry Act, 1908*. In England, the term "tribunal" rather than "commission" is used and, until recently, these tribunals were established under the *Tribunals of Inquiry (Evidence) Act 1921*. Unlike other jurisdictions such as Canada, a resolution was also required by both Houses of Parliament to authorize them: "Generally there has been relatively little debate on parliamentary resolutions establishing tribunals . . . there has been a consensus in the Houses on the need for a particular tribunal."[42] In April 2005 the 1921 statute was repealed and replaced by a new *Inquiries Act 2005*, which removed parliamentary scrutiny of the decision to establish an inquiry and its terms of reference.

Finally, commissions of inquiry also may be established under international political and legal systems. They can be established though *ad hoc* agreements between nations or under international instruments.[43] Section 14 of the *Inquiries Act* specifically authorizes the government to confer on "an international commission or tribunal" the same powers that may be given to commissioners under Part I of the Act.

## F. REFORM

In Chapter 1, reference was made to the work of the law reform commissions of Canada, Ontario, and Alberta in relation to commissions of inquiry. The working papers and reports of all three commissions provide valuable research and discussion but they have had almost no influence on the legislation of their respective jurisdictions, which is, essentially, unchanged.

The Law Reform Commission of Canada proposed the repeal of the *Inquiries Act* and its replacement by a new "system" that would clearly separate "Inquiries to Advise" and "Inquiries to Investigate." Under a proposed new *Inquiries Act*, each type would have different powers. In particular, advisory commissions would not have the power to compel testimony or

42 See, generally, the discussion by the Law Reform Commission of Ontario, above note 9 at 156–70. In Ireland, tribunals are also appointed under the *Tribunals of Inquiry (Evidence) Act 1921*. See also the discussion in Chapter 9, Section D(1).

43 See, generally, K.J. Keith, "Commissions of Inquiry: Some Thoughts from New Zealand" in Manson & Mullan, eds., above note 24 at 153.

the production of evidence, apart from exceptional circumstances. The rationale is that coercive powers are inappropriate in a democracy except where they can be expressly justified and they are seldom useful in developing policy as opposed to conducting investigations.

The lack of enthusiasm for such changes was expressed in a dissent by the commission's then vice-chairman, Justice John Bouck. He was critical of the Working Paper for failing to make a case for repealing the *Inquiries Act* and replacing it with a new statute:

> Throughout, it refers to the present *Act* as being "inadequate," "deficient," "unsound," "giving unnecessary power," etc. Yet, there are very few examples, if any, of actual situations where these allegations can be shown to have substance. Therefore, most of the criticism becomes just a matter of opinion.[44]

He saw no evidence of commissioners having difficulty carrying out their duties under the existing legislation. In a thorough analysis, the Law Reform Commission of Ontario also rejected the creation of two separate classes of inquiry. It recommended that all inquiries should have the same range of powers available but simply exercise good judgment in when to use them.

Recommendations for the reform of commissions of inquiry sometimes may fail to appreciate their underpinnings in government and politics as well as in law. In an excellent analysis and discussion of commissioner independence, Tamar Witelson decried the termination of the Somalia Inquiry. She recommended that the *Inquiries Act* permit the termination of a commission of inquiry only through removal of the commissioner "for cause."[45] The difficulty is that the decision to establish or terminate a commission is not a legal decision but a governmental-political one. A government is entitled to do either and is not legally accountable. But the decision to terminate a commission of inquiry may carry a high degree of political accountability. It could have disastrous political consequences if viewed as an attempt to "cover up." Or it could demonstrate an accurate assessment of public opinion and avoid poten-

---

44 Above note 10 at 89.

45 Tamar Witelson, "Declaration of Independence" in Manson & Mullan, eds., above note 24 at 357.

tially adverse political consequences, as was the case with the Somalia Inquiry.

In December 1996 a draft discussion paper was circulated in the Privy Council Office, entitled "Reforming Commissions of Inquiry." The document appears to have been prepared in the context of the delays in the Somalia Inquiry and its ultimate demise a few months later. It referred to "some factors that have been *irritants* in recent commissions, notably their inability to respect reporting deadlines and budgetary limits, and their occasional tendency to go beyond their terms of reference, at least in the government's view."[46] Some of the possible reforms suggested were to include in the *Inquiries Act* a witnesses' bill of rights, a complete code of procedure for hearings, and a right of appeal against adverse findings.[47] The discussion and recommendations are generally superficial and impractical. For example, they do not recognize the administrative law principle of fairness as a protection for witnesses. Nor do they recognize some of the practices adopted by commissioners who have been successful in conducting thorough and expeditious inquiries.

The last point cannot be overemphasized. There are recurring issues and problems for all commissions of inquiry that must be "managed." There is scope for flexibility and creativity in solving such problems but the process is inquisitorial and the commissioner can seldom play a passive role and be effective. Inquiries that address their terms of reference in a fair and expeditious manner are quite achievable under the existing legislation.

---

46 Jim Bronskill, "Federal Proposals Include Witnesses' Bill of Rights" *Ottawa Citizen* (30 June 1997) [emphasis in original].

47 *Ibid.*

CHAPTER THREE

# Some Canadian Commissions of Inquiry

## A. INTRODUCTION

The previous chapter discussed the nature and purpose of commissions of inquiry by analyzing the characteristics that permit them to perform their unique "residual" role within our system of government. This chapter will add some flesh to that analysis by describing a broad range of commissions that have been established over the past few decades. Since they are *ad hoc* bodies that complete their business and expire, it is difficult to appreciate their collective contribution to Canadian society.

A few years ago, the *Literary Review of Canada* compiled a list "of the 100 most important Canadian books, chosen by a panel of experts."[1] The list contains six royal commission reports! The first of these was Lord Durham's report, described briefly in the first section of the previous chapter. The second is the report of the Kellock-Taschereau Commission into the communication of "Secret and Confidential Information to Agents of a Foreign Power" (1946). This commission was established following the defection of Igor Gouzenko, a cipher clerk at the Soviet embassy in Ottawa, who provided documentation of spying activity to the RCMP. Both commissioners, R.L. Kellock and Robert Taschereau,

1 Matt Goerzen, "List of Top 100 Books Reflects Literary 'Backbone' of Canada" *Ottawa Citizen* (18 November 2005).

were judges of the Supreme Court of Canada at the time. Although the hearings were held entirely in secret, the subsequent release of their proceedings revealed extremely unfair treatment of witnesses. The report led to numerous criminal convictions, including of a Communist member of Parliament, and spawned a number of books when the documentation was made public some thirty-five years later.

The other commissions listed are:

- The Massey-Lévesque Commission on National Development In the Arts, Letters and Sciences (1951), which examined Canadian cultural identity and the protection of its independence from the United States.
- The Hall Commission on Health Services (1964), which led to the adoption of a system of universal health care in Canada.
- The Laurendeau-Dunton Commission on Bilingualism and Biculturalism (1967), which ultimately led to the establishment of legal and constitutional rights to bilingual services and the recognition of "multiculturalism" as a feature of Canadian society.
- The Macdonald Commission on Economic Union and Development Prospects (1985), which led to the Canada-United States Free Trade Agreement.

The last three are described more fully below.

It has been a challenge to determine which commissions to select for this overview because of their diversity as well as their sheer numbers, at both the federal and provincial levels. The descriptions are very brief and general, in contrast to the reports themselves and the media reports, scholarly articles, and books written about them. But they should, cumulatively, provide a good sense of how commissions of inquiry have been deployed in Canada in the past and the circumstances that led to their creation. There are unique features and experiences associated with each of them.

This overview will also provide a broad context for the more detailed analysis in the chapters that follow. To assist the reader, they have been grouped into five broad categories that describe their general roles. These categories are:

- Investigative Inquiries that inquire into specific events and the related conduct of those involved;

- Policy/Advisory Commissions that examine broader societal issues and advise governments on how these should be addressed through public policy;
- Wrongful-Conviction Inquiries that inquire into the factors that resulted in the criminal conviction of an innocent person;
- Inquiries Investigating Crimes; and
- Ongoing Inquiry Bodies that are not commissions of inquiry but have similar powers to conduct inquiries on an ongoing basis.

## B. INVESTIGATIVE INQUIRIES

When conducting investigative inquiries, a commission generally examines events that have occurred in the past and determines how they came about. Usually the inquiry must also examine the conduct of individuals associated with those events in order to reach its conclusions. The Landreville Inquiry examined the conduct of a superior court judge and the Stevens Inquiry examined that of a federal Cabinet minister. The Westray Inquiry investigated the tragedy of a mine explosion and the Walkerton Inquiry that of the contamination of a community's water supply. The Somalia Inquiry was to investigate the behaviour of Canadian troops deployed on a peacekeeping mission and, particularly, the torture and killing of a Somali teenager, but it was unable to complete its mandate.

### 1) Landreville

Leo A. Landreville was a very successful lawyer in Sudbury, Ontario, with a thriving law practice and many lucrative investments. He was elected as mayor in 1954 and appointed as a superior court judge in 1956. The story of his downfall is told in William Kaplan's fascinating book *Bad Judgment: The Case of Mr. Justice Leo A. Landreville.*[2]

At the time of his appointment, all superior court judges in Ontario were required to live in Toronto where they had their offices, in Osgoode Hall. They heard cases throughout the province by going "on circuit." Justice Landreville might be described as "flashy" in his lifestyle, with a villa in Mexico, garish office furnishings, and Cadillac car,

2 Toronto: University of Toronto Press, 1996.

in comparison to his rather staid Upper Canada colleagues. He was also an "outsider" as a French Canadian on the court. Allegations of misconduct were made against him because of share options he received when he was mayor from a company that had obtained the Sudbury council's approval to distribute natural gas in the area. Kaplan documents how the primarily Toronto-based legal and judicial establishment generated pressure on the minister of justice of Canada to have Justice Landreville removed from office.

Section 99(1) of the *Constitution Act, 1867*, provides:

> The Judges of the Superior Courts shall hold office during good behaviour, but shall be removable by the Governor General on Address of the Senate and House of Commons.[3]

Prior to the *Landreville* case, only four others came before Parliament seeking the removal of a superior court judge. None were successful and the last one was in 1881. Section 99(1) is a very blunt instrument for addressing allegations of judicial misconduct. There is no independent and impartial mechanism for fact finding and assessment. As a result, between 1881 and the *Landreville* case, complaints about judicial conduct were dealt with informally and privately, by chief justices and justice ministers, through counselling, reprimand, or resignation under the threat of removal proceedings.[4]

In the case of Justice Landreville, the government decided to establish a commission of inquiry to sort out some of the complex issues and report on his conduct. Retired Supreme Court of Canada Justice Ivan Rand was appointed as commissioner in 1966, at the age of eighty-two. He had a reputation as one of Canada's most eminent judges. Unfortunately, Commissioner Rand did not conduct his commission in a judicial manner. Kaplan writes: "Rand had been given clear terms of reference, but that did not stop him from wandering far off topic. With no restrictions on his right to compel attendance of witnesses, and no fetters on the procedure he decided to pursue, the Commission became nothing more than a fishing expedition desperately searching for something to

---

3 *Constitution Act, 1867* (U.K.), 30 & 31 Victoria, c. 3.

4 Ed Ratushny, "Speaking as Judges: How Far Can They Go?" (2000) 11 N.J.C.L. 293 at 304–5.

justify the recommendation that was reached."[5] He concludes that this commission and its report were "a travesty of justice."

The report found that Justice Landreville had failed in his duty as a judge, and it did so by linking his conduct as mayor to his subsequent reaction to the allegations while a judge. It concluded that Justice Landreville was unfit to continue to hold office as a judge. As a result, the government appointed a special joint committee of the Senate and House of Commons to report on whether there should be an address for removal under section 99(1). The process before the committee provided no greater fairness. Again, Kaplan writes:

> Parliament is equipped for many things, but not for conducting the trial of a judge. The proceedings of the special Joint Committee more than prove this point. The members of that committee did not always take their task seriously, and their attendance record provides persuasive evidence of that. There was also something unseemly about the fate of a judge being thrust into political hands.[6]

The report of the committee recommended removal proceedings and Justice Landreville resigned in 1967. He was denied a judicial pension.

The Landreville Inquiry provides an illustration of the potential unfairness of commissions of inquiry when they are not properly conducted. But it left two legacies. First, subsequent judicial proceedings established that such unfairness could be successfully attacked in court. Secondly, the experience of this case led to legislative amendments to establish a proper process for addressing complaints about judicial behaviour.

Legal proceedings pursued by Landreville were finally successful some ten years after his resignation when Federal Court Justice Frank Collier granted a declaration that Commissioner Rand had failed to comply with section 13 of the *Inquiries Act*. The commissioner, concluded Justice Collier, made findings of misconduct on matters that then Justice Landreville had no opportunity to refute, because he was not given notice of them. It is interesting to note that Collier's respect for Rand did not prevent him from fulfilling his duties as a judge:

---

5 Above note 2 at 192.

6 *Ibid.* at 193.

> I have come slowly to that conclusion. The commissioner was an eminent and renowned Judge of the Supreme Court of Canada . . . .
>
> As a mere trial bench Judge, I feel some reluctance in concluding that this distinguished Commissioner omitted to comply with one of the terms of the statute governing his inquiry; that this was error in law. But my function cannot be affected by diffidence or reluctance. I am required to apply the law, as I conceive it to be, to the issues between the parties to this suit.[7]

The declaration established that Justice Landreville did not have a proper opportunity to refute a finding that was harmful to his reputation. It also assisted him in obtaining an *ex gratia* payment from the government for the pension he had been denied.

The second consequence of the *Landreville* case was the significant impetus it gave to amendments to the *Judges Act* in 1971. These provisions established the Canadian Judicial Council with specific authority to deal with allegations of judicial misconduct.[8]

### 2) Stevens

Sinclair Stevens was a successful lawyer and businessman who was elected to Parliament and became a cabinet minister in the Brian Mulroney government. He was the minister of Regional Industrial Expansion from 19 September 1984 until 12 May 1986, when he announced his resignation in the House of Commons. He resigned in the face of media rumours and allegations of conflict of interest in his role as a cabinet minister. He denied those allegations to the House and went further by asking that there be an impartial investigation into the facts surrounding them.

Three days later, the government appointed Chief Justice William Parker of the High Court of Justice of Ontario as a commissioner to conduct such an inquiry. The terms of reference were brief but very broad in describing the conduct that was the basis for the inquiry and that was then the subject of wide-ranging public controversy: "the facts following allegations of conflict of interest made in various newspapers, electronic media and the House of Commons with respect to the conduct, deal-

7 *Landreville v. The Queen (No. 2)* (1977), 75 D.L.R. (3d) 380 at 405 (F.C.T.D.) [*Landreville*].

8 This council's role is discussed further under Section F(1), below in this chapter.

ings or actions of the Honourable Sinclair M. Stevens." But the standard by which that conduct was to be assessed was very narrow: "whether the Honourable Sinclair M. Stevens was in real or apparent conflict of interest as defined by the Conflict of Interest Post Employment Code for Public Office Holders and the letter from the Prime Minister." In contrast, the Landreville terms of reference were narrower in defining the conduct forming the basis for the inquiry. It was limited to his dealings with a natural gas company or in its shares. The standard was whether he was unfit to be a judge. In Landreville, the commissioner had exceeded his authority by assessing conduct that went well beyond his dealings with the gas company.

In Stevens, the commissioner was able to sort out, without challenge, the conduct to be examined, based on allegations in the media and the House of Commons. But he erred in the standard he adopted for determining whether that conduct amounted to a conflict of interest. Unfortunately, the the post-employment code and letter referred to in the Stevens terms of reference did not contain a definition of conflict of interest. During the course of his deliberations, Commissioner Parker developed his own definition of conflict of interest and then applied it to Stevens's conduct. Stevens learned of the standard that was applied only upon reading the report, which was released in December 1987 and found him in conflict.

Stevens pursued a series of legal actions against the conflict-of-interest findings. Finally, in December 2004, Federal Court Justice John O'Keefe ruled that the commissioner had exceeded his authority by applying the new definition of conflict of interest. Stevens had been denied procedural fairness by not knowing or having a chance to comment on the standard by which he was judged. As a result, the court ruled:

> that the Parker Report is set aside and declared to be of no force or effect in consequence of the excess of jurisdiction by the Commissioner, and a failure to act in accordance with the principles of procedural fairness.[9]

As a practical matter, even though the hearings had ended, it would have been easy for the commissioner to postpone the final writing of his report. He could have informed Stevens of his "proposed" definition and

9 *Stevens v. Canada (Attorney General)*, [2005] 2 F.C.R. 629 at para. 49 [*Stevens*].

invited further submissions on both the definition and its application to the conduct that had been identified as relevant.

The nature of this inquiry was similar to the Landreville Inquiry in one basic respect: it dealt solely with the conduct of a single public officeholder. In one case the officeholder was a superior court judge; and in the other he was a minister of the Crown. There were other similarities. In both cases, the commissioners made adverse findings against the officeholders. In both, the officeholders fought the commission findings in court and in both cases they were successful. Finally, both reviewing courts stressed that, where a commission of inquiry is aimed solely at the conduct of an individual, the standard of procedural fairness required is high.

On being interviewed following the release of the Federal Court decision setting aside the findings of conflict of interest against him, Stevens, then aged seventy-seven, said: "'I think I did the right thing . . . . When you feel a wrong has been done, I feel it's very important that people stand up and try to right the wrong. When you are personally involved, I suppose it's double important.'"[10] Still, he had to wait eighteen years, and it would have been highly preferable for both the Landreville and Stevens commissions to have been properly conducted in the first place.

### 3) Westray

On 9 May 1992 an underground explosion occurred at the Westray Coal Mine in Pictou County, Nova Scotia, leaving twenty-six miners trapped beneath the surface. In spite of frantic rescue efforts, they all perished. Less than a week later, on 15 May, the government appointed Justice Peter Richard to conduct a commission of inquiry into the tragedy. The commission's work was stalled by legal challenges. A number of people who held managerial or supervisory positions with Westray Coal were charged with offences, some under the province's occupational-safety legislation and others under the *Criminal Code*.

The Nova Scotia Court of Appeal held that to proceed with the inquiry would infringe the rights of those charged. The court ordered that the commission's hearings be postponed until after the disposition of

---

10 Gloria Galloway, "Fight Was Worth It, Stevens Says" *Globe & Mail* (18 December 2004).

the penal charges. The Supreme Court reversed the Court of Appeal and allowed the commission hearings to proceed.[11]

The Supreme Court decision is particularly valuable because of Mr. Justice Cory's insights into the crucial importance of commissions of inquiry for communities attempting to cope with a local disaster. His reasons weigh the societal interest in proceeding with the commission hearings against the potential jeopardy to the societal interest in successfully pursuing the criminal charges. In doing so, he articulates the special community interest in this case, arising out of coal-mine disasters. Some of his more general comments about the nature and purpose of commissions of inquiry were quoted in the previous chapter. In the same vein, he said "they are created as needed although it is an unfortunate reality that their establishment is often prompted by tragedies such as industrial disasters, plane crashes, unexplained infant deaths, allegations of widespread child sexual abuse or grave miscarriages of justice."[12]

Justice Cory began his discussion of the context of the disaster in this case by noting that coal mining had been a central feature of the Nova Scotia economy for some three hundred years. Communities were established and grew around coal mines which attracted immigrant workers. Coal provided cargo for ships and attracted steel manufacturers. In Pictou County, the coal industry was the main source of livelihood for inhabitants for almost 100 years, until its decline in the 1950s. It was revitalized by the official opening of the Westray mine in 1991. But coal mining in this area had always been a hazardous undertaking; one author estimates that, since 1827, more than 600 deaths had occurred in Pictou County mines. In one disaster in 1918, eighty-eight men were killed. Early inquiries were conducted by coroner's juries and, following the 1918 explosion, legislation established a special examiner to investigate mining disasters. Since 1938, an inquiry has been created for every major mining disaster in the area. As with similar inquiries in other parts

---

11 *Phillips v. Nova Scotia (Commission of Inquiry into the Westray Mine Tragedy)*, [1995] 2 S.C.R. 97 [*Phillips*]. Justice Cory was joined in his reasons by Iacobucci and Major JJ. The majority (Lamer C.J. and La Forest, Sopinka, Gonthier, and McLachlin JJ.) chose not to address this broader issue because the remaining accused had elected to be tried by judge alone rather than by jury and their trials were proceeding. Justice L'Heureux-Dubé wrote separate reasons.

12 *Ibid.* at para. 60.

of Nova Scotia, they have provided strong impetus for the enactment, implementation, and enforcement of safety regulations.

Justice Cory concluded that there was a "compelling community interest" in having the Westray commission of inquiry proceed as expeditiously as possible. That interest extended beyond the community directly affected by the Westray explosion to the concern of "all caring Nova Scotians." In sum:

> There is a clear and pressing public interest in having, as soon as possible, a broad and open investigation of the events leading up to the deaths of the miners. This is essential in order to reduce the fear that the same thing might happen again to other miners, to identify preventative measures, and to relieve the frustrations and concerns of the families of the victims.[13]

He later emphasized this conclusion, stating:

> In this case the magnitude of the tragedy, its impact throughout Nova Scotia, the extensive publicity which has followed the explosions and accompanied the progress of the Inquiry, and the undeniable importance of the mining industry to the Nova Scotia economy all emphasize the great public significance of the inquiry.[14]

He added that this public interest in learning the truth included doing so as quickly as possible.

The Westray Inquiry did proceed expeditiously and reported in 1997, with the title *The Westray Story: A Predictable Path to Disaster*. The commissioner summarized this story as: "a complex mosaic of actions, omissions, mistakes, incompetence, apathy, cynicism, stupidity and neglect. Some well-intentioned but misguided blunders were also added to the mix."[15] The comprehensive and detailed report assigned responsibility for the disaster at many levels, but primarily with management for failing to operate the mine safely. The mine inspectorate of the Department of Labour was complicit with management by tolerating compliance failures through "apathy" and complaisance." The Department of Natural

---

13 *Ibid.* at para. 71.

14 *Ibid.* at para. 90.

15 Executive Summary at viii.

Resources also failed to discharge its duties and its "wilful blindness" encouraged "arrogance and cynicism" on the part of management.[16]

It remains to be seen whether Commissioner Richard's report on the Westray disaster will help to avoid such tragedies in future. But it is discouraging to realize that this tragedy occurred in spite of so many other tragedies, inquiries, and recommendations in the past. One author, Eric Tucker, argues that "the underlying causes of the Westray Mine disaster are to be found in the particular political economy of Atlantic Canada and Pictou County and in a series of deeply rooted ideological assumptions that inform decision-making by private and public sector actors and . . . unless this social context is addressed, reforms will have only limited impact."[17] Tucker adds that commissions of inquiry often have a broad enough mandate to probe more fundamental questions. He cites the Westray terms of reference, which authorized the inquiry into "all other matters related to the establishment and operation of the Mine which the Commissioner considers relevant to the occurrence." However, this clause appears to have been limited to the particular occurrence rather than inviting broad socio-economic explorations. There are practical constraints on the scope of commissions of inquiry, such as the anxiety of those awaiting the report and the urgency to take whatever immediate remedial steps might be recommended. In these circumstances, investigations with a broad reach can best be undertaken by a policy/advisory commission not related to specific events.

### 4) Walkerton

Another type of disaster occurred in the town of Walkerton, Ontario, in May 2000 when its drinking-water system became contaminated with deadly bacteria, primarily *E. coli*. The result was that "seven people died and more than 2300 became ill. The community was devastated. The losses were enormous. There were widespread feelings of frustration, anger and insecurity."[18] On 13 June 2000 the Ontario government ap-

---

16 *Ibid.* at 11.

17 Eric Tucker, "The Westray Mine Disaster and Its Aftermath: The Politics of Causation" (1995) 10 C.J.L.S. 91 at 95.

18 Walkerton Inquiry, Part One at 2.

pointed the associate chief justice of Ontario, Dennis O'Connor, to conduct a commission of inquiry into this tragedy.

In an article written not long after the commission completed its work, Allan Manson and David Mullan observed that "throughout the course of the Walkerton Inquiry and its immediate aftermath, there has been a general sense that this was a commission of inquiry that worked particularly well."[19] The authors cite many reasons for this observation. There were no criticisms of the process and not a single legal challenge in the courts. In its report, the commission identified four principles it had adopted to guide its process, namely: "Thoroughness; Expedition; Openness to the Public; Fairness." Manson and Mullan describe how the commission addressed a variety of problems in ways that allowed it to achieve the goals established by those principles.

The commission found that the primary source of the water contamination was manure that had been spread on a farm near one of the town's wells. Heavy rainfalls during the time in question contributed to the contamination but the farmer was not at fault. Proper monitoring would have prevented the outbreak but there were shortcomings in the approvals and inspection programs of the Ontario Ministry of the Environment (MOE). The Walkerton Public Utilities operators allowed the problem to become much worse by failing to measure chlorine residuals daily, during the critical period, as they should have done. A whole host of improper operating practices by them were identified as unacceptable and contrary to the established guidelines and directives. Their general manager concealed adverse test results for a short period, an action that caused 300 to 400 illnesses that could have been avoided. All of these findings related to Part One of the inquiry, which addressed what happened "on the ground" in Walkerton. The Part Two report made comprehensive recommendations relating to all aspects of the drinking-water system in Ontario.

But the Part One report did not hesitate to document how the Ontario government's budget reductions had a direct impact on the Walkerton tragedy itself. It identified the privatizing of laboratory testing of water samples as leaving a gap in the reporting of unsafe drinking

19 Allan Manson & David Mullan, "Lessons from Walkerton" in Allan Manson & David Mullan, eds., *Commissions of Inquiry: Praise or Reappraise?* (Toronto: Irwin Law, 2003) at 501.

water to the local medical officer of health. The budget reductions also diminished the effectiveness of the provincial approvals and inspections programs. The consequence was the elimination of steps that could well have "prevented the outbreak or reduced its scope."

This report was damning in placing the responsibility exactly where it belonged: "The reductions were initiated by the central agencies of government . . . and they were not based on an assessment of what was required to carry out the MOE's statutory responsibilities."[20] It pointed out that this decision to slash the budget of the Ministry of the Environment was made in the face of numerous warnings that the cuts could seriously jeopardize the environment and human health. The risks involved were essentially ignored: "There is evidence that those at the most senior levels of government who were responsible for the decision considered the risks to be manageable. But there is no evidence that the specific risks . . . were properly assessed or addressed."[21]

No doubt those "at the most senior levels" of the Ontario government at the time were not amused by these findings. But, for the community to understand what happened and why, this information was important. The commission's findings also represent the central feature of commissions of inquiry, namely, their independence. When governments create them and authorize them to investigate and report on the "public business," government actors must accept that their own roles in the conduct of that business might be scrutinized. This is the very reason why the public has confidence in the residual role of commissions of inquiry as part of the machinery of government.

Perhaps the most distinguishing feature of the O'Connor Commission was its sensitivity to the Walkerton community. As soon as staff were in place, they began meeting with representatives of local groups in Walkerton. Public meetings were held over the course of four days within two months of the appointment of the commission. This is quite extraordinary considering the need not only to engage staff and make logistical arrangements but also to learn about the problem and provide notice. These first public meetings allowed the commission to hear directly from victims "who wished to tell their story about the ongoing impact of the tragedy on their lives."

---

20 Above note 18 at 34.

21 *Ibid.* at 35.

The more focused hearings were conducted over a nine-month period. They were all held in Walkerton and, indeed, both Commissioner O'Connor and his principal counsel, Paul Cavalluzzo, chose to live in the community. The importance of their presence in Walkerton is captured in this passage from an interview given by Cavalluzzo a few years after the commission reported:

> [I]t was a most amazing time. While the stress that inquiry inflicted on our own families was unbelievable, it was somewhat offset by knowing how very much our presence was appreciated. I'd be out jogging and total strangers would wave and call "Hi Paul, how are you today." They knew us from watching the hearings on the local cable, but they regarded us as friends and neighbours. It really meant something to them that we were there. When Justice O'Connor delivered his 2002 statement in the Walkerton arena, local residents packed in and gave him a standing ovation at its conclusion. I've never seen that before or since in any sort of inquiry or proceeding.[22]

This is not to suggest, in the slightest, that Commissioner O'Connor sought personal publicity. On the contrary, he declined any public comment except when presiding over proceedings. He even declined to comment on the Walkerton Inquiry for the article referred to above, some four years after making his report.

Indeed, Commissioner O'Connor demonstrated the same restraint, combined with similar objectivity and toughness, when conducting the Arar Inquiry soon afterwards. This commission attracted not only national but also international attention.

### 5) Somalia

The Somalia Commission was established on 20 March 1995 to inquire into aspects of the deployment of Canadian troops on a peacekeeping mission to Somalia in 1993. Three commissioners were appointed: Justice Gilles Letourneau of the Federal Court of Appeal, Justice Robert Rutherford of the Ontario Court (General Division), and journalist Peter Desbarats. Anne-Marie Doyle had been appointed initially but resigned after a month because of a perception of bias arising from her relation-

22 "Commissioning Justice" *Briefly Speaking/En Bref* (November 2006) at 16.

ship with people associated with National Defence Headquarters who were potential subjects of the inquiry. She was replaced by Justice Rutherford.

The establishment of this commission was largely driven by two events. On 4 March 1993 two Somalis had entered the Canadian compound in an apparent attempt to steal supplies. When discovered, they fled and one was killed when shot by a Canadian soldier at point-blank range. Shortly afterwards, on 16 March, a Somali youth was tortured and murdered in the compound. The circumstances were described in a personal account subsequently written by Commissioner Desbarats:

> The screams of the dying sixteen-year-old Somali could be heard clearly in the Canadian camp in the hot desert night. Many of our soldiers dropped by the bunker, which was not much more than a hole in the ground, protected by a crude roof. They saw the blood, the swollen face and lips. They knew what was going on and they did nothing to stop it.
>
> Many more, dozens of soldiers perhaps, hearing the screams or hearing others talking about what was going on, also did nothing. The agony of Shidane Arone on that night of March 16, 1993, lasted for hours, seemed to go on forever. Before dawn he finally slipped away from his torturers, but his death will be remembered as . . . a symbol of the lowest point in the history of the Canadian military.[23]

The commission's extremely broad terms of reference included "the chain of command system, leadership within the chain of command, discipline, operations, actions and decisions of the Canadian Forces and the actions and decisions of the Department of National Defence in respect of the Canadian Forces deployment in Somalia." In addition, "without restricting the generality of the foregoing," the commission was required to examine nineteen more focused, but still very broad, issues. In the "pre-deployment phase," these included the suitability of the Canadian Airborne Regiment for service in Somalia, its mandate, operational readiness, training, discipline, and leadership. The "in-theater phase" included the influence of cultural differences, attitudes towards lawful conduct and professional values, observance of the rules of engagement, and leadership and reporting. The "post-deployment

---

23 Peter Desbarats, *Somalia Cover-Up: A Commissioner's Journal* (Toronto: McClelland & Stewart, 1997) at 1.

phase" included how the chain of command responded to the problems arising out of the previous phase.

The terms of reference also required that the commission report no later than 22 December 1995. This gave the commissioners nine months to establish offices, hire staff, read the available documentation, determine who should be called as witnesses, provide notices, conduct hearings, give any notices of misconduct and provide an opportunity to respond, write the report, and have it translated. The timeline, even with the short extensions that were subsequently granted, was nothing short of absurd.

The difficulties the commission faced in attempting to fulfill its massive mandate within its short time frame were compounded by the lack of cooperation the commission received from the military and government. The work was also interrupted by a series of court challenges made by individual senior officers. The following account is based on the executive summary of the commission's report.

The commission noted that "many of the leaders called before us to discuss their roles in the various phases of the deployment refused to acknowledge error. When pressed, they blamed their subordinates who, in turn, cast responsibility upon those below them." After acknowledging the courage, integrity, and honesty of many of the military witnesses, the report added:

> However, we must also record with regret that on many occasions the testimony of witnesses was characterized by inconsistency, improbability, implausibility, evasiveness, selective recollection, half-truths, and plain lies. Indeed, on some issues we encountered what can only be described as a wall of silence. When several witnesses behave in this manner, the wall of silence is evidently a strategy of calculated deception.[24]

The problems encountered in obtaining documentation struck at the foundation of the commission's work, namely, the requirement to establish accurate information:

> Perhaps the most troubling consequence of the fragmented, dilatory and incomplete documentary record furnished to us by DND is that, when this activity is coupled with the incontrovertible evidence of document

24 Somalia Inquiry, Executive Summary at 3.

> destruction, tampering, and alteration, there is a natural and inevitable heightening of suspicion of a cover-up that extends into the highest reaches of the Department of National Defence and the Canadian Forces.[25]

The commission indicated that, apart from general legal and public obligations, military laws and regulations impose specific duties related to the reporting and retaining of information, and added:

> In our inquiry, the reporting of significant incidents in theater and the adequacy of the investigations prompted by such reports revealed the existence of one kind of cover-up, while the alteration and falsification of documents and the manipulation of access to information processes led to another. Also, a third variety emerged, as many of the documents to which we were entitled and that were pledged publicly to us by leaders, both governmental and military, reached us with deliberate tardiness, or in incomplete form, or not at all.[26]

The commission described this conduct as shameful and a profound failure of leadership.

The commission's deadline for reporting was extended from six months to nine months at the outset; then by another six months to 28 June 1996; then by an additional nine months to 31 March 1997. On 4 February 1997, the commission was required to finish its public hearings by 31 March but given an additional three months to file its final report. On filing that report, the commission lamented that

> our schedule was aborted just as we were beginning to question the highest levels of leadership of the Canadian Forces and the Department of National Defence and to the allegations of cover-up with respect to some incidents . . . . The Government's decision effectively allowed many of those in senior leadership positions during the deployment to avoid entirely accountability for their conduct, decisions, and actions during and after the mission.[27]

In spite of this unwritten chapter, the commission felt that it had made a number of important recommendations. It also emphasized that the

---

25 *Ibid.* at 37.

26 *Ibid.* at 50.

27 *Ibid.* at 42.

mission to Somalia was not a complete failure and that many soldiers and commanders performed there with honour and integrity. Nor did it detract from the contribution generally made by thousands of members of the Canadian Forces on Canada's behalf.

The decision by the government to terminate the Somalia Inquiry was mentioned in the previous chapter. Normally, a decision to shut down a commission of inquiry would have negative political consequences, but in this case the government went unscathed. Further aspects of this commission are discussed under various headings below.

## C. POLICY/ADVISORY COMMISSIONS

The role of policy/advisory commissions is to explore broad societal issues and advise governments as to the public policies that should be adopted to address those issues. They often involve gathering and conducting research as well as consulting "experts" in various fields. They are usually interdisciplinary in their approach since societal problems seldom fall neatly into a single discipline. They often consist of a "panel" of commissioners who bring their own diverse experience and expertise to the commission's deliberations.

In a sense, they must be "political" if their recommendations are to have any chance of being adopted. That means that they must consult the public but, at the same time, raise the level of public discussion by also educating the public. They must hear from "public interest" groups who often have a very narrow "interest" that is supported by a small segment of the public. They must take into account the consequences of potential changes upon "stakeholders." In the end, their conclusions and recommendations usually will involve compromises among the commissioners. But they must not be too political or they will fail to identify bold policy changes that will address societal issues in a new and beneficial way.

Since such changes are often developed incrementally, the contribution of some of these commissions may not be as direct as others. As the secretary to the Macdonald Commission commented:

> I would not suggest that the main test of the usefulness of a commission is to tally up the recommendations that were adopted by government within the next five years and those that were not. Far more import-

> ant is, "did the work of the commission influence the course of public policy?" a much more difficult question to answer. It is a deeper question and it relates to values and to public policy formation. It also relates to process . . . .[28]

The level of debate may be enhanced by better identifying factual underpinnings and bringing together diverse views. That in itself is a valuable contribution. Policy/advisory commissions also often leave behind a valuable body of research concentrated on issues of broad societal interest. The opportunity for such policy-focused research is seldom available in government and is also limited in universities. As illustrated below, some of these major commissions are the successors or precursors of others in the same or related subject areas.

Three of the royal commissions selected for this section were referred to in Section A: the Hall Commission on Health Services, the Laurendeau-Dunton Commission on Bilingualism and Biculturalism, and the Macdonald Commission on Economic Union and Development. In addition, I have included the Abella Commission on "Employment Equity" and the Le Dain Commission on the Non-Medical Use of Drugs.

Unlike investigative inquiries, policy/advisory commissions do not investigate specific events and the related conduct of individuals. As a result, they seldom have to use their coercive powers or have to worry about legal challenges. They have broad latitude in how they conduct their work and how they interpret their terms of reference. While these commissions have been the subject of numerous articles and books, a few are described here simply to remind the reader of how policy/advisory commissions have come into being and contributed to Canadian society.

### 1) Hall to Romanow

Emmett Hall was one of the many fascinating public figures shaped by Canadian "prairie politics."[29] Although he was born in Quebec, his family moved to Saskatchewan when he was eleven years old, and he called

28 J. G. Godsoe, Q.C., "Comment on Inquiry Management" in A.P. Pross, I. Christie, & J.A. Yogis, eds., *Commissions of Inquiry* (Toronto: Carswell, 1990) at 72.

29 See, generally, Frederick Vaughan, *Aggressive in Pursuit: The Life of Justice Emmett Hall* (Toronto: University of Toronto Press for Osgoode Society, 2004).

Saskatoon "home" for most of his life. He studied law at the University of Saskatchewan, where he became a friend of John Diefenbaker, and then practised law for thirty-five years. In 1957 his friend became prime minister and he, successively, became Chief Justice of the Court of Queen's Bench (1957), Chief Justice of Saskatchewan (1961), and justice of the Supreme Court of Canada (1962). In 1961 he was also appointed by Diefenbaker to conduct a Royal Commission on Health Services.

While practising law, Emmett Hall had been active in local school and hospital boards, the Law Society of Saskatchewan, the Canadian Bar Association, and the Conservative Party. He ran twice as a Conservative and was defeated both times. However, he was far from being a "conservative" Conservative, and indeed on the Supreme Court of Canada he was viewed as a very "liberal" judge. He was the sole dissenting judge in the controversial case of Stephen Truscott and a central figure in the *Calder* case, both discussed below.

The Regina Riot occurred at the height of the Great Depression, in 1935, when police attacked some of the hundreds of unemployed workers who were travelling to Ottawa to protest economic conditions. While the establishment viewed the protesters as dangerous radicals, Hall was sympathetic to them and felt the police were at fault. He took on the defence of a number of them, who were facing criminal charges. His social empathy was, no doubt, a product of his own family's economic hardship. He entered into his working profession at the start of the economic downturn and in the midst of the widespread poverty that took root earlier on the prairies than elsewhere.

During these years, a western-based political party, the Co-operative Commonwealth Federation (CCF), was a strong advocate of "socialized medicine," a cause that also arose out of the economic hardships of the "Dirty Thirties." In 1944 one of the CCF's leading figures, Tommy Douglas, became the premier of Saskatchewan and head of the first socialist government in North America. In 1947 it adopted a system of publicly funded hospital care throughout Saskatchewan, one that steadily developed in other provinces as well with the support of the federal government. However, in 1960, the Saskatchewan government announced plans to expand public medical care to include all services provided by doctors. This caused a bitter confrontation between medical doctors (and their supporters) and the government. Premier Douglas was defeated in his home constituency in 1962.

It was in this economic, social, and political context that the Hall Commission was launched in 1961. Although it is closely identified with its chairperson, Emmet Hall, this commission included six other commissioners: three medical doctors, a registered nurse, a university economics professor, and a Bay Street lawyer-businessman-fund-raiser, Wallace McCutcheon, who resigned when appointed to the Senate in 1962. The Hall Commission held extensive public hearings, received numerous briefs, conducted research, and studied the health care systems of other countries.

Its recommendations were contained in two reports made in 1964 and 1965. They identified numerous inconsistencies, omissions, and other shortcomings of the health-care "system" in Canada and called for a more integrated, comprehensive, and universal approach. This required not only coverage for hospital and physician care but also prescription drugs and dental care for children. The commission's recommendations were considered to be radical by many and their implementation was complicated by the provinces having constitutional responsibility for health care. However, in 1966, under Prime Minister Lester Pearson, federal enabling legislation was passed and negotiations ensued with each province which soon led to the creation of a mutually acceptable system with shared federal financing.

Lingering problems related to "extra-billing" and "user fees" led to Emmett Hall being appointed as a commissioner once more in 1979. His report the next year described these two practices as creating a "two-tiered" system for Canadians and recommended that both be abolished, a recommendation adopted in the *Canada Health Act*[30] of 1984. This appeared to be the final stage in establishing a comprehensive, universal, and accessible health-care system in Canada. Yet the evolution continued.

In 2001 former Saskatchewan premier Roy Romanow was appointed to conduct another commission. The following year, the Romanow Commission issued its report, entitled *The Future of Health Care in Canada*. This additional contribution to the development of health-care policy in Canada was also the result of extensive public consultation and research. The reaction of some members of the public might be: "Another Royal Commission?" But a review of some of the features of the Roma-

30 R.S.C. 1985, c. C-6.

now Commission's report reveals a number of emerging problems and issues that have not been adequately addressed but are important to the future of our health-care system. These include:

- a drop in the federal share of health funding, with related pressures on provincial budgets and service to the public;
- the need to expand publicly insured services to include advanced diagnostic services, which are increasingly being provided by the private sector;
- the need to fund timely access to care in rural and remote areas of the country;
- the need to develop a national home-care strategy;
- the importance of building electronic health-record systems, including personal health records (while protecting privacy) and information for health-care workers and researchers; and
- the need for a concentrated and determined effort to improve primary health care, including timeliness of diagnosis and treatment and greater emphasis on prevention.

In short, successive commissions of inquiry illustrate the evolution of public health-care policy, a process that is bound to continue as new challenges emerge.

### 2) B&B to Aboriginal Peoples

The Laurendeau-Dunton Commission on Bilingualism and Biculturalism, or the "B&B" Commission, was established by Prime Minister Pearson in 1963 in response to rising French Canadian nationalism in Quebec. The context for this commission was the Quiet Revolution that became manifest in the early 1960s following the death of former Premier Maurice Duplessis and the election of the Liberal government of Jean Lesage. The decade included increasing confrontation between Ottawa and the Quebec government, the formation of the Front de Libération du Québec (FLQ), and violent protests including the Saint-Jean-Baptiste Day riot in Montreal on the eve of the 1968 federal election. It culminated in the kidnapping of James Cross, the murder of Pierre Laporte, and the invocation of the *War Measures Act*[31] in October 1970.

31 Since replaced by the *Emergencies Act*, R.S.C. 1985 (4th Supp.), c. 22.

Language rights gained momentum as a central feature of Quebec politics in these years, with numerous provincial commissions and other initiatives leading to provincial legislation and constitutional challenges. But an underlying sense of injustice lay in the inequality of the French language at the federal level. This was recognized in the terms of reference of the B&B Commission, which was directed by the government to report on:

> the existing state of bilingualism and biculturalism in Canada and to recommend what steps should be taken to develop the Canadian Confederation on the basis of an equal partnership between the two founding races, taking into account the contribution made by the other ethnic groups to the cultural enrichment of Canada and the measures that should be taken to safeguard that contribution.

The most direct product of the commission's recommendations was the adoption by Parliament of the *Official Languages Act*,[32] which established English and French as the official languages for Canada at the federal level. The Act gives the Canadian public the right to receive services from federal institutions, including federal courts and tribunals, in the official language of their choice. The B&B Commission also recommended that New Brunswick and Ontario become officially bilingual. New Brunswick did so by passing its own *Official Languages Act* in 1969, the same year that the federal statute was adopted. Ontario and other provinces adopted policies for making government services increasingly available in French. The Trudeau government elected in 1968 also initiated an effective "affirmative action" program of hiring and appointing French Canadians to senior positions in government, agencies, tribunals, and Crown corporations. The result was that the working language of the federal government in Ottawa soon came to include French as well as English.

The *Constitution Act, 1867* had contained very limited language rights in section 133, with respect to the federal Parliament, the Quebec National Assembly, and certain courts. The *Constitution Act, 1982* and particularly the *Canadian Charter of Rights and Freedoms* expand these rights greatly by constitutionally entrenching French and English as the official languages of Canada and New Brunswick. Minority-language education

---

32 R.S.C. 1985 (4th Supp.), c. 31.

rights are also entrenched throughout Canada for children "where the number of those children warrants."

The public hearings and deliberations of the B&B Commission also led to recognition of "multiculturalism" as an important feature of Canadian society. In 1971 the Trudeau government officially adopted a "Policy of Multiculturalism" to replace the "Biculturalism" of the B&B Report, as the partner of "Bilingualism." This policy also became entrenched in the *Charter*, which provides:

> 27. This *Charter* shall be interpreted in a manner consistent with the preservation and enhancement of the multicultural heritage of Canada.

But there also was another element of Canadian society that was omitted from the "multicultural" formulation. This was the rights of the Aboriginal peoples of Canada.

Shortly after the B&B Commission reported, an important case was being argued in the Supreme Court of Canada.[33] Then Indian Affairs Minister Jean Chrétien had published a White Paper in 1969 presenting a new government Indian policy, which rejected Aboriginal land-title and called for the phasing out of Indian special status. This approach would have eliminated the archaic *Indian Act*,[34] instead holding out the alternative of the "integration" of Aboriginal peoples into mainstream Canadian society. When the Indian, Inuit, and Métis peoples immediately attacked this proposal as an attempt to eradicate their identity, the White Paper was quickly abandoned.

Shortly afterwards, in 1973, the *Calder* case was initiated by the Nishg'a First Nation as a claim to ownership of their traditional territories. With neither the courts nor politicians of the time taking Aboriginal rights seriously, the case was viewed as having little chance of success. But in *Calder*, the Supreme Court of Canada was evenly split on the existence of Aboriginal rights. Justice Emmett Hall played a central role in writing a judgment supporting the Nishg'a and persuading three of his colleagues to support him, against the four judges who ruled to

33 See, generally, Douglas Sanders, "Pre-existing Rights: The Aboriginal Peoples of Canada" in Gérald A. Beaudoin & Ed Ratushny, eds., *The Canadian Charter of Rights and Freedoms*, 2d ed. (Toronto: Carswell 1989.) My discussion of the *Calder* case is taken directly from this chapter.

34 R.S.C. 1985, c. I-5.

the contrary. The remaining judge avoided the issue and ruled solely on a procedural basis.[35] However, the *Calder* case had a dramatic impact on both government policy and subsequent judicial decisions. These led to "existing Aboriginal and treaty rights" also being entrenched in the *Constitution Act, 1982*.

But ongoing Aboriginal problems and concerns led to the massive Aboriginal Peoples Commission in 1991, chaired by Aboriginal leader Georges Erasmus and Quebec justice René Dussault and including five additional commissioners. The broad mandate to examine the relationship of Aboriginal peoples with the Canadian government and society resulted in a five-volume report in 1996. It made extensive recommendations in the following areas: self-determination and governance; resolution of land issues and economic stimulation; initiatives to encourage better public understanding of Aboriginal society and culture; and a new relationship between government and Aboriginal peoples based on greater acceptance of their cultures and values.[36]

### 3) Abella

The Abella Royal Commission on Equality in Employment was established in 1983 to examine systemic discrimination in employment in relation to four historically disadvantaged groups: Aboriginal peoples, disabled persons, visible minorities, and women. At the time, human-rights legislation was in place both federally and provincially throughout Canada and had achieved considerable success in dealing with individual complaints of discrimination. The proof of "discrimination" in this context usually involved demonstrating that the complainant had not been treated the same as another. For example, a Black person is told that her qualifications for a job are inadequate; a white person with similar qualifications is then hired for that job.

However, while human-rights legislation confronted blatant discrimination, experience clearly demonstrated the significant under-representation of the four groups mentioned above in both public- and private-sector employment. It was obvious that systemic barriers were at play that would not be overcome by merely treating everyone "the

35 *Calder v. British Columbia (Attorney-General)*, [1973] S.C.R. 313 [*Calder*].

36 The Aboriginal Peoples Commission is discussed further in Chapter 10, Section F.

same." A more sophisticated understanding and application of equality was required.

This was recognized in section 15(2) of the *Charter*, which authorizes special programs or laws for "the amelioration of conditions" of such groups. The provision was intended to ensure that the guaranty of equality in section 15(1) would not prevent such affirmative action. But "affirmative action" had been the subject of considerable judicial attention and public controversy in the United States and some of the negative misconceptions of this approach also became a part of the public discussion in Canada. These included the notion that affirmative action means hiring less qualified workers and amounts to "reverse discrimination." Or that it requires lowering employment standards or setting "quotas."

As minister of employment and immigration, Lloyd Axworthy viewed the Abella Commission as an expedient way to get affirmative-action programs onto the legislative agenda. He also envisioned the process as a vehicle for building understanding and consensus among employers and special-interest groups about the true nature of affirmative action.[37] Commissioner Abella was directed to inquire into "the most efficient, effective and equitable means of promoting employment opportunities, eliminating systemic discrimination and assisting all individuals to compete for employment opportunities on an equal basis." The terms of reference also specified the employment practices of eleven Crown corporations for her review.

Rosalie Abella was the ideal commissioner for this task. At the time of her appointment, she was an Ontario Family Court judge who had already served for five years as a commissioner of the Ontario Human Rights Commission. She had also completed a major report on the accessibility of legal services to disabled persons. In a remarkable legal career, she subsequently became chairperson of the Ontario Labour Relations Board and the Law Reform Commission of Ontario. She served on the Marshall Inquiry Committee[38] before being appointed to the Ontario Court of Appeal and then the Supreme Court of Canada.

---

37 Annis May Timpson, "Challenging Policy Paradigms" in Manson & Mullan, eds., above note 19 at 229. See also Chapter 4, Section C(4) in relation to the Abella terms of reference.

38 Discussed in Sections D(1) and F(1), below in this chapter.

In exploring the barriers faced by each of the four target groups, Commissioner Abella first identified their differences. This in turn reinforced the conclusion that equality in employment could not be achieved by treating everyone "the same." Abella observed that "differences exist and must be respected, equality in the workplace does not and cannot be allowed to mean the same treatment for all." In a stroke of genius, she adopted the term "employment equity" to capture an equality that was sensitive to those differences. This phrase, by itself, contributed to the elevation of the discussion about affirmative action by not mentioning it.

Her conclusions, backed by extensive historical, social, and economic analysis as well as detailed recommendations, resulted in the *Employment Equity Act*[39] becoming law in 1986, only three years after the commission was first appointed. The Liberal government had been defeated in the interim but Axworthy was succeeded as minister by Flora Macdonald, who became a strong advocate for the legislation.

The *Employment Equity Act* has resulted in the establishment of a much better statistical base for measuring the success of affirmative-action programs. It has also created a better understanding and appreciation of their nature and importance, as Axworthy had hoped. Most important, it has contributed gradually to better representation of the targeted groups in the workplace.

## 4) Le Dain

The Le Dain Commission on the Non-Medical Use of Drugs was appointed in 1969 in response to public alarm over increasing use of drugs by young people for recreational purposes. But the widespread public concern went beyond drugs to encompass the threat posed by a "counterculture" that questioned traditional societal values. In some ways, that threat was symbolized by Woodstock, the rock concert captured in a documentary movie of the same name. The fear and paranoia generated among authorities and middle-class parents was fanned by "hippie" symbols such as long hair, beards, distinct clothing, psychedelic vans, and bare feet. But rebellious acts such as smoking marijuana in public places also made the participants easy targets for law-enforcement officers.

---

39 S.C. 1995, c. 44.

The Annual Report of Health Canada for 1968–69 documented an increase in annual narcotic-drug prosecutions from 54 to 2,830 between 1964 and 1968:

> Of these, 2400 were of people under the age of 25. The number of known heroin addicts had also increased. These numbers took another great leap between 1968 and 1969. Convictions under the *Narcotics Control Act* increased from 1779 in 1968 to 3338 in 1969. By far the largest group were marijuana users, 82 per cent of which were under the age of 25. The number of cases involving marijuana had almost doubled in one year.[40]

Simple possession of marijuana was then prosecuted as an indictable offence, leaving thousands of young Canadians with serious criminal records for conduct that many did not view as being even inappropriate.

At the time of his appointment as chairperson, Gerald Le Dain was the dean of Osgoode Hall Law School in Toronto. The other commissioners were Marie-Andrée Bertrand, associate professor of Criminology at the Université de Montréal; Ian L. Campbell, dean of arts, Sir George Williams University, in Montreal; Heinze Lehman, a Montreal psychiatrist who had conducted extensive research in psychopharmacology; and J. Peter Stein, a Vancouver social worker.

The terms of reference were extremely broad. The commission was mandated to:

- gather national and international data and information about the use of such drugs;
- obtain medical knowledge about their effect;
- explore the motivation underlying their use;
- study the "social, economic, educational and philosophical factors" related to their use;
- acquire information about the "age groups involved and problems of communication"; and
- make suggestions for what the federal government could do about the problem.

---

40 Science Council of Canada, *Public Inquiries in Canada* by Liora Salter & Debra Slaco (Ottawa: Supply and Services Canada, 1981) at 118. Much of my discussion of the Le Dain Commission is based on this source.

The commission was required to issue an interim report, which it did in 1970. It then issued a special Report on Cannabis in 1972. Later that year it issued a report on treatment and, in 1973, its final report.

The commissions's public hearings were very informal. Some participants presented formal briefs, others simply spoke and were not required to give their names. The commissioners encouraged questions and engaged in dialogue with the audience. Even more informal "hearings" were held at universities and coffeehouses such as the Penny Farthing in Toronto (Yorkville), the Bistro in Vancouver, and the Back Door in Montreal. In total, the commission conducted forty-six days of hearings in twenty-seven cities, attended by more than 12,000 people.

A problem identified by the Science Council was that the commission was conducting an inquiry into conduct that was essentially illegal. It could provide no guaranty of immunity to "users" who were willing to share their experiences. However, the commission had an informal agreement with the RCMP that persons who provided information would not be charged or investigated based on that information. Researchers also assured subjects that their anonymity would be respected.

In any case, many young people were quite willing to testify and some enjoyed having a platform to advocate drug use as a vehicle for changing social values. To them, drug use reflected a different philosophy of life rather than illegal activity. Obviously, opposing views were expressed by others. Commission Le Dain later spoke of the value of these hearings in a speech to the Empire Club of Canada in Toronto in 1972, shortly before the release of the commission's Report on Cannabis:

> We had the stimulation of direct contact with the kinds of people most deeply involved with the problem. Those hearings made a deep impression upon us. They brought home to us in a way that no amount of library study could do, the seriousness of the problems. People poured out their deepest feelings .... There were many moving occasions. I particularly recall exchanges between young people and adults on the floor—when they were obviously exchanging their points of view for the first time—appealing to one another's understanding. On many occasions there was evidence of a tremendous effort to comprehend and seek reconciliation.

He continued with even greater passion to describe how the hearings had taken on a spiritual dimension:

> We discussed everything, down to the most fundamental values of life, because that is where this inquiry has taken us. We were talking about what it means to be a human being today. People talked freely about spiritual matters . . . .
>
> We look back on this phase with some nostalgia. As commissioners we felt in close contact with the thinking and feelings of people.

Since it is highly unlikely that the commissioners themselves were smoking at the time, this experience suggests the unique "high" that a royal Commission is capable of achieving. Indeed, there is now a public record of the commission receiving secret testimony from John Lennon and Yoko Ono on 22 December 1969, seven months after it was established.[41]

Whatever purpose the public and private hearings may have had, their impact on the commission's reports and recommendations was minimal. The work of the commission became dominated by its in-house research efforts, which at one point involved most of the 200 people on staff. More than 120 research projects were initiated by staff or through other external contracts. Outside experts were invited to attend informal seminars with research staff as a means of providing stimulus and contributing to quality control. The policy-determination function appears to have been overtaken by the ultimate preoccupation with conveying research findings.

The Le Dain Commission admitted to some uncertainty about the interim report it was required to submit: "We have had some difficulty in determining what should be the role of our interim report. In particular, we have been somewhat perplexed as to how far we are justified in coming to conclusions and making recommendations at this time."

The commissioners concluded that they should convey their understanding of the subject matter of the inquiry and any urgent recommendation they felt ready to make. They hoped that identifying certain "attitudes," hypotheses and tentative opinions might serve as a sounding board to elicit further "evidence and opinion." The 320-page interim report stirred considerable controversy in suggesting decriminalization of the possession of all drugs. But, from the public perspective, the whole exercise seemed to be mostly about marijuana.

---

41 Norman Provencher, "Lennon on Drugs Revealed" *Ottawa Citizen* (17 May 2003).

The final Report on Cannabis in 1972 was weakened by a 3:2 split among the commissioners and two separate dissenting recommendations. The majority, consisting of commissioners Le Dain, Lehman, and Stein, recommended that cultivation and possession of cannabis for personal use should not be restrained by law. But the importation and trafficking in cannabis should continue to be serious criminal offences. These commissioners felt that the social cost of criminalizing young people, in particular, for simple possession could not be justified.

However, the majority did not address the inherent contradiction of permitting possession but not distribution unless it was implying that all users should simply grow their own. Commissioner Bertrand tackled that issue squarely by recommending that the sale and distribution of cannabis should be placed under the control of federal and provincial governments. Distribution should be regulated in a manner similar to the controls on alcohol.

Commissioner Campbell went in the opposite direction from the majority by favouring the continued criminalization of simple possession. He recommended that possession be only a summary-conviction offence punishable by a fine of $25 for the first offence and $100 for each subsequent offence. His rationale was that the complete repeal of penal consequences could be "seriously misinterpreted, particularly by young people" as an endorsement of marijuana use as harmless.

It is difficult to assess the contribution of the Le Dain Commission to Canadian society. Its recommendations were never adopted. It may have contributed to calming public fears and to more intelligent public debate. Or society may have simply been "going through a phase" that roughly coincided with the commission's lifespan just as it did with the last gasps of the Vietnam War. The commission certainly left behind a treasure of valuable research and reports that reflect scrupulous analyses and reasoning by the commissioners. It is interesting to note that commissioner Bertrand appeared to be the most kindred spirit of John Lennon, who is quoted as saying: "Let (the establishment) have all the factories. Let it make all the bread in the world. The people only want to smoke. They don't care who makes the money."[42] Lennon added that even modest taxation could generate a great deal of revenue for everything from research to health care to peace projects.

42 *Ibid.*

### 5) Macdonald

The Macdonald Royal Commission on the Economic Union and Development Prospects for Canada—a massive research and policy/advisory commission that became Canada's largest royal commission—was established in 1982 with former federal cabinet minister Donald Macdonald as its head. Despite its size and scope, it appeared to be a model of efficiency and met its three-year timeline for reporting.

As a royal commission on Canada's political economy, the Macdonald Commission had two important predecessors. These were the Rowell-Sirois Commission on Dominion-Provincial Relations, which was established in 1937 largely as a result of the inability of the federal and provincial governments to cope with the consequences of the Great Depression; and the Gordon Commission on Canada's Economic Prospects, which was established in 1955 in response to a sudden economic downturn in the early 1950s and concerns about the potential foreign "takeover" of Canada's economy.[43]

The distribution of taxing powers under the Canadian Constitution of 1867 envisioned a strong central government with dominant spending obligations. But provincial responsibilities for areas such as education, health and welfare, labour, and social assistance grew in importance in the twentieth century without corresponding financial resources. This disparity was accelerated by constitutional decisions of the Judicial Committee of the Privy Council limiting federal jurisdiction and by the effects of industrialization. The Great Depression amplified the consequences of regional disparities and many provincial governments were simply unable to cope with the massive unemployment and poverty that ensued.

The Rowell-Sirois Report, in 1940, recognized the interdependence of the economic collapse, fiscal crisis, and jurisdictional imbalance and recommended strong central government intervention based on Keynesian concepts. Unemployment and fluctuations in income could be reduced by "an intelligent and co-ordinated use of credit, foreign exchange, trade, transportation and taxation policies . . . ." It recommended

---

43 Neil Bradford, "Writing Public Philosophy: Canada's Royal Commission on Everything" (1999–2000) 34 Journal of Canadian Studies 136. This article provides an excellent analysis and discussion of all three of these commissions and I have drawn heavily from it.

that responsibility for unemployment be transferred to the federal government, a proposal that was almost immediately accepted by the provinces and implemented by a constitutional amendment in 1940. It also recommended a realignment of tax fields and the replacement of previous federal subsidies by a national adjustment grant based on norms to encourage national standards in education and social services. Regional disparities would be recognized under the new scheme.

Many of these recommendations were not adopted directly but the underlying concepts led to an evolution of federal-provincial relations. They continue to be an ongoing source of political debate and, most recently, have been stimulated by a shift in the membership of the "have" and "have-not" provinces.

But the unevenness of regional economic activity became pronounced once more with the economic downturn of 1953–54. These conditions again drew attention to the economy's heavy reliance on exploiting rich natural resources without developing the benefits of secondary manufacturing from those resources. A third emerging concern was the potential loss of control of our economy through extensive foreign ownership. Walter Gordon was appointed in 1955 together with four commissioners from different regions of Canada to recommend policies that would best ensure Canada's economic prosperity. Their focus, therefore, was on economic development, wealth creation, and international competitiveness.

The Gordon report in 1958 reflected a commission divided. One perspective was optimistic about the economy's progress and prospects and saw no need to fear foreign ownership or intervene to discourage continental economic integration. The other perspective, articulated best by Gordon, opposed tariff reductions or continental free trade. It recommended specific mechanisms for "micro-managing" aspects of the economy, taking into account Canada's location in the shadow of the United States and its challenges in an era marked by the rise of multinational corporations. But it did little to resolve the debate between the "interventionist nationalists" and "liberal continentalists," which would have to await the next royal commission.

When the Macdonald Commission was appointed in 1982, Canada was facing its worst recession since the Great Depression. Many of the government's interventionist, nationalist policies were diffuse and unsuccessful. The National Energy Program was a disaster. The government seemed unable to cope with the economic conditions of high inflation and unemployment, low productivity and growth, and difficult labour relations.

The Macdonald Commission was highly political in its make-up. In addition to Macdonald, there were twelve commissioners with backgrounds in business, labour, law, economics, government, and politics. The Liberal, Conservative, and New Democratic parties were all represented. The research program was exhaustive, resulting in seventy-two volumes of research comprised of more than 300 studies in nineteen major policy areas. The terms of reference were extremely broad, including "the long-term economic potential, prospects and challenges facing the Canadian federation and its respective regions . . . ," and what these meant for Canada's economic and government institutions, all with an eye on "the appropriate national goals and policies for economic development . . . and the institutional and constitutional requirements for individual liberty and well-being as well as a strong, competitive economy." The specific issues to be addressed seemed to omit very few economic, political, or social topics.

The commission immediately arranged to meet with provincial and territorial premiers and officials and then held private consultations with private-sector groups representing business, manufacturing, finance, labour, resources, agriculture, education, municipalities, volunteers, and Aboriginal communities. It then organized a series of seminars for representatives of many of these groups and distributed 300,000 copies of an information booklet outlining its work and inviting public input. Afterwards, twelve workshops were conducted in universities across the country to stimulate interest in the commission's work, and public hearings were then held in twenty-seven cities and five Arctic communities, where the commissioners heard 759 presentations and received 1,164 briefs. This was followed by a discussion paper grouping the subject areas into eight broad categories. A second round of public hearings was then conducted in the form of round-table debates in five cities, each followed by a "town hall" open forum.

While the public consultations were being conducted, extensive research was also being completed. In the writing phase, working drafts were prepared and revised by eight teams coordinated by policy specialists from various disciplines and analysts who synthesized the testimony and briefs from the hearings. This detail about the process that was followed demonstrates that even such a massive and seemingly unwieldy challenge can be managed. The secretary for the Macdonald Commission subsequently provided the following advice:

> Finally, I would agree totally that you should think early and often about the form and the substance of your report. We had 13 commissioners to sign off on our final report covering three volumes and a bewildering variety of topics. The only way you can do that is by evolving a strategy and trying to get the commissioners and the senior staff together on that strategy very early and then sticking to it.[44]

The experience of this commission certainly indicates the crucial importance of effective management for broad policy/advisory commissions.

The defining feature of the Macdonald report was its recommendation of a free-trade agreement with the United States, in the general context of reduced government intervention and greater reliance on market forces. The immediate adoption of this recommendation by the Mulroney government and its achievement will be a permanent legacy of the Macdonald Commission. Its report also contained recommendations in other areas such as federal-provincial relations, social programs, and even Senate reform (the commission favoured an elective Senate). The report and its research studies continue to be valuable resources, years after they were completed.

## D. WRONGFUL-CONVICTION INQUIRIES

These commissions are simply investigative commissions that are described by their subject matter or role, which is to inquire into the circumstances leading to the wrongful conviction of an innocent person. Our criminal justice system is meant to ensure that this never occurs; there are protections such as the adversary system, the presumption of innocence, the requirement of proof beyond a reasonable doubt, strict rules of evidence, and procedural requirements and limitations now guaranteed by the *Charter*. Recently, however, we have come to recognize the reality that our criminal justice system has convicted innocent people. Some of these victims spent many years in prison before their innocence was officially acknowledged.

---

44 Above note 28 at 73.

In a criminal trial, a finding of "not guilty" is not a finding of factual innocence:

> [A] criminal trial does not address "factual innocence." The criminal trial is to determine whether the Crown has proven its case beyond a reasonable doubt. If so, the accused is guilty. If not, the accused is found not guilty. There is no finding of factual innocence since it would not fall within the ambit or purpose of criminal law.[45]

But evidence of factual innocence may be discovered after a conviction has occurred. DNA evidence might establish that another person was the perpetrator. It also might be demonstrated that the conviction was entirely based on flawed expert evidence. Additional evidence might unequivocally establish that the crime was committed entirely by another person.

It always has been possible for the minister of justice to review cases of alleged wrongful conviction.[46] However, the "system" historically refused to acknowledge that it was capable of making such a serious error. It was only with the decision in the *Marshall* case in 1983 that a wrongful conviction was officially recognized. And even that recognition was tempered by the conclusion that this result was the fault of the accused rather than the "system."

Unfortunately, the *Marshall* decision and the subsequent commission of inquiry came long after the conviction of Stephen Truscott. Truscott was convicted of murder in 1959, at the age of fourteen, and sentenced to death. His death penalty was commuted but he spent ten years in prison followed by a number of years under strict parole conditions. While in prison, a book was published analyzing his conviction and concluding that he was innocent. The ensuing public controversy led the government to refer the case to the Supreme Court of Canada but the Court found no basis to order a new trial.[47]

The controversy over his case was reviewed again at the turn of the century, but this time in the wake of a whole series of commissions on inquiry into wrongful convictions throughout Canada. The Marshall Re-

---

45 Lamer Inquiry, Annex 3 at 342. Adopted in *R. v. Mullins-Johnson* (2007), 87 O.R. (3d) 425 at para. 23 (C.A.) [*Mullins-Johnson*].

46 See the detailed analysis by Kent Roach in the Driskell Inquiry Report, Appendix F.

47 *Reference Re: Stephen Murray Truscott*, [1967] S.C.R. 309.

port had burst the dam. This time, the Truscott case was referred to the Ontario Court of Appeal, which heard new evidence and entered an acquittal in 2007, almost fifty years after his death sentence.[48]

Commissions of inquiry are often instrumental in affecting the compensation that is usually made by a government to the victim of a wrongful conviction. This is done by way of an *ex gratia* payment as a recognition of the injustice and as partial compensation. The commission's report might affect the sum awarded by detailing the conduct of those responsible and the suffering of the victim. The terms of reference for some commissions specifically include the issue of compensation. A separate commission of inquiry might also be established to recommend the compensation that should be awarded or to review the compensation previously awarded.

Commissions of inquiry into wrongful convictions are established by provincial governments since they have the constitutional responsibility for the investigation and prosecution of most criminal offences. Almost all wrongful-conviction commissions have involved the offence of murder. The reports of these commissions have identified many common features of wrongful convictions. In 2005 the federal, provincial, and territorial ministers responsible for justice released a major *Report on the Prevention of Miscarriages of Justice*.[49] This document identifies the key factors that contribute to wrongful convictions as including:

- tunnel vision;
- mistaken eyewitness identification;
- false confessions;
- in-custody informers;
- DNA evidence; and
- forensic evidence and expert testimony.

What follows below are a few random examples of wrongful-conviction inquiries, with certain aspects of each highlighted.

However, it is not possible to refer to wrongful convictions in Canada without recognizing the work of the Association in Defence of the Wrongly Convicted (AIDWYC) and a founding director, James Lockyer. A Toronto lawyer, he has provided great leadership in exposing several

---

48 *R. v. Truscott*, 2007 ONCA 575.

49 Online: www.justice.gc.ca/eng/dept-min/pub/pmj-pej/pmj-pej.pdf.

wrongful convictions in Canada. His work has included the *Morin*, *Milgaard*, *Johnson*, *Parsons*, *Truscott*, and *Driskell* cases and he is currently working on a number of additional cases suggesting miscarriages of justice. His contributions to criminal justice in Canada have been recognized by numerous honorary degrees and other awards.

### 1) Marshall

Donald Marshall, Jr. was convicted of murder and sentenced to life imprisonment in 1971. He was seventeen years of age and Aboriginal. Earlier the same year, he was in a public park in Sydney, Nova Scotia, with a seventeen-year-old Black companion. They were engaged in conversation by two elder men, whom they asked for money. Marshall's companion was stabbed to death by one of the men but Marshall was charged with the murder, convicted, and spent almost eleven years in prison.

A subsequent police investigation based on new information concluded that Marshall was not responsible for the murder. The case was referred to the Nova Scotia Court of Appeal and he was acquitted of the murder in 1983. However, the court concluded its reasons for the acquittal by making a number of gratuitous observations that were critical of Marshall. The court said that "[a]ny miscarriage of justice is . . . more apparent than real" and that his "untruthfullness through this whole affair contributed in large measure to his conviction."[50] This appeared to be a direct response to the following argument in the Crown's factum:

> It is the Respondent's respectful submission that the role of the Court goes much further in this peculiar situation. Here, if the Court does ultimately decide to acquit the Appellant, it is no overstatement to say that the credibility of our criminal justice system may be called into question by a significant portion of the community. It seems reasonable to assume that the public will suspect that there is something wrong with the system if a man can be convicted of a murder he did not commit. A minimum level of public confidence in the criminal justice system must be maintained or it simply will not work.
>
> For the above reasons, it is respectfully submitted that the Court should make it clear that what happened in this case was not the fault

---

50 *R. v. Marshall* (1983), 57 N.S.R. (2d) 286 at 321–22 (S.C.A.D.) [*Marshall*]

> of the criminal justice system or anyone in it, including the police, the lawyers, the members of the jury or the Court itself.[51]

While highly self-serving, this position simply reflected the history of a criminal justice system that refused to accept that it could make such a tragic error.

In 1986 the Nova Scotia government established a "blue chip" royal commission to inquire into the investigation, charging, prosecution, and conviction of Marshall "and such other related matters which the Commissioners consider relevant." The government, wisely, chose three out-of-province jurists of great stature for what proved to be a commission of central importance to the Canadian criminal justice system. It was chaired by Alex Hickman, then Chief Justice of Newfoundland, and included Lawrence Poitras, then associate chief justice of Quebec, and Gregory Evans, retired chief justice of the Ontario High Court.

The commission was blunt in finding:

- that the criminal justice system failed Donald Marshall, Jr. at virtually every turn from his arrest and conviction in 1971 up to—and even beyond—his acquittal by the Supreme Court of Nova Scotia (Appeal Division) in 1983.
- that this miscarriage of justice could have and should have been prevented if persons involved in the criminal justice system had carried out their duties in a professional and/or competent manner.
- that Marshall was not the author of his own misfortune.
- that the miscarriage of justice was real and not simply apparent.
- that the fact that Marshall was an Aboriginal was a factor in his wrongful conviction and imprisonment.

These findings revealed a police investigation that was "incompetent and unprofessional," a prosecution that was inadequately prepared and failed to disclose important evidence, defence counsel that "failed to provide adequate professional representation," and incorrect judicial rulings that denied Marshall a fair trial.

The report was particularly critical of the panel of the Court of Appeal that ultimately entered the acquittal. The commission requested that the

51 Marshall Inquiry Report at 129–30.

Chief Justice of Nova Scotia, who chaired the panel, appear before the commission to explain their observations with respect to the miscarriage of justice. Another issue the commission wished to explore was the apparent conflict of interest of one of the judges on the panel, who had been attorney general at relevant times in the history of the *Marshall* case. The judges claimed judicial immunity from having to testify before the commission and their position was ultimately upheld by the Supreme Court of Canada.[52] But this did not preclude the commission from finding that the Court of Appeal's reasons, on their face, constituted a serious and fundamental error by attempting to defend the criminal justice system at Marshall's expense, "notwithstanding overwhelming evidence to the contrary." The judicial conduct proceedings against the judges on the panel are discussed in Section F(1), below in this chapter.

The release of the Marshall Report in 1990 had a dramatic impact. The "system" officially recognized that it had made serious blunders that tortured an innocent victim. It required the "residual" mechanism of government to expose its shortcomings. That might not have been possible any other way. The Marshall Inquiry exposed the reality of wrongful convictions and opened the door to retrospective scrutiny of the criminal justice system in a way that is not possible through judicial appeals. Over the next decade, cases of wrongful conviction emerged in almost every province and often commissions of inquiry followed. It became accepted that public confidence is best served, not by denying mistakes, but by exposing and analyzing them to determine how they can be avoided in the future.

### 2) Morin

Christine Jessop was nine years old when she was dropped off at her home in a small Ontario town on 3 October 1984. Her parents did not arrive home until about forty-five minutes later. They found her school bag in the house but could not find her in the neighbourhood and called the police. Her body was discovered three months later, some fifty-six kilometres from her home. She had been raped and murdered.[53]

---

52 *MacKeigan v. Hickman* (1989), 61 D.L.R. (4th) 688 (S.C.C.) [*Hickman*].

53 This discussion and related quotations are taken directly from the Morin Inquiry's Report.

Guy Paul Morin lived with his parents as next-door neighbours to the Jessops. He was employed and was a good amateur musician. He had no criminal record but police suspicion focused on him early in the criminal investigation following the discovery of the victim. He was twenty-five years old on 22 April 1985, when he was arrested and charged with the murder. He volunteered samples of his hair, blood, and saliva and was subjected to a six-hour interrogation.

In 1986 Morin was acquitted by a jury but the Ontario Court of Appeal ordered a new trial and was upheld in this respect by the Supreme Court of Canada in 1988. Lengthy pre-trial motions followed but the trial finally proceeded and in 1992 the jury convicted Morin of murder. An appeal was launched and subsequent DNA testing established that sperm recovered from the victim could not have been that of Guy Paul Morin. On 23 January 1995, senior Crown counsel told the Ontario Court of Appeal: "The evidence proves as an indisputable scientific fact that Mr. Morin is not guilty . . . and should be acquitted." On the same day, the deputy attorney general announced that a "public airing" into the case was required.

However, it was not until 26 June 1996 that a commission of inquiry was established with Fred Kaufman as commissioner. Commissioner Kaufman had practised criminal law in Montreal for many years before being appointed to the Quebec Court of Appeal and then "retiring" in Toronto. Since then, in addition to the Morin Inquiry, he has conducted a review of the Nova Scotia public prosecution service as an aftermath of the Marshall Inquiry and a review of the *Truscott* case leading to the reference of this case by the minister of justice to the Ontario Court of Appeal. When announcing the Morin Inquiry, the attorney general said: "An inquiry cannot wipe away the years of pain and turmoil Mr. Morin suffered, but it can examine the complex circumstances surrounding the case, and allow us to learn from it and prevent any future miscarriage of justice."

The terms of reference covered the conduct of the investigation and the criminal proceedings but it also specifically included the Centre of Forensic Sciences. It is this aspect of the report that is briefly discussed here.

At both of his trials, the Crown's theory was that the accused, after coming home from work, lured the victim into his car. Before her parents returned, he drove her some distance from their homes and then sexually assaulted and killed her. At both trials, the Crown relied heavily on hair and fibre evidence presented by forensic scientists employed by the Centre. This included:

> evidence of a hair found embedded in Christine Jessop's necklace which allegedly "matched" Morin's hair, evidence of three hairs found in Morin's car which allegedly "matched" the hair of Christine Jessop, and the "matching" of other fibres and animal hairs found at the murder scene and in Morin's home and car . . . .

Commissioner Kaufman concluded there was no doubt this evidence was crucial to the decision to arrest Morin and contributed to his wrongful conviction.

The Centre of Forensic Sciences in Toronto is a publicly funded institution accountable to the Ontario Ministry of the Attorney General. It is the main laboratory for examining evidence related to criminal investigations. Its public and scientific nature gives an air of credibility to its work and to the presentation of its findings to the courts by its employees. Two of its forensic examiners gave evidence in support of the prosecution of Morin.

The Morin Report devotes over 300 pages to its analysis of forensic evidence, the Centre, and its role in his wrongful conviction. It begins by explaining some basic aspects of hair and fibre comparison (assuming the condition of the hairs does not permit DNA typing). Hair comparisons can definitively *exclude* someone as the donor of an unknown hair. For example, a dark brown hair will exclude a blond person as the donor. But hair comparisons cannot definitely *identify* someone as the donor of the unknown hair. The assessment of hair similarities and differences is highly subjective and statistical "probability" cannot be established. Fibre comparisons raise similar issues.

A problem arises in the courtroom when scientists describe their analysis as demonstrating that a hair found on the victim is "consistent" with the hair of the accused or that a hair found in the accused's car is "consistent" with the hair of the victim. This could mean no more than that they were both brown or both blond. Some scientists even use the word "match" simply to describe consistency, as occurred in this case. The report concluded that the "miscommunication and misapprehension" of such scientific findings contributed to Morin's wrongful conviction.

These findings had not been accurately communicated by the forensic examiners to the police and prosecutors and were misused in the Crown's closing address to the jury. In addition, the fibre evidence had been contaminated at the Centre and there was a cover-up of this contamination by the forensic examiners. Also, further examinations of the contaminated evidence prior to the second trial revealed findings that would have helped the defence, but these were withheld.

The report's exhaustive analysis resulted in thirty-four recommendations related to forensic evidence and the Centre alone, in the following areas:

- the admissibility of hair and fibre comparison evidence in court and the trial judge's instructions on science;
- the form and language used in forensic findings and reports as well as documentation of all related work;
- joint education on forensic issues and a broadly representative advisory board for the Centre;
- improved management of the Centre, including quality controls, a complaint protocol, training, and proficiency testing;
- confidential access to forensic work by defence counsel; and
- adequate resources to eliminate the backlog of cases and permit forensic research and development at the Centre.

The report also addressed other issues such as reliance on jailhouse informants and "junk" evidence that also emerged in other commissions discussed below. But its detailed scrutiny and evaluation of "scientific" evidence was a unique and valuable contribution to the criminal justice system at the time.

### 3) Sophonow

The Manitoba government established the commission of inquiry into the wrongful conviction of Thomas Sophonow in June 2000, with the appointment of Peter Cory as commissioner. He had retired from the Supreme Court of Canada the previous June, in his seventy-fifth year. His judgments in that Court already are frequently quoted above and below, in the cases arising out of the Krever and Westray inquiries. Another "activist" retiree, he followed the Sophonow Commission with a major investigation into allegations that British and Irish security forces colluded with paramilitary groups in committing eight murders in the late 1980s and 1990s. He continues to act as an advisor to the federal Department of Justice.[54]

Thomas Sophonow was convicted of the murder of Barbara Stoppel, whom Commissioner Cory described as a "beautiful, vivacious and friendly sixteen-year-old." She was working alone in a coffee and donut shop in Winnipeg around 8:30 p.m. on 23 December 1981, when she was strangled with a rope in the washroom. Although she was found still alive, there was evidence of a struggle, and she died in the hospital a few days later. The commissioner described Sophonow as "yet another victim." His first trial was aborted when the jury could not reach a verdict. In the second trial, he was convicted but his appeal was allowed and a new trial was ordered. At the third trial, he was also convicted but, again, the appeal was allowed. This time, the Court of Appeal directed an acquittal rather than ordering a fourth trial.

In 1988 the Winnipeg Police Service undertook a second investigation of the Stoppel murder. In June 2000 the police announced that Sophonow was not responsible for the murder and this conclusion was supported by DNA testing. The attorney general apologized to Sophonow for the legal proceedings he had to endure together with the forty-five months he spent in jail for a crime he had not committed. As with most wrongful-conviction inquiries, the Sophonow Commission terms of reference included both the police investigation and the criminal proceedings. But, in addition, Commissioner Cory was directed to determine whether Sophonow was entitled to financial compensation.

At the same time that the police revealed they were satisfied of Sophonow's innocence, they also announced that another suspect had been identified. Commissioner Cory's subsequent report explored how the police had dealt with this alternative suspect at the time of the first investigation. Terry Arnold was linked to Barbara Stoppel in many ways. The circumstantial evidence available to the police that incriminated Arnold was compelling yet he was not pursued as a suspect because of the entire police focus on Sophonow. The report states: "Sergeant Blener, with his usual candor, testified that Terry Arnold slipped through

54 This discussion and related quotations are taken directly from the Sophonow Inquiry's Report. Cory's investigation in relation to Ireland is discussed briefly in Chapter 9, Section D(1).

the cracks of the investigation of the murder of Barbara Stoppel. This is a very sad and telling conclusion . . . . He fairly conceded that he, like other officers working on the case, suffered from tunnel vision." Arnold was a suspected serial killer who was investigated in relation to a number of sexual offences against children before committing suicide in March 2005.

Often, the focus on a single innocent suspect to the exclusion of all others makes it difficult, later, to investigate the person who actually committed the offence. By the time Marshall's innocence was established, the likely murderer in that case had also died. In the *Truscott* and *Morin* cases, no alternative suspects were identified. Exceptionally, as in the *Parsons* case that follows, a second police investigation is successful in identifying and convicting the murderer. Commissioner Cory described "tunnel vision" this way:

> Tunnel Vision is insidious. It can affect an officer or, indeed anyone involved in the administration of justice with sometimes tragic results. It results in the officer becoming so focused upon an individual or incident that no other person or incident registers in the officer's thoughts. Thus, tunnel vision can result in the elimination of other suspects who should be investigated. Equally, events which could lead to other suspects are eliminated from the officer's thinking. Anyone, police officer, counsel or judge can become infected by this virus.

The report illustrates how such an approach undermined the investigation in many respects: the police interviews with Sophonow; the handling of eyewitness identification, alibi, timing, and physical evidence; the failure properly to disclose evidence to the defence; and the reliance on jailhouse informants.

The reliance on jailhouse informants was also the subject of criticism in the Morin Report and in one of the three cases analyzed in the Lamer Report. Commissioner Cory's disgust for this type of witness was expressed in the Sophonow Report:

> They must be recognized as a very great danger to our trial system. Steps must be taken to rid the courts of this cancerous corruption of the administration of justice. Perhaps, the greatest danger flows from their ability to testify falsely in a remarkably convincing manner. In this case, it will be seen that an experienced detective thought that Mr. Martin,

> a very frequent jailhouse informant with a conviction for perjury, was a credible witness. He lied in this case and he has testified in at least nine other cases, undoubtedly with the same degree of mendacity. Jailhouse informants are a festering sore. They constitute a malignant infection that renders a fair trial impossible. They should, as far as it is possible, be excised and removed from our trial process.

The Sophonow prosecution relied on the evidence of three informants. Each claimed that the accused confessed while they were in custody together. Before the third trial, no fewer than eleven jailhouse informants had volunteered their services.

Such "confessions" are easy to concoct since they are alleged to occur when the informant and the accused are alone together. The incentive for the informant is to be in a position to try to negotiate some form of leniency. The police and prosecution are often anxious to use this evidence, particularly as "icing" on a weak circumstantial case. The informants are often "con artists," who are convincing witnesses.

In the Sophonow case, one of the jailhouse informants was cross-examined as to whether he had made a bargain with the police in exchange for his testimony. He denied this and said that, while he hoped he might be treated better for his cooperation, his motivation really was to see a murderer removed from the streets. Unknown to defence counsel, he had previously told the police polygraph officer that his real motivation was to get out of jail and have the charges against him dropped. In fact, he was facing twenty-six counts of fraud that were dropped and he was released from custody on the understanding that he would testify again at the third trial. The failure of the prosecution to disclose this information was a serious error preventing a fair trial.

The Crown sought to hold a second informant in custody to ensure his attendance at trial. This informant responded by threatening to sabotage the prosecution and perjure himself if necessary. The police countered by threatening to expose him publicly as an ongoing police informant. This would place his life in jeopardy on the street, as a "rat." Documentation of the Crown's unseemly dealings with this witness was contained in a police report. It would have significantly affected his credibility but was not disclosed by the Crown to defence counsel.

The third informant who was called as a witness was described as "a prime example of the convincing mendacity of jailhouse informants. He seems to have heard more confessions than many dedicated priests. He has testified as a jailhouse informant in at least nine cases in Canada." When he volunteered his services, the police became aware of his significant criminal record, which included a conviction for perjury. Their inquiries led them to rationalize that he had lied as a witness to protect his wife, and they concluded that "he came across as a truthful type."

The Morin Report made thirty-three recommendations to restrict the use and dangers of jailhouse-informant evidence. These were expressly adopted in the Sophonow Report, which went further. Such testimony, this report stated, should be prohibited except in rare cases. Even where the strict conditions for admissibility are met, strong jury instructions should be required to illustrate the specific dangers inherent in such evidence. The Lamer Report adopted the Sophonow Report's recommendations on jailhouse informants and also recommended that they be adopted as Crown policy for Newfoundland and Labrador.

### 4) Parsons

In March 2003 the former chief justice of Canada, Antonio Lamer, was appointed to conduct a commission of inquiry into three separate murder cases in Newfoundland. The murders had occurred in 1988, 1991, and 1993. In the first case, Ronald Dalton was convicted of murdering his wife. A new trial was ordered on appeal and he was acquitted by a jury on his second trial. The terms of reference specifically directed an inquiry into why it took eight years before his appeal was heard. In the second case, Gregory Parsons was convicted of murdering his mother but a new trial was ordered. The re-testing of exhibits in preparation for the second trial led to his exoneration by establishing that the DNA found at the scene was not that of Gregory Parsons. In the third case, Randy Druken was convicted of killing the woman with whom he lived and, again, a new trial was ordered on appeal. A stay of proceedings was entered but the trial never proceeded. The discussion that follows deals only with the Parsons case.[55]

Gregory Parsons loved his mother and she loved him but she was a difficult person in many ways. She was an alcoholic though had not

55 This discussion and related quotations are taken directly from the Lamer Inquiry's Report.

relapsed for a number of years. She suffered depression and anxiety and had attempted suicide. She saw a variety of doctors and was prescribed thousands of pills, which she hoarded, together with food and beverages. Her psychiatrist described her as a "histrionic" personality type with a tendency to exaggerate and dramatize. She was manipulative and destructive. She would make extreme statements to draw attention to herself and found that she could draw a strong reaction by telling almost anyone who would listen about her fear of her son. She spoke of him abusing and assaulting her and threatening to kill her.

These fears were groundless, as were the allegations of threats and assaults. In fact, Gregory was very respectful of his mother and took care of her in many ways. In March 1990 her demands and erratic behaviour caused him to leave her home and move in with some friends, but he returned briefly in the summer, only to move out again a few weeks later. He turned nineteen in September and arranged to move in with his girlfriend's family, with whom he was very close, in the new year.

He spent New Year's Eve at their home and the next day around midnight called his mother to wish her a happy New Year, when they spoke briefly. He returned to his apartment at 4:00 a.m. and slept until early afternoon. After dinner together, he and his girlfriend drove to his mother's home so he could visit her, but there was no answer to the doorbell and he assumed she was out visiting. They returned the next day and, when there was no response again, he removed a window and entered. He found his mother, half-naked, in the washroom, covered in blood and dead. She had been slashed or stabbed fifty-three times. The investigation and prosecution of Gregory Parsons provides many examples of "tunnel vision" at work.

On the day after her body was discovered, his mother's psychiatrist told the police that he felt Parsons had violent tendencies towards her and repeated her fears that he would kill her. Her lawyer also told the police that she said he had threatened to cut her up with a knife. Attention immediately focused on Parsons as the sole suspect. The crime-scene investigation was a disaster, with twelve to fifteen different people entering the small blood-coated bathroom. There was a broken window in the basement that immediately was ruled out as the point of entry of the killer as being too small. When the murderer was arrested many years later, he turned out to be a former next-door neighbour and friend of Parsons. They frequently entered and exited the basement through this window and he admitted he did so on the night of the murder. The police did not do a "perimeter" search for the weapon but searched only between the murder scene and Parson's residence. The weapon was found years later, nearby, but in the opposite direction, towards the home of the murderer.

The police gathered additional statements by the victim to a wide variety of people about her fear of her son. The police seemed to view these as mutually reinforcing each other as evidence of the identity of the perpetrator and the motive for the murder. However, Commissioner Lamer concluded that every one of the statements came from the same, totally unreliable source. They played an important part in the conviction of Parsons at his trial but never should have been admitted into evidence.

In the conduct of police interviews, witnesses were pressured to tailor their recollections to support a conviction. Innocuous evidence was treated as incriminating. For example, Parsons had told the police that his mother finished their telephone conversation by saying "Goodbye." This was viewed as suspicious because of its air of finality, as opposed to, for example, "See you tomorrow." Moreover, it was her statement not his. Even accepting this far-fetched inference, it would support a suicide rather than a murder. The police report reasoned that the murder was "planned and deliberate" because New Year's morning was selected, when it would not be unusual to see a person on the streets at 5:00 a.m. or 6:00 a.m. Much was also made of Parsons's "suspicious" demeanour shortly after he discovered his mother's body. But the Lamer Report observes that people react in different ways when confronted by tragedies. Some act out emotionally; others, numb with shock, remain silent. Indeed, the same person may react in different ways.

Commissioner Lamer reflected on the insights provided into tunnel vision by previous commissioners Kaufman and Cory. He said:

> Tunnel vision is rarely the result of malice on the part of individuals. Rather it is generated by a police and prosecutorial culture that allows the subconscious mind to rationalize a biased approach to the evidence. Moreover, it is mutually reinforcing amongst police officers, amongst prosecutors and in the interaction between these groups of professionals. It may even affect judges.

He elaborated on the dangers facing the police:

> Once "locked in" to the theory of their case, it is not difficult to understand how some police officers, with "noble" motivation, may move from mere interpretation of the evidence to more malignant practices. These could include "assisting" witnesses in their recollection, ignoring relevant evidence that does not support their mission and using coercion to attempt to obtain admissions from the single suspect, whose guilt is assumed.

During the course of the Parsons hearings, many officers acknowledged the inadequacy of their training and experience, and their limited competence, at the time of the investigation. This was to the credit of the force:

> The good news for the public of Newfoundland and Labrador is that the Royal Newfoundland Constabulary, the RNC Association and many individual police officers approached this Inquiry in an honest and professional manner. Many have gained a great deal of insight and wisdom from this tragedy. Mistakes have been acknowledged and there is strong motivation to establish and maintain a police force whose standard is excellence . . . that is a realistic goal.

Before the Lamer Inquiry had completed its hearings, the Royal Newfoundland Constabulary already had adopted numerous reforms that were approved in the Lamer Report.

The Lamer Report also found tunnel vision to be operative in the Crown's role in the Parsons prosecution. It documented a Crown "culture" that uncritically adopted the police view of his guilt and focused solely on achieving a conviction without adequate consideration for fairness. The report stressed the need for "systemic" changes:

> The emphasis on attitudinal change is well placed and the reference to "culture" properly emphasizes a more systemic approach. The reality is that Crown attorneys are human beings and many criminal trials have stressful and emotional features. Human nature often makes it difficult for professionals working in an adversarial system under such conditions to avoid being "competitive."

In the *Parsons* case, the Crown got caught up in the same vortex as the police and were also driven by the same perceived "noble cause" that led to the tragic result for Parsons.

### 5) Driskell

The Driskell Commission in Manitoba resulted in another important report in relation to wrongful convictions. James Driskell was convicted of murder in 1991 and spent over thirteen years in prison before ultimately being exonerated. To review the case, the government appointed former Ontario Superior Court chief justice Patrick LeSage in December 2005, with broad terms of reference that also had some unique features.[56]

The terms of reference specifically directed an inquiry into the "conduct of Crown Counsel" in this case, as well as the specific question as to whether the Winnipeg Police Service failed to disclose information to the Crown. Advice was sought as to whether the conduct of Crown counsel "fell below professional and ethical standards" and whether the Crown and police conduct should be referred for disciplinary proceedings. Also included was "the role of the RCMP Laboratory" in Driskell's wrongful conviction, including any related systemic issues. Finally, the terms of reference raised the very broad policy question as to whether and when a determination of wrongful conviction could be made in cases such as *Driskell*.

The mandate of the Driskell Commission was both narrower and broader than those given to previous wrongful-conviction commissions. It was directed to examine very specific aspects of Crown and police conduct. Yet it was given a broad, systemic mandate analogous to a more policy/advisory role.

On the *Driskell* case itself, Commissioner LeSage stated at the outset that the failure to disclose information to defence counsel was the central issue of this inquiry. The Crown's case had rested on the evidence of two associates of Driskell, who said he had admitted killing the victim to prevent him from testifying against Driskell on other charges: "At the heart of the disclosure issue is the failure to disclose information to Driskell with respect to matters that were relevant and extremely cogent regarding the credibility of both of these witnesses . . . . " In response to the specific mandate regarding disclosure, the report concluded that the conduct of Crown counsel fell below the professional standards expected of lawyers and agents of the Crown. It also found that the failure

---

56 This discussion and related quotation are taken directly from the Driskell Inquiry's Report.

of police officers to disclose information to the Crown contributed to the miscarriage of justice.

The review of the role of the RCMP Laboratory specifically discussed hair analysis, which had been the subject of considerable review in the Morin Report. It concluded that the laboratory did not fulfill its responsibility to ensure that its conclusions not only assisted the Crown but also set out the limitations and frailties of such conclusions, even though they would assist the defence. Systemic issues related to the laboratory were also examined.

The Driskell Report contained a unique discussion of the broader issues related to whether and how determinations of factual innocence could be made. Since this component of the terms of reference raised a policy issue that did not depend on any adjudicative facts, Commissioner LeSage adopted a special process for addressing it. First, he commissioned a special report by law professor Kent Roach, which was analyzed and discussed with the author by the commissioner and commission counsel. They concluded that the report identified seven major questions or issues arising out of this aspect of the terms of reference. They then invited six additional experts to join the author in a panel discussion that took place at a round-table hearing attended by persons with standing as well as the commissioner and commission counsel. A chapter of the Driskell Report related the views expressed by the panelists and the conclusions of the commissioner.

> In the introductory comments to this section on wrongful convictions, it was pointed out that a finding of "not guilty" is not a finding of "factual innocence." A conclusion of innocence may become apparent from the factual circumstances of the case. When it is available, DNA evidence can be a convincing way to demonstrate factual innocence. But there is no "process" in place for making such determinations. The Ontario Court of Appeal recently confirmed that the criminal judicial process does not permit a formal legal declaration of factual innocence but in that case the evidence did show "beyond question that the appellant's conviction was wrong and that he was the subject of a terrible miscarriage of justice."[57]

57 *R. v. Mullins-Johnson*, above note 45 at para. 26. The issue of determining factual innocence is discussed in Chapter 7, Section A(1).

The court was free to express its reasons in these clear and strong terms but it could not take the further step of declaring innocence. Commissioner LeSage concluded that this broad question of determining "wrongful convictions" or "factual innocence" required further study. But the discussion in the Driskell Report is a valuable contribution to the literature on this subject and to such further study.

## E. INQUIRIES INVESTIGATING CRIMES

The historical background at the start of the previous chapter referred to the ancient use of commissions of inquiry to investigate crimes. This led to the Court of Star Chamber and abuses of its inquisitorial powers, which were replicated to some degree in the Kellock-Taschereau Commission referred to at the start of this chapter. The great attraction of commissions of inquiry to investigate is that they have the power to compel suspects and other witnesses to testify. A police investigation does not have such a power.

The responsibility for investigating most *Criminal Code* offences falls to the provincial governments. But the *Criminal Code* is a federal statute. It not only defines crimes but also establishes the procedures by which they are to be investigated and prosecuted. If a province could use a commission to investigate crimes, it could avoid many of these procedural restrictions by directly compelling witnesses to testify. It could identify suspects through such testimony and then compel the suspects to testify and provide evidence about their criminal conduct. Their subsequent prosecution would then be greatly facilitated.

Provinces have succumbed to this temptation in the past but case law has since established that this is not a permissible deployment of commissions of inquiry. Since criminal procedure is a federal responsibility under the distribution of constitutional powers, a province cannot adopt different procedures to replace those established by the *Criminal Code*. There are now also further restrictions imposed by the *Charter* upon attempts to adopt more intrusive investigative powers, even by the federal government.

The developments discussed below are of mostly historical interest. But they involve some important Supreme Court decisions and provide guidance as to a fine dividing line. This permits inquiries into misconduct that may, incidentally, be criminal but not inquiries for the investigation of criminal conduct.

### 1) Ontario Police Bill

In the early 1960s, concerns mounted about the infiltration of organized crime into Ontario from the United States.[58] The Roach Commission reported in 1963 that, apart from the field of gambling, the degree of such activity was no cause for alarm. But concerns persisted and the government directed the Ontario Police Commission to conduct a further and more intensive inquiry on an ongoing basis. Bill 99 was introduced in 1964 to provide powers to compel testimony *in camera* and to imprison uncooperative witnesses for periods of up to eight days, repeatedly, until they testified.

The legislation was immediately attacked: "The response of the press, and through the press, of the public, was instantaneous. There were charges of a 'police state,' of 'fascism,' of the Star Chamber. First thing next morning the leader of the Liberal Opposition demanded that the government withdraw the Bill or call an immediate election . . . ." The attorney general resigned and another bill was introduced which specified the rights of witnesses. It had the effect of quelling the public controversy even though the legislation still permitted the inquiry to proceed. But the political consequences flowing from the first bill caused the government to abandon its plans for an ongoing organized crime commission.

### 2) Quebec Crime Commission

In 1972 the Quebec government established the Commission of Inquiry into Organized Crime, with a broad mandate to inquire into the activities of "organizations or systems and the persons involved" in a long list of criminal activities. The commission did not view its role as simply to investigate and report; rather, it said that "[w]e consider that an inquiry into organized crime is not intended solely to investigate the organized crim-

---

58 This summary is taken from Walter Tarnopolsky's discussion of "the rise and fall of the Ontario Police Bill, otherwise known as Bill 99" in *The Canadian Bill of Rights*, 2d rev. ed. (Toronto: Macmillan of Canada, 1978) at 57–62.

inal groups in our society, but also to fight against them."[59] The commission subsequently claimed that, through police exposure, it had disrupted the activities of members of organized crime by holding out the prospect that they might have to appear as witnesses. It used its special power of compelling testimony to obtain information for police investigations and claimed credit for a number of criminal charges being brought. Its 1977 report identified specific individuals as being involved in criminal activities.

The Supreme Court of Canada upheld the constitutional validity of the Quebec commission in the *Di Iorio* case.[60] However, the Court did not have before it the 1977 report of the commission or other evidence of its aggressive investigation of specific criminal acts. Then Justice Brian Dickson, with the support of four others, wrote:

> Quebec's Crime Inquiry introduces no new and insidious form of investigation into our judicial system and there is no evidence before the Court that it is a colourable attempt to evade the procedural provisions of the *Criminal Code*.[61]

This observation could only have been characterized as naive had a true record of the commission's activity been before the Court.[62] Dickson added:

> Whether or not one agrees with a result which may force a person to assist in an investigation of his criminal activity, Canadian laws, both federal and provincial, compel such a result.

The judgment of Justice Louis-Philippe Pigeon also contained strong support for the use of provincial commissions of inquiry to investigate crimes and he summarized the *Di Iorio* precedent in the later *Keable* case:

> it appears to me that the majority opinion in *Di Iorio v. Warden of the Montreal Jail*, is conclusive of the validity of the Commission's mandate to the extent that it is for an inquiry into specific criminal activities.[63]

---

59 This quotation and related discussion are taken from Ed Ratushny, *Self-Incrimination in the Canadian Criminal Process* (Toronto: Carswell, 1979) at 366–404.

60 *Di Iorio v. Warden of the Montreal Jail*, [1978] 1 S.C.R. 152 [*Di Iorio*].

61 *Ibid.* at 155, on behalf of Martland, Judson, Ritchie, and Spence JJ.

62 See, generally, above note 59.

63 *Quebec (Attorney General) v. Canada (Attorney General)*, [1979] 1 S.C.R. 218 at 241 [*Keable*].

The door appeared to be wide open for the provinces to establish commissions of inquiry for the purpose of compelling testimony in aid of criminal investigations. It soon slammed shut.

### 3) *Re Nelles and Grange*

A number of infant deaths occurred at the Toronto Hospital for Sick Children in the early 1980s that could not be explained by natural causes. Four charges of murder were laid against one of the nurses on duty when some of the large drug overdoses occurred. The charges were dismissed at the preliminary inquiry but the judge did conclude that some of the deaths were due to deliberate drug overdoses. The government of Ontario established a commission of inquiry with a mandate that specifically asked "how and by what means children . . . came to their deaths . . . ." It also included the circumstances surrounding the police investigation and subsequent criminal prosecution. High Court Justice Samuel ("Sam") Grange was appointed as commissioner.

The terms of reference specifically precluded the commissioner from expressing any conclusions about civil or criminal responsibility for the deaths. When announcing the inquiry, the Ontario attorney general explained:

> This provision was made to ensure that the Commission would not function or be regarded as a criminal or civil trial. Trial by Commission of Inquiry is a concept totally foreign to the Laws of the province. While it is understandable that many members of the public would wish to have an inquiry to determine responsibility for the tragic deaths, this cannot be the function of a Royal Commission. The purpose of a public inquiry is not to attach criminal culpability. It is not a forum to put individuals on trial. The just and proper place to make and defend allegations of crime or civil liability is in a court of law.

He added that there was no precedent in Ontario for a commission of inquiry into deaths caused by deliberate criminal acts of "a person or persons unknown." The Ontario Court of Appeal quoted this statement by the attorney general and specifically endorsed this limitation on commissions of inquiry as being both correct and important:

> A public inquiry is not the means by which investigations are carried out with respect to the commission of particular crimes . . . . Such an in-

> quiry is a coercive procedure and is quite incompatible with our notion of justice in the investigation of a particular crime and the determination of actual or probable criminal or civil responsibility.[64]

In this respect, both the Ontario government and its Court of Appeal implicitly rejected the conduct of the Quebec Crime Commission and its approval by the *Di Iorio* judgment.

The Grange Commission came before the Ontario Court of Appeal because it sought direction as to the scope of its mandate. The commissioner asked whether he was authorized to name any persons who had administered a drug overdose that resulted in death "by accident or design." The court established a five-person panel to hear the case because of its importance. In addition to approving the government's prohibition against findings of criminal responsibility, the court referred to its earlier decision in *R. v. Hoffman-La Roche Ltd.* and quoted extensively from the judgment of Martin J.A., a member of its panel. The passage quoted describes the manner in which police investigations are conducted, without any power to compel testimony. It recognizes that a potential accused person could be compelled to testify at a provincial commission of inquiry, provided it was established and conducted for a "valid provincial purpose" and cited the *Di Iorio* case, but added:

> manifestly it would not be within provincial competence to enact legislation enabling a police officer to summon a suspect before an official and submit the suspect to compulsory examination under oath with respect to his involvement in a crime.[65]

The court pointed out that this passage had received the full endorsement of Chief Justice Bora Laskin, writing for the majority of the Supreme Court in a more recent case.[66] Chief Justice Laskin had written a strong dissent in *Di Iorio*; by this time, however, justices Ronald Martland, Wilfred Judson, and, particularly, Louis-Philippe Pigeon had left the Court, and so Laskin now had a majority.

The Ontario Court of Appeal ruled unanimously and unequivocally that Commissioner Grange could not "name names." However, this deci-

---

64 *Re Nelles and Grange* (1984), 46 O.R. (2d) 210 at 216 (C.A.) [*Nelles*].

65 *R. v. Hoffman-La Roche Ltd. (Nos. 1 & 2)* (1981), 33 O.R. (2d) 694 at 724 (C.A.).

66 *Canada (Attorney General) v. Canadian National Transportation Ltd.*, [1983] 2 S.C.R. 206 [*Canadian National Transportation*].

sion was based simply on its interpretation of the terms of reference. In the circumstances of this commission of inquiry, the naming of individuals who had administered a lethal overdose of drugs would amount to a conclusion that they were criminally responsible. Although it did not rule on the constitutional issue decided in *Di Iorio*, the judgment provided a strong statement about the limitations applicable where criminal conduct may be involved.

### 4) *O'Hara v. British Columbia*

The issue of what may constitute a "valid provincial purpose" where criminal activity is also involved was squarely addressed by the Supreme Court in the *O'Hara* case.[67] A healthy twenty-five-year-old man was arrested for impaired driving and taken to jail because of his drunken state. He left the jail five hours later with a smashed kneecap that resulted in a series of operations and a permanent disability. He complained that he had been assaulted and injured by an officer or officers during his detention. An internal investigation was conducted by the Vancouver City Police but he could not identify his assailant(s) and the police dropped the matter.

He then sought an inquiry by the Vancouver Police Board into his treatment, and particularly into the conduct of the senior police officer on duty while he was detained. The board dismissed the complaint because there was no reliable identification evidence against any of the officers. However, the board did conclude that the complainant had been assaulted by two or more of the officers on duty, causing the injury, and that some or all of them were involved in a "cover-up." The government established a commission of inquiry into the circumstances of his detention and the subsequent related investigations and inquiries. Specifically included in the terms of reference were the persons who inflicted his injuries and the reasons for doing so. The police officers summoned as witnesses challenged the government's constitutional authority to establish a commission because they alleged its primary purpose was to investigate whether criminal offences occurred and, if so, who was responsible. This was a matter for the criminal justice system rather than a provincial inquiry.

---

67 *O'Hara v. British Columbia*, [1987] 2 S.C.R. 591 [*O'Hara*].

Chief Justice Dickson, writing for the majority, began by stating that a matter may fall within federal jurisdiction for one purpose but within the legitimate concern of a province for another purpose. The federal purpose here was to establish and maintain a national procedure for investigating criminal offences. What then was the "valid provincial purpose" that allowed the BC government incidentally to identify the perpetrators of the assault through the procedure of a commission of inquiry?

The provinces are responsible for providing police services and for the control and discipline of police forces. This engages a valid constitutional interest in police conduct, even though it might involve criminal activity, since that is part of the management of police forces. It is the provinces that have responsibility for the professional discipline of the police. In addition to the police, the jail where the events took place is also a provincial constitutional responsibility. Without specifically challenging the position of Justice Pigeon in *Di Iorio*, Chief Justice Dickson noted:

> An inquiry enacted solely to determine criminal liability and to bypass the protection afforded by the *Criminal Code* would be *ultra vires* of a province, being a matter related to criminal law and criminal procedure.

Here, however, the basic purpose was not to determine criminal responsibility. It was clear that wrongful events had occurred in the jail that had to be identified and explained to the public. Public confidence in the administration of justice was at stake. The incidental possibility that criminal charges might be laid did not override the "valid provincial purpose" of this commission of inquiry.[68]

### 5) *Starr v. Houlden*

Although the *Nelles* and *O'Hara* cases spoke of limits upon provincial inquiries, the comments of Justice Pigeon in *Di Iorio*, confirmed in *Keable*, were not directly challenged. And both of those cases, as well as others since *Di Iorio*, have upheld provincial authority to establish commissions of inquiry, even where criminal offences were involved. But none of these commissions could be characterized as essentially focused, in Justice Pigeon's words, on "specific criminal activities." In retrospect, the

68 *Ibid*. at para. 20.

Quebec Crime Commission Inquiry would meet that characterization, but both *Nelles* and *O'Hara* articulated a dominant "valid provincial purpose," apart from criminal activities.

In *Starr v. Houlden*,[69] the Supreme Court laid to rest the ghost of *Di Iorio* and ruled that Ontario had crossed the line into impermissible criminal investigation. Patricia Starr was the chairperson of the Toronto section of a national charitable organization. In February 1989 media reports linked her to a large real-estate development corporation and alleged political contributions that had been made by the charitable organization to the Liberal Party, which then formed the Ontario government. By early June, allegations of impropriety had intensified in the Legislative Assembly, including Ms. Starr's close relationship with some nine cabinet ministers, her public appointment as chairperson of Ontario Place, and a recommendation for her mother to receive a government contract.

On 12 June, the acting solicitor general announced that he had asked the Ontario Provincial Police to conduct a comprehensive investigation into Starr's "contributions and expenditures" in relation to her charitable organization. A special Crown prosecutor was also assigned to the case. Investigations were also instituted by the Commission on Election Finances and the Conflict of Interest Commissioner. But on 22 June the executive director of the Premier's Office resigned and revealed that Ms. Starr had previously arranged for his family to receive a new refrigerator and to have their house painted free of charge. The next day, the premier announced that he was ordering a public inquiry into the entire affair.

Justice Lloyd Houlden, who had served on the Ontario Court of Appeal panel in the *Nelles* case, was appointed as commissioner. The terms of reference were framed in two parts. The first part authorized him "to investigate" the dealings between Patricia Starr and elected and unelected officials as well as private individuals and corporations. Similar dealings of Tridel Corporation were also to be investigated. The second part directed the commissioner "to inquire into and report" on such dealings where "there is sufficient evidence that a benefit, advantage or reward of any kind was conferred upon an elected or unelected public official or upon any member of the family of any elected or unelected public official . . . ."

---

69 [1990] 1 S.C.R. 1366 [*Starr*].

As with the Grange Inquiry, Commissioner Houlden was precluded from expressing any conclusion regarding "civil or criminal responsibility." Starr and others challenged the constitutional authority of a province to establish this inquiry. Once more, the issue was whether the "pith and substance" of the terms of reference served a "valid provincial purpose" or whether they were an attempt to conduct a substitute police investigation where suspects could be compelled to testify.

Then Justice Lamer wrote the majority judgment on behalf of five colleagues as well as himself. Justice Claire L'Heureux-Dubé wrote a sole dissent. Justice Lamer began by finding it "necessary to review the fairly extensive body of jurisprudence" on "the constitutional validity of provincial commissions of inquiry." He soon took dead aim at Justice Pigeon's comments in *Di Iorio* and his interpretation of it as a precedent in *Keable*. Although a majority had upheld the Quebec Crime Commission in *Di Iorio*, Justice Lamer found the number of judgments in that case made it "somewhat difficult to discern the *ratio* of the case." However, he was satisfied that Justice Pigeon's comments in *Di Iorio* were *obiter* since the true basis for that decision was the broader concern with organized crime generally rather than the investigation of specific crimes. Those comments:

> should not be taken to mean that it is within provincial jurisdiction to directly investigate particular individuals in respect of their alleged commission of specific criminal offences.[70]

Justice Lamer also drew on a passage to the same effect from Justice Martin's decision in *Hoffman-La Roche* that was adopted by the Ontario Court of Appeal in *Nelles* and by the Supreme Court in *Canadian National Transportation*.[71] Justice Lamer also found support for his interpretation of *Di Iorio* in the Court's more recent decision in *O'Hara*, just discussed.

Justice Lamer then turned his attention to the specific nature of the Starr Inquiry as defined by its terms of reference. He concluded that this was really an investigation to determine whether Patricia Starr and Tridel Corporation had committed a fraud on the government contrary to section 121 of the *Criminal Code*. Of course, the commission could not enter

---

70 *Ibid.* at 1395.

71 Above note 66.

a conviction but it had been directed to conduct a "substitute police investigation and preliminary inquiry" into whether named individuals had committed a specific offence. There was no broader, policy basis for the inquiry. There was an ongoing police investigation. Although public officials were referred to in the terms of reference, that was only with respect to whether they had dealings with Starr or Tridel, who were private individuals. Moreover, in announcing the commission of inquiry, the Premier stated that "those who have broken the law will be prosecuted."

The wording of the terms of reference bore a "striking resemblance" to the elements of the offence contained in section 121. The structure of the commissioner's mandate established a "two-step" process. The first was to locate and "investigate" the "dealings" of two individuals, much like a police investigation would. The second step was to "inquire" and offer an opinion as to whether there was "sufficient evidence that a benefit" was conferred on an official. This was very similar to the role of a preliminary inquiry judge in deciding whether a *prima facie* case exists against an accused.

In her own inimitable way, Justice L'Heureux-Dubé summarized her dissent this way:

> The case law entirely supports the proposition that the inquiry is *intra vires* the province. Functionally, the Houlden Commission is indistinguishable from those commissions that withstood constitutional attack in *Faber*, *Di Iorio*, *Keable*, and *O'Hara*. The semantic gymnastics used to distinguish the present case from the Court's precedents are not, in my view, sufficient to displace the presumption of constitutional validity.[72]

Undoubtedly, the line is often difficult to draw, but the *Starr* case clearly established that such a line exists by striking down the commission's terms of reference as an attempt to deal with a matter in the exclusive jurisdiction of the federal government.

## F. ONGOING INQUIRY BODIES

A unique feature of commissions of inquiry appointed under the *Inquiries Act* is that they are brought into existence by an order in council and they cease to exist after submitting their reports. But some stat-

---

72 Above note 65 at 1437.

utes also create administrative bodies that function on an ongoing basis and are given the authority to conduct inquiries with similar powers to those granted by the *Inquiries Act*. Indeed, some statutes specifically grant such bodies "the powers of a commissioner under Part I of the *Inquiries Act*." Some examples of this kind of body are the auditor general, the Canadian Judicial Council, the Canadian Transportation Accident Investigation and Safety Board, and the RCMP Public Complaints Commission. The Law Reform Commission of Canada identified almost 100 statutes that gave powers of inquiry to such bodies.[73] Inquiries by two such administrative bodies are discussed below by way of further illustration, even though they are not commissions of inquiry.

### 1) Canadian Judicial Council

The debacle of the Landreville Royal Commission, discussed in Section B(1), above in this chapter, led to the creation of the Canadian Judicial Council in 1971. Its membership includes the chief justices of all of the Canadian superior courts and it is chaired by the Chief Justice of Canada. One of its most important functions is to deal with judicial conduct. It is authorized to hold an inquiry into a judge's conduct and to express its opinion to the minister of justice as to whether a judge "has become incapacitated or disabled from the due execution" of judicial office, and may recommend that the judge be removed from office.[74] The minister of justice may then introduce a resolution into Parliament for the removal of the judge, as discussed above. If the council decides that a judge's conduct was inappropriate, but not so serious as to warrant removal from office, it may simply express its concern about the conduct without recommending removal from office.

The Marshall Inquiry[75] was highly critical of the decision of the Nova Scotia Court of Appeal panel that ultimately acquitted Marshall. The commission reported that the judges had unjustifiably attempted to defend the criminal justice system, at the expense of the victim of a terrible injustice. The five judges successfully claimed judicial immunity

---

73 Law Reform Commission of Canada, *Administrative Law: Commissions of Inquiry*, Working Paper No. 17 (Ottawa: The Commission, 1977).

74 *Judges Act*, R.S.C. 1985, c. J-1, s. 65.

75 Discussed in Section D(1), above in this chapter.

from testifying before the commission. However, the attorney general of Nova Scotia was "deeply troubled by the Commission's finding" with respect to these judges and he wrote to the Chief Justice of Canada, as chairperson of the Canadian Judicial Council, to ask for an inquiry committee to be established under the *Judges Act*. In his letter, he stated: "It is absolutely essential that Nova Scotians have faith and confidence in the highest court in this Province. If that faith has been shaken by the findings of the Royal Commission, as I believe it has been, it must be restored."[76]

As required by the Act and the council's by-laws, an Inquiry Committee was established consisting of three chief justices appointed by the council: Guy Richard C.J.N.B., James H. Laycraft C.J.A., and Allan McEachern C.J.B.C., who chaired the committee; and two lawyers appointed by the minister of justice: Rosalie Abella of Toronto and Daniel Bellemare of Quebec.

Of the five judges who heard the *Marshall* case, one subsequently retired for health reasons and another had reached the mandatory retirement age. The public hearings with respect to the remaining three judges commenced in Halifax in June 1990. Counsel on behalf of one of the judges took the position that their comments and criticism of *Marshall* were completely justified on the evidence. This was a serious error on their part. The Marshall Report was the product of three other chief justices who had conducted a thorough inquiry and persuasive analysis. The response of the judges only suggested that they still "didn't get it" and would be capable of similar misconduct in future. That could support the argument that they were incapable of continuing to serve as judges and should be removed from office.

A basic principle was at stake in this Judicial Council inquiry. Judicial independence requires that judges be free to speak their minds, especially in their reasons for judgment. Could such "judicial speech" constitute misconduct? The majority of the Inquiry Committee had no difficulty in finding that it could and that it did in this case. They said: "the five judges in the collegial decision-making capacity were inappro-

76 The letter is quoted in full in the Inquiry Committee's report, published on the Council's website: www.cjc-ccm.gc.ca, Inquiry Committee Decisions, Hart, Jones and Macdonald (August 1990). See also the detailed analysis, above note 4 at 325–45.

priately harsh in their condemnation of the victim of an injustice they were mandated to correct . . . ."[77]

It is important to keep in mind that the principle of judicial independence exists to maintain public confidence in the judicial role. But it does not exist in isolation. Independent judicial speech can also detract from public confidence when it appears to be grossly unfair. The majority concluded that public confidence would be undermined in this case if it did not criticize the improper conduct of the judges on the panel.

However, the majority did not recommend that the three remaining judges be removed from office. They collectively had served as judges for fifty-eight years prior to the Marshall Reference. And they each continued to sit for seven years afterwards, without similar inappropriate conduct. Counsel on behalf of Marshall submitted to the Inquiry Committee that he did not wish to see the judges removed from office. He only sought that the judges' conduct be admonished as official recognition that it was wrong. After the committee's report was released, the same lawyer said that Marshall was pleased by the strong public disapproval it had expressed.

Like a commission of inquiry, an inquiry committee established by the Canadian Judicial Council ceases to exist after it has reported. But the Council itself continues to exist and to appoint new inquiry committees as required, in conjunction with the minister of justice and in accordance with the *Judges Act*.

## 2) RCMP Public Complaints

The Royal Canadian Mounted Police Public Complaints Commission consists of a full-time chairman, a member from each RCMP-contracting province, and three additional members who may be appointed on a full-time or part-time basis.[78] The commission is authorized to receive complaints from any member of the public about the conduct of an RCMP member. The commission chairman may also initiate an investigation

---

77 Chief Justice McEachern wrote a dissenting report while the other four Committee members constituted the majority. The report is available on the Council's website, *ibid*.

78 *Royal Canadian Mounted Police Act*, R.S.C. 1985, c. R-10, s. 45.29.

without a public complaint if he/she considers it advisable in the public interest. The chairman may also institute a hearing to inquire into such matters and assign a member or members of the commission to conduct the hearing. In doing so, the panel acts as "the Commission."

Upon completion of a hearing, the commission is required to submit a written report of its "findings and recommendations." In this respect, the commission is similar to a commission of inquiry. It has no authority to make binding decisions or orders. It cannot grant remedies. It merely investigates, makes findings of fact, and issues recommendations arising out of those findings.

Interesting hearings were conducted by the commission in relation to the conduct of RCMP officers responsible for security at the Asia-Pacific Economic Cooperation (APEC) conference in Vancouver in November 1997. The University of British Columbia's beautiful campus in suburban Vancouver had been selected as the site for the summit. It was an inspired choice in many respects, bringing Pacific Rim leaders into an academic community that had burgeoning programs in almost every discipline, that reached out to APEC countries, and, of course, that was located in Canada's city gateway to the Pacific. Unfortunately, it also created difficulties in maintaining the level of security required for such a gathering of world leaders. The logistical challenges were exacerbated by the status and role of one of those leaders, President Suharto of Indonesia. After thirty-two years in power, he was on the verge of a downward spiral that would see him deposed within six months. But he was still in a position to make demands for "security" that translated into protection from political embarrassment on a world stage:

> the dictator made it clear he did not want to see any protests against him, and threatened to boycott the summit unless that was assured. Aides say Chrétien grew increasingly exasperated by Suharto's demands—but he could hardly ignore them. Indonesia has the world's largest Muslim population, and Suharto was the most influential leader in southeast Asia. A summit without him might be deemed a failure.

The officers responsible for security appeared to go out of their way to make Canada's guests feel comfortable: "The pretty pictures of the back-slapping leaders are long-forgotten. Canadians now remember the APEC summit for its images of young protesters being blasted with pepper spray by RCMP officers, and signs urging democracy and free speech being torn down by Canadian police."[79] Some fifty-two complaints were made about RCMP conduct and the chairman of the commission decided in February 1998 to appoint a three-member panel to conduct a hearing. A series of bizarre twists followed.

At the pre-hearing conference, a number of the complainants, who were student protesters, sought public funding for legal representation at the hearings. In April, this author provided a legal opinion to commission counsel for the panel conducting the hearings. The opinion advised that the panel was not authorized by law to pay the legal fees and disbursements of counsel retained by a complainant appearing at the hearing. The application for legal funding was denied and the complainants sought judicial review. My legal opinion had been distributed to the complainants and was before the Federal Court, which heard the application for judicial review on 13 July. Judgment was delivered one week later, on 20 July, since the hearings were scheduled to commence on 14 September.[80]

Justice Barbara Reed accepted the view that the commission did not have the authority to pay legal costs itself and noted that the applicants had shifted their ground in no longer pressing the claim for an order to provide funding. They now sought an order to compel the commission "to request the Federal Government to provide funding." Justice Reed did not consider such an order to be appropriate since such a request fell within the complete discretion of the commission. However, she declared that making such a recommendation certainly fell within the commission's authority if it chose to do so. She also offered some personal observations that legal representation of the complainants would improve the quality of the proceedings.

The next day, the panel wrote to the solicitor general requesting that funding be provided, but this was denied in September. The complainants persisted and the panel wrote again on 6 October. On 16 October, the solicitor general again rejected the request. The panel was faced with having to proceed without the complainants having legal representation. Shirley Heafey, the chairperson of the commission, discussed this problem with the author in the context of favourable comments made by Justice Reed about an alternative process for legal representation,

---

79 Bruce Wallace, "APEC Protest Controversy" *Maclean's* (21 September 1998).

80 *Jones v. Canada (Royal Canadian Mounted Police Public Complaints Commission)* (1998), 154 F.T.R. 184 (T.D.).

described in the earlier letter of opinion. The chairperson decided to recommend this alternative process to the panel. At her request, on 17 October, the author prepared a "Draft Opening Statement for the Panel's Consideration" which would transform the role of commission counsel so as to have them act at arm's length from the panel and provide representation for unrepresented parties.[81]

In her judgment, Justice Reed explained the *rationale* for this proposal by quoting at length from my earlier legal opinion which had taken issue with the Justice lawyer:

> He also pointed out that there was nothing wrong with Commission members cross-examining witnesses. While that may be legally correct, aggressive questioning by Panel members may seriously detract from the perception of impartiality of the Panel and the credibility of its subsequent recommendations. Similarly, Commission counsel is an extension of the Panel and must avoid the perception of favouring some parties over others. It is true that an inquiry is not, essentially, adversary [*sic*]. But there are occasions during inquiries when aggressive cross-examination of witnesses or protection of witnesses from overly aggressive cross-examination must be undertaken by Commission counsel.
>
> It is difficult to maintain a perception of impartiality when taking on an adversarial role in public and then meeting in private with the Panel to discuss the proceedings. This is an inherent dilemma for Commission counsel where there is a dual role of presenting the evidence and advising the Panel. The example provided by Mr. Arvay at page 219 with respect to the Securities Commission is preferable. Counsel who present the case to the Panel acts at arm's length from the Panel, which may draw upon its own counsel for advice as may be required. Similarly, counsel for some human rights commissions have the statutory responsibility for "carriage of the complaint" before a tribunal panel.

Justice Reed found this description of the limitations on the role of counsel to be "instructive."[82] These observations are directly relevant to the discussion of the role of commission counsel discussed in Chapter 6 below.

---

81 The entire Draft Opening Statement is reproduced in Gerald M. Morin, "Personal Reflections on the Ill-Fated First APEC Inquiry" in W. Wesley Pue, *Pepper in Our Eyes: The APEC Affair* (Vancouver: UBC Press, 2000) at 168–70.

82 Above note 80 at para. 12.

The proposal was that commission counsel, who was by then intimately familiar with the parties and evidence, would act as independent counsel, with instructions

> to marshall and present the evidence on behalf of the complainants and to advance such evidence and present argument in accordance with the law and the public interest and to act at arm's length from the Panel . . . where necessary, Independent Counsel will rigorously cross-examine witnesses who are represented by counsel and intervene to protect the interests of those who are not represented.

Justice Reed raised some of the issues surrounding public funding of counsel and observed:

> one of the attractive features of Professor Ratushny's suggestion that Commission counsel be appointed to act as advocates for all of the complainants avoids many of these administrative questions.

However, the decision whether or not to adopt this solution to the government's denial of funding was not before her and rested with the panel. The panel was free to reject this proposal, and in fact it declined to read the Draft Statement when hearings resumed on 19 October. The chair of the panel later stated publicly that he felt the commission chair had interfered with the panel's independence in making the proposal. In my view, it was completely appropriate for the commission chair to make such a suggestion to a panel.

Meanwhile, in parallel developments, on 5 October the solicitor general, Andy Scott, was charged in Parliament with prejudging the outcome of the APEC Inquiry by stating that the RCMP had used "excessive force" and that one officer would take the "fall" for it. An NDP member of Parliament claimed he had been sitting two seats from the minister, in the same row, of an Air Canada flight when he overheard the comments to an unidentified passenger. The MP claimed he had taken two pages of notes of the conversation. Ongoing controversy and demands for the minister's resignation led to him submitting a sworn affidavit on 19 November in which he denied having made inappropriate comments. That was followed by an affidavit from the passenger with whom he had the conversation, confirming the allegations. The minister resigned.

In late October, counsel for the RCMP raised allegations of bias against the chair of the panel. An RCMP constable from the chair's hometown of Prince Albert claimed he overheard remarks made by the chair to fellow gamblers in a casino the previous spring. He claimed the chair stated the police were wrong to pepper-spray the protesters and knew what his findings would be, even though the hearings had not yet commenced. The chair denied the allegations and adjourned the hearings. But he then hired a private investigator to gather evidence against the RCMP officer who had alleged his improper comments. When he submitted a bill to the chair of the commission for $8,000, she refused to pay and insisted that the secret investigation be made public. He had also arranged for a private investigation into break-ins into his automobile and the panel's offices. On 4 December the chair resigned from the panel, citing interference from the commission chair rather than his initiation of the private investigation into the person who had alleged bias against him.

Later that month, the remaining two panel members also resigned. A new panel was appointed consisting of a single commissioner, former judge Ted Hughes, who had extensive experience in conducting public inquires. The new solicitor general agreed to a modified proposal for funding legal counsel for the complainants. And the panel completed its hearings and submitted its extensive report without further significant incident.

### 3) Other Ongoing Inquiry Bodies

There are a great many additional administrative bodies at both the federal and provincial levels with ongoing powers to conduct inquiries and to compel testimony. They are also cast into the public spotlight for a variety of reasons.

A national and international tax expert, Professor Vern Krishna Q.C., has decried the "Orwellian" powers granted to a hearing officer under the *Income Tax* Act.[83] Section 231.4 gives the minister broad powers to conduct an inquiry into the financial affairs of a taxpayer, with all of the powers of a commissioner under the *Inquiries Act*. The Act allows:

> the hearing officer to inquire into every aspect of an individual's private and business life without any assurance of privacy or natural justice.[84]

---

83 R.S.C. 1985 (5th Supp.), c. 1.

84 Vern Krishna, "Canadian Taxpayers Subject to Orwellian Law" *Law Times* (14 September 1997).

These powers permit "fishing expeditions" which place the burden on the taxpayer when Revenue Canada does not have reasonable and probable grounds. Krishna refers to the dangers of permitting regulatory processes to encroach upon criminal investigations and notes that the courts have more recently extended *Charter* protections against unreasonable search and seizure to this process.

The Military Police Complaints Commission[85] has powers analogous to those of the RCMP Public Complaints Commission discussed above. In 2007 it had initiated investigations into the transfer of detainees to Afghan custody and, in particular, whether the military knew they were likely to be tortured. The commission was unsuccessful in obtaining relevant government documents, for over a year, and in March 2008 it announced that it would hold public hearings in order to engage its subpoena powers to force disclosure. In April the government countered with a Federal Court challenge to the commission's jurisdiction to conduct such hearings.[86] However, the commission decided to commence hearings on 25 May 2009, before the court ruling was given. They began with general introductory matters and commission counsel announced that the controversial issues would be postponed until October. This "soft" approach drew strong criticism from University of Ottawa law professor Amir Attaran, who first called for an investigation into the prisoner transfers but now questioned the utility of the hearings.[87]

The Canadian Transportation Accident Investigation and Safety Board reported publicly almost two years after a BC Ferry struck an island, resulting in two deaths, in March 2006. The board's report indicated that it some fourteen minutes elapsed between the ferry's missing a crucial course change and two crew members noticing that the ferry was about to strike the island. It also revealed that the two had recently ended a romance and were engaged in a "personal conversation"; however, it refused to release details, merely asserting that they had been "distracted." The fifty-three surviving passengers and relatives of the two deceased were left with an incomplete explanation of what hap-

85 R.S.C. 1985, c. N-5, Part IV.

86 Steven Chase & Joe Friesen, "Panel to Continue Probe Despite Ottawa" *Globe & Mail* (15 April 2008). See also Paul Koring, "Ottawa Still Not Co-Operating in Detainee Inquiry" *Globe & Mail* (5 December 2008).

87 Bill Curry, "Skepticism Greets Launch of Afghan Detainee Inquiry" *Globe and Mail* (26 May 2009).

pened and why, leading to calls for a full commission of inquiry. One of the board's investigators described interest in the conversation as "prurient" and the board chairman, in effect, took the position that it was sufficient that the board knew the details.[88] While the report did make a number of specific findings and recommendations, its paternalistic approach fell far short of inspiring public confidence.

Finally, the Indian Claims Commission provides an interesting variation on the theme. It was established as a commission of inquiry under the *Inquiries Act* with a mandate to assist in settling land claims. But that was in 1991. For eighteen years it functioned in a manner analogous to the category of established administrative bodies with ongoing inquiry powers. It had an annual budget and a regular staff. In fact, for many years, the commission called on the federal government to set up a permanent independent claims body. Finally, the Specific Claims Tribunal was created under the *Specific Claims Tribunal Act*.

88 Justine Hunter, "Unhappy with Ferry Report, Family Wants Full Inquiry" *Globe & Mail* (12 March 2008); "Undue Discretion," editorial, *Globe & Mail* (14 March 2008).

CHAPTER FOUR

# *Establishing a Commission of Inquiry*

## A. THE DECISION TO ESTABLISH

In Chapter 2, Section B, the commission of inquiry was described as a "residual" institution within the machinery of government which is established when other institutions of government and their processes are found to be inadequate. For the reasons discussed there, a commission of inquiry gives the public confidence that it will achieve what the others cannot. In that respect, a commission of inquiry is often the result of a crisis in public confidence. We are speaking here of commissions exercising primarily investigative functions. The genesis of primarily policy/advisory commissions is usually different.

### 1) A Political Decision

Since it is the Cabinet that decides to establish a commission of inquiry, that decision is inherently political. There are often significant political advantages to invoking this exceptional response to public confidence in the government. But there is also a potentially serious disadvantage. During the hearings and because of the commission's report, the government loses control of the information given to the public and the manner in which it is expressed.

The primary political advantage in appointing a commission of inquiry is to take the heat off the government in relation to a problem with a high public profile. The government can say it has "done something" without having to admit to wrongdoing, at least temporarily. The government also avoids having to commit to any more specific response to the problem.[1] Still another advantage is that it then becomes difficult for critics to continue to attack the government since, inevitably, part of their earlier attacks included the demand for such an inquiry. Once that demand has been met, they are not in a position to continue their criticism before the commission can report.

But such demands are so numerous that the government will first respond by denying that the problem is significant or stating that existing processes are addressing it. In seeking to retain control, the government may be concerned that the obligation to provide information could lead to wider problems being revealed. In addition, the cost of a commission of inquiry does not merely involve its own expenses. Other government officials must gather information, monitor the hearings, brief ministers, attend as witnesses, and deal with public and media requests. Finally, the government must assess its "exposure." Is the problem limited to a few individuals? Does it reach into senior and ministerial levels? Will the exposure put the government in a bad light even if there is no clear evidence of wrongdoing? Is there a strong public suspicion of a "cover-up" that can be confronted only by independent fact finding?

The government must assess not only the scope of the problem but also whether it has "legs." Can the government weather the storm by simply repeating its position until the media and public grow tired of the issue? There is the danger of having the worst of both worlds—taking a prolonged political beating and then having to succumb to an inquiry anyway if the issue should gain momentum rather than losing it.

In *Starr*,[2] Justice L'Heureux-Dubé described in some detail the momentum that increased and ultimately forced the Ontario government to establish a commission of inquiry. Media reports led to the government announcing a criminal investigation into the allegations of misconduct:

---

1 See, generally, John D. McCamus, "The Policy Inquiry: An Endangered Species?" In Allan Manson & David Mullan, eds., *Commissions of Inquiry, Praise or Reappraise?* (Toronto: Irwin Law, 2003) at 211 and Michael J. Trebilcock *et al.*, *The Choice of Governing Instrument* (Ottawa: Economic Council of Canada, 1982).

2 *Starr v. Houlden*, [1990] 1 S.C.R. 1366 [*Starr*], discussed in Chapter 3, Section E(5).

> However, it quickly became apparent that the matter was far from being so limited in its nature, scope or effect. The record reveals that the allegations intensified almost daily from May 15, 1989 until the establishment of the inquiry.[3]

It was alleged that four Cabinet ministers had received campaign contributions or other benefits from Ms. Starr. By 19 June, additional ministers were implicated and allegations were made of public funds being diverted into a Liberal "slush fund." Ms. Starr had received a public appointment and it was alleged that efforts were made for her mother to receive a government contract. But the fatal blow came three days later when the executive director of the Premier's Office resigned after disclosing he had received financial benefits from her. The premier announced the commission of inquiry the next day.

The following passage describes a completely different rationale for the establishment of a commission of inquiry:

> A government may also have an incentive to establish a commission of inquiry where the incident in question happened on the watch of a previous government. A government may believe that political risks associated with an inquiry are mitigated when the events in question predate its election. However, given the independence of a commission of inquiry, and the unpredictable nature of its investigation, this incentive may not be as strong as it would at first seem.[4]

A case in point is the Somalia Inquiry. Although the Liberal government established that inquiry to address events under the previous Conservative government, the Liberals decided to terminate the commission before an impending general election. Presumably, the ongoing "bad news" of the hearings was having a negative effect on the public's perception of the government, even though the events had occurred when the previous government was in power.[5]

Similarly, the Ipperwash Inquiry was established by the Ontario government to address events under a previous Conservative administra-

---

3 *Ibid.* at 1414.

4 Robert Centa & Patrick Macklem, "Securing Accountability through Commissions of Inquiry: A Role for the Law Commission of Canada" in Manson & Mullan, eds., above note 1 at 79.

5 Discussed in Chapter 3, Section B(5).

tion. One journalist expressed the view that this decision was not really motivated by a desire to find "the truth about what happened" or "what lessons we might draw from the tragedy." Rather, " . . . the subtext was clear: It was to put Mr. Harris and his government on trial. The charge: that he had personally ordered the Ontario Provincial Police to use force to break up a native occupation of Ipperwash Provincial Park, and thus was directly responsible for Mr. George's death at the hands of an OPP sniper."[6] However, the commission's report specifically absolved the former premier from giving inappropriate directions to the police or encroaching on the domain of law enforcement. In fairness to the Liberal government of the time, it had aggressively demanded the appointment of a commission of inquiry as the opposition and during the previous election campaign. It would have been difficult for the Liberals to avoid establishing one after they subsequently gained the power to do so.

But investigative commissions are not always established in response to allegations of government wrongdoing. The decision to establish a commission will also be influenced by the "nature of the problem." Some specific examples follow.

### 2) Nature of the Problem

The commissions of inquiry described in the previous chapter were established in response to a variety of problems. The Landreville and Stevens inquiries were into the conduct of individuals in relation to the offices they held. One was a superior court judge and the other a minister of the Crown. The Nelles, O'Hara, and Starr inquiries also involved individual conduct but in a context that involved as well the commission of a crime. Nelles was a nurse who worked in a hospital where a number of babies had been murdered. O'Hara was one of the police officers on duty when a person was taken into custody and released the next morning with a smashed kneecap. Starr was a political operative whose conduct involved her relationship with members of the government. These last three cases demonstrate the fine legal line that prevents commissions of inquiry from being deployed primarily to investigate a crime.

The Westray and Walkerton inquiries involved disasters within local communities, namely, a deadly coal-mine explosion and the deadly

6 Andrew Coyne, "Native Violence Becomes Blameless" *National Post* (2 June 2007).

contamination of the drinking-water supply. Coincidentally, while the Walkerton Inquiry was under way, another commission of inquiry was established in relation "to the current contamination of the public water supply of the City of North Battleford" in Saskatchewan.[7] Public confidence in its supply of drinking water is a problem that is obviously suited for the invocation of this residual institution. All of the existing safety measures suddenly prove to be inadequate. The public needs a fast and authoritative response.

And Justice Cory eloquently described the "compelling community interest" in the Westray Inquiry proceeding expeditiously.[8] Indeed, the history he relates of coal-mining disasters suggests that a commission of inquiry has now become an almost automatic response to them. While such a response may be necessary for the local community, historian Eric Tucker notes that it does not resolve the larger problem:

> [T]he tragic cycle of disasters, public inquiries, recommendations and more disasters warns us that, despite its greater possibilities, other factors operate to limit the effectiveness of inquiries. Although generally good at identifying the immediate technical causes of disasters, the treatment of systemic causes of occupational health and safety disasters by inquiries has been much less consistent.[9]

The Westray Inquiry's report did make a number of systemic recommendations, including the adoption of a new regulatory regime. This would involve consolidation of the federal and provincial regimes, updated regulations, and aggressive enforcement.

Commissions of inquiry into wrongful convictions may become less frequent in future. Many lessons have been learned from past commissions. Some common features were referred to in Chapter 3, Section A. Terms such as "tunnel vision" and "noble cause corruption" have become more widely understood. Past reports have sent strong messages to police, prosecutors, and other officials. At the time of writing, the Ontario government had still left open the possibility of an inquiry into

---

7 North Battleford Inquiry.

8 *Phillips v. Nova Scotia (Commission of Inquiry into the Westray Mine Tragedy)*, [1995] 2 S.C.R. 97 [*Phillips*], discussed in Chapter 3, Section B(3).

9 Eric Tucker, "The Westray Mine Disaster and Its Aftermath: The Politics of Causation" (1995) 10 C.J.L.S. 91 at 117.

the case of Robert Baltovich although it does not appear likely. Of special concern was the role of the trial judge in his conviction: "Any inquiry into the Robert Baltovich case must focus closely on the dangerous bias that some trial judges develop when presiding over murder trials, Mr. Baltovich and his defence counsel, James Lockyer said yesterday."[10] However, the Ontario Court of Appeal had already addressed the judge's conduct in its decision quashing the conviction. The court criticized him in no uncertain terms and referred to his "contempt for the defence position."

In the Sophonow Inquiry, Commissioner Cory concluded that the accused had been denied a fair trial and added:

> It is not necessary for me to comment upon the conduct of the trials by the presiding Trial Judges. That has been done by the Manitoba Court of Appeal . . . . I agree with and endorse their findings pertaining to the conduct of those trials.

Commissioner Lamer commented directly on the contribution of the trial judge to the wrongful conviction of Gregory Parsons. He observed that the trial was not conducted with the rigour warranted for the serious charge of murder and described the judge's conduct towards defence counsel as "petulant and unfortunate" in contrast to his treatment of the Crown.

The Ontario Court of Appeal identified another wrongful conviction in *R. v. Mullins-Johnson*.[11] The court declined to make a declaration of "factual innocence" but expressed profound regret that the accused was wrongly convicted as a result of "flawed pathological evidence." It added that the accused had committed no crime and that no crime had been committed against the deceased. That flawed evidence included the work of Dr. Charles Smith, who was the subject of a review by the chief coroner for Ontario six months prior to the Court of Appeal decision. The chief coroner found that, in a number of cases of suspicious child deaths in which Smith was involved, the factual conclusions were not reasonably supported by the available materials.

---

10 Kirk Makin, "Baltovich Probe Should Focus on Judge's Bias, Lawyer Says" *Globe & Mail* (24 April 2008).

11 (2007), 87 O.R. (3d) 425 (C.A.) [*Mullins-Johnson*].

Rather than a commission of inquiry into this wrongful conviction, the government adopted a "systemic" approach. Justice Stephen Goudge of the Ontario Court of Appeal was appointed to conduct "a systemic review and assessment" of Ontario's paediatric forensic pathology system as it related to the criminal process. The terms of reference specifically precluded reporting on any individual cases. A separate process was established for reviewing particular cases, by Crown and defence counsel, with a view to pursuing processes under the *Criminal Code* for addressing potential wrongful convictions. The Goudge Inquiry's mandate specifically established the period from 1981 to 2001 for its review.

Policy/advisory commissions are seldom established as a result of a single precipitating event although such events may be contributing factors. For example, the Oka crisis contributed to the creation of the Aboriginal Peoples Commission. But, generally, as with this commission, the problems they are handed are complex and of long standing in our society. Some of the features of their work include extensive research, public dialogue, and the objective of crystallizing and advising on policy options. The policy/advisory commissions briefly described in Chapter 3, Section C illustrate the broad scale of the societal problems they address: medicare, language and culture, equality in the workplace, non-medical use of drugs, and the Canadian economy.

These commissions are not suitable for resolving an essentially political problem. Unless they involve issues of broad policy or public education, political problems should be addressed in political arenas. If an issue already has been defined and refined and is well understood, a commission of inquiry will have little to contribute. Indeed, issues that already have been well developed may simply be awaiting a political choice. Similarly, "a commission of inquiry will be less helpful in resolving an issue involving ethical or value choices. Neutrality lends little authority for the making of choices that clearly depend primarily on values."[12] Such choices should be made by the government, with its ultimate accountability to the electorate.

12 Frank Iacobucci, "Commissions of Inquiry and Public Policy in Canada" in A.P.I. Pross, I. Christie, & J.A. Yogis, eds., *Commissions of Inquiry* (Toronto: Carswell, 1990) at 25.

### 3) The Air India Approach

The Air India Inquiry provides an example of the government appointing an independent adviser to recommend whether a commission of inquiry should be established. On 26 April 2005 the then minister of public safety and emergency preparedness, Anne McLellan, appointed Bob Rae, then a practising lawyer, to conduct a review and provide such advice, with respect to the bombing of Air India Flight 182. His mandate was expressed in broader terms, being to report on "the questions and answers that have already been determined . . . whether there are any outstanding questions of public interest that can be answered . . . options for addressing such outstanding questions." But the real purpose was to respond to pressure from the families of some of the victims, leaders in the Sikh community, and others to establish a formal commission of inquiry. These pressures had intensified with the acquittal the previous month of the last two suspects who had been criminally charged in the murders.

The Air India disaster had occurred almost twenty years earlier, on 23 June 1985, killing all 329 passengers and crew. One person had been convicted and imprisoned but two others were acquitted and the criminal investigation had reached an impasse. Two potential witnesses had been murdered and there were threats of violence in the Vancouver Sikh community. Concerns were expressed that most Canadians did not take this tragedy seriously because of the race of most of the victims, even though most of them were also Canadian. There was no sense of closure.

Rae's report[13] was released on 23 November 2005, seven months after the review was commenced. While the work had proceeded expeditiously, seven months would ordinarily be a long period to wait for a government to decide whether to establish a commission of inquiry into a disaster. But the adoption of this approach, as well as the process of the review and resulting report, were well received by those affected. The decision whether to establish a commission of inquiry finally had become focused.

---

13 *Lessons to Be Learned*, The Report of the Honourable Bob Rae, Independent Advisor to the Minister of Public Works, on Outstanding Questions with respect to the Bombing of Air India Flight 182, online: www.publicsafety.gc.ca/prg/ns/airs/rep1-eng.aspx.

The report recommended that a commission of inquiry be established but emphasized that it could not be used as a vehicle for further investigation into who had committed the crime. It quoted extensively from the *Nelles* and *Starr* judgments to emphasize that the law was clear in that respect. It also recommended against an inquiry into the conduct of government, security, and police officials, because of the length of time that had passed. In some respects this was a cruel irony since governments had resisted such an inquiry for years on the basis that it could affect the investigation into the bombing and subsequent criminal proceedings. However, as Rae stated:

> The great distance of time is important because government policies have changed, practices have been amended. Many of the individuals involved in aspects of the case have retired, left public service, or died . . . a micro-examination of decisions made twenty years ago . . . would be a massive, multi-year undertaking that would immediately become embroiled in extensive litigation.[14]

An inquiry that was "too open-ended" would be quickly derailed after raising false expectations.

The report recommended "a focused, policy-based inquiry." A number of facts and details were clearly established and did not need to be revisited. Instead:

> What we need to know more about is how Canada assessed the threat, how its intelligence and police forces managed the investigation and how its airport safety regulations did or did not work. Twenty years later, these questions are still worth asking. The Air India bombings were the worst encounter with terrorism Canada has experienced. We cannot leave any issues unresolved.[15]

The focus should be on what the responsible government departments and agencies have learned, what changes were made, and what further changes are still required.

Upon receiving the report, Minister McLellan announced that Rae had now been appointed as "Chairperson of the Air India Flight 182 Review and Inquiry." This was a popular choice since he appears to have

14 *Ibid.*

15 *Ibid.* at 2.

developed a credible rapport with those most affected by the disaster. But a general election was called a few days later and he stepped down to run as a Liberal candidate. On 1 May 2006, the new prime minister, Stephen Harper, announced the appointment of retired Supreme Court justice John Major as the commissioner for this inquiry. The terms of reference are specific but relate to systemic issues as recommended by Bob Rae.[16]

## B. ALTERNATIVE PROCESSES

This section examines alternatives to the establishment of a commission of inquiry to address problems with a high public profile that have shaken public confidence. It begins with the Mulroney-Schreiber affair as an illustration of an unsuccessful attempt to address the problem through a parliamentary committee. The story has a number of interesting and bizarre twists but also demonstrates the inadequacy of such a forum for addressing this kind of problem. It certainly has political overtones because a former prime minister of Canada was the central figure. But the gist of the task was to investigate very specific conduct and related events.

This section then canvasses criminal investigations, existing statutory mechanisms, departmental investigations, and informal inquiries. Each has features more suitable for different kinds of problems than the others.

### 1) Legislative Committees

The Mulroney-Schreiber saga provides a useful illustration of the nature of a parliamentary committee as a forum for addressing problems of public interest. It also illustrates its limitations. The committee that attempted to deal with this matter ended up with a single recommendation, namely, that the government appoint a commission of inquiry to deal with it.

The context is familiar to Canadians. Former prime minister Brian Mulroney stepped down from that office in 1993. In 1995 the subsequent Liberal government sought information from a Swiss bank and, in support of the request, claimed that Brian Mulroney had been engaged in

16 Air India Inquiry.

criminal conduct. The allegation related to kickbacks from the sale of Airbus aircraft to Canada for some $1.8 billion, while he was prime minister. When the investigation became public, Mulroney sued the government and the RCMP and received both an apology and a substantial cash settlement.

The details of these events are chronicled by legal historian William Kaplan in *Presumed Guilty*.[17] Receiving unprecedented cooperation from the former prime minister and unlimited access to his files, Kaplan found a wide range of corroborating information for Mulroney's version.[18] He concluded that Mulroney had been the subject of an unfair investigation and supported his attempts to restore his reputation. However, one element had been omitted by Mulroney. He failed to disclose to Kaplan or to the public that he had received some $300,000 in cash payments, commencing shortly after he ceased to be prime minister but while he was still a member of Parliament.

This subsequent revelation and others led Kaplan to write a second book, *A Secret Trial*.[19] The author admitted, frankly, that he had been "duped" and concluded that the government of Canada and Canadians also had been misled. Although the disclosure of the $300,000 cash payments occurred in 2004, for a variety of reasons[20] it did not gain significant political interest and momentum until 7 November 2007, when Karlheinz Schreiber filed an affidavit in a lawsuit confirming that he had made payments to Mulroney.

On 9 November, Prime Minister Stephen Harper announced that he would appoint an independent adviser to recommend an appropriate course of action. On 12 November, Mulroney publicly requested that a commission of inquiry be established. On 14 November, the prime minister announced the appointment of Waterloo University President David Johnston as his independent adviser. However, in light of Mulroney's

---

17 William Kaplan, *Presumed Guilty: Brian Mulroney, the Airbus Affair, and the Government of Canada* (Toronto: McClelland & Stewart, 1998).

18 J.L. Granatstein, "Foreward" in William Kaplan, *A Secret Trial: Brian Mulroney, Stevie Cameron and the Public Trust* (Montreal & Kingston: McGill-Queen's University Press, 2004).

19 Kaplan, above note 17.

20 Norman Spector, "We Need More Than an Investigation into an Investigation" *Globe & Mail* (10 November 2007). See, generally, Norman Spector, "Afterward," in Kaplan, above note 17 at 191 and following.

request, Harper also announced that a commission of inquiry would be appointed. The independent adviser was now directed only to "make recommendations as to the appropriate mandate for a public inquiry into those allegations, including the specific issues that warrant examination under the *Inquiries Act*."[21] He was also directed to determine whether there was any "*prima facie* evidence of criminal action" and, if so, how this should be accommodated in relation to the formal public inquiry; and he was invited to recommend "whether any additional course of action" was appropriate. His report was to be submitted by 11 January 2008, and the path ahead appeared to be set.

Meanwhile, the fearless House of Commons Standing Committee on Access to Information, Privacy and Ethics decided that it wanted in on the action. On 22 November, the committee agreed it would examine whether there were ethical violations "by any office holder in relation to the Mulroney Airbus settlement." Its review would include any information not available at the time of the settlement, including the Schreiber allegations and how these were handled by the current government. It proceeded with stunning alacrity and commenced its hearings one week later, on 29 November.

A commission of inquiry normally would take months to gather and analyze all of the relevant documentation, to review the entire history of the relevant events, and to interview all witnesses who might cast light on the subject matter as well as those who might be called as witnesses. In addition, witnesses would be given notice of the specific matters that would be explored in their testimony and any related documentation would be disclosed to them. They would be advised of possible allegations of misconduct and the expected testimony of other witnesses in support of such allegations. But the committee members plunged ahead, no doubt to the chagrin of the parliamentary counsel responsible for advising them.

The hearing on 29 November was a disaster.[22] Karlheinz Schreiber was facing extradition proceedings on serious criminal charges in Ger-

21 *Report of the Independent Advisor into the Allegations Respecting Financial Dealings Between Mr. Karlheinz Schreiber and the Right Honourable Brian Mulroney, First Report*, Schedule 2, online: www.pco-bcp.gc.ca/index.asp?lang=eng&page=information&sub=publications&doc=ria-rci/table-eng.htm.

22 House of Commons Standing Committee on Access to Information, Privacy and Ethics, Meeting 5, 29 November 2007, Evidence, online: www2.parl.gc.ca/House-

many. He was transferred from custody in Toronto to an Ottawa jail and then brought to the hearing room to testify as the first witness. He began his opening statement by saying he had been transported wearing an orange jumpsuit, in handcuffs and in leg irons. He elaborated on the legal proceedings that had denied him bail and the bail review to be conducted by the Ontario Court of Appeal. He pointed out that the Speaker's warrant to compel his attendance authorized him to go to his home to retrieve documents related to his testimony but he was denied that opportunity. As a result, he could not properly prepare to testify and would not speak. The chair ruled that questioning would commence but that, if necessary, Schreiber could answer some of the questions at future hearings.

The chair pointed out that the committee would meet from 11:00 a.m. to 1:00 p.m. on Tuesdays and Thursdays. Questioning would consist of two rounds, alternating from one political party to another. There would be a limit of seven minutes each during the first round and five minutes each during the second. Around 11:30 a.m., the questioning was ready to proceed but a motion was introduced to add extra hearing times to the schedule. After another thirty minutes, it was defeated. There were a half-dozen interventions on points of order. In the two-and-one-half-hour hearing on this first day, thirteen different members spoke at least once. The chair spoke 117 times. Schreiber declined to answer on at least two dozen occasions. The time allotments were sometimes shared between more than one member of the same party. There was no logical order in pursuing the subject matter or time of the events that had occurred over the previous twenty-five years. No meaningful development of any line of questioning occurred. There were disruptions as members "signed in" to replace others.

The next hearing was five days later and Schreiber by then was free on bail. The chair began by apologizing to him:

> Let me begin, Mr. Schreiber, by letting you know that we have received a very, very large number of faxes and e-mails from Canadians all across the country. They were expressing their disgust at the failure of the responsible policing authorities to ensure your personal dignity while being in handcuffs when led to your Ottawa residence to access your

---

Publications/Publication.aspx?DocId=3153843&Language=E&Mode=1&Parl=39&Ses=2.

> documents. This unacceptable incident was also exploited by some, as you know, who also subjected you to ridicule and mockery. This matter was internationally reported, and in our view, the committee's view, the shaming of one Canadian has shamed all Canadians.[23]

The witness then distributed numerous documents that he had chosen to present and elaborate on. The lack of preparation of members, loose format for questioning, and time limits gave both Schreiber and, subsequently, Mulroney great latitude to avoid precision and consistency. Witnesses were permitted to have legal counsel present but only to provide direct advice to their clients. Counsel were not permitted to address the committee or to question other witnesses.

The partisan nature of the questioning was obvious. At one of the last hearings, on 25 February 2008, former Conservative Cabinet minister Elmer MacKay began his testimony by stating: "there's a growing consensus that this committee has become irrelevant. People are turned off. Some committee members even seem to share this view."[24] The witness then took the chair to task for "disparaging and demeaning comments you made about me" prior to his appearance that day. The chair did not deny that he had made public comments suggesting that MacKay had faked an injury to postpone his appearance in order to have more time to rehearse his testimony. He offered to step down as chair and simply to listen to MacKay's testimony and he did.

Schreiber was then recalled as a second witness that day and used his opening statement to attack the testimony of Mulroney. He said Mulroney had used the "old trick" of taking Schreiber's previous testimony out of context. He provided transcripts of his earlier testimony in a court case that members did not have when Mulroney testified. Schreiber pointed out that Mulroney's lawyers had declined to cross-examine Schreiber on his affidavit in that case. He accused Mulroney of lying and said his claim to have done work to sell armoured vehicles internationally was a complete fabrication. He stated that the $300,000 given to Mulroney was trust money for services that were never performed.

---

23 *Ibid.*, Meeting 6, 4 December 2007, online: www2.parl.gc.ca/HousePublications/Publication.aspx?DocId=3168619&Language=E&Mode=1&Parl=39&Ses=2.

24 *Ibid.*, Meeting 18, 25 February 2008, online: www2.parl.gc.ca/HousePublications/Publication.aspx?DocId=3296992&Language=E&Mode=1&Parl=39&Ses=2.

In late January, Mulroney's counsel wrote to the chair to complain of bias and unfair treatment during his earlier appearance.[25] A second letter from him, a few days later, alleged that the committee was going beyond its proper mandate. It sought assurances of protection from "irrelevant or abusive questions or comments" if Mulroney should appear again.[26] He subsequently announced that Mulroney would not appear again and added that since he had not been implicated in any wrongdoing, a public inquiry was no longer necessary.[27]

Meanwhile, on 9 January 2008, while the committee hearings were under way, independent adviser Johnston submitted his report. He recommended that the commission of inquiry be established with narrow terms of reference. They should be restricted to the cash payments to former prime minister Mulroney by Schreiber and the nature of their business and financial dealings.[28] This would preclude a review of the Airbus sale, the Bear Head Project, or any of Schreiber's other dealings. The report listed seventeen more detailed questions arising out of the cash payments and business dealings between the two principals.

The parliamentary committee presented its report on 2 April and included a comment on the Johnston recommendations with respect to the scope of the terms of reference: "The Committee does not agree . . . that a politically charged inquiry such as this should be limited in scope. On the contrary, we believe that a broad mandate should be granted the Commissioner so that he or she is not unduly limited in terms of the scope of the inquiry."[29] It recommended that a commission of inquiry with such a broad mandate be established at the earliest possible date. The partisan nature of the committee is reflected in the "Dissenting

---

25 Brian Laghi & Gloria Galloway, "Mulroney's Future Appearance before Ethics Committee in Doubt" *Globe & Mail* (25 January 2008).

26 Allison Hanes, "Federal Ethics Committee Going Beyond Scope: Mulroney" *National Post* (30 January 2008).

27 Nicole Baer & Jack Aubry, "Mulroney Now against, But Would Co-Operate with Public Inquiry" *National Post* (28 February 2008).

28 Above note 21 at 25.

29 Canada, House of Commons, Standing Committee on Access to Information, Privacy and Ethics, *The Mulroney-Schreiber Affair—Our Case for a Full Public Inquiry* (2 April 2008), online: http://cmte.parl.gc.ca/Content/HOC/committee/392/ethi/reports/rp3376356/ethirp05/ethirp05-e.pdf.

Opinion of the Conservative Party." Supplementary opinions of the Bloc Québécois and the NDP were also included.

Finally, Johnston submitted a second report to the prime minister that took into account the committee's report and the evidence before it. Submissions were invited from Mulroney, who now argued that there should be no commission of inquiry, and Schreiber, who recommended additional questions for such a commission to consider. Johnston's second report essentially confirmed the first. It concluded that the seventeen questions listed in the first report should define the scope of the commission of inquiry.[30]

It is ironic that Mulroney now argued against a public inquiry when he previously calld for one and said he would appear "with bells on." Sinclair Stevens also had called for a commission of inquiry into his conduct. Such moments of bravado can lead to prolonged periods of grief.

The involvement of the Ethics Committee in the Mulroney-Schreiber affair was unfortunate. A legislative committee is totally unsuitable for a detailed investigation into complex events and conduct where the credibility of witnesses is important. Most of the participants lack adequate preparation, skills, and focus to conduct a thorough investigation and the questioning protocol is superficial. Although the committee considering the Mulroney-Schreiber affair included some very good lawyers, such as Joe Comartain and Serge Ménard, the forum rendered their legal skills of little value. Many members are also preoccupied with media and partisan considerations and are burdened with other onerous duties. This is simply a reality of political life and the necessity of getting re-elected. Some elected officials might see short-term benefits through the publicity attendant upon an exercise such as the Ethics Committee hearings on the Mulroney-Schreiber affair, to say nothing of the opportunity to score partisan points. But the exercise becomes counter-productive when this political process demonstrates its inability to meet the real challenge in a thorough and fair manner.

Indeed, it is a wise legislative committee that recognizes when it has reached the frontier of its capacity and recommends from the start that the task at hand is more suitable for a commission of inquiry. It was the subcommittee of the Standing Committee of the House of Commons on Health that led to the establishment of the Krever Inquiry into Canada's

---

30 Above note 21, Second Report 16.

blood-supply system. The subcommittee's report acknowledged that it simply could not answer certain questions and strongly recommended that a commission of inquiry be appointed.[31] Another potential problem is that, in attempting to deal with a large and complex problem such as this, a parliamentary committee could "die" with the dissolution of Parliament, before being able to complete its work.

## 2) Criminal Investigation

In recommending that the circumstances of the Airbus sale not be further explored, Independent Adviser Johnston said: "I would not recommend terms of reference that charge a Commissioner to go over this well-tilled ground. The public inquiry should not be used to repeat what has already been done in the extensive RCMP investigation."[32] He later added: "To launch a public inquiry into those matters would be tantamount to reopening the extensive RCMP investigation that reviewed these dealings in detail to determine if evidence existed on which criminal charges could be based, something that a public inquiry is not permitted to do."[33]

With respect, this conclusion begs the question of whether the Airbus sale should have been included in the terms of reference. If it were included *only* for the purpose of investigating a crime, Johnston would be correct. But if it were included for another valid purpose, it would be in the public interest to have this event examined.

A variety of valid issues could be explored. Was the sale conducted in accordance with government regulations and policies and are these adequate? Was it influenced by political considerations that were not in the public interest? Was it a "good deal" for Canada? After all, some $1.8 billion of public money was spent. Millions of dollars were paid in commissions. If the inquiry should, incidentally, learn of bribes, it would be able to report them, provided it does not characterize them as criminal. A commission of inquiry has the extraordinary power to compel testimony, which a criminal investigation does not have. A commissioner could also be given

---

31 *Canada (Attorney General) v. Canada (Commission of Inquiry on the Blood System in Canada - Krever Commission)*, [1997] F.C.J. No. 17 at para. 20 (C.A.).

32 Above note 21 at 4.

33 *Ibid.* at 22.

access to privileged documents that the police did not have at the time of their investigation. An unsuccessful criminal investigation does not mean that the relevant issues have been adequately examined.

On occasion, legitimate "transcending" issues, warranting a commission of inquiry, may arise directly from potentially criminal activity. For example, in August 2008, a young Aboriginal man was shot to death by Winnipeg police. The previous month, an Aboriginal teenager had died after being "tasered" by the same police force. Aboriginal leaders immediately called for a public inquiry.[34] Oddly enough, the first victim was related to J.J. Harper, whose killing in 1988 led to the creation of the Aboriginal Justice Inquiry in Manitoba that same year. That inquiry's massive report in 1991 contained some 140 recommendations addressing a broad range of systemic issues as well as police responsibility for Harper's death and the conduct of the earlier case involving Helen Betty Osborne.[35] A commission of inquiry was established in Ontario the following year to inquire into systemic racism in the criminal justice system, with "anti-black racism as a focal point."[36] A major impetus to that commission was the shooting of Black youths by police officers, particularly in Metropolitan Toronto.

Issues of timing may arise where there is both a criminal investigation and a commission of inquiry. In response to the most recent call for an inquiry, Winnipeg Police Chief Keith McCaskill responded: "We all learned from the Aboriginal Justice Inquiry. One of the things we learned was not to draw conclusions on an instant or release details prior to the completion of an investigation. Doing so compromised the investigative process and many believe tainted the outcome of that investigation."[37]

Different consequences may flow from the issue of timing. In the Air India case, the time lost while awaiting completion of the criminal proceedings reduced the scope of the commission's mandate. In *Phillips v. Nova Scotia (Commission of Inquiry into the Westray Mine Tragedy)*,[38] the Supreme Court held that a compelling public interest required the commission of inquiry to proceed in spite of concurrent criminal proceed-

34 Steve Lambert, "Aboriginals Urge Public Inquiry" *Globe & Mail* (6 August 2008).

35 Online: www.ajic.mb.ca/volume.html.

36 Systemic Racism Commission.

37 Above note 34.

38 [1995] 2 S.C.R. 97.

ings. The Starr Inquiry was established in response to intense political pressure, even though the launching of a criminal investigation had been announced earlier by the government.

Where criminal investigation and prosecution may have significant political implications, an option for the government is to appoint an independent special prosecutor. The BC government appointed a special prosecutor to assess the allegations of polygamous criminal conduct in the community of Bountiful. In 2006 the RCMP had recommended criminal charges against members of the community under the sexual-exploitation provisions of the *Criminal Code*, but Crown counsel concluded there was not a substantial likelihood of conviction. The special prosecutor agreed but felt a prosecution under the polygamy section might succeed. Earlier reservations about proceeding under this section were based on the likelihood that it would be contrary to the *Charter*'s protection of freedom of religion. However, based on increasing evidence that polygamy is socially harmful, the special prosecutor recommended a constitutional reference to determine the section's validity.[39] In early January 2009, the attorney general decided to proceed directly with polygamy charges.

Recently, the appointment of a special prosecutor in Winnipeg has actually led to a commission of inquiry being established to inquire into his own conduct in carrying out that role. A police officer was accused of drunk driving, resulting in a car crash that killed a young woman. A lawyer in private practice was appointed as a special prosecutor and agreed to a plea arrangement. The result was a conditional sentence of house arrest for two years. The reaction of the family and others led to the appointment of retired Justice Roger Salhany of the Ontario Superior Court to inquire into the conduct of the police investigation and the prosecution as well as the treatment of the victim's family.[40]

### 3) Existing Statutory Processes

Some statutory bodies have ongoing powers to conduct inquiries.[41] These are not "alternative approaches" in the sense of a government being able

39 *Report of the Special Prosecutor for Allegations of Misconduct Associated with Bountiful, B.C.*, online: www.llbc.leg.bc.ca/public/PubDocs/bcdocs/418439/070801-Bountiful-Summary.pdf.

40 Taman Inquiry.

41 See Chapter 3, Secion F.

to select one as an alternative response to a problem. The statutes that create them also dictate when an investigation or inquiry is authorized or required. Occasionally, there are calls for a commission of inquiry to be established even where one of these processes has assumed its jurisdiction over a particular problem.

Such demands occurred during the first RCMP APEC Inquiry and during the investigation into the sinking of a BC ferry. In the latter case, the families of the victims were highly critical of the Canadian Transportation Accident Investigation and Safety Board, with some justification, in view of its insensitive and bureaucratic response to criticism of its report.[42] Such ongoing bodies may be in danger of losing their "edge" when responding to disasters that become relatively "routine" for them. When dealing with a particular industry, they can also become familiar with the businesses and people involved on a regular basis, with corresponding loss of sensitivity to the general public.

But where such bodies are given statutory authority, it may not be possible to establish a commission of inquiry. Section 3 of the *Inquiries Act* states that such an inquiry may be created only where the subject "is not regulated by any special law." This would prevent the government from establishing a commission of inquiry when the same subject matter already falls within the explicit statutory jurisdiction of an existing body.

Similar provisions are contained in some, but not all, of the corresponding provincial inquiry Acts. For example, section 2 of the Ontario Act adopts the same language: "is not regulated by any special law." It does seem logical that the exceptional, residual power to create a commission of inquiry should not be invoked where the existing machinery of government already provides a mechanism to address the specific problem.[43]

### 4) Departmental Investigations

Part II of the *Inquiries Act* is headed "Departmental Investigations" and is followed by section 6, which states:

---

42 Chapter 3, Section F(3).

43 This issue is revisited in Chapter 7, Section B.

> The minister presiding over any department of the Public Service may appoint at any time, under the authority of the Governor in Council, a commissioner or commissioners to investigate and report upon the state and management of the business or any part of the business, of such department, either in the inside or outside service thereof, and the conduct of any person in such service, so far as the same relates to his official duties.

This differs from the public inquiries, under Part I, that must be established by the Governor in Council rather than a single minister. Part II investigations are also limited in scope to the business of the minister's department and the conduct of official duties in the service of that department. Other powers granted under Part II are broader in some respects but narrower in others than those under Part I. Both authorize compelling attendance and testimony and the production of documents.

Part II appears to be directed more towards internal management than to issues of broad public concern. When such internal management also raises issues of broad public interest, a Part I inquiry may be established even though it could also have proceeded under Part II. This occurred with the McDonald Commission into the RCMP.[44]

### 5) Informal Inquiries

The term "informal" is simply used to describe inquiries that have no powers to compel testimony or the production of evidence. The variations are unlimited. A single official could be directed to gather information and prepare a report. A departmental, interdepartmental, interprovincial, federal-provincial, or international committee could be formed for the same purpose. Often the term "task force" is adopted to illustrate the limited and focused mandate involved.

On 29 March 2007 the minister of public safety announced an independent investigation into aspects of the RCMP Pension Plan Funds and, two weeks later, named the former chairman of the Ontario Securities Commission, David Brown, to lead this investigation. On 15 June Brown reported that the RCMP's management was "horribly broken." He recommended that a task force be created to study the appropriate

---

44 McDonald Inquiry.

governance structure and culture for the force. On 16 July, Brown was appointed to chair the Task Force on Governance and Cultural Change in the RCMP, which had a specific mandate, not unlike that of a commission of inquiry, but without the powers of such a body. The other members consisted of a former RCMP commissioner, a federal deputy minister, and two additional lawyers. The task force released its report, *Rebuilding the Trust*, on 14 December 2007.[45] Its work demonstrates the speed with which such an informal task force can fulfill a substantial mandate.

The best exposition of this kind of process is "The Bernardo Investigation Review," by the late Justice Archie Campbell.[46] Following the conviction of Paul Bernardo on two counts of first-degree murder, he was also declared a dangerous offender. But public concerns remained about the police investigation and related issues such as the handling of forensic evidence. More generally, why did it take six years before he was caught and tried? Justice Campbell, then of the Ontario Superior Court, was a former Crown counsel and had served as deputy minister for both the attorney general and correctional services departments. His review was conducted without any statutory authority, hearings, or formal evidence. He considered all of the documentation and relied on interviews of those involved by his own investigators. All of the interviews were voluntary but with prior notice of the "ground rules," including the interviewees' option to have the interviews recorded and to have counsel present. Justice Campbell observed that all of the organizations affected realized that "they had problems that had to be addressed" and gave their complete cooperation.

Another key factor in the success of the Bernardo Review was that "there were no significant conflicts of evidence to be resolved." There were no real disagreements as to what actually happened and, therefore, no need to compel testimony or test credibility through rigorous questioning. As a result, this process had the great advantages of speed, low cost, and focus on the issues without the distractions of "sideshows." It was completed in six months at a cost of approximately $362,000, rather

45 Online: www.publicsafety.gc.ca/rcmp-grc/_fl/Task_Force_Report-English.pdf.

46 In Manson & Mullan, eds., above note 1 at 381. See also Margaret Allars, "Procedural, Strategic and Legal Constraints upon a Non-statutory Inquiry" in Manson & Mullan, *ibid.* at 407.

than the millions of dollars that a commission of inquiry would have cost. Moreover, all of its recommendations were implemented.

But without the cooperation Justice Campbell received, evidence would have to be compelled, and if there were conflicting evidence, it would have to be tested and resolved. Justice Campbell observed that, in some situations, public hearings are necessary to "secure public confidence" in the effectiveness of the review: "This is particularly so if there is a suggestion of cover-up or it is alleged that some lower official is taking the fall for someone in high places."[47] For a policy/advisory commission, public hearings might also be necessary to engage in public education and consultation.

In contrast, there is a recent example of an informal inquiry that achieved very limited success. Canadians are familiar with the plight of former Minister of Foreign Affairs Maxime Bernier, arising out of his romantic relationship with Julie Couillard. Upon his return from a NATO Summit Conference in Europe on 4 April 2008, Bernier went to Couillard's residence, where he spent the night. He left the next day with the briefcase that had accompanied him to Europe and into her residence the previous evening. On 8 May, media reports commenced, describing Couillard's past associations with members of outlaw biker gangs. These led to calls for the minister's resignation but the official response was that such ties no longer existed and nothing more was involved than the private lives of two people. At some point, their relationship ended.

On 25 May, through her lawyer, Couillard contacted a member of Bernier's staff to return documents he had left in her residence and they were collected the same day. The documents had been prepared for the NATO conference and some were classified as "Secret." They had been left at her place upon his return from Europe on 4 April. He met with the prime minister on 26 May and submitted his letter of resignation later the same day. The leader of the opposition and others called for a full public inquiry into the circumstances and possible consequences of the security breach. The prime minister dismissed opposition MPs as "gossipy old busybodies" who were more interested in salacious details of the affair.[48]

---

47 *Ibid.* at 391.

48 Canadian Press, "Dion Calls for Bernier Public Inquiry" *CTV.ca* (28 June 2008).

On 27 May the clerk of the Privy Council instructed the deputy minister of Foreign Affairs "to conduct a comprehensive review into the incident," working closely with the director of security operations in the Privy Council Office (PCO). The security officer of Foreign Affairs engaged two consultants from a private investigation and security firm. Their final report was submitted on 16 July 2008.

The report concluded that the documents were in Bernier's briefcase when he arrived at Couillard's residence but were no longer in his briefcase when he left the next morning and he was not aware they were missing. Bernier had previously stated publicly that he had no recollection of leaving the documents behind. Couillard's lawyer was contacted but she declined to be interviewed. In these circumstances, the report further concluded: "In the absence of evidence to refute the Minister's version of events and based on a balance of probabilities, the Minister did not, at any time after the NATO Summit Conference, remove the briefing material from the briefcase." The report added, rather ominously, that "Ms. Couillard may have put herself in potential jeopardy of having contravened a provision of the *Security of Information Act*,"[49] and that there were two subsequent occasions when she could have told Bernier about the documents but failed to do so. Couillard's lawyer publicly rejected the clear implication that she had stolen the documents and asserted that, if necessary, she would respond to the RCMP publicly, or in court, with statements "supported by external, documented facts."[50]

The report also concluded that publication of the documents after the conference was over would not have caused significant injury to the national interest. The incident did tarnish Canada's "good reputation within NATO circles" for the careless handling of classified information. But it would be viewed as an individual error rather than "a systemic failure of the Government."

---

49 *Final Report on the Administrative Review into the Security Incident Reported by Maxime Bernier—Classified Documents Left at a Private Residence*, online: www.international.gc.ca/about-a_propos/report-rapport.aspx.

50 Daniel LeBlanc, "Couillard's Lawyer Dismisses Federal Report" *Globe & Mail* (7 August 2008). In her subsequent book, *My Story*, Couillard claimed that before leaving that morning, Bernier gave her the documents, said they were confidential, and asked her to put them in the garbage. Daniel LeBlanc, "Couillard Told to Trash NATO Briefings, Book Reveals" *Globe and Mail* (1 October 2008).

This report was extremely unfair to Couillard and gives the impression of a clumsy attempt to "spin" the incident in favour of the embarrassed former minister. What was "the minister's version" that created evidence against her? The mere fact that he does not remember removing the documents from his briefcase is not evidence that he did not do so. It is evidence that he did not know. He simply may have been distracted or suffering from jet lag. What was the evidence that tipped the scales "on a balance of probabilities"? A suggestion of misconduct, amounting to criminal conduct, should never be made without a clear statement of the evidence in support of such a charge. Couillard had no obligation to submit to an interview and it probably was good legal advice for her not to do so in the circumstances. Did the authors take into account that provisions of the *Security Information Act* recently had been struck down as unconstitutional?[51] The report is vulnerable to a judicial declaration that it denied the principle of fairness.

This clearly was not an appropriate situation for an informal inquiry. It required both the powers and the protections of the *Inquiries Act*. It would seem to be ideally suited for a departmental investigation under Part II of the Act, with one exception: section 6 contemplates the conduct of officials rather than a minister or former minister. But a commission of inquiry under Part I was a much better alternative to the informal inquiry that was conducted. It could have compelled the testimony of both Couillard and Bernier and provided both of them the protection against findings of criminal conduct. The credibility of each of them could have been tested. It also would have required notice and an opportunity to respond to allegations of any kind of misconduct.

It would have been necessary, however, to "design" the commission to address this very specific incident. The terms of reference could have narrowly defined the inquiry as a specific investigation into a specific incident. There are good reasons why public hearings were not necessary or appropriate. A commission of inquiry could have reported just as quickly as the informal inquiry did, but more effectively and more fairly. The flexibility of the government to craft the terms of reference allows it to use a commission of inquiry for a very narrow purpose as well as for very broad purposes.[52]

---

51 *O'Neill v. Canada (Attorney General)* (2006), 82 O.R. (3d) 241 (S.C.J.).

52 Iacobucci Inquiry.

## C. TERMS OF REFERENCE

### 1) Importance and Consultation

On 3 May 2006, following release of the Gomery Inquiry Report, the University of Ottawa and the Institute of Public Administration of Canada (IPAC) jointly sponsored a round table of leading academics with practical experience in public administration and policy. This led to a report entitled *Commissions of Inquiry in Canada: Lessons Learned from Recent Experience*.[53] Participants noted that:

> launching a royal commission of inquiry is a risky process—a bit like sending a ship out to sea. You don't know where it will go, how long it will take, how much it will cost or what it will bring back. And trying to relocate a ship lost at sea and bring it back to port can be a costly experience (especially if the captain is not in a hurry to come home).

A government cannot control what a commission will "bring back" in its final report. But it has control of two crucial elements prior to the ship's departure. These are the terms of reference and the appointment of the commissioner. Getting both of these right will help to ensure a successful voyage rather than a meandering cruise or even a shipwreck.

The terms of reference are crucial because the mere appointment of a commissioner tells us little. The entire life of a commission is dictated by its terms of reference, which are legally binding. They establish the jurisdiction of the commission. The boundaries of that jurisdiction dictate what the commission must do and what it cannot do. And they are legally enforceable by the courts. How should the government go about establishing the terms of reference?

An important aspect of developing appropriate terms of reference is to ensure proper consultation on their content. An official in the PCO is normally responsible for commissions established under Part I of the *Inquiries Act*. The orders in council establishing them are commonly issued on the recommendation of the prime minister but that is not always the case. For example, Mulroney-Schreiber was on the recommendation of the prime minister but Somalia was on that of the minister of defence.

53 Peter Larson, Larson Associates, September 2006. Available online: http://74.125.95.132/custom?q=cache:voozMx_5ddsJ:www.ipac.ca/documents/Ex-Brief3Commissions31.pdf+larson&cd=2&hl=en&ct=clnk&client=google-coop.

The mere fact that the recommendation is from a minister rather than the prime minister does not make the commission of inquiry a departmental investigation under Part II of the Act.[54]

Consultations as to the terms of reference will vary, depending on the nature of the inquiry. Broad policy/advisory commissions do not usually proceed with the same urgency as investigative commissions and permit more extensive consultations with those affected. For example, the Royal Commission on Aboriginal Peoples[55] was established with terms of reference developed following a report by the former chief justice of Canada, Brian Dickson. He had consulted with Aboriginal groups and leaders, politicians at all levels, experts in various disciplines, and members of the public. Investigative commissions, established as a direct response to a crisis generated by tragic events, do not have the luxury of such extensive consultations. As occurred in the Walkerton Inquiry, the needs of those most directly affected may have to be identified as well as met, primarily as part of the inquiry process itself.

At a minimum, however, internal consultations will occur with all government departments and agencies that might be affected. In some situations, federal-provincial or interprovincial cooperation may be required, indicating the need for such communication and consultation at an early stage. A first draft of the terms of reference should be circulated for comment before being sent for legal drafting and the legal document also should be circulated to ensure it does capture the intent of the earlier draft.[56]

Occasionally, an investigative commission will not be faced with a sense of urgency but will examine a problem that had remained unresolved for some time. This may allow for a more formal consultative process as occurred prior to the establishment of the Mulroney-Schreiber Inquiry. [57] Prime Minister Harper first announced that he would appoint an independent adviser to recommend an appropriate course of action

---

54 "Ruling on Jurisdictional Issue" (3 January 2006), Arar Inquiry.

55 Aboriginal Peoples Commission.

56 See, generally, H.A. Wilson, *Commissions of Inquiry: A Handbook of Operations* (Ottawa: Privy Council Office, 1982). Consultation with the commissioner is discussed in Chapter 5, Section A(1).

57 Discussed in Section B(1), above in this chapter. The Rae Report discussed in Section A(3), above in this chapter, also contains recommendations on the terms of reference.

to address the Schreiber allegations. When Mulroney then requested the appointment of a commission of inquiry, the mandate changed and the independent adviser, David Johnston, was directed to recommend the appropriate terms of reference. This was done and the commission of inquiry was established with the terms of reference flowing directly from his recommendations. Reference is made to his reports in the preamble to the terms of reference and his name is mentioned five times.

The process of appointing an independent adviser to recommend the scope of the terms of reference was successful in this case. It was possible because it could be accommodated within the time frame necessary for the Ethics Committee hearings to run their course, prior to the commission being established. David Johnston was a credible adviser in the eyes of the public. His reports were thorough and helped to cut through the superficiality of the committee's report. I disagree with his recommendations concerning Airbus [58] but that does not detract from the value of such a process, where the circumstances allow it to be adopted.

### 2) Objectives and Scope

The first report of Independent Advisor Johnston provides a useful approach to determining what should be included in a commission's terms of reference. Johnston wrote that "[t]he issue I have struggled with is whether and to what extent a public inquiry exploring these further details would be in the public interest, keeping in mind the purpose and constraints on such inquiries. The answer depends on what public interest is legitimately engaged."[59] He concluded that the broad public interest here was the integrity of government. The more specific issue was whether there was a breach of the constraints related to conflict of interest of former high officeholders after they left office. This would also raise the issue of the adequacy of existing constraints and whether further rules should be adopted.

This approach can be used as a backdrop for assessing the terms of reference of most commissions. What is the broad public interest that will be served? In the factual circumstances of concern, what specific

58 Section B(2), above in this chapter.

59 Above note 21 at 19.

issues arise that will advance that public interest? What must be examined to address those more specific issues? Another dimension to be considered is public perception. Even though some significant conduct or events may appear to the government to be capable of straightforward and satisfactory explanation, the stage may have been reached where such an explanation has little credibility when made in the political forum. The "public interest" may require that the explanation be assessed by the commission in order to respond to that public perception, even if it is clearly erroneous in the eyes of the government.

Bryan Schwartz highlights the danger that a government will overreact when establishing a commission of inquiry:

> Faced with public outrage and loss . . . a government may initiate the inquiry without sufficient planning and forethought. Instead of thinking through its mandate, purpose, and mission, and installing safeguards for civil liberties, a government may create an inquiry with an ill-defined and potentially vast mission. The victims of the tragedy, and their families, may be temporarily placated by a hastily created inquiry. But as the inquiry drags on unreasonably, due to poor planning, the financial cost and emotional stress on the wronged will be exacerbated, not tempered.[60]

At issue is not only the breadth of the terms of the mandate but also the time within which it must be fulfilled. The Somalia Inquiry provides an example of terms of reference that were simply impossible to complete even within the extensions given to the initial time deadline.[61]

It is reasonable to impose a date by which a commission is required to report but it should be realistic in relation to the breadth and complexity of the terms of reference. It should not take into account that a time extension is always possible. The government has to decide whether the terms of reference should be reduced in scope to meet a desired deadline. If not, the deadline should be sufficient to allow the commission to fulfill its mandate. A government also may well have under consideration the likely date of the next election when establishing a commission's reporting date.

Schwartz adds that governments may also attempt to avoid accountability by carefully crafting the terms of reference: "The mandate of the

60 Bryan Schwartz, "Public Inquiries" in Manson & Mullan, eds., above note 1 at 447.

61 See Chapter 3, Section B(5).

inquiry can be subtly manipulated to avoid certain especially embarrassing matters." In my view, this is difficult to achieve. Governments often establish commissions of inquiry in response to pressure from the public, media, and opponents. Once that occurs, the next line of attack is the inadequacy of the terms of reference. They will receive intense public scrutiny and governments are likely to want to avoid further embarrassment through valid criticisms that they tried to avoid crucial issues.

An exception may occur when terms of reference are circumscribed on the basis of the report of a credible independent adviser. Although not legally bound to follow such a report, the government may effectively lose control from a political perspective. But it also may be shielded from criticism if the report is adopted, even though its recommendations may coincide with the government's political interests. In Section B(2), above in this chapter, I took issue with David Johnston's justification for excluding Airbus from the Mulroney-Schreiber terms of reference. He said it would be tantamount to reopening a criminal investigation but ignored other legitimate purposes as well as intervening events.

In his successful lawsuit after the investigation, Mulroney testified about his relationship with Schreiber (during Mulroney's examination on discovery). His description of that relationship was less than forthright and there was no mention of the secret cash payments he received from Schreiber. William Kaplan testified before the Mulroney-Schreiber Inquiry that he had asked the head of the RCMP Airbus investigation when he first learned of these payments. Inspector Al Matthews responded that it was on 10 November 2003, long after the investigation had been terminated and the lawsuit settled in Mulroney's favour.

Was there a connection between Airbus and the Mulroney-Schreiber relationship? There is no evidence of that and both protagonists deny it. Perhaps ironically, they had a common interest in doing so. But the Mulroney-Schreiber Inquiry was precluded by its terms of reference from attempting to resolve that issue conclusively. This omission could leave perpetual doubts about the relevance of any findings this commission might make.

Still, the contours of the terms of reference may be restrictively designed for specific purposes that are understandable. In the Lamer Inquiry, they responded differently to each of the three murder cases being examined. But these different mandates and related limitations were justified by the unique circumstances of each of the cases. They could not be criticized as an attempt to "gerrymander" the boundaries, but did raise other problems.[62]

Some terms of reference contain "open-ended" or "basket" clauses that give their commissions a potentially unlimited scope. The substantive terms of reference for the Marshall Inquiry[63] were short but far-reaching. They simply referred to:

> the investigation of the death of Sanford William Seale on the 28th–29th day of May, A.D., 1971; the charging and prosecution of Donald Marshall, Jr. with that death; the subsequent conviction and sentencing of Donald Marshall, Jr. for the non-capital murder of Sanford William Seale for which he was subsequently found to be not guilty; and such other related matters which the Commissioners consider relevant to the Inquiry.

This landmark commission was extremely successful and the absence of constraints in its terms of reference might have encouraged the commissioners to explore important issues such as racism and the role of the Nova Scotia Court of Appeal, which were not specifically included.[64] There was no deadline for reporting and the report was released approximately three years after the commission was established.

Although it did not create a problem in relation to the Marshall Inquiry, the last clause of the terms of reference may have been unnecessarily broad. The phrase "related matters" does denote relevance to the Donald Marshall, Jr. case, but the phrase "which the Commissioners consider relevant" is wide open. Particularly with no time deadline, it would be difficult to control a "rogue" commission that wandered far beyond the government's intentions. This subjective test of relevance would make judicial review difficult and terminating the inquiry could lead to charges of "cover-up." Although the government escaped negative consequences when it shut down the Somalia Inquiry, the electorate might not be so forgiving in other circumstances.

---

62 Some of the challenges posed for Commissioner Lamer by these terms of reference are discussed in Chapter 5, Section D(4).

63 See Chapter 3, Section D(1).

64 See the passage from the opening remarks of Chairperson Hickman, quoted in *McKeigan v. Hickman* (1989), 61 D.L.R. (4th) 688 at 712 (S.C.C.). They reflect an early willingness to pursue such broader issues.

There may well be circumstances in which the government will want to give a commissioner discretion to extend the scope of an inquiry. This should be done advisedly and on the basis of objective criteria. It is not necessary to anticipate every possible issue of interest in the terms of reference. A commissioner is always able to recommend areas worthy of further examination by another body, issues that are related but fall outside her mandate or capacity to address. For example, the finding in the Lamer Report of a Crown "culture" that reflected unfair attitudes led to a subsequent independent review of the Public Prosecutions Division in Newfoundland by retired chief justice William Marshall.

In the final report of the Arar Inquiry, Commissioner O'Connor identified the cases of three additional men who were imprisoned and allegedly tortured in Syria. But he did not favour another public inquiry into these cases: "[T]here are more appropriate ways than a full scale public inquiry to investigate and report on cases where national security confidentiality must play such a prominent role."[65] On 23 January 2008 the government appointed former Supreme Court justice Frank Iacobucci to conduct an "Internal Inquiry" into these three cases.[66]

In establishing the objective and scope of terms of reference, it has been argued that

> [g]overnments should generally avoid mixing inquiries into particular episodes with larger policy inquiries. The intermixture may greatly protract the investigation of the particular episode, to the detriment of both the victims of alleged wrongdoing and those who are under suspicion. Moreover, casting a commissioner in the role of a social reformer may undermine confidence in his or her role as an impartial judge of past conduct.[67]

In my view, there is little public interest to be achieved in appointing commissions of inquiry merely to investigate specific incidents or conduct. Such investigations gain their value mainly from the lessons they teach in terms of future practices and policies:

> To state the point boldly: identifying who (and what) might have been at fault in a drug-related hospital tragedy is of little consequence if the

65 Arar Inquiry.

66 Iacobucci Inquiry

67 Above note 60 at 455.

> practices that led to the misconduct, oversight, or inaction are not reformed. Often, it is the system that is guilty, as much as, or even sometimes instead of, individuals and organizations. However valuable the adversarial process in serving the interests of justice, as conventionally understood, it rarely provides much guidance on how to deal with systemic problems likely to be of greatest interests in policy inquiries.[68]

In fact, it is becoming increasingly rare not to include, with investigative powers, an examination of systemic issues and any corresponding recommendations. Drafters of terms of reference should give careful thought to the kinds of systemic issues that could be at play. They may first seem intangible but may be manifest in such issues as leadership, relationships, morale, past practices, and institutional "culture." There seldom will be a downside to giving commissioners latitude to explore any potential systemic issues that may be relevant. But some specific guidance may also be helpful.

### 3) Some Specific Provisions

The terms of reference for past commissions of inquiry provide a cornucopia of precedents that could be considered for future inquiries. Of course, the subject matter to be examined will vary with each one. There are also a number of generic standard provisions authorizing the commissioner to, among other things, rent space and facilities; engage the services of lawyers, advisers, and other staff; grant standing; and recommend funding for participation. Potential expenditures are tied to standards set by the Treasury Board or the provincial equivalent. Federal inquiries recently have been directed to use a specific document-management program and to follow standards for record management.

The commissioner may be given authority to rely on previous inquiries or reports in making findings. For example, Commissioner Iacobucci was authorized to act "as he considers appropriate with respect to accepting as conclusive, or giving weight to, the findings of other examinations that have been conducted." The Air India Inquiry was given similar authorization and seven such earlier "examinations" were specified, including the report of Bob Rae, the proceedings before the su-

---

68 Liora Salter, "The Complex Relationship between Inquiries and Public Controversy" in Manson & Mullan, eds., above note 1 at 185.

perior courts, a review by the Security Intelligence Review Committee, and a report by an Indian High Court justice into the disaster. The Cornwall Inquiry into allegations of abuse of young people was given broad latitude to rely on transcripts of court or tribunal proceedings as well as "medical, professional, social science and similar evidence and background information related to the causes, consequences, and responses to the abuse of young people."

Such provisions probably are not legally necessary but may discourage undue reliance on oral testimony. Unless specifically restricted, a commissioner would be entitled to consider such evidence and give it such weight as deemed appropriate. Whether or not such authorization is given, the principle of fairness would have to be observed before relying on such evidence for findings of misconduct. Perhaps provisions of the kind just mentioned give the commissioner some guidance as to what is expected and a reminder not to reinvent the wheel.

An important recent innovation is the encouragement of Ontario commissions to rely upon "overview reports." The procedural rules for the Air India Inquiry elaborate on such an approach by authorizing commission counsel to present a "commission dossier" of evidence and conclusions for the proposed adoption of the commissioner. The procedural rules for the Iacobucci Inquiry also authorize commission counsel to prepare "proposed findings" for possible adoption by the commissioner. Since these procedures relate to the important function of gathering, marshalling, and disclosing the evidence, they are discussed in greater detail in relation to the role of counsel in Chapter 6, Section B(2).

The federal *Inquiries Act* does not specify that hearings are to be conducted in public. A variety of approaches have been taken in the terms of reference. Almost all of them authorize the adoption of "any procedures and methods that he [the commissioner] may consider expedient for the proper conduct of the inquiry." The Gomery terms of reference did not mention public or private hearings. The Mulroney-Schreiber terms assume that hearings will be in public since they specifically authorize "the holding of hearings in private." The Somalia terms also assumed that hearings would be in public by directing that "the proceedings of the inquiry be held *in-camera* where necessary to protect information relating to national security or in any matter where the commissioners consider it necessary in the public interest." Both the Arar and Air India terms contain more detailed provision for the conduct of hearings *in camera* where disclosure of information could be injurious to international relations, national defence, or national security. While Commissioner Iacobucci was also appointed under Part I, he was directed to take "all steps necessary to ensure that the inquiry is conducted in private." But he was also authorized to conduct portions in public when "satisfied that it is essential" to the effective conduct of the inquiry.

In contrast, section 4 of the Ontario Act specifically addresses the question of public and private hearings:

> 4. All hearings on an inquiry are open to the public except where the commission conducting the inquiry is of the opinion that,
>
> (a) matters involving public security may be disclosed at the hearing; or
> (b) intimate financial or personal matters or other matters may be disclosed at the hearing that are of such a nature, having regard to the circumstances, that the desirability of avoiding disclosure thereof in the interest of any person affected or in the public interest outweighs the desirability of adhering to the principle that hearings be open to the public,
>
> in which case the commission may hold the hearing concerning an such matters in the absence of the public.

In spite of this provision, the Cornwall Inquiry's terms of reference specifically directed it to balance "the public interest, the principle of open hearings, and the privacy interests" of those affected in relation to the disclosure of evidence.

It is now common for both federal and provincial terms of reference to specify that no conclusion or recommendation should be made regarding the civil or criminal liability of any person or organization. The terms of reference for the Goudge Inquiry added a third prohibited category, namely, "professional discipline matters involving any person." It is reasonable that any conclusions or recommendations on matters falling within the statutory jurisdiction of other bodies should be avoided on the same basis as civil liability. Provisions in some terms of reference also direct that any criminal investigations or proceedings not be jeopardized, where that may be relevant.

It is common now too for Ontario terms of reference to include a requirement that government bodies and officials cooperate with the commission. The Walkerton Inquiry terms stated: "All ministries, Cabinet Office, the Premier's Office and all boards, agencies and commissions of the government of Ontario shall assist the commission to the fullest extent so that the commission may carry out its duties." The commission reported that many provincial officials "worked long and hard" to produce some one million documents" in remarkably short periods of time. The government asserted Cabinet privilege over some documents, but the commission took the position that the privilege had been waived by the breadth of its mandate. A practical agreement was ultimately reached that avoided the need for a Divisional Court ruling. The terms of reference for the Cornwall and Goudge inquiries contained a similar provision but added: "subject to any privilege or other legal restrictions."

The terms of reference for the Driskell Inquiry in Manitoba contained the following provision: "Government departments and agencies, and any other bodies established under the authority of the Manitoba Legislature, including the Winnipeg Police Service, must assist the commissioner to the fullest extent permitted by law." Federal terms of reference have avoided such provisions even though non-cooperation by governments and military officials was a serious problem for the Somalia Inquiry.

The terms of reference may authorize a commission of inquiry to submit one or more interim reports or may require it to do so. Where there is no mention of an interim report, there is nothing to prevent the commission from making one. But it is entirely up to the government when (and if) to release it. The Krever Inquiry was appointed on 27 October 1993 and required to submit an interim report no later than 31 May 1994 "on the safety of the blood system, with appropriate recommendations on actions which might be taken to address any current shortcomings." The safety of the blood-supply system was a matter of national concern but the time frame was unrealistic. The interim report was not released until March 1995 and the final report in November 1997, after some 250 days of public hearings involving more than 350 witnesses. In Chapter 3, Section C(4), reference was made to the Le Dain Commission being "perplexed" about how to handle its requirement to submit an interim report.

The Gomery Inquiry's terms of reference had two aspects. The first was an investigative inquiry into the sponsorship scandal and those involved. The second concerned systemic aspects of public management. With respect to the sponsorship program, the commissioner was directed "... to submit, on an urgent basis, one or more reports, interim or final, of his factual findings." A separate report was to be submitted on the systemic aspects. The first report was published in early November 2005 and the reaction forced the government to call an election in January, which it lost. The final report was released shortly after.[69]

These are but a few of the many examples of provisions in terms of reference that guide the manner in which the specific subject matter of a commission of inquiry is to be addressed. They continue to evolve in nature and in different jurisdictions based on the cumulative experience of previous commissions. Their formulation depends upon legal and practical considerations as well as political judgment.

### 4) Interpretation and Amendment

Once a commission of inquiry has been established, the interpretation of its terms of reference is the role of the commissioner rather than the government. This is so even though the commission owes its entire existence and its mandate to the government: "It is for the Commissioners to interpret the instrument that gave birth to the Commission."[70] The reason is that the terms of reference are legal in nature; they define the commission's jurisdiction. This means that an erroneous interpretation by the commissioner is subject to judicial review by one of the parties or by the government.

Such a successful attack on a commissioner's interpretation of his mandate occurred in the Cornwall Inquiry.[71] The Ontario Court of Appeal unanimously agreed that Commissioner Normand Glaude's interpretation simply was not logical or reasonable and constituted jurisdictional error. The court said that "a high degree of deference" would be given to a commissioner by a reviewing court provided the evidence he sought to explore was reasonably relevant to the subject matter of the inquiry."

69 Gomery Inquiry.

70 *Re Commission of Inquiry* (1979), 94 D.L.R. (3d) 365 at 370 (Comm. of Inq.).

71 *Ontario (Provincial Police) v. Cornwall (Public Inquiry)*, [2008] O.J. No. 153 (C.A.) [*Cornwall*]. See also *Bortolotti v. Ontario (Ministry of Housing)* (1977), 15 O.R. (2d) 617 (C.A.).

But the definition of that subject matter goes to jurisdiction and must be correct. This ruling by the commissioner was not reasonably based and was incorrect.[72]

May statements made in a legislative assembly be taken into account in interpreting the terms of reference? In certain circumstances, they may. In the Cornwall Inquiry case, Justice Michael Moldaver said:

> Given the unclear language used in the [order in council], the Commissioner was entitled to and should have looked beyond the four corners of the document for assistance in interpreting its meaning. Had he done so, he would have gained valuable insight into the scope of his mandate from the background circumstances and context in which the Commission was created.[73]

Justice Moldaver added that it was necessary to have careful regard to the circumstances that had led to the establishment of the inquiry. He quoted a number of passages from Hansard, both prior and after the formation of this commission, and observed: "They provide valuable insight into the background and purpose of the [order in council] . . . and should have been used in determining the legislative purpose for creating the Commission."[74] It should be emphasized that the resort to Hansard flowed from the "unclear language" of the terms of reference. Where the wording is clear, it would prevail over contradictory statements, even by the minister responsible for the inquiry or the premier or prime minister.

In the *Nelles* case, the Ontario Court of Appeal endorsed the statement of the attorney general when announcing the commission of inquiry. He had emphasized that the commission could not be used to investigate crimes. The majority of the Supreme Court of Canada focused on the Ontario premier's statement in announcing the Starr Inquiry, that "those who have broken the law will be punished." It supported the interpretation that the primary focus was to attempt to create a substitute police investigation and preliminary inquiry.[75]

---

72 See also the discussion of this case in Chapter 5, Section D(2).

73 Above note 71 at para. 27.

74 *Ibid.* at para. 42.

75 See the discussion of the *Nelles* and *Starr* cases in Chapter 3, Sections E(3) and (5).

It is always open to the government to amend the terms of reference. Just as it may terminate a commission of inquiry, it may also modify its mandate. However, that would be an unusual step to take, apart from extending its time for reporting, which is common. Once an inquiry has set its course, changes may be disruptive, unless the amendment removes some area of investigation or is a simple "add-on." As described under the previous heading, it is possible to establish a secondary or follow-up inquiry to address any unfinished or new business that arises out of a commission's work. The Starr terms specifically authorized the commissioner to request an amendment to the terms of reference:

> nothing set out above shall be taken as in any way limiting the right of the Commissioner to petition the Lieutenant Governor in Council to expand the terms of reference to cover any matter that he may deem necessary as a result of information coming to his attention during the course of the investigation or inquiry.

Generally speaking, the amendment of the terms of reference is not a common practice and is probably not usually desirable.

Rigid adherence to the jurisdiction established by the terms of reference is seldom an issue for policy/advisory commissions. Indeed, their mandates are generally very broad and the challenge for their commissioners will be to determine which authorized issues to pursue and to what extent. Two exceptions were the Royal Commission on the Status of Women (RCSW) and the subsequent Abella Commission on Employment Equity. Although both were heavily involved with the issue of women's employment, including equality issues, neither was authorized to deal with questions about childcare. In addressing those questions, they went beyond their terms of reference, but there never was a practical likelihood that they would be subject to judicial review.

In "Challenging Policy Paradigms," Annis May Timpson analyzes the work of these landmark commissions. She notes that "the RCSW attracted a public debate about non-maternal child care that the framers of the Commission's mandate had hoped to avoid."[76] Its report ignored the terms of reference and called for a national child care system, leading the two male commissioners to file minority reports. This was taken a step further by Commissioner Abella, who was given a very narrow

76 In Manson & Mullan, eds., above note 1 at 236.

mandate but integrated child care into her work from the start, including a massive survey and commissioned research that investigated the "broader societal factors" that influenced employment inequalities. Her report produced the "master-strategy" of employment equity applicable to all four target groups, but it indicated that child care was particularly important for the equity context of women. Commissioner Abella described child care as "the ramp that provides equal access to the workforce for mothers." She also emphasized that it should be "a public service to which every child has a right." Building on the work of Commissioner Florence Bird and her colleagues in the earlier commission, she recommended a blueprint for implementing a national child care system.

## D. SELECTION OF COMMISSIONER

As discussed in Chapter 10, a panel of commissioners is often desirable for a policy/advisory commission. But it is difficult to appreciate why more than one commissioner would be necessary or desirable for an investigative commission. Any "representational" interests could conflict with the perceived independence required for fact-finding and findings of misconduct. The task of controlling contentious hearings is also best achieved by a single commissioner.

The role of a commission of inquiry in gaining public confidence means that the person appointed as commissioner must have some stature. This might arise from the appointee's past experience and achievements or her position or both. In Canada, the office of a judge, by itself, carries with it a degree of public confidence. There are guarantees of judicial tenure, financial security, and administrative independence that inspire and reinforce such confidence. It is difficult to find examples in the Canadian judiciary of the kind of corruption that plagues many other jurisdictions throughout the world. It has become a Canadian tradition for judges (and retired judges) to conduct commissions of inquiry.

When a government is facing a public crisis, the appointment of a reputable commissioner to conduct an inquiry has a calming effect. Apart from judges, there are other distinguished persons other than judges who could also meet the public expectation of independence and impartiality and have done so in the past. Recently, Bob Rae was a practising lawyer with a distinguished political career behind him when he was asked to act as an independent adviser in relation to the Air India disaster. David Johnston had been a law professor, dean, and university president when called upon to play a similar role regarding the Mulroney-Schreiber matter. Apart from judges, there are many other lawyers with distinguished careers and reputations who would also inspire public confidence in their ability to conduct investigative inquiries. Some also have had extensive experience in conducting administrative hearings in a matter better suited to inquiries than rigid trial-like settings. But when, for example, there is an inquiry into a wrongful conviction, the entire criminal justice system comes under scrutiny and a judicial commissioner is almost a necessity.

The appointment of a suitable judge has little downside for a government, but it may have considerable downside for the judge and the judge's court.[77] Yet it is essential to realize that, when acting as a commissioner, the judge is merely an appendage of the executive branch of government. The government creates the commission, establishes its mandate, provides funding for its operation, and may terminate it if that should become politically expedient. Unlike the office of judge, the office of commissioner has no legal guarantees of its ultimate independence, even when the commissioner is also a judge.

It is important that persons appointed as commissioners be free of past associations or conduct that could result in a judicial challenge of bias. One of the three commissioners originally appointed to the Somalia Inquiry resigned a month after her appointment: "Ms. Doyle was apparently closely aligned with the Liberal government that appointed her, and close friends with some of the key players who worked at National Defence Headquarters during the period under review."[78] The panel of the McDonald Inquiry into the RCMP was challenged on the basis of the close ties of all three commissioners to the Liberal government that appointed them. The court held that a commission of inquiry was not subject to judicial review for bias since it only had authority to make recommendations.[79] This is no longer good law since judicial review, especially in relation to the principle of fairness, has evolved a great deal

---

77 This is discussed in relation to a judge's decision to accept such an appointment in Chapter 5, Section A(2).

78 Tamar Witelson, "Declaration of Independence: Examining the Independence of Federal Public Inquiries," in Manson & Mullan, eds., *ibid.* at 301. See also Chapter 3, Section B(5).

79 *Re Copeland and McDonald* (1978), 88 D.L.R. (3d) 724 (F.C.T.D.).

since then. The experience of Commissioner Gomery related in Chapter 5, Section B(3) provides a graphic example. The resignation of Commissioner Doyle was justified in the circumstances but it raises the question of why she was appointed in the first place.

Potential appointees as commissioners should scrutinize their past to determine whether there is personal history that could lead to a reasonable apprehension of bias. If the inquiry has a high public profile, it would be embarrassing and disruptive for such revelations to occur after the work has commenced. The extent of the scrutiny that can be expected from the media was illustrated following the appointment of Associate Chief Justice Jeffrey Oliphant to conduct the Mulroney-Schreiber Inquiry. He declined to be interviewed personally but journalists made extensive inquiries in light of his previous appointments as a judge and as associate chief justice while Mulroney was prime minister. The most that could be found of a political association was that he was "moderately active in Progressive Conservative circles" and had been urged to run as a candidate but declined. The Prime Minister's Office told the media that he had never met Mulroney.[80] Commissioner Oliphant simply did what all good citizens should do by participating in the political process. And that was prior to his twenty-three subsequent years' service as a distinguished judge.

Such considerations are not likely to be as significant for policy/advisory commissions where commissioners usually are part of a panel and may "represent" a particular community or point of view or have some special expertise. Such expertise may occasionally be helpful for investigative commissions. For example, an inquiry into a small plane crash might be assisted by the commissioner's experience as a pilot.

Commissioners for investigative inquiries should have legal qualifications and experience, particularly in conducting hearings. But the hearings of commissions of inquiry require greater flexibility than that called for in judicial trials. The commissioner should be willing and able to adapt procedural fairness to achieve expeditious hearings. A commissioner must also have the ability to "manage" not only the hearings but the entire operation of the inquiry. This includes delegation of administrative responsibilities but without any loss of control or direction.

---

80 Greg McArthur, "A Judge Known for Separating Truth from Theatrics" *Globe & Mail* (11 July 2008).

Finally, there are some intangible qualities that may be difficult to anticipate. A degree of humility is a good place to start. In this respect, the Gomery Inquiry and the Walkerton Inquiry provide a helpful contrast. The Gomery Inquiry seemed to be largely about Gomery while the Walkerton Inquiry was about the people of Walkerton. Dealing with the media is an important part of a commission's role. But it should not be part of a commissioner's attempt to become a media "star." In the appointment of a commissioner, basic human qualities should be taken into account for a role that requires restraint, discipline, sensitivity, and respect for those affected. This theme is discussed further in the next chapter.

CHAPTER FIVE

# *Role of the Commissioner*

The first three chapters were a general introduction and provided an overview of Canadian commissions of inquiry. The last chapter examined the establishing of a commission of inquiry from the perspective of a government.

This chapter moves to how a commission should fulfill its mandate, commencing with the role of the commissioner. The next chapter then examines the related role of legal counsel.

The next three chapters then shift the focus to the legal framework; the conduct of hearings; and the actual report, including findings of misconduct. The final chapter examines broader policy/advisory mandates.

The reports of past commissions of inquiry provide a valuable resource in guiding the practice of future inquiries. The Walkerton Report and the Goudge Report, in particular, have been helpful in the preparation of this study, for each devotes an entire chapter to discussing how these commissions carried out their mandates.[1] I have borrowed liberally from both, but those involved in inquiries are also encouraged to read these chapters directly.

---

1 Walkerton Inquiry, "The Process of Part I of the Inquiry," Part One, c. 14; Goudge Inquiry, "The Scope and Approach of the Inquiry," vol. 4, c. 23.

## A. DECISION TO ACCEPT

### 1) Prior Consultation

It is important that a person who agrees to conduct a commission of inquiry does so with as much knowledge as possible of what will be involved. It is often a difficult challenge to address the terms of reference adequately within the time available. The process and the commissioner will be subjected to the glare of public scrutiny and some of the parties may be emotionally involved. The manner in which the inquiry is conducted and the report may both be criticized publicly and may affect the commissioner's future reputation. The attitude of the government to the commission may be supportive at the beginning, but that may change if public opinion does.

In a gem of a presentation entitled "The Bernardo Investigation Review," the late Justice Archie Campbell observed: "The commissioner's first task is to ensure that the terms of reference will work, and to secure a clear understanding that the inquiry will be independent and will be supported by reasonable resources."[2] He added: "One veteran of Royal Commissions is noted as saying that your bargaining position never gets better than it is the minute before you say yes."[3]

It is important for the prospective commissioner to meet with the responsible minister and/or senior officials to review the terms of reference at an early opportunity.

Justice Gilles Letourneau agreed to conduct the Somalia Inquiry without any advance knowledge or input into its terms of reference. In fact, he appears to have considered that it would not be appropriate for a commissioner to see them in advance: "I had accepted it before seeing the terms of reference so it wouldn't be proper to be involved in defining the terms of reference because it is a Cabinet decision."[4] When he and his colleagues informed the government that the terms would be impossible to fulfill in the six months proposed, they were given nine months and told the deadline would be reviewed after that. While Justice Letourneau felt that the commissioners should have been consulted on

---

2 In Allan Manson & David Mullan, eds., *Commissions of Inquiry, Praise or Reappraise?* (Toronto: Irwin Law, 2003) at 385.

3 *Ibid.* at 388.

4 Interview with Mr. Justice Gilles Letourneau, *ibid.* at 363.

the time frame in advance, they placed themselves in a difficult position by accepting their appointments without first insisting on a realistic deadline for reporting.

Contrary to the suggestion by Justice Letourneau, it is perfectly appropriate for a prospective commissioner to discuss the draft terms of reference with the government. Commissioner O'Connor specifically addressed this issue in a ruling in the Arar Inquiry, after it was suggested that such consultation was unfair to the parties:

> I disagree. In my view, there is no significance to the fact that I reviewed the terms of reference before Order-in-Council PC 2004-48 was finalized. This was done as part of a practice that has evolved when governments ask someone to undertake the task of being a commissioner. Adherence to this practice is not unfair, nor does it create an appearance of unfairness.[5]

The same practice is encouraged in the Canadian Judicial Council policy discussed in the next section.

In his own inimitable fashion, former Commissioner Gomery described his "negotiations" with federal officials to establish his mandate. He said that he "felt a little like David against Goliath . . . There were three or four deputy ministers around the table with their teams of associates and assistants and I was alone."[6] However, he obtained important concessions. First, he requested that there be no time limit in light of the experience of the Somalia Inquiry. Second, he wanted assurances that he could examine all facts that he considered to be relevant to fulfilling his mandate. He was also given this subjective authority. In his words: "That left me with almost absolute power."

Finally, he requested that privilege be waived for relevant Cabinet documents. When the officials balked, he suggested that they talk to the prime minister's staff since he had given assurances that all necessary powers would be granted for a complete investigation. They conceded that he would have access to Cabinet documents.

Justice Gomery was in a very favourable negotiating position since the news release announcing his appointment said that he would assist in setting the terms of reference. But every commissioner should insist

5 Arar Inquiry, "Ruling on Jurisdictional Issue" (3 January 2006).

6 Rollande Parent, "At 75, Gomery is Shifting Gears" *Globe & Mail* (6 August 2007) A6.

on having a frank discussion about the draft terms of reference before agreeing to proceed. And governments should accept this as a valuable step in ensuring that the terms of reference are effective. The prospective commissioner may have special insights into process that can assist the officials in drafting the terms of reference. That is particularly true if that person has had experience with past commissions or processes that went beyond simply conducting judicial trials. It is also important for that person to learn of government requirements and restrictions and, if not a judge, to establish the personal honorarium.

In some circumstances, there is little flexibility for altering the proposed terms of reference. An example is the Mulroney-Schreiber Inquiry, where detailed terms of reference were developed through an independent consultative process. A basic policy decision was taken to confine the inquiry to the dealings between the two main actors rather than to include the Airbus affair. It would be difficult to revisit such a decision after the highly publicized consultative process that occurred.

In this example, the breadth of the mandate was extremely politically sensitive. This made it much more difficult for a judicial commissioner to participate in establishing the commission's scope. A judge should not be involved in making political choices. The dilemma is that a judge still may be vulnerable to criticism for even accepting a mandate based on partisan political choices.

The most difficult aspect of getting the terms of reference "right" is often the scope of the subject(s) to be examined and the time permitted for doing so. Even the Goudge Inquiry, which was conducted with almost military precision, required an extension of five months beyond its original one-year mandate. The Walkerton Inquiry had no time limitation in its terms of reference but managed to fulfill its massive mandate in just under two years. In contrast, the Cornwall Inquiry had no reporting date in its terms of reference but the government imposed one after it was well into its fourth year.

It is understandable that a government should include a reporting date in the terms of reference and this is probably a responsible decision as well. What is irresponsible is to establish impossibly broad terms of reference with unrealistic time limits. A sad illustration of the potential consequences of a commissioner attempting to push forward in the face of unrealistic time constraints was the Erebus Inquiry in New Zealand. The Judicial Committee of the Privy Council praised the commissioner for "brilliant and painstaking investigative work" and conducting hearings with "patience and courtesy." But he laboured under a "severe handicap," the "pressure of time," which led him to adopt findings in the final report that could not be supported by the evidence or logic.[7]

Nor should a commissioner accept the assurance that "we can always give you an extension." That is true but circumstances change and a government might decide that it really doesn't want the kind of inquiry the commissioner was originally asked to conduct. The decision to "review" the Somalia reporting date after the first nine months led ultimately to the embarrassing termination of the commission. It is far better for the commissioner to insist on a realistic time period and assure the government that she will try to finish ahead of time.

One important policy/advisory commission had been given a six-month mandate, which was inadequate for the task. After the work was under way, the commissioner sought a six-month extension but the responsible minister had changed and an election call was now likely to be imminent. The new minister was not as interested as the previous one in the substantive aspects of the ultimate report. But he thought its very subject would sell well in his constituency. He refused the extension so he could release the report before the election and take credit for it in his campaign. The commissioner explained to him that to issue the report within the six months allotted would emasculate its value. But the minister held firm until finally the commissioner threatened to make public the constraints imposed on completing the task and the circumstances of the denied extension. The minister capitulated, the extension was granted, and the landmark report was completed within the six-month extension.

The problem of time deadlines faced by the Somalia Inquiry was compounded by a lack of cooperation on the part of the government. The final report referred to the "fragmented, dilatory and incomplete documentary record" that was disclosed by the Department of National Defence. The late Justice Campbell explained why government cooperation may be lacking:

> Once the Government secures and announces your commitment to conduct the inquiry, many forces within government can militate against

7 *Re Erebus Royal Commission; Air New Zealand Ltd. v. Mahon*, [1983] N.Z.L.R. 662 (P.C.) [*Erebus*]. Discussed further in Sections B(1) and (3), below in this chapter.

> co-operation. There is always the question of cost. Some government officials regard an independent inquiry as the enemy. Some institutions feel threatened by independent scrutiny. Many officials prefer internal inquiries over which they can exercise more control. Some officials consider it their particular duty to advise their minister and are unfriendly to outside advice, particularly when it is offered publicly.[8]

Sometimes, differences can be worked out informally, as the Walkerton Inquiry did in relation to privileged Cabinet documents. But it is better if such issues can be anticipated and addressed in advance.

A broad provision in the terms of reference requiring government cooperation may be helpful. But where such cooperation is subject to "any other privilege or other legal restriction,"[9] the restrictions pertinent to a specific inquiry should be anticipated, discussed, and addressed in the terms of reference or otherwise. In the case of the Gomery Commission, the waiver of privilege over Cabinet deliberations was not included in the terms of reference but established by two separate orders in council.

### 2) Judges

Manitoba Chief Justice Richard Scott has served admirably for many years as the chairperson of the Judicial Conduct Committee of the Canadian Judicial Council, which deals with complaints of misconduct on the part of judges. He recently observed that a number of judges are of the view that judges simply should not accept appointment to commissions of inquiry.[10] In this respect, he reflects the comments of the late Justice Campbell, whose wisdom requires that he be quoted yet again: "There is a growing reluctance in the Canadian judiciary to see judges serve on Royal Commissions . . . rooted in the principle that judges are appointed and paid to judge cases in court, not to help governments solve political or social problems, and not to preside over extrajudicial proceedings." This reluctance was magnified by governmental responses

---

8 Above note 2 at 388–89.

9 See Chapter 4, Section C(3).

10 Janice Tibbetts, "Judges Warned of 'Hot Potato' Inquiries" *Canwest News Services* (18 August 2008).

to the Krever and Somalia inquiries, which Campbell described as "gratuitous and unfair commissioner-bashing." He added:

> Quite apart from the spectre of agreeing to a difficult task only to get beaten up by the government that appointed you, serious problems can arise when a judge steps off the bench and enters the arena of public controversy. There are practical problems, such as the disruption in the work of the judge's court, the potentially partisan implications of a judge's findings of fact, the potentially adversarial situation between the judge and the government, and the judicial review by other judges of the judge's conduct as a commissioner, which makes the judge a defendant in proceeding in his or her own court and exposes him or her to allegations of error or unfairness.[11]

The Somalia Inquiry demonstrated most graphically how vulnerable judges are when agreeing to serve as commissioners. Commissioner Letourneau was subjected to judicial review by a Federal Court trial judge, who found a reasonable apprehension of bias and ordered that the commissioner be prohibited from making findings of misconduct against one of the parties. Three judges, and colleagues of Justice Letourneau on the Court of Appeal, then overruled the trial judge. Aside from the merits of the case, the public optics of such a process could do little for public confidence in the judiciary and must have been embarrassing for Justice Letourneau.

But this is a real potential consequence of a judge agreeing to become a commissioner and thereby an appendage of the executive branch of government. In the case of the Somalia Inquiry, the commissioners were placed in the public light as operating inefficiently and constantly pleading for more time and money. Then they were told to file an incomplete report and disband. Nor did it end there. Judicial review continued after the report was published, which included attacks on the credibility and integrity of the commissioners. Justice Letourneau subsequently commented that he should have obtained a written undertaking from the government, in advance, that he would be represented by counsel in any challenge to the report. Instead, the government was represented by lawyers who had little knowledge of the inquiry, and, indeed, the government itself was also highly critical of the report when it was released.

---

11 Above note 2 at 392.

There are many reasons why judges agree to act as commissioners. In doing so, they perform a public service. But it is a service that lawyers, arbitrators, and academics with practical experience could easily fulfill without potential institutional harm to the judiciary. Some judges would view the opportunity to conduct a commission of inquiry as a unique and interesting opportunity that would be a pleasant "sabbatical" from their usual judicial diet. There is professional satisfaction in conducting an effective inquiry and leaving behind the legacy of a thorough report with important recommendations. Occasionally, a judge may be driven by ego, with potentially unfortunate consequences for his reputation, the commission, and the judiciary.

In recent years, some chief justices have adopted a policy that effectively prevents their judges from acting as commissioners in future. In 1998 the Canadian Judicial Council instituted a policy on the appointment of superior court judges to commissions of inquiry.[12] This policy provides that requests for a judge to undertake such a task should first be made to the chief justice or other administrative head of the judge's court. The chief justice and judge would then consider whether the judge's absence would "significantly impair the work of the court." They would also assess whether the reporting date is realistic, and, if not, "the proposed appointment should not be accepted." It reminds the chief justice that this might be an opportune time to ask the government to add an additional judicial position to the court's complement!

The chief justice and judge are also to consider whether the appointment "could impair the future work of the judge" as a judge. Factors to consider in this respect are:

- whether the issues are essentially partisan;
- whether they involve the conduct of agencies of the appointing government;
- whether they essentially involve criminal conduct or civil liability;
- whether the judge has any unique experience required or whether a supernumerary or retired judge would suffice; and

---

12 Canadian Judicial Council, *Annual Report, 1997–98* (Ottawa: Canadian Judicial Council, 2008) Appendix F at 59, online: www.cjc-ccm.gc.ca/cmslib/general/news_pub_annualreport_1997-1998_en.pdf. See also the Council's publication *Ethical Principles for Judges* (Ottawa: Canadian Judicial Council, 1998) at 11. At the time of this book's publication, this policy was under review by the Council.

- whether a judge is necessary at all or whether a senior lawyer could "perform this function equally well."

It is difficult to envision circumstances in which a senior lawyer could not perform the functions equally as well as a judge. Indeed, most judges who act as commissioners rely very heavily on their senior lawyers and do not hesitate to say so in their reports. However, the judicial office in itself brings an added degree of statute and credibility to a commission of inquiry.

## B. NATURE OF ROLE

### 1) Legal Status

The office of commissioner is an "appendage of the executive branch of government" even if the commissioner is also a judge, since any judicial authority is not carried over to the role of commissioner except to the extent specifically provided in the *Inquiries Act* or terms of references. The authority of a commissioner is derived entirely from the *Inquiries Act* and the terms of reference established for each commission. These define the jurisdiction of a commission and impose legal constraints as well as authority. A third legal constraint upon a commissioner is the principle of fairness.

The principle of fairness provides two broad protections to a person who may be adversely affected by a commission of inquiry. First, the commissioner must be independent and impartial, in the sense of being free of any actual bias or even a reasonable apprehension or perception of bias. This could arise from the commissioner's past activities or associations. One of the commissioners initially appointed to the Somalia Inquiry resigned after a month because of her previous associations with officials in the Department of National Defence.[13] But a legal bias may also be inferred from the manner in which the commissioner conducts the proceedings or conducts himself.[14] The second broad protection is the legal requirement of procedural fairness in the conduct of hearings.[15]

---

13 Chapter 3, Sections B(5) and D(4).

14 Such personal conduct is an important aspect of the role of a commissioner. See Section B(3), below in this chapter.

15 See Chapter 7, Section D.

Another feature of the role of a commissioner arises from the legal distinction between adversarial and inquisitorial proceedings. Judicial trials are conducted in an adversarial manner, where each side gathers its own evidence, presents it as favourably as possible, and emphasizes weaknesses in the evidence of the other side. The judge plays a passive role, primarily listening, and then rendering a decision. A commission of inquiry is an inquisitorial process that requires the commissioner to conduct an active search for the evidence as well as to present it publicly, assess it, and make findings in a final report.

The distinction between the two processes is not rigid. A judge may personally pursue a line of questioning of a witness that she considers important to the issues and that opposing counsel has not adequately explored. A commission of inquiry may (and should) conduct most of its search for evidence prior to the public hearings. At these hearings, the commissioner may play a more passive role, relying on the parties and commission counsel to explore the strengths and weaknesses of the evidence. But the essential difference is that the parties are responsible for collecting and presenting the evidence to a judge. The commissioner is responsible for collecting and presenting the evidence to the public, while providing a fair opportunity for affected parties to participate. Lord Diplock, in the *Erebus* case, described the "marked contrast" between civil litigation and an investigative inquiry:

> Where facts are in dispute in civil litigation conducted under the common law system of procedure, the Judge has to decide where, on the balance of probabilities, he thinks that the truth lies as between the evidence which the parties to the litigation have thought it to be in their respective interests to adduce before him. He has no right to travel outside that evidence on an independent search on his own part for the truth . . . .[16]

If the evidence is inconclusive, the judge must simply apply the rules as to onus of proof and make a decision. In contrast, the Erebus commissioner was required to inquire into and report on "the cause or causes of the crash." In doing so:

16 Above note 7 at 666.

> [I]t is inevitable, particularly if there are neither survivors or eye-witnesses of the crash, that the emergence of facts, and the realisation of what part, if any, they played in causing the disaster and of their relative importance, should be more elusive and less orderly, as one unanticipated piece of evidence suggests to the Commissioner, or to particular parties represented at the inquiry, some new line of investigation that it may be worth while to explore; whether, in the result, the exploration when pursued leads only to a dead end or . . . . The discovery of other facts which throw a fresh light on what actually happened and why it happened.

In this case, the pressure of time, combined with the initial adoption by commission counsel of a flawed process for marshalling the evidence, led to the evidence emerging piecemeal. This, in turn, "had unfortunate effects in colouring" the commissioner's view of that evidence, leading to successful judicial review.[17]

At common law, judges are given absolute immunity from being sued for their actions as a judge. This covers the entire range of their functions from pre-trial matters to what they say in their judgments. Since the immunity is absolute, it applies even if the judge acts in bad faith or with malice. Qualified privilege would not protect acts done in bad faith or with malice.

The inquiries legislation throughout Canada varies in its protection of commissioners from being sued for acts done as commissioners. The provinces of Alberta, Saskatchewan, Nova Scotia, and Newfoundland and Labrador all grant their commissioners the "same privileges and immunities" as a superior court judge. Quebec uses the words "protection and privileges," to the same effect. The Supreme Court of Canada held[18] that the Quebec Act granted its commissioners the same absolute immunity that protects superior court judges. The Manitoba Act states directly that "no action shall be brought" against a commissioner.

The British Columbia and New Brunswick Acts adopt a qualified rather than an absolute immunity for its commissioners. Each articulates the applicable qualification to the privilege. The British Columbia Act states that the immunity granted to a commissioner:

---

17 The role of commission counsel in marshalling the evidence is discussed in Chapter 6, Section B(2).

18 *Morier v. Rivard*, [1985] 2 S.C.R. 716.

> does not apply . . . to anything done or omitted by that person in bad faith.

The qualification in the New Brunswick Act is:

> unless it appear that the act was done by the commissioner without reasonable cause, and with actual malice, and wholly without jurisdiction.

The Acts of Ontario, Prince Edward Island, Canada, and the three territories make no reference to the immunity of commissioners. The Law Reform Commission of Ontario has reported that, in such circumstances, the common law is applicable. But it declines to state its view of the protection afforded by common law to Ontario commissioners.[19]

The leading authority in this respect still appears to be the Supreme Court of Canada decision in *Harris v. Law Society of Alberta*.[20] There, a lawyer sued the Law Society for damages after it disbarred him without complying with a statutory condition precedent. The Law Society was clearly in error and its decision was held to be "an absolute nullity" since it was made without jurisdiction. However, "under the circumstances of this case," the Law Society was not liable in damages.

The Court does not use the term "qualified privilege" but that clearly was the basis for its decision not to find liability. Chief Justice L.P. Duff adopted the view that, since the benchers were exercising a judicial power, "no action would lie in the absence of malice."[21] Here, "they acted in entire good faith." Justice Thibaudeau Rinfret added that, in fulfilling their role in this case, they were "only endeavouring to do their duty to the public and the profession."[22] This decision is authority for the conclusion that a statutory body exercising a judicial function is protected by qualified privilege.

The following statutory provisions limit the immunity protection when carrying out the duties of a commissioner:

- Newfoundland and Labrador—section 24: "in carrying out an inquiry "
- Quebec—section 16: "in the execution of their duty."

19 Ontario Law Reform Commission, *Report on Public Inquiries* (Toronto: The Commission, 1992) at 62.

20 [1936] S.C.R. 88 [*Harris*].

21 *Ibid.* at 94.

22 *Ibid.* at 104, writing for himself, Lamont, Crocket, and Kerwin JJ.

- New Brunswick—section 12: "purporting to be done by him in his capacity as such commissioner."
- British Columbia—section 32(1)(a): "in the performance or intended performance of any duty"; and section 32(1)(b): "in the exercise or intended exercise of any power."

In this respect, it is interesting to note that, in *Harris*, the Court did not find liability even though the benchers acted outside their jurisdiction. The words "purporting" and "intended" in the last two provisions seem directed at acts that are beyond the capacity or duties of a commissioner. But the Harris decision appears to have extended "good faith" to defining the scope as well as manner of fulfilling these functions.

Another consideration raised by *Harris* is whether a commission of inquiry can be characterized as acting "judicially." If not, it could be argued that the common law qualified privilege would not apply to it. Historically, there is a great deal of case law attempting to sort out when a statutory function is "judicial" or merely "administrative." If not judicial, the rules of natural justice would not apply. Under that historical analysis, a commission of inquiry would not be considered to be exercising judicial functions because it does not make decisions that affect rights. It merely recommends. With the replacement of the rules of natural justice by the principle of fairness, it is no longer necessary to find a "decision" that "affects rights" in order invoke procedural protections. A "recommendation" that may "affect interests" is a sufficient threshold.

Commissions of inquiry should be protected by qualified privilege even if they do not meet the previous rigid criteria to be classified as "judicial." They must comply with a fairly high standard of fairness.[23] They also may make findings of misconduct against individuals and report them publicly. More important, the underlying rationale for granting immunity is highly applicable to commissions of inquiry. It is necessary for the proper administration of justice. A commissioner must be free to speak and report freely and objectively so the truth may be discovered and reported objectively. The same considerations apply to the protection of witnesses and counsel.

Indeed, recent Canadian authority has tended to ignore the *Harris* case and grant absolute rather than qualified privilege to statutory bodies exercising quasi-judicial functions. For example, the Prince Edward

---

23 See Chapter 7, Section D.

Island Court of Appeal[24] did not refer to the *Harris* case, or to any other Canadian cases, in support of this conclusion but cited some British cases and the following passage from *Gatley on Libel and Slander*:

> General. The doctrine that an absolute immunity exists in respect of statements made in the course of proceedings before a court of justice has been held to apply to statements made in the course of any proceedings before a tribunal (which word covers a commission of inquiry) recognized by law which, though not a court in the ordinary sense, exercises judicial functions.[25]

There are similar examples from other provinces,[26] so it seems to be generally accepted that it is absolute rather than qualified privilege that applies at common law. Of course, qualified privilege would apply to commissions of inquiry in New Brunswick and British Columbia because of the express statutory provisions in those provinces. Their adoption of qualified rather than absolute privilege is based on sound policy reasons. The Supreme Court should consider restoring the qualified privilege established by *Harris* but subsequently ignored. The policy reasons adopted by the majority of the Court in *Nelles v. Ontario*[27] for granting only qualified privilege to crown attorneys appear to be equally applicable to statutory bodies exercising judicial functions.

### 2) Basic Functions

A commission of inquiry has no authority to decide legal rights or obligations; the fact-finding function of a commissioner has an intrinsic value quite apart from that of serving as the foundation for determining rights or obligations. The public is entitled to know why its supply of drinking water became dangerous, causing illness and death in the community. It wants to know why a mine explosion occurred that killed workers in the community. It must know how and why our criminal justice system could convict and imprison someone for a heinous crime that he did not commit.

---

24 *Ayangma v. NAV Canada* (2001), 203 D.L.R. (4th) 717 (P.E.I.S.C.A.D.).

25 9th ed. (London: Sweet & Maxwell, 1998) 295.

26 *Boyachyk v. Dukes* (1982), 136 D.L.R. (3d) 28 (Alta. Q.B.); *Perry v. Heatherington* (1971), 24 D.L.R. (3d) 127 (B.C.S.C.).

27 (1989), 60 D.L.R. (4th) 609 at 640–44 (S.C.C.).

A commissioner does not merely "find" facts. All of the facts must be assessed individually and collectively, including their interrelationship. The commissioner must analyze the primary facts and then draw conclusions about what happened, how it happened, and why it happened. These conclusions and the reasons for reaching them, as articulated in the commissioner's report, then become a part of the public record, available for all to see.

But it would be a sterile exercise merely to record these conclusions since they provide a unique opportunity to go one step further. That is to make recommendations to avoid similar problems occurring in future. The commissioner must become educated throughout the inquiry process in order to draw lessons from the events. The recommendations can relate to laws, administrative practices, relationships, and organizational structures and can inform future public and political discussion and debate.

In many respects, the journey of a commission of inquiry is as important as the destination. The commissioner becomes the face, and often the name, of the inquiry as its hearings proceed with public visibility and scrutiny. The hearings should represent only a relatively small part of the work of a commission. Yet they are of crucial importance as an opportunity for those most directly affected, and for the general public, to become educated. In this respect, the hearings should also enhance public confidence in the ability and integrity of the commissioner to come to the correct conclusions in her final report. An important element of such confidence will be the fairness of the manner in which the commissioner proceeded.[28]

### 3) Fairness: Impartiality

When all other processes are incapable of satisfying public confidence, one of the most important features the commissioner brings to the table is her independent and impartial status. A commissioner must be credible in the public eye, when appointed, but must also maintain

---

28 *Stevens v. Canada (Attorney General)*, [2003] F.C.J. No. 1589 (Fed. Ct.); and *Beno v. Canada (Commission of Inquiry into the Deployment of Canadian Forces in Somalia)* (2 May 1997), Ottawa T-408-97 (F.C.A.). The trial decision was reported at [1997] 1 F.C. 911 (T.D.).

that credibility throughout the work of the inquiry, including the final report. This is done by acting fairly and objectively and without demonstrating any personal bias. The round table that assessed the work of commissions of inquiry, in the wake of the Gomery Inquiry, observed:

> In our highly mediatised world, the commission and in particular the commissioner inevitably becomes a subject for intense media scrutiny. Everything about the commission—from how much the commissioner is paid, to the political connections of those he engages to assist him or her, his style of handling witnesses, his capacity to respect the commission's budget, will be considered for media coverage.
>
> Furthermore, the commissioner needs to be acutely aware of the political implications of any statements s/he makes to the press during the course of the commission's work.[29]

The commissioner must set the tone for the operation of the commission, which also includes commission counsel and all others working on its behalf. A good starting point is the resolve to treat every individual who deals with the commission, or may be affected by it, with dignity, respect, and sensitivity.

This is not a legal requirement but a human response. It is a basic value that can be overlooked under the pressure of time and volume of work as well as in routine tasks.[30] It was this human response that led Commissioner O'Connor's staff to begin meeting with representatives in the Walkerton community within weeks of his appointment and to hold public meetings within two months for the sole purpose of allowing those tragically affected to tell their stories.[31] It was also reflected in Commissioner Goudge's private meetings with individuals and families affected by paediatric forensic pathology practices during the initial period of his systemic review. Although he was not authorized to inquire into specific cases, he chose to meet with those directly affected to provide them that opportunity and also to "anchor my work in real human

---

29 Peter Larson, Larson Associates, September 2006. Available online: http://74.125.95.132/custom?q=cache:voozMx_5ddsJ:www.ipac.ca/documents/ExBrief-3Commissions31.pdf+larson&cd=2&hl=en&ct=clnk&client=google-coop. Discussed in Chapter 4, Section C(1).

30 Ed Ratushny, "Beyond Our Own Workshop: Dignity, Respect and Kindness" (2006) Advocates' Soc. J. 20.

31 See Chapter 3, Section B(4).

experience." The terms of reference for the Air India Inquiry specifically requires opportunities for appropriate participation by the families of the victims.

Emotions may run high in some inquiries. There may be victims who seek "revenge" by attempting to use the hearings to attack those they perceive as the perpetrators of their plight. Others may seek to deflect responsibility away from themselves by blaming others. Justice Cory, delivering the judgment of the Supreme Court of Canada, summarized Commissioner Krever's approach when inquiring into how thousands contracted HIV and Hepatitis C as a result of Canada's blood system:

> In describing his mandate and intention, the Commissioner emphasized that the Inquiry "is not and it will not be a witch hunt. It is not concerned with criminal or civil liability." He said the reason the Inquiry was called was not to advance the interests of those involved with or contemplating litigation of any kind, and that he would not permit the hearings to be used for ulterior purposes. At the same time, he made it clear that he interpreted his mandate as including a fact-finding process focusing upon the events of the early 1980s and that he intended to "get to the bottom" of those events.[32]

Twenty-five interested parties had been granted standing, which posed a massive challenge for conducting fair and efficient hearings yet keeping the focus on the terms of reference rather than on other personal or corporate interests.

In the court below, Justice Robert Décary had observed that a commissioner also may have to focus on keeping himself on track. He adopted the following comment by Bryan Schwartz as correctly noting "the dangers that lie in wait for a commissioner":

> Again, an interest in promoting a general cause may distort the judgment of even the most judicious person. The danger of distorted perception is especially serious for those who obtain ego-gratification by feeling righteous and being perceived as such. Most public inquiries are about rooting out something every [one] thinks is bad, "drug-use in sports, political corruption, bad police behaviour" and a commissioner

32 *Canada (Attorney General) v. Canada (Commission of Inquiry on the Blood System in Canada—Krever Commission)*, [1997] 3 S.C.R. 440 at para. 5.

> can be carried away with the general enthusiasm for reform to the point that individual conduct cannot be fairly evaluated.[33]

The Erebus Royal Commission in New Zealand provides an example of a commissioner succumbing to this danger when investigating a plane crash. The Judicial Committee of the Privy Council commented on the commissioner's mental process:

> These appalling blunders and deficiencies, the existence of which emerged piecemeal in the course of the 75 days of hearings, had caused the loss of 257 lives. Their Lordships can well understand the growing indignation of the Judge when, after completing the hearings and for the purpose of preparing his Report, he brought them together in his own mind and reflected upon them.[34]

Unfortunately, he concluded that there had been a pre-determined plan to deceive him and a conspiracy to commit perjury at the hearings, which he described as "an orchestrated litany of lies." The Committee concluded that there was no evidence of any probative value on which such findings could be based and set them aside.

A similar example of misguided investigative zeal occurred in the case of *R. v. Elliott*[35] where the Ontario Court of Appeal ordered a new trial because of the conduct of the trial judge. The accused was charged with murder and dismemberment of the dead body. Justice Paul Cosgrove, in effect, had allowed a series of defence motions to transform the criminal trial into an investigation into the conduct of the police and those involved in the prosecution. He found misconduct on the part of fifteen named police officers and others unnamed, Crown counsel, and officials of the departments of the attorney general, solicitor general, and immigration as well as the Ontario Centre of Forensic Sciences. His findings included: witness tampering, non-disclosure, deceitful destruction and fabrication of evidence, perjury, false and misleading submis-

---

33 *Canada (Attorney General) v. Canada (Commission of Inquiry on the Blood System—Krever Commission)*, [1997] F.C.J. No. 17 at para. 32 (C.A.), Strayer and McGuigan JJ.A concurring. Citing Bryan Schwartz, "Public Inquiries" in *Public Interest v. Private Rights: Striking the Balance in Administrative Law*, 1990 Isaac Pitblado Lectures (Winnipeg, Law Society of Manitoba, 1990) at 264–65.

34 Above note 7 at 685.

35 (2003), 181 C.C.C. (3d) 118.

sions to the court, and other serious misconduct. He found over 150 *Charter* violations and ordered a stay of proceedings and costs against the Crown.

The Court of Appeal set aside his findings and ordered a new trial. The judgment elaborates on how misguided his conduct was. There was no factual or legal foundation for his conclusions and he did not even attempt to explain the legal basis for many of them. He was totally misguided and acted in an unfair manner to those he had castigated. His bizarre conduct led to an inquiry by the Canadian Judicial Council into whether he should be removed from the office of judge, a recommendation for his removal, and his resignation.

This incident is recounted here even though it arose out of a criminal trial rather than a commission of inquiry. If such crusading zeal is possible within the confined structure of criminal proceedings, it poses a much greater danger for a commissioner with a far broader mandate, discretionary coercive powers, and often multiple constituencies affected. And it is a danger not only with respect to the broad direction of an inquiry but also in relation to discrete issues within broader subject areas.

The public scrutiny to which commissioners may be subjected when conducting hearings was illustrated in an article in the *Ottawa Citizen* on the chairman of the Somalia Inquiry entitled "Gilles Létourneau: Feisty and Fair or Heavy-Handed?" It said that

> [C]ritics have accused the chairman of browbeating witnesses with heavy-handed tactics that have prompted several heated exchanges, including a verbal altercation last month with Vice-Admiral Larry Murray, the country's acting top soldier. Létourneau told Murray he shouldn't expect special treatment. Murray later shot back: "As CDS (chief of the defence staff) I'm appalled at the way you treat junior officers who come to testify."[36]

Another incident involving Chairman Létourneau was the subject of judicial review. During the examination of Brigadier General Beno by commission counsel, the chairman intervened. He told the witness his testimony contradicted an earlier answer he had given to a question by the chairman. The witness denied any contradiction and the chairman

---

36 Jim Bronskill (26 February 1997).

responded: "I might as well tell you that you won't gain much by fiddling around. It was a clear question and you won't gain much." The witness's lawyer then objected and the chairman dropped the matter.

The following week, the chairman visited Calgary with three commission staff members to interview soldiers. They all attended a breakfast meeting at the Calgary Base Officer's Mess. Another general, who had watched the testimony on television, told the chairman he thought Brigadier General Beno had been treated aggressively and unfairly. The general later swore an affidavit stating that the chairman's reply expressed the opinion "that Brigadier General Beno had not given straight answers and that perhaps Beno had been trying to deceive." A retired general, who expressed a similar criticism on the same occasion, later swore that the chairman responded to him that when Beno testified, he was "very tense . . . he seemed to be hiding things . . . he didn't seem to want to cooperate with the Commission." On judicial review, the trial judge concluded that there was a reasonable apprehension of bias on the part of the chairman in relation to General Beno.

The Federal Court of Appeal reversed this finding. It observed that the chairman must have been shocked to hear criticism of his behaviour, and added:

> It is easy now to say that he should have remained silent. But it is not abnormal for a person in that situation whose impartiality is openly put in question to try to explain the reasons that motivated his behaviour.[37]

This rationalization is not convincing. The chairman had engaged in discussions about the credibility of a witness before the proceedings had been completed. He suggested that the witness had lied and that this was reinforced by the demeanour of the witness on the stand. The "fiddling around" statement was inappropriate and it would have been better to have commission counsel challenge the witness rather than the chairman entering the fray at the hearing.

Furthermore, it is not clear why the chairman of the three-member commission was travelling to Calgary to interview prospective wit-

---

37 *Beno v. Canada (Commission of Inquiry into the Deployment of Canadian Forces in Somalia—Létourneau Commission)*, [1997] 2 F.C. 527 at para. 33 (C.A.). All of the discussions and quotations regarding the case are taken from the Federal Court of Appeal decision.

nesses to see what evidence they might give before him. This was a task normally done by investigators or by commission counsel. Visiting the base for a breakfast meeting might have been a nice gesture, but it placed Chairman Létourneau in a vulnerable position when he became engaged in discussions about the credibility of a witness before that determination was made.

There is nothing sinister in this conduct but it appears to be ill-conceived. Apart from the possibility of judicial review, it gives a public impression of not acting fairly and impartially. The "fiddling around" comment was no doubt born of frustration. Some witnesses, and the military generally, were uncooperative in many respects. But any public impression of unfairness would only make it easier for the government to shut down the commission, which it ultimately did.

While Commissioner Létourneau's conduct may have been influenced by frustration, Commissioner Gomery appears to have been driven by ego. The participants in the round table referred to above felt strongly that the public policy aspect of the Gomery Report was significantly weakened by "[a] fascination with the media role of the Commission. In this regard, rapid publication of a book by the former Communications Chief of the Commission with a foreword by Judge Gomery, was regarded as particularly unseemly."[38]

This commissioner's behaviour in relation to the media was documented in a recent decision of the Federal Court. There, Justice Max Teitlebaum found that his comments to the media demonstrated a reasonable apprehension of bias towards former prime minister Jean Chrétien. As a result, his findings with respect to Chrétien were treated as void and set aside.[39]

The judgment points out that Commissioner Gomery was aware that the evidence emerging throughout the inquiry could reflect badly on

---

38 Above note 29.

39 *Chrétien v. Canada (Commission of Inquiry into the Sponsorship Program and Advertising Activities, Gomery Commission)*, 2008 FC 802 [*Chrétien*]. Justice Teitlebaum also set aside the findings related to the prime minister's chief of staff: *Pelletier v. Canada (Attorney General)*, 2008 FC 803. He dismissed a similar application by the minister then in charge of the sponsorship program on the basis that the commissioner's bias was not directed against him personally: *Gagliano v. Canada (Commission of Inquiry into the Sponsorship Program and Advertising Activities, Gomery Commission)*, 2008 FC 981.

the conduct of individuals. He stated at the outset that the potentially unfavourable impact on individual reputations made it "of paramount importance that the Inquiry's process be scrupulously fair." He added that his media spokesperson would be "the only person who will speak on behalf of the Commission." But when the opportunity presented itself, he could not resist breaking his own rule and embarking on a path that was accurately portrayed in the argument of counsel for Chrétien and summarized in the judgment as follows:

> Commissioner Gomery was seduced by the media and the limelight to such an extent that the judicial instinct for fairness, objectivity and restraint . . . gave way to a preoccupation on his part with focusing media (and public) attention upon himself.[40]

Justice Teitlebaum concluded that the comments made by the commissioner had the cumulative effect of prejudging the issues and demonstrating a bias against Chrétien.

In late September 2008 the government announced that it had appealed this decision. But even if the appeal is successful, the circumstances provide a classic illustration of how a commissioner should *not* behave in dealing with the media.

The problem began on 15 December 2004, when Commissioner Gomery gave what was described as his "first-ever media interview."[41] The inquiry had heard just over three months of evidence and was about to break for Christmas. The following quotes were reproduced in the judgment and Gomery did not contest their accuracy. In a newspaper article appearing the next day he said: "Does anyone have a different opinion on that subject? . . . I simply confirmed the findings that [Auditor General] Sheila Fraser had made, which I think I'm in a position to do after three months of hearings." Justice Teitlebaum rejected this contention since there were six more months of hearings to come, his mandate was much broader than the auditor general's, and his mandate required him to consider "all levels" of officials in his investigation. He had not yet heard from those he found to be in charge of the program, particularly the prime minister's chief of staff. As a result, he had prejudged the matters he was required to investigate before hearing all of the evidence.

---

40 *Chrétien, ibid.* at para. 78. The quotations that follow are taken from this judgment.

41 Don Martin, "Gomery Calls Guité A Charmer" *National Post* (16 December 2004).

In another interview, after his report had been published, Justice Gomery made this comment on Chrétien's testimony: "And the very answer he gave me was the only answer that counted as far as I was concerned .... So with this answer I had everything that I needed." This did not convey the perception of an impartial and objective adjudicator. Rather, it suggested to a reasonable observer, according to Justice Teitlebaum, that

> the Commissioner had a plan or checklist of the evidence that was expected and which was required in order to support pre-determined conclusions.

In his initial interview on 15 December 2004, Gomery had also said that the "juicy stuff" was yet to come. Justice Teitlebaum concluded that this comment "trivialized" the proceedings, which were of "enormous" importance to the witnesses who had yet to testify and bore a "pejorative connotation" towards them.

When counsel for Chrétien brought an application for the commissioner's recusal following those statements, his media spokesperson announced that the commission had received a flood of e-mails from the public. He described them as saying: "What's Chrétien got to hide?" In rejecting the motion, the commissioner said that this comment was made without his knowledge but he also purported to confirm the accuracy of the comment by saying it was simply a statement of fact.

Justice Teitlebaum reviewed those e-mails and concluded that they simply did not support the comment. Moreover, they had raised suspicions and doubts about Chrétien's integrity before he had testified. But the commissioner had also insulted Chrétien directly: "It's such a disappointment that the Prime Minister would put his name on golf balls. That's really small-town cheap, you know, free golf balls." In addition to insulting the former prime minister and his background, it suggested improper conduct even before he testified.

Chrétien was not the only party subjected to the commissioner's extra-curricular musings. The newspaper report of his first interview included the following passage:

> "Judge Gomery singled out Chuck Guité, the former senior bureaucrat who presided over the sponsorship program, as a highlight of the Ottawa hearings. Testimony has suggested Mr. Guité operated the secret-

> ive program with little oversight on how he spent the government's money."
>
> "It's impossible not to like Chuck Guité," Mr. Gomery grinned. "Let's face it, he's a charming scamp and he had his department mesmerized. He got himself promoted just before his retirement and thereby built up his pension. I'm going to hear more about Mr. Guité. He'll probably have to testify again."

The next day, he denied he had prejudged any issues and characterized this as simply "a comment on the personality of one of the witnesses." Justice Teitlebaum's judgment documents a number of attempts by the commissioner to deny he had prejudged any issues. Some of these can be described as sheer sophistry. For example, Gomery stressed that he said he "was coming" to the same conclusions as the auditor general, not that he had done so. He argued that this demonstrated an open mind! He also argued that his press interviews were in the spirit of judges coming "out of their ivory towers" to help the media better understand what was taking place. But they were really about the commissioner, not the process. He referred to the proceedings as a "show" or "spectacle" and said he had "the best seat in the house for the best show in town." Upon his retirement from the bench in the summer of 2007, he gave another interview in which he repeated this comment: "I was criticized for saying it, but I stand by what I said: I had the best seat in the house for the best show in town. It was an amazing spectacle. It was a drama with surprise discoveries almost every day, with eminently competent lawyers. It was an ideal situation for the person running the show."[42] This article demonstrates how much Gomery enjoys the kind of celebrity status his appointment as commissioner brought. He spoke of being known across Canada, getting the best table when going out for dinner, giving the odd autograph, and being recognized everywhere—which he did not find "disagreeable."

It appears that his ego was firmly in place well before his appointment as a commissioner. In reflecting on his career, he found something special in conducting "a high profile" criminal trial: "I adored all of it . . . But you know, it pleases the ego to preside over a trial that makes headlines." He felt that his commission was popular because it exposed

---

42 Parent, "At 75, Gomery Is Shifting Gears," above note 6.

his personality to the public. In reality, he played fast and loose with the reputations of others for self-aggrandizement. He is probably a good person and does have a good reputation as a judge but the conduct described above is a demonstration of how a commissioner should not act. Besides the danger of having findings struck down, a commissioner has a legal obligation to treat witnesses with fairness, and a human obligation to treat them with dignity, respect, and sensitivity.

Commissioner O'Connor, who conducted the highly successful Walkerton and Arar inquiries, recommended that commission counsel should assume the role of speaking to the media. He added that it is "a very bad idea" for the commissioner to do so.[43]

## C. IMMEDIATE REQUIREMENTS

### 1) Staff and Facilities

Following his experience with the Somalia Inquiry, Justice Létourneau emphasized that, at the time of appointment, a commissioner has absolutely no infrastructure of support to assist him in fulfilling his mandate:

> [Y]ou are left with nothing. You have no offices, no staff, no personnel, no computers, not even a pen, and not even a piece of paper. You have got nothing. So you have got to set up everything and organize everything. That is what I call the administrative aspect of it, the analytical aspect of it. You still have nothing. You have no evidence, you have to gather the evidence; the purpose is to gather evidence. You have to organize your workforce once you have hired your workforce. What it is you are going to be doing and who is going to be doing what and get the whole thing organized. So that takes at the very least three months before you can even put a single witness in the box.[44]

The late Justice Archie Campbell elaborated:

> You need counsel and staff; you need investigators and researchers. You need office space outside the ministry or agency involved. You need reliable contact people in the organization you are looking at. You may

---

43 Justice Dennis O'Connor, "The Role of Commission Counsel in a Public Inquiry" (2003) 22 Advocates' Soc. J. 9 at 11.

44 Above note 2 at 362.

> be confronted immediately with requests to pay the legal costs of those who are the subject of your inquiry. There may be documents or other evidence that needs to be preserved. People may come forward right away and try to make some kind of deal to give you information in exchange for something they want. You need a budget; you need financial and expenditure controls; you need security systems, document storage and control systems, computer systems, and the like. You need, you need, and you need.[45]

Many commissioners have stressed the importance of the contribution of their counsel and administrative staff to successfully fulfilling their mandate.[46] In the Gomery Commission, the role played by the commissioner's media spokesperson contributed to some of his findings being struck down on judicial review.

The commissioner must put together a team that understands it must work together, often under time constraints and other pressures. It seldom is a "nine-to-five" job, except, potentially, where the commissioner has no deadline for reporting and is a bad manager. Counsel and other staff must also appreciate that they are an extension of the commissioner and their conduct may reflect on her. There must be rigorous screening to avoid real or apparent conflict of interest. Even though legal conflict of interest may not exist, there may be past associations that could cause reasonable members of the public to conclude it would be better for someone not to be on the commission's staff. Once engaged, there must be a clear understanding of their specific roles and responsibilities. What they should not do may be as important as what they are expected to do. That would include avoiding close social relationships with the parties involved during the course of the inquiry. Staff should demonstrate a sense of public service and treat everyone with courtesy, while maintaining appropriate boundaries such as confidentiality.

The task of putting together such a staff may at first seem daunting, but there are two key positions that the commissioner should be able to fill almost immediately. These are the executive director and the senior counsel. This might include both a senior hearings and a senior advisory counsel.[47] The commissioner may then work with them in developing

---

45 *Ibid.* at 385–86.

46 *Ibid.* at 386; above note 43 at 9 and see Chapter 6, Section A(1).

47 See discussion in Chapter 6, Section A(3).

the organizational structure and engaging qualified personnel. The following discussion is only introductory but may provide some preliminary guidance in this respect.

Of course, there is considerable latitude in how each commission organizes its infrastructure. The equivalent of the executive director has also been called the chief administrative officer, executive officer, executive secretary, secretary, and registrar. While the commissioner has ultimate responsibility for all aspects of the commission, the executive director is delegated responsibility for all administrative and financial aspects of the commission's operations. At the federal level, terms of reference usually use phrases such as "in accordance with Treasury Board policies" and "that may be approved by Treasury Board." In Ontario, the reference is to "Management board of Cabinet Directives and Guidelines" and possibly "other applicable government policies" for expenditures. It is important that the executive director understand these requirements and how corresponding decisions are made in order to facilitate administration and avoid unnecessary delays. Experience and knowledge of how government works are invaluable.

The Executive Director will play a major role in developing the commission's budget. It must be realistic and meet government policies such as those referred to above. Procedures for approving expenditures must be adopted. There is little evidence of governments attempting to encroach on commission independence through budgetary interference, but budgets must be prepared and submitted for government approval.

A commission's budget must be based on estimates of the work involved and time required. As former Commissioner O'Connor has observed:

> In a sense, budgets are really self-imposed time limits . . . . Preparing a budget and being prepared to explain it through commission counsel is a good exercise in planning and discipline.[48]

It may be necessary to start with an interim budget and provide modifications and a final budget later. But commissioners should be prepared for the possibility that their budgets will become the subject of public comment and criticism.

Appropriate hiring practices must be followed. If people are retained to conduct a specific task, appropriate contractual provisions are re-

48 Personal correspondence between the author and Justice O'Connor.

quired. For example, if research contracts are given, they should address issues such as conflict of interest, confidentiality, publication rights, and ownership. A hearing room will have to be found and commission offices established, both with appropriate equipment. Some construction modifications may be required that have to be done expeditiously. The Goudge Inquiry reported on the hearing room it had designed and constructed:

> Our hearing room accommodated approximately 27 counsel. Each counsel table had two electronic monitors, which displayed the documents that were before a witness . . . the Commission's registrar . . . easily piloted the Inquiry's electronic database to retrieve documents from it quickly and have them available on the hearing room monitors. This allowed us to conduct a largely paperless process. Counsel tables were wired to Internet hook-up, and wireless Internet was also available in the hearing room. A seating plan was prepared for the hearing room.

Although there also was a small public gallery, many more people were able to follow the proceedings through the commission's webcasting. Also, rather than delay the hearings until construction was completed, the preliminary hearing was conducted in a hotel meeting room.

While the executive director would have staff to fulfill specific administrative duties, he would normally report directly to the commissioner on any financial or administrative matters requiring her attention. It also is helpful for the executive director to establish good communication with senior officials in the central agency responsible for commissions of inquiry as well as in the department of the minister primarily responsible. That might assist in early identification of any misunderstanding or concerns that could arise.

The senior or lead commission counsel is generally responsible for the marshalling and presenting of the evidence and managing the hearings. In general, she is the operational control centre for the substantive work of the commission.[49] This includes assisting in the selection, deployment, and supervision of the legal team. If investigators are retained, they would also fall under her supervision. The Goudge Inquiry had a lead commission counsel, a special criminal law counsel, two assistant commission counsel, seven staff lawyers, a special counsel for privacy law, and additional lawyers and law clerks retained for specific projects.

---

49 Discussed in greater detail in Chapter 6, Section B.

While the challenges of coordination must have been difficult, Commissioner Goudge reported that this number of lawyers allowed him to complete his report in an expeditious manner, which he certainly did.

Commissions of inquiry that deal with massive documentation require a skilful information manager. The Walkerton Inquiry reported receiving as many as one million documents from the government and scanning 200,000 into its database. The identification, classification, storage, and retrieval of relevant documents can be important for the expeditious operation of a commission as well as the thoroughness of its findings. Different levels of access may also be required. Some may be restricted to parties with standing, while others could be made available on the commission's website after they are entered onto the record.

The Goudge Inquiry's terms of reference specifically provided that "[t]he Commission shall establish and maintain a website and use other technologies to promote accessibility and transparency to the public." In addition to webcasting, such websites also allow access to daily transcripts, rulings of the commissioner, and other information. The Walkerton hearings were televised on local cable television to an eager audience. The Air India hearings were available on the Cable Public Affairs Channel (CPAC). This public access is highly desirable but the federal privacy commissioner expressed concerns in a recent speech when she said that "it's time to find the 'right balance' between privacy rights and the sacrosanct 'open court' principle in the Google age.[50] One suggested approach has been to disclose the sensitive information but not 'name names' on the internet."[51]

Traditional media is still an important information avenue to the public for commissions of inquiry. It is important that adequate assistance is provided by a commission to media representatives in carrying out their functions. At the time of writing, the Cornwall Inquiry website has the most detailed information about such assistance. It provides this helpful information:

- General Information: Photo opportunities in the hearing room; Cameras not permitted after hearings in progress; Confidentiality agreements for *in camera* hearings.

50 Kathryn May, "Former Bureaucrat Investigated For Fraud Fights to Keep Name Secret" *Ottawa Citizen* (1 September 2008).

51 *Ibid.*

- Audio and Television Feeds: Video and audio feeds available.
- Media Room: Television and audio monitor; Telephone Lines; daily transcriptions available.
- Media Relations: Media advisories; Commissioner will not grant interviews; Spokespersons for commission; Requested sensitivity to personal experiences of witnesses.
- Parking availability.
- Media contact for commission.

These features appear to have been developed from the precedent of the Arar Inquiry.

The Goudge Inquiry described the role of its "Communication and Media Relations Officer" as follows:

> Given that this was a public inquiry which was likely to draw significant media attention, it was important to retain an individual with excellent media contacts and prior experience working with public inquiries. I found both qualifications in Peter Rehak, who was retained as the Commission's communications and media relations officer. Mr. Rehak's duties included drafting press releases, coordinating with the media regarding their attendance during the inquiry process, answering questions from the media about the inquiry process, overseeing the design and operation of the Inquiry's media room, and designing and maintaining the Inquiry's website.

Rehak is, indeed, a seasoned and respected journalist and consultant, who played a similar role in the Toronto Leasing Inquiry, the Walkerton Inquiry, and others.

A media-relations officer can also identify any problems or concerns the media might have about the process or their access to information. Any such concerns can be addressed or, if necessary, brought to the attention of commission counsel or, ultimately, the commissioner.

In my view, the media-relations officer should not speak publicly on behalf of the commission. I agree with Associate Chief Justice O'Connor that, when necessary, that role should belong to commission counsel. It appears that the media spokesperson for the Gomery Inquiry did not understand the role of a commissioner. He seemed to view the process as some sort of political contest where the purpose was to gain headlines and win public support for the commissioner at the expense of the parties. Reference was made in the previous section to his summary of the e-mails the commission had received: "What's Chrétien got to hide?" In his subsequent book, he altered the wording to "What is Jean Chrétien trying to do?" but added: "That remark won me a headline, an angry response from Jean Chrétien's lawyers, and a new wave of support."[52] A commission of inquiry should not be an adversarial political campaign, and should never feed false information to the public.

Other possible commission personnel might be indicated by the nature of the task assigned by the terms of reference. The Goudge Inquiry, like the ongoing Cornwall Inquiry, had an "outreach" component requiring special skills and experience. A research director may be necessary if there are systemic or policy dimensions involved. Translation services may be necessary in some jurisdictions.

### 2) Game Plan

At the earliest opportunity, the commissioner, with the assistance of her advisers, must establish a "game plan" as to how the commission will go about fulfilling its mandate. Careful analysis and preparation at the outset can avoid delay and confusion as the process progresses. While minor adjustments are inevitable along the way, it may be difficult to change the main course once it has been set. Some inquiries, such as Mulroney-Schreiber, are relatively narrow in focus and straightforward. Others, such as Somalia, are extremely broad and complex. Sometimes, there must be at least a preliminary assessment of some of the evidence before this general approach can be crystallized. But the game plan should be in place and operational by the time of the opening hearings.

The first basic question to be asked is what this commission is really about. What were the politics that led to its creation and what are the political implications of the hearings and the final report? Did these influence the terms of reference or timelines? Are there individuals or institutions likely to be in conflict with each other? What are the potential sources of cooperation or resistance? What has been the public/media reaction and expectations?

To ask these questions is not to suggest that the commissioner must react to the answers. Rather, it is to provide a broader context of under-

52 Above note 40 at para. 89.

standing and may help to identify and avoid potential pitfalls. For example, with the wisdom of hindsight, one could draw the conclusion that the Somalia Inquiry was designed for failure. The breadth of the terms of reference was staggering. The initial time frame of six months was ridiculous and the first extension to nine months was also completely unrealistic. While the first defence minister was supportive, the commission soon encountered layers of resistance within the government and military. Is it possible that the Starr Inquiry's terms of reference were designed to be struck down on a constitutional challenge? This may seem a bit far-fetched, but the attorney general of Ontario at the time was Ian Scott, a brilliant constitutional lawyer and tactician. And the terms of reference were designed almost as a criminal indictment. Such an approach could be justified as an attempt to test the limits of provincial constitutional jurisdiction in such inquiries.

The work of previous commissions of inquiry provides a rich source of precedents for future inquiries. It may be helpful for commissioners and their advisers to consult the websites and reports of previous commissions with similar mandates. Commissioner O'Connor mentioned in both his Walkerton and Arar reports that he and his staff learned as they went along, and he has also spoken of the "evolutionary" nature of the work of public inquiries. To some extent that will always be the case since unique issues and problems will continue to arise. Solutions will have to be found along the way. But the more such matters can be anticipated and addressed as part of the game plan, the more efficient, effective, and fair the commission's work is likely to be.

In this respect, a detailed scrutiny and analysis of the terms of reference is crucial. Although the commissioner should have had a preliminary discussion with the responsible minister and/or senior officials in advance, a more thorough analysis with commission advisers should now take place to inform the manner in which the commissioner should proceed. If the terms involve technical issues, requiring expertise, the commissioner may wish to create an informal advisory group to assist in this process. The members of such a group could also be a source of future advice or expert testimony as required and they would already be familiar with the terms of reference.

The analysis of the terms of reference should also consider potential constitutional limitations, vagueness, internal inconsistencies, difficulties in obtaining information and evidence, and similar issues. The

Cornwall terms gave a discretion to rely on "factual overview reports." The Goudge terms said "shall rely wherever possible" on such reports and had a similar requirement for "representative witnesses on behalf or institutions." In either event, the commission is bound by the principle of fairness. But the Goudge terms established a "systemic" inquiry, making the adoption of summary processes much easier. Where the terms involve investigation into potential, individual misconduct, different considerations often apply.

The subject matter in the terms of reference may provide direct guidance as to how the game plan should be approached. The Walkerton terms referred to three aspects: What caused the tragedy? What was the responsibility of the government for this? How to ensure the safety of Ontario's drinking water? Commissioner O'Connor divided the inquiry into two parts. The first two questions would be addressed in Part I since they were Walkerton-related and highly investigative. Each area would be addressed, in turn, in adjudicative style hearings in Walkerton. Part II would deal with policy issues and involve broader considerations, including "issues, practices, and experience in other jurisdictions." This required a different procedural model and would be addressed in a separate report. Both Parts proceeded simultaneously. The decision to hold the hearings in the community (and for the commissioner and lead counsel to live there) has been recognized as an important factor in its success.

Where the terms of reference are broad, they must be broken down into manageable components. The Goudge Inquiry provides a good illustration. At a preliminary hearing, less than two months after it was established, the commissioner outlined nine broad subject areas he saw as guiding his systemic review.[53] These included the nature of the science, best practices, key institutions and their interaction, the evolution of investigation procedures, role of experts, role of the courts, and other matters. This was not an exclusive list but it provided a broad road map of where the commission was heading. Such an overview can be valuable for the public, the parties, and the commission in the gathering and assimilating of information. The "headings and subheadings" then evolve over the course of the inquiry and ultimately find expression in the commission's final report.

---

53 Opening Statement by Commissioner Goudge (18 June 2007).

The broad manner of dealing with the terms of reference also should be considered. Often there is not such a clear separation of investigative and policy components. Where systemic aspects arise out of specific conduct, two phases may be established. Some evidentiary exploration of systemic aspects may occur during the investigative stage but further systemic evidence and expertise, as well as policy aspects and systemic recommendations, are often left for a second phase.

The use of "town hall meetings" may be therapeutic for a community but they must be carefully considered. The Cluff Lake Uranium Inquiry structured them in the form of public debates with speakers representing opposing views. The commissioner wanted to provide a fair opportunity for the public to hear both sides, and the meetings did achieve that. But such an approach will be difficult to manage where there are highly polarized positions.[54] Perhaps they are more valuable where there are shared community needs and goals, as in Walkerton. If one of the purposes is to provide information to the community, then it is important that the meetings be scheduled at a time when the commission has information to share.

The order of addressing the issues also may be significant. If a finding of misconduct is possible, efforts should be made to present any evidence in support of such allegations before the person in question is called to respond. Counsel for the Ontario Provincial Police Association (OPP) was critical of the Ipperwash Inquiry for failing to address the involvement of the premier and other politicians at the outset:

> That was why the inquiry was primarily called. That was really, I think, the central focus that one would have expected from the inquiry, and I would have thought that the inquiry, with that central focus, could have been done much more quickly without going into such detail about the interactions between individual officers and individual occupiers and others.
>
> I would have thought that the more sensible way of conducting the inquiry would have been to start with the politicians and start with the central issue, instead of spending, I don't know, over a year, before you got to that.

---

54 Liora Salter & Debra Slaco, *Public Inquiries in Canada* (Ottawa: Supply and Services Canada, 1981). See, generally, Chapter IV.

The inquiry followed a chronological timeline dealing with a broad range of events and going into great detail for each. The OPP counsel described the approach as "fairly inefficient" in view of the focus of the ultimate report.[55]

The process of marshalling the evidence for the hearings is often a massive task for commission counsel, but, of course, it is important to start this aspect of the commission's work as quickly as possible.[56] There may be other matters that can be addressed at the outset, without much preparation time required. For example, the attendance of Walkerton Inquiry staff in the community and Commissioner Goudge meeting with individuals adversely affected by the subject of his inquiry basically involved "listening." The manner of dealing with "victims" will vary with the circumstances of each inquiry. The Cornwall and Air India inquiries provide other recent examples. The Walkerton Inquiry commissioned an issues paper to document and explain the "machinery of government" in Ontario for dealing with safe drinking water. Such a study could provide a valuable road map for exploring systemic issues through a labyrinth of government laws, officials, agencies, policies, procedures, and practices.

Other research needs should also be set in motion as quickly as possible since it will take time for studies to be completed. The Driskell Inquiry was required by its terms to review the use of the Crown's "stay" power where a new trial has been directed under section 696 of the *Criminal Code*. Commissioner Le Sage initially commissioned a report on the subject by a law professor. This report ultimately became the framework for dealing with the "stay" power in a panel including the author and six other experts. In assessing research needs, apart from broad policy/advisory commissions, it is important that the research be practical and directly related to the terms of reference, as was the case in Driskell. If the commission is to conduct any surveys, it is also important that they be initiated at an early stage.

In the introduction to this chapter, it was mentioned that the Walkerton and Goudge reports each devoted an entire chapter to how they carried out their mandates. The subsequent references to these inquiries demonstrate how valuable it was for them to share insights into their

55 Helen Burnett, "Participants Give Thumbs Up to Ipperwash Probe" *Law Times* (11 June 2007).

56 See Chapter 6, Section B(2).

processes. In the course of doing so, both described "Principles" that should guide the conduct of public inquiries.

The Walkerton Inquiry was designed with the following four principles in mind: Thoroughness, Expedition, Openness to the Public, and Fairness. Commissioner O'Connor's elaboration of these principles provides a form of "mission statement" (there is a two-page elaboration in the report itself).[57] The goal of proceeding expeditiously can be "bogged down in procedural wrangling" but often this can be avoided simply by balancing expedition with fairness. While the principle of fairness is a legal requirement, it may be achieved informally and with flexibility. Federal statutes that establish tribunals often contain a provision similar to the following:

> All proceedings before a board shall be dealt with by the board as informally and expeditiously as the circumstances and considerations of fairness permit.[58]

Openness to the public and thoroughness go to the very heart of the nature of a commission of inquiry. In Chapter 2, Section B, they were described as public confidence in the "effectiveness" of the inquiry to get to the root of the problem and in the "transparency" of the process that followed in doing so. While such principles can be expressed in different ways, the Walkerton formulation provides an excellent starting point for all commissions to consider. In discussing "thoroughness," Commissioner O'Connor referred to independence and impartiality, which also could be considered an aspect of fairness or a separate principle.

Commissioner Goudge adopted the same principles and expressed them as fairness, efficiency, transparency, and thoroughness. However, he added that "it is important not to confuse thoroughness with exhaustiveness" and also adopted the principle of "proportionality." The inquiry's preparation and hearing times "were allocated in proportion to the importance of the issue to my mandate." That importance might also be described as the degree of relevance. The comment quoted above by one of the counsel to the Ipperwash Inquiry suggests that its hearings could have been more expeditious if it had paid greater attention to

---

57 Walkerton Inquiry.

58 See, generally, Ed Ratushny, "Rules of Evidence and Procedural Problems before Administrative Tribunals" (1989) 2 Can. J. Admin. L. & Prac. 157.

sorting out issues of relevance prior to the hearings. It appears that the hearings simply proceeded to cover, in chronological order, all events related to the commission's mandate.

In contrast, Commissioner Goudge reported: "Commission counsel did not follow every conceivable lead, interview everyone with any information that might be relevant, or collect all documents of possible relevance. Rather, we focused on what was significant." He observed that this approach was "instrumental" to the commission fulfilling its mandate expeditiously and that the proper balance had been achieved by using "proportionality" to guide "thoroughness." However, that balance will be different for each inquiry and for different issues within each inquiry. The Goudge Report acknowledges two key features of its terms of reference: "it was to be systemic in nature, and it had a strict time limit." Different considerations may have applied, or at least the same considerations in a different way, had the mandate included the examination of specific cases. For example, the Grange Inquiry into the unsolved murder of babies in a hospital did require an exhaustive investigation of every conceivable lead.

Once the "game plan" has been established, flexibility often will be required in its execution. But to quote the famous words of Yogi Berra: "If you don't know where you're going, you might not get there."

### 3) Standing and Funding

Standing determines who will participate in the proceedings and to what extent. Persons or institutions who are granted standing are described as "parties." They are usually represented by legal counsel and that raises the questions of funding for their participation. It is important to note that the participation of "parties" does not change the nature of a commission of inquiry. It is still an inquisitorial process conducted at the direction of the commissioner. Every witness is a witness of the commissioner, not of a party, although a party may request that a particular witness be called and may be allowed to lead the evidence of that witness.

The grant of standing allows a party's special interests to be protected and advanced. The participation of parties may also contribute to the thoroughness of hearings. Commissioner O'Connor reported in Walkerton that "I wanted to ensure that a broad range of interests and perspectives would be represented so that the Inquiry was inclusive and thorough." At the same time, he recognized the need to proceed expeditiously. This means that the extent of participation by parties must be restricted:

> [H]olding that the [town] council has standing, in general, does not mean that every single time the council wishes to produce a witness or ask a question in cross-examination that they have the right to do so indiscriminately. The commissioner remains in charge of the inquiry. He is in control of its process, thus he is obligated to rule on the relevance of any questions to the interest of the council (or such other individuals as are given standing).[59]

The participation must be restricted by relevance to the terms of reference and the purpose for which standing was granted. Where the basis for standing is limited, counsel normally will not attend for unrelated hearings. Of course, commission counsel also have standing since they act according to the instructions given by the commissioner and are responsible for adducing the evidence before her.

The basis for granting standing may be established by statute, the terms of reference, the principle of fairness, or the overriding discretion inherent in the role of commissioner. The first category is represented by section 12 of the *Inquiries Act*, which provides:

> The commissioners may allow any person whose conduct is being investigated under this Act, and shall allow any person against whom any charge is made in the course of an investigation, to be represented by counsel.

Section 13 provides that no finding of misconduct may be made unless notice and a full opportunity to be heard is provided. Where there is no statutory provision to this effect, such notice and opportunity to be heard still must be given under the principle of fairness.[60]

A second and broader category requiring standing is represented by section 5(1) of the Ontario *Public Inquiries Act*:

> A commission shall accord to any person who satisfies it that the person has a substantial and direct interest in the subject-matter of its

59 *Re Royal Commission on the Northern Environment* (1983), 144 D.L.R. (3d) 416 at 421–22 (Ont. Div. Ct.).

60 Lamer Inquiry.

> inquiry an opportunity during the inquiry to give evidence and to call and examine or to cross-examine witnesses personally or by counsel on evidence relevant to the person's interest.

Although the *Inquiries Act* does not contain such a provision, the terms of reference of the Gomery Inquiry state:

> the Commissioner be authorized to grant to any person who satisfies him that he or she has a substantial and direct interest in the subject-matter of the Inquiry an opportunity during the inquiry to give evidence and to examine or cross-examine witnesses personally or by counsel on evidence relevant to the person's interest.

The Arar terms of reference are almost identical. The Air India terms also speak of "a substantial and direct interest" but refer to "appropriate participation" rather than to giving evidence, examining, and cross-examining. It should be noted that the Air India terms of reference also specifically granted standing to the families of victims. Where there is no stated requirement to permit participation based on such an interest, a commissioner is still likely to do so as a matter of discretion.

What is a "substantial and direct interest in the subject matter" for the purpose of granting standing? Obviously, the interest must be measured against the terms of reference, which represent the "subject matter." In Arar, the commissioner ruled that merely being a witness, having a genuine concern, or having expertise in relation to the subject matter does not satisfy the test. Potential findings that could affect legal or property rights or interests would do so, but the standard is broader. Commissioner Gomery elaborated that the interest "may be as insubstantial as the applicant's sense of well-being or fear of an adverse affect upon his or her reputation. Even if such a fear proves to be unfounded, it may be serious and objectively reasonable enough to warrant party or intervener standing in the inquiry." The Walkerton Inquiry included in the definition: "anyone whose reputation might be damaged by the findings of the commissioner and who has a greater interest in the proceedings than that of an interested member of the public." In the end, even where there is a statutory requirement, there is a zone of broad discretion on the part of a commissioner to grant or deny standing.

Where standing is granted, based on a potential adverse finding or other special interest, the party is entitled to participate in the hearings.

If standing is limited, it is important that the commissioner articulate the scope of the interest on which standing is based. This will be the measure for the extent to which a particular party will be permitted to participate.

There are many diverse rulings on standing left by past commissions. An interesting example occurred in the Milgaard Inquiry into his wrongful conviction for murder. Larry Fisher was subsequently convicted of the same murder and received standing pending his appeal, to protect his legal interests in the event of a new trial. The inquiry might have uncovered evidence that would help in his defence, which meant he had a direct and substantial interest. However, during the inquiry's hearings, the Supreme Court denied leave to appeal and a new trial was no longer possible. Since the original basis for standing was gone, Fisher sought continued standing on the basis that he would be blamed by other parties for remaining silent while Milgaard had been convicted and imprisoned. In short, his reputation was at stake. Commissioner Edward McCallum said in his ruling: "Given the savagery of the Gail Miller murder and Fisher's notoriety as a violent sexual offender, I feel compelled to observe that reputation is not his most vulnerable asset. But the argument goes further . . . . Procedural fairness is for all, not just the upright."[61] Fisher was an ubiquitous presence throughout the course of events and no other party was likely to defend his interest. The commissioner further observed:

> Even with inspired advocacy on his side, it will not likely be Fisher the person who lends moral force and legitimacy to the process. Rather the fact and appearance of procedural fairness in allowing standing to such a person might demonstrate that the Commission is determined to protect human dignity and self-respect wherever resident.

Fisher's standing was extended for the rest of the investigative, but not the systemic, phase of the inquiry.

Another category of standing is for "intervenors." The Arar Inquiry's rules of procedure and practice provide: "The Commissioner may grant intervenor standing to persons who satisfy the Commissioner that they have a genuine concern about issues raised by the Factual Inquiry mandate and have a particular perspective or expertise which may assist the

61 Milgaard Inquiry.

Commissioner." Commissioner Gomery described intervenors as having "clearly ascertainable interests and perspectives essential to the commission's mandate," even though they have no direct and substantial interest: he denied party status to the Conservative Party of Canada and the Bloc Québécois but he granted intervenor status to both. The Walkerton commissioner had denied standing to the Ontario New Democratic Party for two reasons. First, those who were granted standing would bring a sufficiently broad range of perspectives to the table. Secondly, it is undesirable to use public inquiries as a forum for political parties to advance their positions or policies. Although he accepted assurances that this was not the applicant's motivation, there remained a danger of the public perceiving the inquiry as becoming politicized in a partisan way. Commissioner Jeffrey Oliphant denied intervenor standing to the Bloc Québecois in the "factual" hearings since it failed to demonstrate it had a particular perspective or expertise that might assist.

The Association in Defence of the Wrongly Convicted[62] was given standing before the Morin and Sophonow inquiries but denied standing in the Lamer Inquiry. Commissioner Lamer first explained that, in spite of its "national prominence and advocacy" for the wrongly convicted, it had no direct and substantial interest in any of the three cases under consideration. He added:

> Two, AIDWYC has already made a substantial contribution to our understanding of wrongful convictions, especially with its work in the Morin and Sophonow Inquiries. Fortunately, the fruits of its efforts are available to me through the reports of those two inquiries and the literature on the subject. There was therefore no need for me to repeat what had already been done. Third, AIDWYC did submit a written submission on systemic issues, introduced through Jerome Kennedy's submission on behalf of Gregory Parsons, and James Lockyer of AIDWYC was called as a witness.

Indeed, Lockyer's testimony was referred to substantially and favourably in the report. Although standing had been denied, the association was still in a position to make a valuable contribution to the work of the commission.

Intervenors are subject to the commissioner's direction regarding their participation. Normally they do not participate in the hearings but

---

62 See Chapter 3, Section D.

make written submissions and may be called upon by the commissioner as required. Their contributions are likely to be more relevant to systemic aspects although they might also be able to bring perspectives to bear on the investigative side.

The number of parties granted standing may be reduced by grouping common interests. In the Walkerton Inquiry, Commissioner O'Connor reported: "In cases in which several applicants for standing appeared to have similar perspectives, they were given a single grant of standing on the understanding they would form a coalition." This approach can avoid duplication by encouraging cooperation. O'Connor ruled that there was "a significant congruence of interest" between the Walkerton Public Utilities Commission and the town. The possibility of a conflict arising was recognized but a single grant of standing was to be shared, with only one set of cross-examination between them. However, an adversity in interest did arise, making cooperation difficult, and the original ruling was amended to permit separate cross-examinations. At the same time, the commissioner encouraged these parties to agree on a single cross-examination in the many areas where a congruence of interest would continue to exist.

Along the same vein, for example, a police association might represent the interests of all of its members. As an inquiry progresses, the evidence might raise issues of possible misconduct by individual officers that had not been anticipated. Such individuals would have to obtain separate standing and representation to protect their specific interests.

Finally, a witness who is not represented as a party is usually permitted to have personal counsel present while testifying. Such counsel are allowed to address the commissioner but it is still within the discretion of the commissioner whether such counsel may question the witness. The Gomery Inquiry gave such counsel full standing while the witness/client was on the stand.

Before leaving the issue of standing, reference should be made to the Acts in Newfoundland and Labrador and in British Columbia. Both address the issues of findings of misconduct in substantially the same way as the federal and Ontario Acts. But, on standing, the language of "substantial and direct interest" in the Ontario Act and recent federal terms of reference is not adopted. The wording does refer to individual interests and also anticipates intervenor standing. The Newfoundland and Labrador Act permits persons who "believe they have an interest" to apply to participate. In determining whether to permit participation, the commissioner must consider whether "the person's interests may be adversely affected by the findings"; whether participation would "further the conduct of the inquiry"; and whether it would contribute to its "openness and fairness." The British Columbia Act uses the phrases whether, "and to what extent, the person's interests may be affected by the findings"; whether it would "further the conduct of the inquiry"; and whether it would contribute to its "fairness." The Acts of Saskatchewan, Manitoba, Quebec, Nova Scotia, and Prince Edward Island make no reference to standing.

Beyond all of these approaches is an overarching discretion on the part of a commissioner to grant standing or participation in a variety of ways. In view of the common features of commissions of inquiry, that discretion is likely to be exercised in a similar way in similar circumstances.

Related to the issue of standing for parties is the funding of legal counsel to represent them. Section 5(5) of the Newfoundland and Labrador Act is the only statutory reference to such funding:

> A commission may recommend that the government of the province provide funding for counsel and other expenses of a person who is permitted to participate in an inquiry.

Most terms of reference now authorize a commissioner to make recommendations regarding funding for parties with standing. Such recommendations are usually conditional on the commissioner's view that the party would not otherwise be able to participate. The extent of the recommendation is also restricted by the extent of the party's interest and government financial regulations.

In the absence of such a provision, there is nothing to prevent a commissioner from making such a recommendation anyway. But where such recommendations are expressly invited, there may be a greater obligation on the government to accept them. That obligation might extend to accepting them as long as they are reasonable in the circumstances. In practice, they are almost inevitably accepted.

The terms of reference for the Morin Inquiry contained no reference to funding. Commissioner Kaufman reported that this "proved to be a contentious issue" and "threatened to derail the Inquiry in its earliest stages." Funding was ultimately cobbled together from provincial and municipal governments and the commission's budget (for intervenors). However, it was a rocky start for a complex and important commission of inquiry.

In contrast, the North Battleford Inquiry's terms of reference gave the commissioner authority to determine applications for funding and to set the rates for the services of counsel. This is unusual but proved to be successful as the commissioner acted in a fair but restrained manner. Usually, a member of the commission's staff, or an independent lawyer retained for that purpose, will serve as taxing officer to verify accounts for payment by the government. Funding also may be granted to parties for research or retaining expert witnesses. But most commissioners will prefer to engage such services directly rather than have parties do so.

The commission's rules of procedure and practice usually contain its criteria for granting standing and recommending funding. The recommendations for parties will depend upon the extent of their interest and expected involvement in the proceedings. The recommendations for intervenors will depend on such factors as expertise and experience in the subject area and any track record of contributing to public discussion and reform. Intervenors with similar interests and attributes may also be grouped together for the purpose of shared standing and funding.

The cost of participation in a commission of inquiry can be a huge burden for individuals who are not granted funding. Some may obtain legal representation through their employers or unions. The federal government has a policy of receiving requests for counsel from public servants who may be parties or called as witnesses. The Department of Justice reviews such requests to determine whether legal representation is required and, if so, whether departmental counsel should be assigned. If there is a potential conflict between the positions of the individuals and the government, private counsel may be retained. Where an individual has no such support for legal representation, fairness and the public interest in a full inquiry should dictate a large and liberal interpretation of the criterion "not otherwise able to participate." Commissioners are usually given a subjective discretion in this regard. Of course, they should also circumscribe the actual extent of participation in the interests of expedition as well as economy.

The Goudge Inquiry established rules of standing and funding separate from its rules of procedure. This is a good idea. It permits the commission to resolve this preliminary aspect very soon after the commission is established and the terms of reference are analyzed. This then creates a "community" to work with commission counsel in preparation for the hearings and provides some certainty for the parties.

Notices of the standing and funding stages should be published in newspapers and on the commission's website. References could also be made on the website to the complete rules for standing and funding. The commission's criteria for granting standing and recommending funding should be specified. Most applications should be clear enough to be resolved through written or electronic submissions. Applicants who might be unsuccessful should be given an opportunity to make oral submissions. The rules of procedure and practice may specify that compliance with them is a condition of standing and that standing may be revoked for non-compliance. If that is the case, notice of this should also be contained in any separate rules for standing and funding.

### 4) Preparation for Opening Hearing

Once the issues of standing and funding have been resolved, two preliminary matters should be addressed with the assistance of the parties. These are the adoption of rules of procedure and practice and the interpretation of the terms of reference.

It has now become standard practice for investigative commissions of inquiry to adopt their own "rules" or "practices" to govern how they will carry out their business. The rules of procedure and practice of previous commissions are easily accessible on their websites as precedents for commission counsel to consider as they prepare a draft for consultation with the commissioner. The draft is circulated for comment and suggestions from the parties and can then be revised and adopted by the commissioner. There is no need to use hearing time for this purpose since there is likely to be little public interest in such matters. Submissions simply can be made in writing and copied to all parties. The media-relations officer likely will discuss with media representatives those aspects of the draft rules that affect them. These rules are usually flexible in providing the commissioner an overriding discretion to deal with unanticipated circumstances. They also reflect the "generous interpretation" given by the courts to the powers of commissioners to control their own proceedings.[63]

---

63 *Phillips v. Nova Scotia (Commission of Inquiry into the Westray Mine Tragedy)*, [1995] 2 S.C.R. 97 at para. 175, Cory J. [*Phillips*].

It was suggested, at the outset of this chapter, that a prospective commissioner should discuss the proposed terms of reference with the minister and/or senior officials before agreeing to serve. However, once appointed, the commissioner has the sole responsibility for interpreting the terms of reference, subject to potential judicial review.[64] Following internal analysis and discussion among the commissioner and advisers, the parties should be invited to provide submissions on the terms of reference. In doing so, commission counsel might identify aspects that may be vague or ambiguous as to the scope of the mandate or whether particular subjects or conduct should be included. If the government is not a party, it also should be given this opportunity as a matter of courtesy but also since it might have helpful perspectives.

Even if the terms appear relatively straightforward, this opportunity should be provided at the outset, to discourage interventions about the scope of the inquiry after the course has been set. If serious issues are raised, then submissions on them should be received at public hearings. These would be a matter of public interest if they relate to the concerns that gave rise to establishing the commission.

An example of a preliminary ruling on the interpretation of terms of reference occurred in the Lamer Inquiry, prior to its phase dealing with the wrongful conviction of Gregory Parsons. The relevant term required the commissioner "[t]o inquire into the conduct of the investigation into the death of Catherine Carroll, and the circumstances surrounding the resulting criminal proceedings commenced against Gregory Parsons for the murder of Catherine Carroll." At issue was the meaning to be given to the phrase "circumstances surrounding" the criminal proceedings that followed the investigation. It was argued that this phrase precluded an examination of what occurred "in the face of the Court." This view was reinforced by the ordinary meaning of the word "surround," which implies being "outside."

Commissioner Lamer rejected this contention. First of all, the Sophonow Inquiry's terms of reference contained an identical phrase but Commissioner Cory did not hesitate to review the trial proceedings, including the role of the trial judge. Secondly, the phrase "criminal proceedings" is very broad. It extends prior to the trial back to the laying of the charge. To avoid that entire period would preclude examining the

---

64 See Chapter 4, Section C(4).

dealings of the police with the prosecution and the prosecution with defence counsel, particularly on the important question of disclosure. Thirdly, the terms of reference authorized reliance on any "transcript or record of pre-trial, trial or appeal proceedings" which supported the examination of matters "inside" the criminal proceedings. Finally, to interpret "criminal proceedings" so restrictively would undermine the very purpose of the inquiry. It was to find out how the wrongful conviction occurred in order to inform the public and recommend how improvements could be made to the administration of justice. Commissioner Lamer therefore interpreted the phrase "circumstances surrounding" as being expansive rather than restrictive of his jurisdiction.

The actual task of preparing for the public hearings falls more to commission counsel and staff than to the commissioner but the commissioner still must provide overall direction. An important decision will be the extent to which the public hearings should be delayed to permit "adequate" preparation. If the information to be examined is voluminous, it is difficult to start calling witnesses before gaining a bigger picture of what is involved. Tens of thousands of documents may have to be gathered, analyzed, stored, and disclosed. Witnesses must be identified and interviewed. Institutions and practices may have to be examined. At the same time, public concern and even anxiety may require that hearings commence as quickly as possible.

The Walkerton Inquiry was able to commence its public hearings four months after it was established, in spite of the need to review hundreds of thousands of documents and call over 100 witnesses. Three counsel worked intensively to interview witnesses after the hearings commenced. One would lead the evidence of witnesses at the hearings for a week, while the other two would interview the witnesses whose evidence they would lead at the hearing in each of the following two weeks. It was important to the community that the circumstances surrounding the tragedy started to unfold as soon as possible.

While the Goudge Inquiry was also focused on proceeding expeditiously, it delayed commencing public hearings. The commissioner reported:

> I took the advice of my counsel and did not rush to commence our oral hearings. Oral hearings are costly and have the potential to take on a life of their own if they are not carefully structured. Considerable pres-

> sure is often put on a commission to begin public hearings. Although we began with a 12-month mandate, my counsel recommended that we allocate six-and-a-half months to conduct the investigation and to prepare for the hearings. My counsel predicted that this process would allow us to keep the public hearings relatively short and efficient. This proved absolutely correct.

Again, it is important to bear in mind that this was a systemic inquiry. It did not report on individual cases. And the commissioner did arrange to meet privately with individuals and families who suffered from the processes he was investigating. These meetings commenced within two months of his appointment.

The Lamer Inquiry examined three unrelated murder cases and was really three separate inquiries. The events had occurred some ten years previously. It was possible to complete one phase and leave a period of a number of weeks to prepare more intensively for the next phase. This was important since each involved considerable detail as well as many of the same lawyers and, in two of the cases, many of the same witnesses. In these circumstances, the sequential preparation contributed to more focused hearings.

The public hearings normally commence with an "Opening Statement" by the commissioner. Again, there are examples of a variety of opening statements on the commission websites. They give the public an opportunity to learn what the commission is all about, what it has been doing from the time it was established until the commencement of the hearings, and what to expect over the course of the hearings.

The matters covered will vary with the nature and approach of each commission but there are many common themes that need to be touched upon. The first objective should be to explain the nature of a commission of inquiry. It is important to emphasize that the commission is not a court and cannot make findings of criminal or civil liability. It may be helpful to state briefly the circumstances leading to the commission's creation (sometimes found in the "whereas" part of the order in council). But the commission's sole purpose is to examine all relevant information, make findings, and set out recommendations arising out of those findings. It will examine individual and institutional conduct and may conclude that some conduct was inappropriate. Such a conclusion, however, has no legal consequence. Nor is it reached to embarrass or attempt to "punish" anyone. It would be made only to explain what happened and to avoid similar unfortunate consequences in future.

It should be explained that the process is that of the commissioner, and not of the government or the parties. Although created by the government, the commissioner acts completely independently of the government and is free to make adverse findings against anyone, including the government. The commissioner has legal powers to compel documents to be produced and witnesses to testify. But the commissioner expects that the inquiry will proceed in a spirit of cooperation. The commission's governing principles or "mission statement" could be presented with a request for support, from everyone involved, in achieving its goals.

Witnesses should be assured that they have certain protections in law and will be treated with fairness, dignity, and respect. Occasionally, difficult questions will be asked but they will not be for any personal motive and only to serve the public interest. Persons allowed to participate as "parties" should be invited not only to assist the commissioner in assessing their conduct objectively but also to take opportunities to contribute to other aspects of the commission's mandate. Parties should be assured that it is not necessary that their lawyers question every witness in order to protect their interests. The allocation of opportunities to question will be designed to ensure that all interests are protected and issues addressed.

Parties should be advised that neither they nor their lawyers are permitted by the rules of procedure to make public comments on the evidence and, particularly, on the credibility of witnesses. Any observations or submissions must be made in the hearing room, through counsel. Failure to observe this requirement could result in the loss of standing. This restriction is necessary in the interests of fairness to everyone involved. Once the inquiry ends after publication of the report, any person, whether a party or not, may make any public comment they desire. This issue is discussed further in Section D(3), below in this chapter.

The public should be informed of access to the hearings and the availability of information such as transcripts and rulings on the commission's website. The commission's staff and their responsibilities should be introduced.

The commissioner may wish to inform the public of what has been done prior to the commencement of the hearings. For example, Commissioner Goudge mentioned:

- his private meetings with affected individuals and families;
- steps taken to provide counselling services for them;
- a one-day education session on forensic pathology for all counsel; and
- his visits to two Aboriginal communities in northern Ontario.

In addition, he reported on his rulings on standing and on motions for publication bans.

This also provides an opportunity to report on the investigative steps taken to gather documents and interview witnesses to that date. The manner in which the commission intends to proceed might include a preliminary agenda of topics to be addressed, as derived from the terms of reference and the order of proceedings. The general plan for scheduling hearings, witnesses, and breaks could be introduced and qualified as subject to modifications available on the website. In addition to the commissioner's opening statement, commission counsel might also make an opening submission to deal with some of these matters, instead of the commissioner.

If necessary, the opening hearing could then hear any necessary submissions on the terms of reference, followed by evidence that would not be affected by any potential ruling on the terms of reference.

## D. MANAGING THE COMMISSION

### 1) Management

This section is intended to emphasize the commissioner's responsibility for the entire operation of a commission of inquiry. A commissioner should not attempt to "micro-manage" every aspect of that operation but should provide direction and leadership. Reference was already made to establishing a "game plan" and adopting broad guiding principles, but the plan also must be executed. The financial and administrative aspects can be delegated through the executive director and the evidentiary and substantive aspects can be delegated through senior counsel.

Even so, the commissioner should approve any major decisions and should be informed of significant problems as they arise. For example, the processes that counsel plans to adopt for gathering evidence as well as its disclosure and presentation should be approved together with the manner in which other lawyers and staff are to be generally deployed.

Similarly, decisions about the budget and administration should be discussed with the executive director since the commissioner is still the chief executive of the commission.[65]

The commissioner must also demonstrate leadership in meeting timelines. The cooperation of lawyers for the parties must be gained, initially through commission counsel but with the full support of the commissioner. A pattern should be established of resolving procedural issues prior to the hearings and only raising them at hearings when such resolution simply was not possible. An atmosphere and practice of fairness to witnesses should be established through the leadership of the commissioner and the counsel who appear on his behalf. The message must be sent to all participants that the hearings will not be used as a forum to attack or embarrass witnesses, no matter how strong the personal emotions of some parties might be. Nor should hearings be allowed to be exploited for subsidiary agendas such as discovery for future civil litigation.

One commissioner included a chapter in his report entitled "Why So Long? Problems and Frustrations of an Adversarial Inquiry." The following are some excerpts:

> [S]everal of the parties took a very adversarial and sometimes bitter confrontational approach to one another . . . Witnesses were cross-examined endlessly . . . there was an overall problem that some counsel appeared to be frequently playing to the press and television cameras . . . . Counsel were frequently at each other's throats . . . the Inquiry was forced to accept the "leave no stone unturned" position, and to chase down many blind alleys.[66]

In both of his reports on the terms of reference for the Mulroney-Schreiber Inquiry, David Johnston referred to the Rae Report's concern that any inquiry not become a "circus of lawyers." No elaboration was given as to what this meant, but presumably it meant an inquiry such as the one referred to above. The actual conduct of hearings is addressed in Chapter 8 but "managing" other aspects of the inquiry is also important and may influence the conduct of counsel at the hearings.

---

65 Harry Williams, *Commissions of Inquiry: A Handbook of Operations* (Ottawa: Privy Council Office, 1982) at 13.

66 Report of the Niagara Regional Police Force Inquiry (Toronto: Ministry of the Attorney General, 1993) at 345–46.

Managing the timelines necessary to report expeditiously is a basic challenge for most commissions and requires constant reinforcement from the commissioner. As the secretary (executive director) of one complex inquiry observed:

> A commission of inquiry is a race against time from start to finish and there is very little opportunity to learn on the job as progression through each of its stages provides fresh challenges of a different kind. The organizational pattern and policy approaches adopted at the outset will probably persist, therefore, throughout the life of the commission. As it is a relatively short-term enterprise, the tendency will be to live with a problem rather than risk change in the expectation of benefit which will accrue over time. For these reasons, it is obviously preferable to start out right and it is, therefore, at the outset that most good can be done in organizational and administrative terms.[67]

In other words, most commissions must quickly get on the right track and go "flat out" to meet their reporting deadline.

A newspaper article about the Cornwall Inquiry, which asked whether this inquiry had "gone off the rails,"[68] illustrates the kind of criticism a commission may expect if it is not operating effectively. The commission was then well into its third year, not close to completion and likely to cost as much as $50 million. The article reported a change in its approach following criticisms of its "plodding pace" and "sprawling reach," and described the commissioner and his lead counsel as "inexperienced in the complex world of public inquiries." It criticized the organization and management of the hearings:

> [T]he inquiry moved quickly—arguably, too quickly—into public hearings. The first few months were consumed by experts who provided context about pedophilia. More months passed as a stream of complainants gave lengthy, often emotional testimony. Critics believe it all should have been compressed or summarized.

This article quoted the earlier comments of a local columnist:

---

67 David Grenville, "The Role of the Commission Secretary" in A.P. Pross, I. Christie, & J.A. Yogis, eds., *Commissions of Inquiry* (Toronto: Carswell, 1990) at 70.

68 Kirk Makin, "Has Pedophile Probe Gone off the Rails?" *Globe & Mail* (6 November 2007).

> "The circus is in its second year, and nobody is sure when it is going to fold up the tent, round up the clowns and elephants, and head out of town—leaving behind a tab that will be in the millions, and a lot of innocent people who have once again had their reputations dragged through the muck," Claude McIntosh, a columnist for the Cornwall Standard Freeholder, wrote last August. "For all that money, we are going to get a report that will talk about how the institutions should have handled cases . . . 25 and 30 years ago."

The circus metaphor seems to have a broad appeal for inquiries that are perceived as inefficient.

It is difficult to appreciate why the commissioner of the Cornwall Inquiry found it necessary to move directly into court-like hearings for "contextual" testimony from some eleven expert witnesses. This type of evidence could have been consolidated in written reports. The same is true of much of the evidence of some nineteen corporate officials representing various public institutions. The terms of reference specifically authorized reliance upon "factual overview reports" but they were not utilized effectively. These could have been used for the twenty-eight alleged victims of historical abuse as well as their relatives who testified. Perhaps a few "representative" witnesses would have sufficed. All of these witnesses were called from mid-February 2006, when the commission began hearing evidence, to mid-July 2007.[69] A few weeks after the above column was published, the commissioner made a public statement attempting to justify the necessity of calling these alleged victims of abuse. Essentially, he said it was necessary: "Because we have to listen to as much as we can." The Goudge Inquiry provides a striking contrast in its approach to the necessity of oral testimony. Even taking into account the systemic nature of the Goudge Inquiry's terms of reference, its reporting time of seventeen months was very expeditious. The Cornwall Inquiry's report will take more than three times as long and it also is, essentially, systemic. It had no reporting deadline in its original terms of reference, but a deadline was subsequently imposed.

The Cornwall Inquiry commissioner's statement, referred to above, is one of a series made periodically over the course of the inquiry and posted on its website. This can be a valuable avenue for reporting on the

69 *Ontario (Provincial Police) v. Cornwall (Public Inquiry)*, [2008] O.J. No. 153 (C.A.) [*Cornwall*].

commission's plans and progress. Unfortunately, in the case of the Cornwall Inquiry, some of the commissioner's statements take on the tone of political rhetoric used to justify delay. For example, on 12 May 2008, just over three years after the commission was established, a statement was made about the "big picture." The commissioner said:

> This is an inquiry that will be thorough and look at matters methodically and carefully. This means we will take the time needed to do it right. I will not be deflected from doing my work with diligence. I will not be distracted from ensuring my work is complete.
>
> We are here to get to the bottom of divisive and heart-wrenching issues that have troubled this community. Doing this right takes time and money. Not doing it right is a disservice for those who have lived theses issues for decades .... The work of this inquiry—the public's inquiry—will stay on track.

On 17 September 2007 he had reinforced the commission's commitment to thoroughness:

> It is my responsibility to ensure your inquiry completes a thorough examination of the matters within its terms of reference. We do need to take time to see everything. At the end of the day, we want a thorough job to be done. If there are better ways for the future, we do not want to miss out on a single improvement.

He also commented on his personal credibility: "I think you know me as a straight-talker. That's partly because it's how I am—I like to get on with things. But also I like straight talk because I see giving everyone the same information as being fair." On 28 November 2007, the commissioner reiterated the purpose of the inquiry and the manner in which he was proceeding and noted: "What public inquiries do is take the time to thoroughly examine complex and sensitive issues .... Knowing what we came for, we stick to it. Our principles and our schedule have been consistent."

Thoroughness is an important goal for most commissions. But in Section C(2), above in this chapter, reference was made to Commissioner Goudge's warning not to confuse "thoroughness" with "exhaustiveness" and his adoption of the principle of "proportionality." Properly managing a commission should include balancing thoroughness with expedition.

### 2) Scope of the Inquiry

An important aspect of conducting an expeditious inquiry is to remain strictly within the terms of reference in defining the scope of the subject matter. The commissioner must be constantly vigilant by questioning how each proposed avenue of inquiry assists in fulfilling the mandate established by the terms of reference. Departures from the commission's jurisdiction must be avoided, no matter how relevant a subject may be to some other important public purpose or how inherently interesting.

Even if a matter does fall within a commission's terms of reference, judgment may have to be exercised as to whether it is worth pursuing and, if so, to what extent. Lord Salmon emphasized the importance of focusing on the most important issues for the sake of effectiveness as well as expedition: "To attack on an over-wide front means dissipating one's powers; the attack tends to slow down, lose driving force and finally effectiveness. It is, as a rule, the best policy, whether in war or law[,] to concentrate one's forces on attacking what really matters."[70] This also requires vigilance and good judgment on the part of the commissioner.

The Cornwall Inquiry also provides an example of an ill-conceived attempt to expand a commission's mandate. The commissioner sought to call as a witness a woman who alleged that some fifteen years earlier, when she was sixteen, she had been sexually assaulted at knifepoint by two teenaged boys. She was to testify as to her treatment by the police officer who took her complaint and commenced the investigation. She alleged that she was badly treated, lost confidence in the police, decided not to proceed with the charges, and suffered emotional difficulties. The commissioner ruled that his terms of reference extended to all cases involving allegations of abuse of young people at any time prior to the date the commission was established.

On judicial review, the Ontario Divisional Court upheld this ruling by a margin of two to one. The majority simply took a deferential approach to the commissioner's broad interpretation of the scope of his mandate. The Ontario Court of Appeal strongly disagreed. The "definition of the subject matter of the Inquiry" is an issue of jurisdiction on

70 Sir Cyril Salmon, *Tribunals of Inquiry*, Lionel Cohen Lectures, The Hebrew University of Jerusalem, Fourteenth Series—1967 (Jerusalem: Magnes Press, Hebrew University, 1967) at 11.

which the commissioner must be correct. In this case, the commissioner misconstrued the terms of reference:

> and in doing so he enlarged the subject matter of the Inquiry and conferred a much wider jurisdiction upon himself than the legislature contemplated.[71]

The mandate the commissioner ascribed to himself was described as "truly breathtaking in its scope." It would encompass every such allegation since "Cornwall's inception in 1834."

The judgment also responded to the commissioner's comment that it was not his intention to "open the floodgates":

> I fail to see how, on the Commissioner's view of his mandate, he could reasonably hope to keep the floodgates from opening . . . . It would open the door to similar testimony from hundreds of complainants and their family members . . . . In short, the Commissioner's view of his mandate runs the risk of standing the so-called "main focus" of the Inquiry on its head and creating an unwieldy, if not unmanageable, mega-inquiry that could go on for years at great public expense.[72]

At the outset of its judgment, the court had expressed concern that the commissioner should be seeking to expand his mandate after the commission had been in existence for over two years and heard evidence for some eighteen months:

> Against that backdrop, it is hard to believe that the Commissioner, his counsel and the parties would, at this late stage, be involved in a debate about the subject matter of the Inquiry and the breadth of the Commissioner's mandate. And yet that is precisely the issue that lies at the core of this appeal.[73]

These observations are a warning of the potential pitfalls in attempting to expand the scope of an inquiry beyond its terms of reference.

In a statement of 31 March 2008, the commissioner referred to the Court of Appeal decision. He had decided not to appeal the decision to the Supreme Court of Canada in the interest of avoiding further delay

---

71 Above note 69 at para. 24, Moldaver J.A., Doherty and Gillese JJ.A. agreeing.

72 *Ibid.* at paras. 60 & 61.

73 *Ibid.* at para. 3.

and uncertainty. He also decided to accept the "guidance" given to him by the court. He then spoke publicly to the young woman who was prevented from testifying because of the court's decision. He expressed his sympathy to her and thanked her for her willingness both to testify and to offer her recommendations for future change!

Another aspect of the Cornwall Inquiry also raises a jurisdictional question. In his Opening Statement of 7 November 2005, the commissioner indicated that he would divide the inquiry into two parts. Part II would "take a more remedial approach, one where we can explore the healing and reconciliation of this community." The related aspects of the terms of reference include the Preamble, which states: "Community members have indicated that a public inquiry will encourage individual and community healing." This is merely an observation that the conduct of a public inquiry could, in itself, encourage healing. Item 3 states: "The Commission shall inquire into and report on processes, services or programs that would encourage community healing and reconciliation in Cornwall." This authorizes an inquiry to explore avenues that would encourage these goals. But it authorizes only the presentation of the commission's findings. It does not authorize the commission actually to implement such "processes, services or programs." Item 4 states: "The Commission may provide community meetings or other opportunities apart from formal evidentiary hearings for individuals affected by the allegations . . . to express their experiences of events and the impact on their lives." This appears merely to authorize providing sensitive opportunities for people to tell their stories. That, in itself, could be therapeutic. But Item 4 does not authorize the commission to establish other therapeutic services for such individuals. The jurisdictional issue is whether the commissioner transcended his terms of reference by providing such services and others without authority.

In his statement of 28 November 2007 the commissioner reported:

> My advisory panel and commission staff have been asked by me to contribute to our unique and demanding mandate—to further healing and reconciliation. We have planned for and are carrying out an ambitious agenda. This includes professional training opportunities that have already started and have had excellent registration. It includes community and neighborhood meetings, mentorship training, establishment of a counselling transition committee and workshops on important and relevant topics.

The professional-training opportunities include a two-day training program on male sexual victimization, a two-day training program for professionals who work with assaultive men, and intensive four-day training for health professionals working with trauma. Another training program is for mentors who are then matched with adults who suffered childhood abuse in a "one-to-one supportive relationship." There is a witness-support program for helping people testifying before the inquiry, which would be reasonably incidental to the terms of reference. But there is also a Counselling Support program for persons and their families "who are affected by the Cornwall Public Inquiry." Counselling support is made available, free of charge, "wherever you live."

No one can argue with the importance of healing and reconciliation. But, apart from investigating and reporting, is it appropriate for the services described above to be provided by a commission of inquiry? If so, was this commission authorized to do so? The Goudge Inquiry was specifically authorized by its terms of reference to provide for counselling services. The Cornwall Inquiry appears to have had no additional authority beyond investigating and reporting. The government of Ontario finally imposed a time limit, requiring this inquiry to cease hearing testimony in by 30 January 2009, to complete closing submissions by 27 February 2009, and to report by 31 July 2009.[74]

### 3) Publicity

A commissioner should be interested in the publicity her inquiry is receiving but not for the reasons demonstrated by Commissioner Gomery and his media spokesperson. Nor should a commissioner respond to criticisms that simply reflect views on such matters as whether a public inquiry is necessary, whether it is effective, or the cost. Engaging in this kind of public discussion in the media is seldom productive, and is unseemly for a commissioner. But it is important to correct the factual record where reports of the evidence before the commission are inaccurate or witnesses are unfairly characterized. This is usually best done by commission counsel, even if one of the parties is affected, to ensure objectivity.

---

74 O.C. 1787/2008, approved 22 October 2008. See also Kirk Makin," A Tale of Two Inquiries—And How One Lost Its Way" *Globe & Mail* (25 October 2008).

Journalists usually try hard to get the facts right. And they are increasingly conscious of their obligation for fairness and the need to respect a degree of privacy as well as publication bans. A commissioner who appreciates and helps to facilitate their important roles is even more likely to receive fair and objective coverage of the inquiry. Of course, their fare is "news" rather than ordinary events, but newsworthy stories will be generated by most inquiries by their very nature. There is no proper role for the commissioner or his staff in helping to "make news" for the media apart from carrying out their respective roles fully, fairly, and objectively.

The same is true for the parties and their counsel. The commissioner should be vigilant in reminding the parties that any evidence or submissions should be given in the hearing room and not to the media. During the Taman Inquiry in Winnipeg, members of the family of the victim made a number of comments to the media about the evidence. Her husband, who had full standing, made this comment on the testimony of the former police officer who drove the vehicle which caused his wife's death: "I see a lack of remorse. I see somebody very robotic and not a lot of caring . . . I don't feel for him. Not ever. Not since that day. There is no sympathy for what he and his family is going through."[75] Any such public comments on the evidence or on witnesses or other parties should be chastised by the commissioner at the first opportunity.

Of course, it may be difficult to chastise the family of a victim but the concept of fairness should be explained. Comments about evidence interfere with the role of the commissioner, who must make findings about the credibility and reliability of the evidence of witnesses. Similarly, counsel should not be permitted to comment publicly on the evidence. Any attempts to comment on inferences that should be drawn or how evidence should be interpreted must be confined to the hearing room for the ultimate determination by the commissioner.

It was suggested in Section C(4), above in this chapter, that the rules of procedure and practice should prohibit such public comments. This is revisited in Chapter 7, Section E, with reference to revocation of standing for non-compliance with a "deemed undertaking." Such a rule could be helpful to the commissioner and counsel in reminding parties of their

---

75 Joe Friesen, "Memory Virtually Blank on Crash, Ex-Officer Says" *Globe & Mail* (7 August 2008).

responsibility. In practice, it is difficult to envision the extreme circumstances that would warrant the revocation of standing.

In most circumstances, the moral suasion of the commissioner should suffice to control such behaviour by reminding parties and their counsel that the restriction is based on fairness. The commissioner has a responsibility to protect the integrity of the hearings and to protect witnesses from unfair collateral attacks by parties in the media. In an extreme situation, if a party continues to attack witnesses publicly after admonitions from the commissioner, a revocation of standing could be justified. Such conduct could warrant forfeiture of the right to participate in the hearings on the basis that procedural fairness to such a party is outweighed by the overall fairness and integrity of the process.

A variation on this theme arose before the Air India Inquiry. Apparently, the commissioner's staff had contacted the office of Canada's privacy commissioner but was told she had no testimony to offer. The commissioner then announced on 13 June 2007 that he had issued a subpoena for her to testify because of a "free-wheeling" media interview she gave the previous day. She was responding to testimony before the commission about a Canadian "no-fly" list and said she was surprised about the testimony of a Transport Canada official. She said the list could become a "nightmare" and the commission could have benefitted from hearing "informed points of view" on the subject.

The inquiry's commissioner, John Major, was not amused and said: "She apparently had no hesitation in giving information to the public and the press that should have properly been given to this commission when the opportunity presented itself."[76] This is simply another example of the value of a commissioner monitoring the commission's publicity in order to protect the integrity of its hearings.

### 4) Government Relations

A commission of inquiry must operate with complete independence from the government but should try to avoid being perceived by the government as an adversary. The IPAC round table, described in Chapter 4, Section C(1), observed in its report:

---

76 Kim Bolan, "Privacy Chief Called on Carpet over No-Fly List" *National Post* (14 June 2007).

> To be credible, the commission must be its own person—independent of the pressures on government agencies. Yet, to be effective, it must have easy access to government information—both formal and informal. Based on experience it was noted that as soon as a commission is established, it becomes an "external organism" in the eyes of government departments and agencies. Friendly collaborative relationships quickly trend toward prickly, even hostility, as departments and agencies sense a threat to their decisions or challenges to their current policies. It is extremely important for the Commissioner to anticipate the challenges of developing effective working relationships with the appropriate government departments and agencies, and plan proactively.

Government officials may fear that they will be easy targets as scapegoats. It should be demonstrated that they will be treated with the same openness and fairness as all other potential witnesses and parties.

The executive director should have open lines of communication with appropriate officials in the department of the minister and the responsible central agency. If there are unusual budgetary or administrative problems, they may be able to assist or at least will understand unexpected delays. If problems are anticipated in meeting the reporting deadline, it is better for these to be raised early. Commission counsel must also have good lines of communication with senior officials to establish and maintain cooperation in relation to the gathering of information, including documents and the identification of persons to be interviewed.

A problem arose with respect to the terms of reference of the Lamer Inquiry that inquired into events related to three separate murder convictions in Newfoundland in the early 1990s. Each case presented a unique situation in comparison to the others. Gregory Parsons was subsequently acquitted. The government had acknowledged his factual innocence and awarded compensation to him. Ronald Dalton was also acquitted but he spent eight years in prison before his appeal was brought on for a hearing before the Court of Appeal and a new trial was ordered. The terms of reference for this case were limited to inquiring into why the appeal was delayed for eight years, whether Dalton should receive financial compensation for the delay and, if so, the amount of such compensation. The Court of Appeal also ordered a new trial for Randy Druken but a stay of proceedings was entered by the Crown. The stay expired and no further charges were laid. The terms of reference included the criminal investigation and prosecution as well as whether he should receive financial compensation "in the circumstances" and, if so, the amount.

The dilemma facing Commissioner Lamer was the basis on which he was to determine compensation in the last two cases. Dalton was acquitted and therefore entitled to an "irrebuttable presumption of innocence" (because he could not be charged again). But many people are in that situation and are not compensated. Compensation is normally paid where there is a demonstration of "actual" innocence and where the wrongful conviction has been shown to be the consequence of the criminal justice system not operating the way it should have. The government had not reached these conclusions in Dalton's case (except for the obvious malfunction of the system regarding delay). There may be a significant difference between awarding compensation for delay, resulting in imprisonment, to one who is factually innocent and extending the same treatment to one who was potentially guilty but acquitted because the Crown could not prove its case beyond a reasonable doubt.

Similar concerns arose in relation to potential compensation for Druken, with the added complication that he had not even been acquitted. It was still open to relay the charges against him for the murder in question.

On the eve of the hearings to receive submissions from the parties on the terms of reference, the premier-elect of the province issued a press release. It suggested that the government would be pleased to hear any recommendations the commissioner might want to make by way of amendments to the terms of reference. While this might seem like an unusual form of communication, there were special circumstances. The government that established the commission had been defeated just days before the hearings opened. The new premier was giving the parties and the public, as well as the commissioner, notice that the new government would welcome his advice, not only on matters within his terms of reference, but also on how those terms of reference might be improved.

In his ruling, the commissioner concluded that the terms of reference did not authorize him to inquire into the factual innocence of Dalton or Druken. He noted that it would be constitutionally valid for a province to grant that mandate to a commission of inquiry but that was not done here. He cautioned that, if such a mandate were to be given for these two cases, substantial additional time and resources would be required. And there still would be a possibility that the findings would be inconclusive. The ruling stated that he did not have any recommendations by way of amendments but added: "In the event any changes to those Terms are proposed, I trust I will have an opportunity to comment on any such proposals." The commissioner subsequently was invited to meet with the new attorney general and a senior official to discuss this problem further. He did so but no other options were identified.

The government then did amend the terms of reference to the effect that the compensation phase of the inquiry would be postponed until after the commissioner reported his findings on the administration of justice in these cases. The government would have a period of "not more than six months" to review the findings. This proved to be an effective manner of proceeding since the government subsequently negotiated compensation with Dalton for the delay. It then concluded from the findings that Druken was factually innocent and compensated him on that basis. And it also concluded from the findings that Parsons's previous compensation had been inadequate. It made an additional *ex gratia* payment to him.

This example demonstrates that communication between the commission and government can lead to practical solutions for difficult problems. There was never any discussion of the merits of the evidence or issues nor whether the commissioner had any preliminary views on them. That would be inappropriate. Such views should await a consideration of all of the evidence and only be expressed in the commissioner's report.

Obtaining full and timely disclosure of documents from governments is a recurring problem for commissions of inquiry. From the government's perspective, the volume involved may require a great deal of coordination as well as "legwork." This added responsibility may be burdensome for officials who also have their ongoing responsibilities to fulfill. But it must be understood as a cost the government incurs as part of its decision to establish a commission of inquiry.

Difficulties also may be encountered where the government refuses disclosure on the basis of privilege. When the Walkerton Inquiry was told that the Ontario government would assert Cabinet privilege, the commission threatened to seek judicial review. This would be a public process that could put the government in a bad light. An informal agreement was reached as to how the issue would be resolved, which is discussed in the next chapter. As described in Section A(1), above in this chapter, Commissioner Gomery was able to negotiate a waiver of Cabinet privilege by orders in council. The Arar Inquiry had to address and work around national-security confidentiality issues throughout its proceedings and in its report.

This issue also became a preoccupation in the course of the Air India Inquiry. On 19 February 2007 Commissioner Major announced that it would be impossible for him to continue if he could not use large portions of documentation that had been blacked out by the RCMP and the Canadian Security Intelligence Service (CSIS). He ordered a two-week adjournment to give the government an opportunity to reconsider its position with respect to the massive censoring of thousands of pages of documents. He said that, if the government refused to make much more of the information available to the public, his task could be "meaningless." The commissioner was in a strong position in taking such a firm stand since the commission was established in fulfillment of an election promise by current Prime Minister Harper to the families and communities of the victims. A spokesperson for the families was offended by this development: "How dare the government on the one hand say that it insists in getting to the bottom of what happened and on the other hand withhold crucial information that will lead to the truth? How dare the government of Canada play this charade?"[77] In responding on the same date to the commissioner's actions, the prime minister told the House of Commons that he had directed his national-security adviser to meet with the responsible officials. They would be instructed to adopt a "non-restrictive interpretation of the law" and to resolve the dispute.

When the hearings resumed two weeks later, the government lawyer reported that people were working nights and weekends to declassify parts of the documents. But he argued that the security concerns were very real, even though the events occurred over two decades previously. The commissioner responded that he had some scepticism "about the troops behind you being able to follow your command." A few witnesses were called for whom the documents were not required, but commission

77 Jeff Sallot, "Secrecy Thwarting Air-India Probe, Judge Says" *Globe & Mail* (20 February 2007).

counsel observed that there was no benefit to "a stuttering commission that starts, stops, starts, stops."[78] Following further adjournments, the hearings continued and were completed. Because of the importance of this commission to the families of the victims, it might be difficult for someone in Commissioner Major's position simply to "walk." He began his proceedings, as did Walkerton and Goudge, by hearing voluntary testimony from the people affected. And, in spite of possible leverage with the prime minister, he may have been accurate in identifying "the troops" as a significant element of the problem. In these situations, it may be more difficult to make them accountable since they operate behind the lines rather than in the trenches.

The ultimate example of confrontation between a commission and the government probably was the Somalia Inquiry. The lack of cooperation by the government and military was discussed in Chapter 3, Section B(5) and some of the examples are shocking. The frustration of the chairman may have led to his manner of treating some witnesses and the declining confidence in his perceived fairness, as discussed in Section B(3), above in this chapter. Counsel to the commission later commented: "The problem that has arisen more recently, and particularly with Somalia, is the fact that the commissioners came into very direct and very public conflict with the Government."[79] This is an awkward position for a commissioner to be in, particularly when the commissioner is also a judge. The massive terms of reference and inadequate time deadlines and extensions left the commissioners in a battle they could not win[80].

But the saga provides some valuable lessons and insights for future commissions. It demonstrates that government relations can become one of the most difficult and treacherous challenges for a commissioner and cannot be ignored.

---

78 Jeff Sallot, "Slow Release of Air India Papers Threaten to Sink Inquiry, Judge Says" *Globe & Mail* (6 March 2007).

79 Tamar Witelson, "Declaration of Independence" in Manson & Mullan, eds., above note 2 at 351.

80 See Section A, above in this chapter and Chapter 3, Section B(5).

CHAPTER SIX

# *Role of Counsel*

## A. COMMISSION COUNSEL

### 1) General Role

In the previous chapter it was suggested that the commissioner begin by appointing, almost immediately, the executive director and the senior counsel to the commission. Under the former, the entire administrative and financial plans are developed and executed. In general, senior (or "lead") counsel is the "operational control centre" for the substantive work of the commission. In his article "The Role of Commission Counsel in a Public Inquiry," former Commissioner O'Connor's first words were: "I made what I think turned out to be the most important decision in the Walkerton Inquiry within the first week after my appointment. I selected commission counsel."[1] He added that his three counsel "did an outstanding job." It is common to see acknowledgments in commissioners' reports of the important role their counsel have fulfilled. In the Arar Inquiry, Commissioner O'Connor reported that his legal team met the same standard: "They were outstanding. They performed their duties with great skill, professionalism and, importantly, the balance that is essential

1 (2003) Advocates' Soc. J. 9.

to the role of Commission counsel in a public inquiry. They worked long hours and made great personal sacrifices. I am deeply grateful."[2]

Similarly, Commission Kaufman spoke of his three counsel as: "the Dean of the Criminal Bar . . . a highly skilled criminal counsel . . . [and] an experienced and well-respected civil and commercial litigator . . . . They approached the daunting task of marshalling thousands of pages of evidence with skill and determination."[3] Commissioner Lamer:

> I appreciated very much the assistance and advice of my legal counsel . . . who provided great service in organizing the evidence and hearings so that they flowed smoothly and efficiently . . . [another] provided wise counsel and guidance . . . . I selected him for his intellectual honesty and sense of fairness. He is an outstanding lawyer and a good friend.[4]

Commissioner Goudge:

> I am convinced that a talented legal team of this size was instrumental to my ability to complete my mandate in an expeditious manner . . . . These tasks could not have been accomplished in such an efficient manner without the skill, size and dedication of my legal team.[5]

Commissioner Cory:

> Commission Counsel conducted themselves in an exemplary manner . . . they so organized the presentation of material and witnesses that the hearings proceeded as smoothly, fairly and efficiently as possible. They worked long and hard in the presentation of evidence. As well, they were of invaluable assistance in their reviews of the evidence and issues. All this was accomplished quickly and cheerfully. I could not have had better counsel.[6]

These comments reflect the unique challenges of a commission of inquiry when it faces massive and complex information, unanticipated complications, and a challenging deadline. The legal team, under senior commission counsel, must come together quickly and have an attitude

---

2 Arar Inquiry, "Acknowledgments."

3 Morin Inquiry, "Acknowledgments."

4 Lamer Inquiry, "Acknowledgments."

5 Goudge Inquiry, "The Scope and Approach of the Commission."

6 Sophonow Inquiry, "Acknowledgments."

of "whatever it takes" to get the job done. An intense commitment is required.

A commissioner may be authorized to engage counsel either directly by the inquiry's legislation or by the terms of reference. Both will also authorize broad latitude as to how the inquiry is to be conducted. Recent federal terms of reference authorize the commissioner "to adopt any procedures and methods that he may consider expedient for the proper conduct of the inquiry." This includes the role to be undertaken by commission counsel. It would be open to a commissioner to question witnesses directly, without the assistance of commission counsel. But it is difficult to assess evidence objectively when adducing it and the manner of questioning may be perceived as partisan.[7]

In the above article, Commissioner O'Connor explained the relationship of counsel to the commissioner: "It is with the assistance of commission counsel that the commissioner carries out his or her mandate, investigating the subject matter of the inquiry and leading evidence at the hearings. Throughout, commission counsel act on behalf and under the instructions of the commissioner."[8] In carrying out this role, commission counsel, in effect, become an extension of the commissioner:

> And this is where commission counsel play such an important role. Commission counsel are on the very front line of doing much of what is necessary to gain the public confidence about the process and about the integrity and impartiality of the inquiry itself. . . . As a result, commission counsel's role is not to advance any particular point of view, but rather to investigate and lead evidence in a thorough, but also completely impartial and balanced, manner. In this way, the commissioner will have the benefit of hearing all of the relevant facts or evidence unvarnished by the perspective of someone with an interest in a particular outcome.[9]

He added that a perceived lack of impartiality on the part of commission counsel "could seriously impair the credibility of the whole exercise."

The role of commission counsel also was addressed in a ruling by Commissioner Major in the Air India Inquiry. The association repre-

---

7 John Sopinka, "The Role of Commission Counsel" in A.P. Pross, I. Christie, & J.A. Yogis, eds., *Commissions of Inquiry* (Toronto: Carswell 1990) at 77.

8 Above note 1 at 10.

9 *Ibid.*

senting the families of the victims asked that security-cleared counsel be admitted to *in camera* hearings and have access to privileged information. But the commissioner ruled that the public interest in a full exploration of all the facts would be adequately addressed by commission counsel's responsibility to act on behalf of that public interest.

Commissioner William Parker of the Stevens Inquiry equated the role of commission counsel to that of a prosecutor, but that is, generally, viewed as an incorrect comparison.[10] A prosecutor acts as a proponent in an adversary system while commission counsel does not. In fairness, the former commissioner's comparison was probably limited to the context of a duty to put forward all relevant evidence.[11]

However, there are occasions where credibility may be an issue and the task of testing that credibility through cross-examination falls upon commission counsel. In some hearings, there may be enough diversity of interest that the parties may be relied upon to do this. But that is not always the case and it certainly was not the case for the *in camera* hearings upon which Commissioner Major ruled and which were ubiquitous in the Arar hearings. A perception of partiality or unfairness cannot arise from what actually happens during *in camera* hearings where the parties and the public are excluded. But during public hearings, if commission counsel is in the position of having to cross-examine a particular witness or related witnesses extensively, the "credibility of the whole exercise" could be impaired. The late Justice John Sopinka warned of the danger: "In carrying out this duty . . . commission counsel must guard against becoming the advocate exclusively for one point of view. This is a natural tendency for counsel, generally, whose entire experience and training is to be on one side or the other."[12] This danger may be exacerbated by sympathy for an innocent victim or a particular perspective. It also can be difficult for such counsel to be loaded with ammunition and having to hold fire, especially after having to fight many past battles with limited firepower.

---

10 *Ibid*. See also Sopinka, above note 7 at 77–78.

11 Alberta Law Reform Institute, *Public Inquiries*, Issues Paper No. 3 (Edmonton: The Institute, 1991) at 67.

12 Above note 7 at 82.

In his article, former Commissioner O'Connor divided the functions of commission counsel broadly into six areas, which can be summarized as follows:

1) To provide advice and guidance to the commissioner throughout the process. This includes acting as a "sounding board."
2) To supervise and conduct the investigation into all of the information relevant to the terms of reference including gathering documentation and interviewing witnesses.
3) To develop and maintain open communication with all parties and to encourage cooperation in facilitating the disclosure and presentation of evidence.
4) To call evidence at the hearings, including witnesses the parties seek to call. Cross-examination by the parties is likely to be limited if the prior examination by commission counsel has been thorough and fair.
5) To assist the commissioner in writing the report. This role varies with different commissioners but is easier to accept when commission counsel has acted in an "impartial and even-handed way" throughout the inquiry.
6) To serve as media spokesperson for the commission to the media.[13]

All of these responsibilities of commission counsel will be addressed now, but under different headings, and in a different way.

### 2) Fundamental Problem

The fundamental problem for commission counsel is the dilemma that they may have to take on both an impartial and an adversarial role. It is almost inevitable that, at some point in most investigative commissions of inquiry, commission counsel will have to cross-examine the commissioner's witnesses. In some inquiries that will be occasional but in others it may be frequent. In some, the cross-examination will be mild and in others it will be intense. I am not talking about a cross-examination that is unfair. It is assumed throughout that commission counsel is treating the witness with respect and fairness. The problem is that commission counsel is asking questions that are adversarial in nature. This means that they are opposed in interest to the witness, who, in these circumstances, is usually a party.

---

13 This role was discussed in Chapter 5, Sections B(3), C(1), and D(3).

Commission counsel acts "on behalf and under the instructions of the commissioner." In other words, counsel is an extension of the commissioner. Accordingly, if commission counsel is acting in opposition to the interests of a party, it is reasonable for that party to perceive that the commissioner is also opposed in interest. And in this respect, "the credibility of the whole exercise," and confidence in the impartiality of the commissioner, may be disturbed, threatened, or lost.

Justice Ian Binnie made the following observation in delivering the judgment of the Supreme Court in *Consortium*:

> Indeed, judicial inquiries often defend the validity of their existence and methods on the ground that such inquiries are inquisitional rather than adversarial, and that there is no *lis* between the participants. Judicial inquiries are not, in that sense, adversarial. On this basis the appellants and others whose conduct is under scrutiny can legitimately say that as they are deemed by the law not to be adversaries, they should not be treated by Commission counsel as if they were.[14]

This is a fair and legitimate objective. But it often meets practical difficulties.

The problem arose in the Stevens Inquiry and it is interesting to note how Commissioner Parker addressed it in his final report:

> A true understanding of the inquiry process therefore must reflect the need to balance considerations of due process with the investigation required of an inquiry.
>
> This tension raises the question of the proper role of Commission counsel in such proceedings. I am satisfied that his or her task is to ensure that all of the evidence, all the issues, and all possible theories are brought forward to the Commission. In this context, counsel's obligation is most often described as the duty to be impartial.
>
> During the course of this Inquiry, some parties accused Commission counsel of being too adversarial . . . . Their complaint lay with the manner in which certain cross-examinations were conducted as well as Commission counsel's submission that certain inferences, adverse to their clients, should be drawn from the evidence . . . . In this Inquiry, although numerous parties were granted standing, no one appeared who

14 *Consortium Developments (Clearwater) Ltd. v. Sarnia (City)*, [1998] 3 S.C.R. 3 at para. 41, Binnie J. delivering the judgment of the Court [*Consortium*].

> was adverse in interest to Mr. Stevens. In these circumstances there was no one to ask the "hard questions" in a probing and thoughtful manner unless this task was undertaken by Commission counsel.[15]

So, essentially, considerations of due process or fairness had to give way to necessity. Parker added that this conduct of commission counsel had to be weighed in the context of counsel's impartial selection of witnesses and disclosure of documents to the parties. He also expressed the view that the duties of commission counsel are "virtually identical" to those of a prosecutor and concluded that counsel had acted "in the best traditions of the Bar." The discussion included reference to a similar rationalization from a Manitoba commission of inquiry where the unfairness was also justified on the basis of necessity and "the best traditions of the Bar."[16]

It is true that, in the past, many commissions have been able to "live with" this problem. The impeccable approach and attitude adopted by some commissioners and the sensitive approaches taken by commission counsel have allowed public confidence in these commissions' fairness to prevail. But on occasion that confidence has not been shared by some of the parties most directly affected. Of course, the public does not always make fine distinctions about the fairness of who is conducting the cross-examination. They may be satisfied with the superficial impression that someone is "getting what he deserved." The commissioner has a special responsibility to protect such vulnerable witnesses from actual unfairness.

Commissioner Parker essentially said that there really was no problem with commission counsel acting as a "prosecutor" because commission counsel really was impartial and acted impartially in other respects. In another inquiry, Commissioner Denise Bellamy explained the impartiality of commission counsel in this way:

> Impartiality on the part of commission counsel is not to be confused with a lack of rigour and vigilance in seeking the truth. Commission counsel must still act forcefully wherever necessary to overcome resistance that could obscure truth. This persistence is particularly important wherever the transparency of public inquiries motivates resistance

---

15 Stevens Inquiry, "The Inquiry Process."

16 Also referred to by Sopinka, above note 7 at 82.

> on the part of those with something to hide. What makes commission counsel's role unique is that they must take into consideration the public interest, the interests of all parties, and furthermore, must explore conscientiously all plausible explanations and outcomes regardless of whose interests are advanced. We have now reached a point in the evolution of commission counsel's role where it can be confidently asserted that every task they undertake must be infused with an impartiality inseparable in degree from that of the commissioner.[17]

She also described as a "core principle" that "commission counsel is the commissioner's *alter ego*."

But the reality is that rigorous cross-examination can be rough business, as a matter of necessity, "for some witnesses are so penurious of the truth that they will only part with it when torn from them by violence."[18] It is not a role that a commissioner should perform and, when performed by commission counsel, it should be done at arm's length from her. The reality is also that rigorous cross-examination cannot be impartial. It is adverse in interest to the witness. It is adversarial.

Some commissioners have attempted to address potential partisan perceptions of commission counsel at hearings by limiting their role in other respects. The role of commission counsel in the Somalia Inquiry was defined in this way by the commission: "At the end of the hearings, Commission Counsel will summarize the issues and evidence for the Commissioners but will not make submissions regarding their views of the evidence or on the findings or recommendations which the Commissioners should make." Moreover, commission counsel would not participate in drafting the final report. Counsel for the Gomery Inquiry made no submissions at the conclusion of the hearings (of the investigative phase). However, counsel for former prime minister Chrétien did not consider this to enhance the fairness of the process. On the contrary, he brought a motion (unsuccessful) before the commissioner to require his counsel to make public any private submissions regarding factual findings that could be supported on the evidentiary record. The concern was that commission counsel was familiar with a significant body of information not introduced in the hearings as well as having met many people not called as witnesses. This information could find the commis-

17 Toronto Leasing Inquiry, Ruling (15 October 2003).

18 *Murray v. Haylow* (1927), 60 O.L.R. 629 (C.A.).

sioner's ear in counsel's advisory capacity without being identified for the parties, to allow them to respond.

Another party to the Gomery Inquiry claimed that he walked out of a meeting with commission counsel that was to review his upcoming testimony "because he felt the Gomery Commission's lead counsel was trying to bluff him into believing the inquiry had documents that linked Mr. Gagliano with the sponsorship scandal." He felt the counsel was "insulting" him by warning that he should be afraid that incriminating documents would be found: "The lead counsel threatened me . . . that he would continue the preparation session not only for the rest of the day, but also for the rest of the night."[19] This incident illustrates that the conduct of commission counsel may be made public even where it occurs outside the hearing room. Aggressive conduct at this stage poses the same problem for the commissioner's credibility.

A commission of inquiry in Newfoundland and Labrador recently came under public criticism from the premier of the government that created it. Premier Danny Williams described the hearings as being conducted like a prosecution and elaborated:

> "I know a prosecution when I see one . . . . The tone of this inquiry has been excessive. There have been witnesses who have been on the stand for five days, which is an unusual length of time." Williams said his opinion was directed more at the inquiry's counsel than at its commissioner, Justice Margaret Cameron. "This is more of a comment on the nature of the tone of counsel at the inquiry and the manner in which they're conducting themselves," Williams said.[20]

Commission counsel had taken an aggressive role in cross-examining politicians and government officials in relation to the treatment of cancer patients by the health-care system. The premier's comments were inappropriate, and even more so since they were made prior to him being called as a witness. However, even assuming that such rigorous cross-examination was necessary, it would have been desirable for the

---

19 Jack Aubry, "Gomery's Lead Counsel Bullied Me: Gagliano" *Canwest News Service* (19 July 2007).

20 Tara Brautigam, "Williams Defends Statement that N.L. Breast Cancer Inquiry a Prosecution" *Canadian Press* (9 May 2008).

commissioner to be able to draw a clear line between her own role and that of commission counsel.

The Taman Inquiry involved the investigation and prosecution of an off-duty police officer who killed a young woman by smashing into her car after a night of drinking. An opening statement provides a typical example of the self-definition by commission counsel of their role in forthcoming hearings:

> My role as Commission counsel, as you are well aware, Mr. Commissioner, is to assist you. I am not to be partisan, I am to provide a neutral and dispassionate presentation of the evidence. And the overriding obligation that I have is to assist you in uncovering the relative truth about the facts that have occurred and to marshall the evidence that is required in order for you to discharge this Commission. It is not an adversarial proceeding from this particular seat that Mr. Clifford and I are occupying. It is our function to ultimately contribute to a truthful and complete record so that you can make appropriate recommendations.
>
> It has certainly been the experience in the Canadian criminal justice system and the civil justice system that having an adversarial approach can contribute to the finding of the truth. Since we are not in a position to do that, it has become the practice of Commissions of Inquiry to invite individuals who do have an interest to come forward and to participate.[21]

Prior to the hearings, commission counsel had conducted full-scale examinations for discovery of the witnesses under oath. These were transcribed and used by commission counsel frequently to engage in aggressive cross-examination in direct pursuit of adverse findings.

The nature of these cross-examinations is reflected in commission counsel's final submissions, which were blunt in alleging a lack of credibility on the part of a number of witnesses as well as misconduct in the police investigation. The conduct of the prosecutor was also criticized, but to a much lesser degree. The following are a few excerpts from the start of the closing submissions of the same commission counsel:

---

21 Taman Inquiry, Transcript (4 February 2008). The discussion that follows should be interpreted not as a criticism of commission counsel but as a demonstration of the frequent need for rigorous cross-examination and consequential submissions. Indeed, commission counsel here was Professor David Paciocco, one of Canada's outstanding scholars and lawyers.

- [The investigation] was a colossal failure of justice
- It was stymied by a botched investigation
- It was stymied by uncooperative police witnesses
- It was nothing less than a betrayal of the rule of law
- It was the product of a lack of courage . . . suppressed information and revisionist history
- [A] collage of individual self-interest, misguided loyalties and peer pressures that coalesced into the mess described to you in the evidence.

Counsel also referred to the responsibility of the police officers involved "to honour the memory of the victim and to support her family and their community."

Commission counsel clearly adopted an adversarial role contrary to that described in his opening statement. And counsel obviously was "partisan." But this departure from counsel's depiction of his role must be qualified by another element of that depiction. That relates to the "overriding obligation" to assist in uncovering the facts and to contribute to "a truthful and complete record." In fact, these cross-examinations and related submissions formed the core findings of the report, which in turn were the foundation for the commission's recommendations that were accepted in their entirety by the government of Manitoba.

Commission counsel may conclude that an aggressive, adversarial approach is necessary to assist the commissioner in fulfilling her mandate. If so, he can justify the situation as leaving no choice but to abandon the "neutral and dispassionate" goals originally articulated. The manner and degree to which that is done is a matter of judgment for commission counsel, subject to the ultimate supervision of the commissioner. But the bottom line is that the laudable goals of both neutrality and truth seeking may come into direct conflict with each other through the conduct of commission counsel. Commission counsel should not be put in such a conflicting role.

The late Justice Sopinka referred to the consequences this may have for a commissioner, who must "bear in mind that if he allows his gladiator to thrash about in the arena, the latter's transition to the dias [*sic*] may evoke a public clamour."[22] This comment was made in the context

---

22 Above note 7 at 85.

of commission counsel assisting in writing the final report. It is also applicable to other advisory functions.

The Law Reform Commission of Canada articulated the conflict in commission counsel's role in this way:

> Their duties may easily extend to advising the commissioners about testimony or on the course the inquiry should take, assisting the commissioners in assessing evidence, and writing some or all of the final report. To some witnesses, and perhaps to the public, counsel's apparent dual role may seem grossly unfair; we all know that no man should be a judge in his own cause.[23]

A problem for the commissioner is that the areas where aggressive advocacy is required are also likely to involve some of the most difficult and controversial issues to be determined. These are often the critical issues on which the commissioner could most use a sounding board to explore alternative approaches and offer advice. There is a strong perception of unfairness if commission counsel participates in the deliberative process after taking adversarial positions against parties during the hearings.

An attempt was made to prevent counsel for the Krever Inquiry from participating in the preparation of the final report. This was done on the basis that counsel had access to information not available to the parties and that, by preparing notices of misconduct, they had adopted a position adversarial to some parties. The Federal Court of Appeal had said that wide latitude should be given to commission counsel participating in writing the report in this broad *obiter* statement:

> We must be careful not to impose too strict standards on a commissioner who is conducting a public inquiry of the nature and scope of this Inquiry, in terms of the role he may assign to his counsel once the actual hearings have concluded. A final report is not a decision and the case law that may have developed in relation to decisions made by administrative tribunals, particularly in disciplinary matters, does not apply. We must be realistic and pragmatic. The Commissioner will not likely be able to write all of his report himself, or verify the accuracy of the facts set out in it on his own, any more than he could reasonably have asked

23 Law Reform Commission of Canada, *Administrative Law: Commissions of Inquiry*, Working Paper No. 17 (Ottawa: The Commission, 1977) at 40.

> all the questions during the examination of witnesses or sift through the hundreds of documents that were introduced. What is important is that the findings he makes in his report be his own. If, in order to make those findings, he considers it advisable to seek the assistance of one or more of his counsel, including those who conducted the examination of witnesses, in relation to questions of fact, evidence and law, he must have broad latitude to do so.[24]

In light of the subsequent decision of the Supreme Court, it is doubtful how valid these observations may be. The Court rejected the distinction between a "report" and a "decision" by emphatically stating that procedural fairness applied to the hearings of a commission of inquiry. The Court also noted that the potential consequences for a person's reputation were serious.[25]

However, Justice Cory rejected this attempt to exclude commission counsel as premature since there was no indication that the commissioner intended to rely on his counsel in drafting the report or that counsel had access to undisclosed information. Nor was there unfairness in the process of giving notices of misconduct. However, he added that the commissioner "should not seek advice regarding the report" if counsel did receive undisclosed evidence.[26] It should be noted that this was not a situation where commission counsel had taken strong adversarial positions against individual parties during cross-examination and in final submissions, as occurred in the Taman Inquiry, or where commission counsel had participated in writing the report.

In my view, participation of commission counsel as both a partisan advocate against a party and then assisting the commissioner in making adverse findings against that party at the deliberation stage could well constitute a reasonable apprehension of bias sufficient to strike down such findings.

---

24 *Canada (Attorney General) v. Canada (Commission of Inquiry on the Blood System in Canada—Krever Commission)*, [1997] F.C.J. No. 17 at para. 102 (C.A.), Décary J.A., Strayer and MacGuigan JJ.A. agreeing. See also Chapter 7, Section D(1).

25 *Canada (Attorney General) v. Canada (Commission of Inquiry on the Blood System—Krever Commission)*, [1997] 3 S.C.R 440 at para. 55, Cory J. delivering the judgment of the Court. See also Chapter 7, Section D(1).

26 *Ibid.* at para. 72.

The issue of commission counsel participating in the writing of the final report was also raised as a second ground of attack on the report of the Stevens Inquiry. Stevens sought a declaration to set aside the report that found him in conflict of interest. The first ground of attack was that the commissioner adopted and applied a new definition of conflict of interest after the hearings ended and without notice to Stevens. Justice O'Keefe granted the declaration on this basis and did not address the second ground. But it is worth examining here since it alleged that commission counsel had played an improper role by taking an adversarial approach at the hearings and then participating in drafting the final report.[27]

The basis of this challenge was simply a denial of fairness by counsel acting as "a judge in his own cause" or as "both prosecutor and judge." It was not difficult to establish the adversarial manner in which the hearings proceeded. Former commissioner Parker appeared as a witness before a parliamentary committee on the subject of conflict of interest after his report was completed. This exchange occurred:

> Mr. Layton: My memory goes back those four years, to watching the situation, the atmosphere, on T.V. To me it was adversarial.
>
> Mr. Parker: It was.
>
> Mr. Layton: So the legal counsel you would have called on was really almost like a prosecutor.
>
> Mr. Parker: Yes, and on the other side, he was like a defendant. What I tried to do was get somewhere in between. I had a lot of good lawyers making suggestions. It is only my opinion. What I decided was fair and reasonable in the right way. I respect the opinions of other people.

In my view, it would be unfair for commission counsel, who acted as a "prosecutor," then to "judge" the person he prosecuted by participating in making findings against him. The inquisitorial nature of the proceedings does not alter the basic principle. The process still must be fair.

However, Stevens had difficulty in establishing the factual basis for this challenge. He was not able to determine exactly what role commission counsel actually played in writing the report. There was strong circumstantial evidence that this role was substantial. Justice O'Keefe

---

27 *Stevens v. Canada (Attorney General)*, [2005] 2 F.C.R. 629 (Fed. Ct.).

accepted that, during the deliberative phase of the inquiry, commission counsel docketed approximately 1,700 hours. However, the legal accounts, provided under access-to-information legislation, expurgated the narrative portions that identified the work performed. This was based on solicitor-client privilege, which was upheld by the Federal Court of Appeal. Attempts to join the commissioner and counsel as parties, in order to obtain discovery, were unsuccessful.

An effort to examine the commissioner as a third party also failed on the ground of deliberative secrecy. Although this privilege was not absolute, the prothonotary ruled that there was insufficient evidence of a breach of the rules of natural justice to override the privilege. Stevens was in a "Catch-22" situation. He needed the testimony to establish counsel's participation in writing the report. But he had to establish that participation to obtain the testimony he needed. The 1,700 hours of billing during the deliberative phase certainly raised a strong inference that counsel was helping to write the report. What other extensive legal services would he be providing at that stage?

Justice Elizabeth Heneghan upheld the prothonotary's ruling by applying the "patently unreasonable" standard, requiring "extremely high deference." She was not prepared to conclude that the ruling was "clearly wrong" in not finding a breach of fairness. She added that commission counsel's participation in writing the report was "not necessarily a violation of procedural fairness." But she did not address the crucial question of the actual role played by counsel during the hearings that preceded the report.[28] In my view, it was unseemly for the former commissioner to refuse to disclose the true role played by commission counsel to prevent a determination of its fairness.

Even assuming that judicial review were not possible on this ground, the perception of unfairness should be avoided. This applies to commission counsel, not only at the deliberative stage, but throughout the inquiry. It is difficult for the parties and the public to have confidence in a process where commission counsel opposes a motion by a party in the hearing room, only to step into the commissioner's private office to discuss the issue further and offer private advice. The problem for the commissioner is that further advice, possible research, and assistance in

---

28 *Stevens v. Canada (Attorney General)* (2002), 215 F.T.R. 228 (T.D.).

drafting the ruling may be very helpful. The challenge is to reconcile the competing advocacy and advisory functions.

There is also a problem with the perception of fairness where counsel initially announces that he will act in a neutral and dispassionate manner and subsequently takes on an adversarial role. That may well be justifiable as being necessary to find the truth by rigorously testing the evidence. But it would be better to articulate that role at the outset rather than having to abandon the original depiction after having embraced it.

### 3) Solution: Bifurcation

A solution to this problem is simply to bifurcate these advocacy and advisory roles by assigning them to different commission counsel. Commission counsel (hearings) would be responsible for marshalling and presenting the evidence at hearings and would be free to cross-examine witnesses and make full submissions. She would still act under the broad direction of the commissioner in relation to the evidence to be adduced. But she would not discuss the weight or quality of that evidence with the commissioner in private. Any such opinions would be expressed publicly in the hearing room so that counsel for any of the parties could respond if they disagreed.

In contrast, commission counsel (advisory) would attend the hearings but would not participate in them. He would be free to act as a sounding board for the commissioner and to provide advice and opinions privately on any matters the commissioner might choose. Advisory counsel would assist in drafting both rulings and the final report.

This approach has been adopted by some administrative tribunals such as professional disciplinary boards. Where most or all of the panel members are not lawyers, they often require an advisory counsel to assist them in dealing with difficult legal issues. Another lawyer then takes on the role of presenting the evidence of misconduct against the professional in the public hearing but does not meet with the panel in private.

To provide context for this separation of roles, it may be useful to examine the evolution of the concept in relation to the Canadian Judicial Council and then the Lamer Inquiry. The Marshall Inquiry led to an Inquiry Committee established by the Canadian Judicial Council under the *Judges Act* to inquire into the conduct of the judges of the Nova Scotia Court of Appeal who heard the Marshall reference.[29] Although the court acquitted Marshall, it had commented that he was largely to blame for his wrongful conviction and almost eleven years of imprisonment. This was the first time that a public inquiry committee was established under the *Judges Act* and I was appointed to advise on the novel legal and constitutional issues that it raised. Harvey Yarosky, QC, a distinguished Montreal lawyer with extensive experience in public inquiries, was retained as counsel to the Inquiry Committee. We worked closely together and I joined him at the counsel table during the hearings.

At the commencement of the hearing, counsel for one of the judges took a very aggressive and adversarial approach, which included an attack on Donald Marshall, Jr., who was not a party to the proceedings but received standing as a result. Counsel for the judge, in effect, argued that the court was perfectly justified in claiming that Marshall was the author of his own misfortune and that any injustice was "more apparent than real." With this turn of events, the Inquiry Committee decided that it would no longer meet privately with Yarosky and me and would maintain an arm's length relationship with us for the remainder of the proceedings. Yarosky was left in the position of having to respond to this judge's criticism of Marshall and did so, forcefully, arguing that it was improper for the court to blame Marshall for the injustice that occurred.

Three years later, the Canadian Judicial Council appointed a second Inquiry Committee, this time to inquire into the capacity of Justice F.L. Gratton to continue to hold office. The Chief Justice of Saskatchewan, Ed Bayda, was appointed as chair and the other members were Chief Justice Ben Hewak of Manitoba and Chief Justice Lawrence Poitras of Quebec, both as members of the council, and Fran Kitely and Gilles Guenette, both members of the bar appointed by the minister of justice. I was appointed as counsel to the Inquiry Committee.

In this capacity, and in light of our experience with the Marshall Inquiry Committee, I recommended that "independent counsel" be appointed to present the evidence at the hearing. The intention was that such counsel would present the relevant evidence in an objective and impartial manner. However, an arm's length relationship would be maintained between such counsel and the Committee in the event that circumstances might arise that could affect the perception of fairness. The

---

29 See Chapter 3, Sections D(1) and F(1).

Committee accepted this recommendation and Chief Justice Bayda wrote to Chief Justice Lamer, in his capacity as chairperson of the Canadian Judicial Council, to request that the Council appoint such counsel.

Yarosky was subsequently appointed as "independent counsel" to gather, marshall, and present any evidence relevant to the allegation of incapacity. Although he was appointed by the Council, he did not receive specific instructions from it. Rather, he was directed to be guided only by the law and his view of the public interest in these proceedings. The inquiry proceeded on this basis but Justice Gratton resigned after the preliminary determination of a constitutional issue.[30] I continued to act as counsel to the Committee itself and assisted in drafting the constitutional ruling.

In light of these experiences, I subsequently assisted the Canadian Judicial Council in drafting by-laws and policies to codify these procedures related to inquiry committees. It will be most illustrative simply to quote the relevant by-laws, subsequently established as a regulation under the *Judges Act*, and the corresponding policy. The *Inquiries and Investigations By-Laws* of the Council provide:[31]

> 3. (1) The Chairperson or Vice-Chairperson of the Judicial Conduct Committee shall appoint an independent counsel, who shall be a member of the bar of a province having at least 10 years standing and who is recognized within the legal community for their ability and experience.
>
> (2) The independent counsel shall present the case to the Inquiry Committee, including making submissions on questions of procedure or applicable law that are raised during the proceedings.
>
> (3) The independent counsel shall perform their duties impartially and in accordance with the public interest.
>
> 4. The Inquiry Committee may engage legal counsel to provide advice and other assistance to it.

The Council's related Policy[32] elaborates on the respective roles of these counsel, as follows:

---

30 Online: www.cjc-ccm.gc.ca/cmslib/general/conduct_inq_Gratton_DecisionIC_199402_en.pdf.

31 *Canadian Judicial Council Inquiries and Investigations By-Laws*, online: www.cjc-ccm.gc.ca/cmslib/general/lawyers_bylaw_outline_en.pdf.

32 Canadian Judicial Council, *Policy re Counsel Retained in Judicial Conduct Matters* (September 2002) (unpublished).

> The role of *Independent Counsel* is recognized by the By-laws and is unique. Once appointed by the Chairperson or a Vice-Chairperson of the Judicial Conduct Committee, Independent Counsel does not act pursuant to the instructions of any client but acts in accordance with the law and counsel's best judgment of what is required in the public interest. This is an important public responsibility that requires the services of Counsel of high ability, experience and stature in the legal community.
>
> Independent Counsel is, of course, subject to the rulings of the Inquiry Committee, but is expected to take the initiative in marshalling and presenting the evidence before the Committee.
>
> Although Independent Counsel "shall present the case to the Inquiry Committee," this does not mean that Counsel acts on behalf of the complainant or the Council. Nor does Counsel act on behalf of the Minister or Attorney General who may have initiated the constitution of the Inquiry Committee.
>
> Independent Counsel does not act as a "prosecutor." Rather, such Counsel presents the evidence and related submissions to the Inquiry Committee with full appreciation of the objective concerns underlying the complaint or allegations, with complete fairness to the judge who is the subject of the Inquiry Committee, and conscious of the importance of conducting the proceedings in a manner that will enhance public confidence in the judiciary.
>
> . . .
>
> The role of *Counsel to the Inquiry Committee* is to act on the instructions of the Committee in any way that may be helpful. Counsel would attend the hearing, but not as a participant. Nor would such counsel participate in the adjudicative deliberations, although he/she is available to provide advice and assistance for those deliberations. This might include acting as liaison with other legal counsel, providing research, assisting in the recording of deliberations and preparing drafts of rulings and the Committee's report.

Independent counsel acts in an impartial manner in marshalling and presenting the evidence but also has complete freedom to be rigorous in testing the evidence of witnesses through cross-examination without being perceived as reflecting the views of the Inquiry Committee. Nor will she have the ear of the Committee outside of the hearing room. The application of this concept can best be illustrated by the Lamer Inquiry.

When appointed to conduct a commission of inquiry into three murder convictions in Newfoundland, Commissioner Lamer adopted this bifurcation of the advocacy and advisory roles of counsel. In his final report, he described these respective roles as follows:

> There are three Commission lawyers: two to handle the hearings and one to be my legal advisor and to assist me in the preparation of this Report. Since in Canada our Commissions, at times, proceed in a manner analogous to an adversarial process, I decided to keep Professor Ratushny at arm's length from the production and the examination of witnesses. He and not the Counsel (Hearings), gives me advice, when sought, to deal with interlocutory matters, such as the disposition of objections. He also assisted in developing the Commission's Rules of Practice and Procedure, in accordance with the requirements of the *Public Inquiries Act* found at Annex 5. He often acted as a liaison, on my behalf, with my staff in St. John's. Finally, he assisted in the preparation of this Report.
>
> This division of responsibilities allowed Counsel (Hearings) considerable latitude, under my general direction, to gather all relevant documentation, interview potential witnesses and marshall the evidence at the hearings. They were also free to take strong positions in their submissions before me and counsel for the parties were free to challenge such submissions. The parties knew that I would not be receiving any "private" submissions from Commission Counsel (Hearings).[33]

He also made the following observations in his earlier "Ruling on the Terms of Reference":

> The parties will observe that I have not adopted some of the submissions made by Commission Senior Counsel (Hearings). That should not be viewed as surprising but rather as a reflection of the division of responsibilities I have established. Commission Counsel (Hearings) makes submissions in the hearing room, together with counsel for all of the parties and there may be strong disagreement reflected in those submissions. However, once those submissions have been made, I rely only on Commission Counsel (Advisory) to provide legal and constitutional advice and to assist in formulating my reasons.

---

33 Lamer Inquiry, "General Introduction."

What are some of the implications of the separation of these responsibilities? Essentially, the role of commission counsel (hearings) is the same as that fulfilled by lead counsel in other commissions of inquiry, with one exception. This counsel is not permitted to discuss the credibility of witnesses or merits of alternate findings in private with the commissioner. Any related opinions or advice are expressed only publicly in the hearing room and may be disputed by parties to the hearings. In contrast, advisory counsel plays no role in the hearings, apart from attending. He is, generally, "seen but not heard" except by the commissioner in private.

This approach has considerable benefits for both the commissioner and such counsel. Hearings counsel is free to cross-examine without her approach being interpreted as reflecting some pre-conceived views of the commissioner. It is easier to explain such a role to the parties and the public when this counsel will not participate in making findings or writing the report. Similarly, hearings counsel is completely free to make whatever submissions she deems appropriate without the concern that she will be interpreted as speaking on behalf of the commissioner. These submissions are extremely valuable for the commissioner, particularly in final submissions, since they come from counsel with the most comprehensive and detailed knowledge of all of the relevant facts and issues. What is doubly valuable to the commissioner is that all of the parties hear those submissions and may respond to them. Such responses may help to determine the extent and manner that commission counsel's submissions may be adopted in the final report. Comprehensive and detailed submissions from hearings counsel can provide an invaluable frame of reference for writing the final report.

This arm's length relationship also permits a party to seek a ruling from the commissioner when there is a concern that commission counsel may be acting unfairly. This should very seldom be necessary but it may provide a good safety valve in some situations. Another advantage arises in relation to the notices that must be given of potential findings of misconduct. They are discussed further below but, generally, it reflects better on the commissioner's impartiality if they originate with hearings counsel rather than with the commissioner.

Hearings counsel still must deal directly with the commissioner outside the hearing room on other matters. Such counsel must establish, with the approval of the commissioner, the manner in which the investigation and presentation of the evidence will be carried out. The commissioner must be briefed on an ongoing basis as to the nature of the evidence and the witnesses to be called and other aspects of the management of the hearings. In her role as media spokesperson, there may be matters requiring the approval of the commissioner. These are all functions under the ultimate direction and control of the commissioner but delegated to hearings counsel and the other lawyers and staff reporting through her.

Advisory counsel will, generally, "stay out of the way" of hearings counsel in carrying out her operational and advocacy responsibilities. Occasionally, though, the commissioner may find it useful to have advisory counsel discuss some matters with her on his behalf. Hearings counsel may also find it helpful to have a preliminary discussion with advisory counsel on an issue that relates to the merits of the evidence. There is flexibility for these roles to evolve while respecting the principle of separating the advocacy and advisory functions with the goal of achieving real and perceived fairness.

### 4) Advisory Counsel

Former Commissioner O'Connor listed six broad functions for commission counsel in the article referred to at the beginning of this chapter. Two of these would fall within the role of advisory counsel. The first is to provide advice to the commissioner throughout the inquiry process. Of course, hearings counsel also provides advice on issues like the evidence and witnesses that should be called and other aspects of managing the hearings. But her advice on the merits of the evidence adduced should be given only in the hearing room. In contrast, advisory counsel may act as a sounding board, on any issue, in complete confidence. Perceptions, insights, and suggestions may be offered from the perspective of an impartial observer to the proceedings, not preoccupied with the presentation of evidence. The commissioner will have a full opportunity to discuss proposed rulings and, later, proposed findings. Advisory counsel might follow up in checking the transcripts or doing further research or analysis before rulings are made.

In this respect, advisory counsel may contribute to the commissioner's critical analysis and thinking. Sometimes, this may be helpful in sorting out facts from assumptions. It is difficult to believe that the commissioner in the Erebus Inquiry or the judge in the *Elliott* case would have wandered so far astray if they had the benefit of such a sounding board.[34] While these are extreme examples, the benefit of independent private advice will be valuable even in less dramatic circumstances.

The second major role for advisory counsel is to assist in drafting the final report. Since counsel did not participate in the hearings but attended them, there can be no perceived unfairness in him assisting in this regard. Some commissioners may prefer to tell counsel his views and have a first draft prepared. Others might prefer to do the first draft themselves. But a collaborative effort will both reduce the burden on the commissioner and result in a better end product.

There are other drafting functions that can be served as well, such as the Opening Statement and rulings over the course of the proceedings. To provide maximum assistance, advisory counsel should be a senior lawyer with extensive experience and a track record of writing, rather than a recent law graduate, falling into the category of a law clerk to a judge.

Section 11(2) of the *Inquiries Act* provides that a commissioner may authorize and direct a qualified person to inquire into specific matters within the terms of reference. The commissioner of the Arar Inquiry appointed a law professor to act as a fact finder in relation to the torture of Maher Arar. It might be appropriate in some circumstances to utilize advisory counsel in such a capacity as well. Any meetings with the responsible minister, as referred to in Chapter 5, Section D(4), would better be attended by advisory rather than hearings counsel.

A New Zealand report had suggested that sole commissioners should not be appointed for the following reason:

> Even the most expeditious inquiries take some time, expend significant sums of public money, and take up the valuable time of witnesses and counsel. If a sole commissioner should become incapacitated or die when an inquiry is at an advanced stage, the whole process would have to begin again with all the disruption and cost that this would entail. One has only to reflect on the costs and disruption to say nothing of the distress to the relatives and friends of the victims . . . .[35]

---

34 See Chapter 5, Section B(3).

35 M. Probini, "Administrative Arrangements for Setting up and Conducting Royal Commissions and Commissions of Inquiry" (Wellington, NZ: Department of Internal Affairs, 1989) at para. 38. Section 84 of the Manitoba Act authorizes replacement of a sole commissioner but not to continue the work of the previous one.

Although this might be a remote possibility, having an advisory counsel in place would provide an easy solution to such a problem. The advisory counsel could simply be appointed as commissioner to continue and complete the inquiry. There could be no objection based on fairness since he would have attended the hearings from their inception but not participated in any way.

Finally, amicable relations are valuable between the commissioner and all counsel and staff but may be particularly important for advisory counsel, with whom the commissioner is likely to spend more private time. As former Commissioner Grange observed:

> I have not only had extremely competent counsel but very genial ones as well. And that latter quality is vital if you're going to spend most days and many nights . . . together for a year or so. The last one I found to my delight was just as fond of food as I am. Besides he could drink more and hold it better.[36]

## B. HEARINGS COUNSEL

What follows is a discussion of the role of lead counsel or senior counsel to the commissioner in an investigative inquiry. The term hearings counsel is used to distinguish that role from the role of advisory counsel. If a separate advisory counsel is not appointed, the role of hearings counsel does not change. But, if it is necessary to assume adversarial positions, that may impose limitations on such counsel in providing private advice to the commissioner on the merits or in participating in drafting rulings or the final report. This simply means that the commissioner may not have the advice and assistance that advisory counsel otherwise could provide.

### 1) Operational Control Centre

The role of hearings counsel was described as the "operational control centre" for the substantive work of the commission.[37] This means that the commissioner has delegated to this counsel all aspects of "getting

---

36 Justice Samuel Grange, "The Joys and Woes of a Public Inquiry" (Paper presented to the Second Annual Conference of Canadian Administrative Tribunals, Kingston, ON, 5–8 May 1986).

37 See Chapter 5, Section C(1).

the job done," subject to the broad direction of the commissioner. In addition to the two functions referred to in the previous section (providing advice and assisting in writing the report), former Commissioner O'Connor listed four additional responsibilities for commission counsel. These are: investigating all relevant information and marshalling the evidence to be disclosed and presented at the hearings; maintaining open and continuous communication with all of the parties to the inquiry; presenting the evidence at the hearings, including cross-examination of witnesses when necessary; and serving as spokesperson for the inquiry to the media.

In fulfilling these responsibilities, hearings counsel must also assume a managerial role. This goes beyond the role of counsel as an advocate, although "management" may also be important in complex litigation. It requires that a team be established, deployed, and coordinated to assist the commissioner in fulfilling the mandate dictated by the terms of reference. Strategic planning is required of the commissioner to establish the framework for proceeding.[38] Generally, this will involve three stages, namely, the investigative stage of gathering and marshalling the evidence prior to the hearings, presenting the evidence at the hearings, and presenting comprehensive and detailed submissions at the end of the hearings, which will assist the commissioner in writing the final report. A systemic stage may also be adopted by the commissioner, requiring additional organization on the part of hearings counsel.[39]

The team that hearings counsel must lead may consist not only of lawyers but also of investigators, researchers, and experts. The Goudge Inquiry provides an example of a very large legal staff that was allocated specific areas of responsibility and assignments and was able to function expeditiously. This requires the supervision of hearings counsel since the executive director will not be directly involved in dealing with substantive issues.

The function of maintaining communication with all of the parties to the inquiry is important. Such communication must include providing ongoing information about the manner in which the inquiry will proceed and full disclosure of the relevant evidence. Issues that might be of particular concern to some of the parties should be identified and

---

38 See Chapter 5, Section C(2).

39 See Chapter 9, Section B(4).

discussed with them. It may be possible to work out expeditious and fair ways of addressing such issues that will avoid taking up extensive time at the hearings. Creating an atmosphere of fairness and openness both with and among the parties will contribute greatly to the smooth functioning of the hearings.

The very nature of a public inquiry means that there will be considerable media interest. The media-relations officer plays an important role, with the caveat that it is commission counsel who should act as commission spokesperson to the media.[40] Again, former Commissioner O'Connor explains why:

> The media and public should be fully informed about what is happening. Someone needs to be available to speak to the media, often on a daily basis . . . . Many lawyers are not accustomed to or comfortable in facing media scrums; however, it is necessary to have someone familiar with the inquiry process and the evidence who can handle the reasonable inquiries that regularly arise. Commission counsel are the logical choice to assume this role.[41]

We have seen the disastrous consequences that may result from an excessively garrulous commissioner attempting to fulfill this role.[42]

### 2) Marshalling the Evidence

To marshall the evidence is not merely to gather and present all of the available evidence. It must be analyzed, assessed, disclosed to the parties, and then presented in an orderly fashion. Much of the success of a commission of inquiry will depend upon how well commission counsel fulfils this role prior to the actual hearings. The challenge in doing so was described recently by the Supreme Court of Canada:

> Unlike an ordinary lawsuit or prosecution where there has been preliminary disclosure and the trial proceeds at a measured pace in accordance with well-established procedures, a judicial inquiry often resembles a giant multi-party examination for discovery where there are no pleadings, minimal pre-hearing disclosure (because commission counsel, at

40 See Chapter 5, Section C(1).

41 Above note 1 at 11.

42 See Chapter 5, Section B(3).

> least at the outset, may have little to disclose) and relaxed rules of evidence. The hearings will frequently unfold in the glare of publicity. Often, of course, at least some of the participants will know far in advance of the commission counsel what the documents will show, what the key witnesses will say, and where "misunderstandings" may occur. The inquiry necessarily moves in a convoy carrying participants of widely different interests, motives, information, involvement, and exposure.[43]

A commission of inquiry may not have the benefit of civil pre-trial procedures but it has the power to compel the production of documents and the testimony of witnesses. These powers are often persuasive in encouraging cooperation from parties and witnesses prior to the actual hearings.

In marshalling the evidence for presentation at the hearings, commission counsel should strive to avoid them becoming a "multi-party examination for discovery" by providing maximal pre-hearing disclosure. A commission of inquiry should be governed by the principle of complete and open disclosure in the absence of exceptional circumstances. In some circumstances, this may be not only desirable but required by the principle of fairness. This requirement was examined recently in relation to a New Brunswick inquiry into allegations of sexual abuse in the Kingsclear Youth Training Centre. The applicant sought judicial review to quash findings against him and one of the grounds was a denial of procedural fairness because of inadequate pre-hearing disclosure.

There was no dispute that the applicant was entitled to some degree of procedural fairness but the issue was the extent required. Similar to the *Inquiries Act*, and other provincial and territorial Acts, the New Brunswick Act precludes any findings against an individual who has not received adequate notice and an opportunity to respond. It does not explicitly provide for disclosure of the related adverse evidence. Chief Justice Joseph Daigle concluded that the principle of fairness imposed such a duty of disclosure, one that went beyond the statutory requirement of notice.[44] This case is discussed further below in relation to interviewing witnesses.

While fairness requires the parties to know the case they have to meet, there is flexibility in how a commission or other tribunal may fulfill that obligation. The Ontario Divisional Court recently said:

---

43 *Consortium*, above note 14 at para. 41.

44 *Richards v. New Brunswick (Commission of Inquiry into the Kingsclear Youth Training Centre* (1996), 180 N.B.R. (2d) 1 at para. 24 (Q.B.) [*Kingsclear*].

> A tribunal is the master of its own procedure. It is not required to adopt the procedural rules of the civil court system in order to achieve fairness. Tribunals are not courts, and are fully entitled to streamline their disclosure procedures in keeping with their objective to provide a timely and cost-effective adjudication of the rights of the parties.[45]

In this case, the party sought full oral discovery of witnesses under oath prior to the hearing. This was not granted since the pre-hearing disclosure process of exchanging all relevant documents was found to be fair and reasonable in the circumstances.

In seeking judicial review of the Gomery Inquiry findings against him, former prime minister Chrétien alleged a deliberate attempt by commission counsel to ambush him by using a "document dump." The Memorandum of Fact and Law of the Applicant[46] stated that he had been provided with "two binders, each three and a half inches thick" of documents that might be raised during his testimony. He was then interviewed by commission counsel on 1 February 2005 and told that, if any new documents were to be produced, he would be advised prior to his testimony. On the day before he was to testify, one week later, his counsel received an additional four volumes, totalling 889 pages. The last twenty-five pages contained documents about political donations that were never disclosed previously nor drawn to his attention prior to this testimony. This allegation of a denial of fairness through inadequate disclosure was not addressed by the court since the findings were quashed on another ground.

### a) Documents

The task of gathering and sorting through the documentation relevant to the terms of reference must be commenced as quickly as possible. This will establish most of the information base for the inquiry so it will influence planning and when the hearings may commence. Of course, the volume and importance of the documentary evidence will vary with the nature of the inquiry but often it will be massive. It will suggest the order in which the evidence should be called and will identify potential witnesses to be interviewed. Ideally, the gathering and analysis

---

45 *Clifford v. Ontario (Attorney General)* (2008), 90 O.R. (3d) 742 at para. 10 (Div. Ct.) [*Clifford*], Molloy J. (Murray J. concurring, Pitt J. dissenting).

46 *Chrétien v. Canada (Commission of Inquiry into the Sponsorship Program and Advertising Activities, Gomery Commission)*, Federal Court File: T-2118-05.

of documentation would be completed before the hearings commence. But there are bound to be delays in obtaining documents and the commissioner usually must make a "judgment call" to schedule the start of hearings, even though the gathering and analysis of all documents is not likely to be completed beforehand.

Normally, the first step is simply to gather and review every document that is potentially relevant. The Walkerton Inquiry reported as many as one million documents obtained from government alone. Of these, some 200,000 were scanned into the commission's database and some 3,000 entered into evidence in the Part I hearings.

The Somalia Inquiry faced problems in obtaining documents from the Department of National Defence.[47] It described the documentary record provided as "fragmented, dilatory and incomplete" and found "incontrovertible evidence of document destruction, tampering and alteration." Many of the documents that government and military leaders pledged to provide "reached us with deliberate tardiness, or in incomplete form or not at all." These problems contributed to significant delays and, ultimately, the shutting down of the inquiry. It is within the power of a commissioner not only to summon documents but also to subpoena witnesses to testify as to why they were not produced and to explain the efforts made to provide them. But such a formal, confrontational approach is usually not practical within an inquiry's limited lifespan.[48] A better approach is to encourage cooperation through preparation, focused requests, and persistence on the part of commission counsel and staff.

The Walkerton and Goudge inquiries did a great service to future commissions by describing how they carried out this task of gathering and organizing their documentation.[49] The following discussion describes, generally, how they proceeded. Not only must the information be "gathered" but it must be analyzed to determine what is of significant relevance. The relevant evidence must then be organized and classified

---

47 See Chapter 3, Section B(5).

48 The Somalia Inquiry devoted a phase of its public hearings to determining why it was not receiving necessary documents and "whether this deficiency was deliberate." Chapter 39 of its report documents its findings in this respect. The lack of cooperation and outright obstruction on the part of government officials may have left the commission with little choice but to proceed in this way.

49 Walkerton Inquiry, "The Process of Part 1 of the Inquiry," Part One, c. 14; Goudge Inquiry, "The Scope and Approach of the Inquiry," vol. 4, c. 23.

into a coherent body that allows easy access to any information that is sought during the preparatory or the hearings stage. Issues of privilege must be resolved and privacy interests must be considered. A system must be established for comprehensive access by the parties. In recent years, the development and application of information technology has been invaluable in facilitating these objectives.

The Walkerton Inquiry's Report describes the task of obtaining all of the relevant government documents as "an enormously complicated experience." The commissioner made seventeen detailed document requests to the government. The first of these was to the Ministry of the Environment, some two weeks after the commission was created. This request established a time frame going back some seven years and forward "to the present time and continuing." It requested all documents relevant to forty-one categories, for example:

> 4. All warnings, citations, or concerns expressed by MOE staff to the Town of Walkerton or the [Public Utilities Commission] with respect to drinking water, drinking water testing or the water works.

Some of the categories were much broader, but they reflect considerable analysis of the issues likely to flow from the terms even at that early stage.

The government responded with "many waves of document production" that continued after the hearings were commenced and even concluded. The government was warned that, if necessary, additional hearings would be scheduled to call or recall witnesses necessarily arising out of late production. But the hearings were able to proceed expeditiously. The commissioner obtained search warrants from the superior court, as authorized by the Ontario Act. These were provided at the request of the government to accommodate issues arising out of privacy and freedom-of-information legislation. Since they were not the result of any lack of cooperation on the part of government, they were described as "friendly" warrants to expedite production. The government at first claimed Cabinet privilege over some documents but the commission asserted that the privilege had been waived by the terms of reference and was prepared to have the issue resolved in court. However, the government agreed to allow commission counsel to inspect each document and, if privilege were claimed, to attempt to work out an agreement to remove some portions of the document that would meet the commission's needs. It became unnecessary to resolve any of these issues in court.

The commission took precautions to ensure that the government's search for electronically stored documents was thorough. It obtained a list of the keywords used by each of the ministries and agencies to locate documents requested by the commission. In some instances, the commission considered the keywords to be unduly narrow and sought additional searches based on an expanded list of keywords. On the advice of RCMP personnel, the commission even searched the hard drive of some computers for any relevant files that had been deleted. The commission also obtained "certificates of production" from senior government officials verifying that officers were directed to conduct a diligent search, that this was carried out, and that, if any information was found to be inaccurate, it would be corrected forthwith.

The Goudge Inquiry took a different approach to the gathering of relevant documents. In view of the systemic nature and strict time limit in its terms of reference: "my counsel did not set out to collect every document that could be potentially relevant to our work . . . . Instead, my counsel applied a more focused criterion and collected only those documents that appeared to be relevant to the systemic nature of the inquiry." Counsel commenced by consulting with the institutions and individuals from whom production was sought. The approach varied with the parties and nature of the documents. Although summonses were served for the production of documents, commission counsel also pursued discussions with each of the sources.

These discussions proved to be very "productive." Marginally relevant documents were not accumulated nor was time spent in analyzing them. Additional documents or categories of documents, not originally contemplated, were identified and produced. Just as in Walkerton, all claims of privilege were resolved informally. The government of Ontario provided commission counsel with direct access to its files, without waiving claims of privilege, which were made and resolved subsequently. As the scope and nature of the issues became more clearly defined, additional requests were made for more specific documents.

This approach of the Goudge Inquiry proved to be highly successful, no doubt through the skill, preparation, and persistence of commission counsel. It is one that might be more difficult to follow where the government refuses to cooperate and is obstructive, as in Somalia. Nor would it likely resolve the claims of national-security confidentiality that plagued the Arar and Air India inquiries. Finally, the systemic nature of the Goudge Inquiry may have made this approach less threatening than might be the case for some other investigative inquiries.

A related issue is the need for a commission of inquiry to make these relevant documents available to the parties, particularly the documents that are selected to form part of the record as exhibits. The Goudge Report describes the process it adopted for this purpose. Each document was scanned into litigation-management software with a unique document number as well as other objective identifying features such as author, recipient, date, and source. This permitted those with access to search the content of the documents. The documents were stored on a secure server that permitted the parties to download them over the Internet through a strict security system.

Counsel and their clients who had access to these documents were required to sign undertakings of confidentiality. In turn, if counsel wanted to share these with others such as law clerks or secretarial assistants, they would have to sign a "third-party" undertaking, tailored to the particular circumstances of each third party and prepared by commission counsel. Documents would be available to the public when entered into the record.

Documents did not have to be entered as exhibits during the hearings. They were simply identified by their unique document number, referred to above, and became a part of the record if they fell into one of the specified categories. These included, for example, certain reports, affidavits, written evidence, documents referred to in a documentary notice, and documents referred to in testimony. This efficiency in storing and making documents available electronically was imported into the hearing room to permit the hearings to proceed as "a largely paperless process."[50] It has now become standard for the terms of reference of federal commissions of inquiry to require the commissioner, as the Mulroney-Schreiber terms state, "to use the automated document management program specified by the Attorney General of Canada and to consult with records management officials within the Privy Council Office on the use of standards and systems that are specifically designed for the purpose of managing records."

When an investigative commission is examining potential misconduct, some parties may be concerned that commission counsel is not

---

50 See Chapter 5, Section C(1).

adequately taking their interests into account in assessing relevance. Hearings counsel might not consider a document to be relevant but counsel to a party might find in it some aspects that are important to the party's interests. In such inquiries, hearings counsel should cast the net of potential relevance very broadly. Consideration should be given to the interests of the parties both when making demands for documents and when assessing their potential relevance. Even when she does not intend to introduce a document into the record, it should be available for the parties to assess. They should then be permitted to demonstrate its relevance to them and request its introduction into the record.

Where an issue of privilege cannot be resolved informally, it is within the authority of a commissioner to examine the documents, hear submissions on the issue, and make a ruling on its admissibility.[51] However, a practice appears to be developing in Ontario, at least, of commission counsel reviewing such documents with counsel for the party claiming privilege. If agreement is not reached, the issue is referred to a judge other than the commissioner for a ruling. This process was adopted by consent during the Walkerton Inquiry. The Goudge Inquiry's rules of procedure specifically designated, for this purpose, "the Associate Chief Justice of Ontario or his designate" (although, the commissioner also retained the authority to make a ruling). The Cornwall Inquiry's rules designated "a Judge of the Superior Court of Justice of Ontario." The Toronto Leasing Inquiry referred the question of privilege to the "Regional Senior Justice or his designate." In *Lyons*, the court described the rationale for this approach as follows:

> [T]he Commissioner has deputized Commission counsel to screen the sealed documents to determine privilege, in part for reasons of efficiency and in part to shield herself from seeing any privileged documents.[52]

In this situation, any adversarial aspect of commission counsel's role is marginal and it is carried out in private with opposing counsel. But it suggests another reason for bifurcation of the role of commission counsel.

---

51 *Lyons v. Toronto (Computer Leasing Inquiry—Bellamy Commission)* (2004), 70 O.R. (3d) 39 (S.C.J.) [*Lyons*], Swinton J. for the court (O'Driscoll and Then JJ.). National Security Confidentiality falls within a separate category, discussed further in Chapter 8, Section D(2).

52 *Ibid.* at para 38.

Advisory counsel, in contrast to hearings counsel, would be in the same position as the commissioner in not seeing any privileged documents.

### b) Witnesses

Commissioner Goudge identified the purpose of witness interviews during the process of gathering and marshalling the evidence:

> Some interviews help to identify those who should be called as witnesses. Many interviews assist with fact finding and document production. Others are simply educational, assisting the Commission staff in understanding the context or identifying issues. Interviews also allow individuals interested in the work of an inquiry to express their views and concerns.

Commissioner O'Connor described the role of commission counsel in interviewing witnesses:

> [T]here is a huge advantage to having commission counsel thoroughly interview the witnesses and prepare very detailed witness statements for two reasons. First, there should be no surprises to others who are involved in the process. The proceeding is entirely investigatory and not adversarial. Nothing is gained by surprise, and there is a danger of unfairness if witnesses are examined on areas in the evidence for the first time in the midst of the public hearing. Because of the media attention that often accompanies a public inquiry, the potential for unfairly damaging a witness's reputation must always be kept in mind.
>
> The second reason that witnesses should be thoroughly interviewed and detailed witness statements prepared is that doing so will likely significantly shorten the time taken in the actual hearings. When it is understood in advance what a witness's evidence is likely to be, the examinations of commission counsel and the cross-examiners tend to get to the point much more quickly.[53]

The need to commence the Walkerton hearings as quickly as possible resulted in the three commission counsel acting as a "tag team" by leading evidence sequentially. While one was doing that in the hearing room, the other two were interviewing the witnesses they would each call in turn. The Goudge Inquiry's interviews also continued after the public hearings began but the increased period of preparation before commen-

---

53 Above note 1 at 10.

cing the hearings, the large legal staff, and the systemic nature of the issues suggest an intense but less frenetic pace.

A variety of approaches have been taken to the recording of interviews and their use at the public hearings. The systemic nature of the Goudge Inquiry also allowed a less adversarial approach to the recording of interviews:

> The interviews were neither transcribed nor recorded. My counsel rejected this procedure for at least three reasons: a concern that transcribing the interviews would add a level of formality to the interviews which might make witnesses uncomfortable; a concern that it might even create an adversarial atmosphere; and a concern that generating transcripts would be costly and lead to delay. Instead, one of the Commission lawyers kept notes during the interview and prepared a draft summary for the person interviewed to review. After the person interviewed was satisfied with the summary, it was circulated for parties with standing . . . . Neither parties nor Commission counsel were permitted to cross-examine a witness on any interview summary.

In contrast, in the Taman Inquiry, the witnesses were examined under oath or affirmation with a reporter present. The interviews were transcribed and used by commission counsel throughout the hearings in cross-examining the witnesses.

The manner of interviewing witnesses by commission counsel or investigators became a focus of the *Kingsclear* case, referred to at the beginning of this section. At issue was whether the witness had sufficient notice of the allegations and evidence against him and a full opportunity to respond to them.

The commission investigators were given written guidelines and instructions for conducting interviews. Potential witnesses were contacted and informed they were not required to give interviews. If they did so voluntarily, they could be given in writing or taken down in writing or by means of a taped recording. The witness was entitled to receive any written or electronic recording of the interview and a transcript of any taped interview. In this case, the witness, Richards, was interviewed three times by two different investigators over a three-week period.

> Throughout the three interviews, the investigators repeatedly informed Mr. Richards what other witnesses had told them and pointed out that

> his testimony differed from that of many others . . . . Prior to his testimony, a Commission counsel, Mr. Goss[,] met with him and pointed out to him that his evidence differed in a number of important respects with that of previous witnesses. During his testimony before the Commission, Mr. Goss pointed out to him again the conflict between his testimony and that of previous witnesses.[54]

After several hours of questioning at the hearing, commission counsel told him that it would be left to the commissioner to determine who was telling the truth. But he also emphasized that the witness's conduct was in question and he was in jeopardy of an adverse finding. The serious discrepancies in his evidence on crucial issues was brought out extensively throughout his interviews and testimony.

The court held that, in these circumstances, the witness had received sufficient "actual notice" of potential findings of misconduct as well as a fair opportunity to respond. The investigators and counsel had "meticulously" put to him all of the discrepancies and contradictions that might be prejudicial to him and that were known by commission staff at the time in question. He had "actual notice of the substance of the misconduct alleged against him" and had a full opportunity to be heard. Both the statutory requirement of notice and compliance with the requirement of pre-hearing disclosure had been met.

What if a potential witness declines to be interviewed? The *Inquiries Act* would appear to be broad enough to permit a commissioner to compel a witness to testify in the form of a private interview. A subpoena simply could be issued to require the witness to attend at the commission offices and be questioned under oath or affirmation. This certainly can be justified as a matter of fairness since questioning a witness for the first time at the hearings could produce unpredictable results as well as be a waste of time. The witness might, for example, reveal personal misconduct or unfairly criticize another person who received no advance notice. Or the witness could have no relevant evidence to give.

### c) Facilitating Evidence

The procedural flexibility available to commissions of inquiry provides opportunities to expedite hearings by presenting evidence in different

54 Above note 44 at para. 40.

ways. It is not necessary to adduce all evidence through traditional witness testimony and primary documents. Reference was made in Chapter 1 to the approach adopted by the National Energy Board almost fifty years ago to facilitate the presentation and testing of scientific and expert evidence. The only limit on how a commission of inquiry may present evidence is the principle of fairness.

An example was given in the first part of this section as to how documents could be introduced into the record without witnesses having to identify each one and then marking them as exhibits. Where the testimony of a witness is not controversial and there is no need for cross-examination, such testimony can be introduced in the form of an affidavit or the transcript or written statement from the witness's interview prior to the hearings.

The Cornwall Inquiry was authorized, in its discretion, to rely on any "factual overview report" filed by a party. The Goudge Inquiry was required to do so: "the Commission shall rely wherever possible on overview reports submitted to the inquiry." It was authorized to consider such reports "in lieu of calling witnesses." The Goudge Inquiry followed up in its rules of procedure by stating that commission counsel would prepare such reports containing "core or background facts, together with their source(s)." Commission counsel would consult with the parties on the accuracy of these reports and modify them, if necessary, prior to filing them. The parties also would be given the opportunity to propose witnesses "to support, challenge, comment upon or supplement" these reports.

The Goudge Inquiry enthusiastically reported the success of this process, for the benefit of future commissions of inquiry. The terms of reference established that this commission was to conduct "a systemic review and assessment" and specifically precluded a report on any individual cases. At the same time, the systemic issues arose out of eighteen individual cases reviewed by the chief coroner, so they could not be ignored. Commission counsel spent four months preparing overview reports of these cases, setting out "the core and background facts in a neutral, non-argumentive way . . . . It was essential that there be scrupulous accuracy and no evaluation." The draft reports, mostly over 100 pages in length and summarizing thousands of documents, were provided to the parties for comment but there were few suggested revisions. This was a testament to the skill and industry of commission counsel and their ability to gain the confidence and cooperation of counsel to the parties while conducting this process.

The final reports were filed on the first day of the public hearings. They greatly reduced the number of documents and witnesses required and contributed to more focused testimony from the witnesses who were called: "One of the reasons that witness examinations were so concise and effective was because the Overview Reports anchored every examination. I understand that many of the witnesses found it easy to prepare for their testimony by reviewing these reports." The reports did contain information that could not be treated as reliable evidence, including potentially unreliable opinions and spurious allegations that were later refuted. But even these contributed to a better understanding of what happened at various times over the twenty-year period under review. Both the parties and the commissioner simply accepted these documents for what they were and they contributed greatly to the effectiveness of the inquiry.

Another effective innovation of the Goudge Inquiry was the creation of "institutional reports." It was important for the inquiry to understand the policies, procedures, and practices of Ontario institutions such as the Office of the Chief Coroner, the College of Physicians and Surgeons, and Sick Children's Hospital. Rather than call all of the individuals working in each of the relevant components of each of the institutions, it would have been possible to call one "representative" witness to testify in detail about the workings of each institution. But even that was not necessary. Instead, the commission asked each institution to prepare a written report on itself, documenting what otherwise would have been required in testimony. Instead of commission staff attempting to prepare such reports, it was left for the parties to do so. This permitted the staff to join the other parties in analyzing and assessing the accuracy of the reports and the effectiveness of the institutions. Representative witnesses then introduced the reports at the hearings and were available for cross-examination on them, but "very little" cross-examination was required. These reports provided a clear example of the superiority of written reports over oral testimony for the purpose in question.

The Air India Inquiry adopted another innovative approach to expediting hearings. Its rules of practice and procedure included the following:

> At the commencement of any phase . . . Commission Counsel may present to the Commissioner a statement of evidence, facts or conclusions together with the sources or basis for the evidence, facts or conclusions that Commission Counsel proposes that the Commissioner adopt for purposes

> of the Commission's findings or conclusions with respect to that phase . . . (a "Commission Dossier").

Commission counsel could also call witnesses to support or supplement the dossier, whom the parties could cross-examine. As well, the parties could propose witnesses to be called in relation to the dossier. The rules of the Iacobucci Inquiry contained a variation of this approach, described as Proposed Findings: "To facilitate the expeditious conduct of the Inquiry, Inquiry Counsel may prepare proposed findings for the Commissioner's consideration based on documents, interviews and the findings of other examinations that may have been conducted . . . ." The basis for such findings were to be set out "with reasonable particularity" and such findings could be adopted by the commissioner as his own, subject to the notice provision of the *Inquiries Act*. Such adoption would also be subject to compliance with the principle of fairness.

There are a number of factors to consider when replacing oral testimony with written documentation. If the credibility or reliability of the witness is at issue, oral testimony and the opportunity for cross-examination may be required. If the area of contention is narrow, it might be possible to limit oral testimony to that area. Even where there first appears to be an area of contention, it may be resolved by consent of the parties. Or it may be of marginal relevance and not worth pursuing. Finally, even where a witness's evidence is not contentious, commission counsel still may wish to call her simply because she was a key player in the events and should be heard by the public.

### 3) Role regarding Hearings

While the commissioner retains overall responsibility for the management of the commission, it is hearings counsel who has "hands-on" responsibility for the management of the hearings. This requires organizational skills, ongoing supervision, and flexibility. In addition, she must play a central role in participating in the hearings as commission counsel. Finally, she has an important role in making comprehensive and detailed submissions and ensuring procedural fairness in relation to any potential findings of misconduct.

The importance of properly managing the hearings cannot be overstated. Since they often proceed in the glare of publicity, they provide the greatest opportunities for unfairness to individuals and generate criticism when they do not proceed in a smooth and efficient manner. They also present the greatest opportunities for delay and falling behind in meeting deadlines. Once a course has been set for the hearings, it is difficult to proceed in a different direction.

The New Zealand Erebus Inquiry provides a sad example of commission hearings that simply fell apart.[55] Commission counsel had proposed that witnesses be called, not by him, but by the interested parties. The order of witnesses was to follow the chronology of the events about which they would speak. That approach proved impractical. It was then decided that the parties would provide commission counsel with written briefs of their proposed testimony well in advance of them being called. This also broke down and the briefs were distributed only as each witness took the stand. The Judicial Committee of the Privy Council observed:

> This procedure . . . had the inevitable consequence that facts to which the Judge, in his Report, was ultimately going to attach the utmost significance seemed to be emerging only piecemeal as successive witnesses were called.

Their Lordships concluded:

> the procedure adopted had unfortunate effects in colouring the Judge's view . . . .[56]

This, in turn, led to his conclusion of a pre-determined plan to deceive him and a conspiracy to commit perjury at the hearings. These and other findings were struck down.

After gathering the documents, interviewing the witnesses, and engaging in ongoing consultations with counsel to the parties, commission counsel will have a full appreciation of the nature and scope of the relevant evidence. The next step is to prepare a general plan for discussion with the commissioner as to how the hearings should be scheduled and the evidence called. They already may have had ongoing discussions in this regard and decisions already may have been taken to divide the hearings into broad phases or stages to correspond with the require-

---

55 See Chapter 5, Section B(3).

56 *Re Erebus Royal Commission: Air New Zealand Ltd. v. Mahon*, [1983] N.Z.L.R. 662 at 665–66 (P.C.).

ments of the terms of reference. A system will be in place for ongoing disclosure to the parties since, as suggested above, the marshalling of the evidence is likely to continue even after the hearings commence.

In developing a schedule for the calling of witnesses, the order of presentation and estimates of time required must be established. There must be flexibility to accommodate illness or other complications. Ongoing consultation and communication with all counsel is crucial and the relevance and significance of some evidence may shift as other evidence unfolds. Since counsel must also prepare and participate as counsel at the hearings, it is important that a junior commission counsel or other staff member is available to ensure rapid communication of scheduling changes and corresponding updates to the website. Every effort should be made to avoid calling a witness more than once, although that might be appropriate when different evidence is to be given in relation to different phases.

In terms of the order of calling witnesses, it is important to be conscious of parties against whom allegations of misconduct are expected from some witnesses. Efforts should be made to call such witnesses before such a party is called. In that way, the party will have full knowledge of the case against him and be in a position to respond to the allegations when he testifies.

A related concern is to try to avoid lengthy intervals between the time when such allegations are made and when the party is able to testify to respond to them. Where possible, the witnesses making such allegations and those responding should be presented as a "bundle." It would be unfair, for example, to have all of the allegations presented before a lengthy Christmas break and allowed to "hover" until the party is called to respond to them many weeks later. David Scott made this suggestion:

> and of course television and the print media play up with headlines what is going on and the poor "victim" has to wait months for the opportunity to respond. This buttresses the development of the idea of holding *in camera* hearings where very sensitive information is given which could damage a person or be prejudicial to a person, and leaving its release to the public until closer to the moment that that person will be entitled himself to give evidence.[57]

---

57 David W. Scott, Q.C., "The Rights and Obligations of Those Subject to Inquiry and of Witnesses" in Pross, Christie, & Yogis, eds., above note 7 at 146.

While this might be a reasonable option in extreme circumstances, sensitive scheduling by hearings counsel can usually minimize this problem.

The order in which counsel examine or cross-examine witnesses is usually established in the commission's rules of procedure but with some flexibility. Commission counsel normally lead the evidence of each witness. Other counsel then question, to the extent of their interest, as reflected in their standing. If the witness is represented by counsel, that counsel usually questions last, subject to the right of re-examination by commission counsel. The Ontario Court of Appeal has ruled that a party, who had made serious allegations against the government, was entitled to be examined in the first instance by his own counsel rather than by commission counsel.[58] Where a number of parties have the same interest, only one of their counsel should question the witness on behalf of all of them. These are matters which should be established in advance by commission counsel in consultation with all counsel on the basis of common sense and fairness.

Special considerations arise when commission counsel intends to cross-examine a witness. Commission counsel should not be permitted both to examine and cross-examine the same witness. Lord Salmon addressed this matter in his classic "Royal Commission on Royal Commissions." He reported:

> No witness should ever be examined and cross-examined by the same counsel. This presents an air of unreality. The purpose of examination in chief is to establish the evidence being given by the witness. The purpose of cross-examination is to test and if necessary to destroy it. If both these tasks are undertaken by the same counsel, however brilliant the *tour de force*, the witness may be perplexed and left with the feeling that he has not been fairly treated.[59]

In these circumstances it would be most fair to permit counsel for the witness to lead the evidence, with commission counsel questioning last, subject to the right of re-examination by counsel for the witness. Where the

---

58 *Re Shulman*, [1967] 2 O.R. 375 (C.A.). Compare Goudge Inquiry, Ruling on the Application of Dr. Charles Smith to be Examined in Chief by His Own Counsel (20 November 2007).

59 Great Britain, Royal Commission on Tribunals of Inquiry, *Report of the Commission under the Chairmanship of the Rt. Hon. Lord Justice Salmon* (London: H.M.S.O., 1966) Cmnd 3121.

witness is not represented by counsel, a second member of the commission's legal team should conduct the examination and re-examination.

One of the advantages of bifurcation of the roles of commission counsel[60] is for the commissioner to receive comprehensive and detailed submissions from commission counsel at the conclusion of the hearings. The parties granted standing have a "substantial and direct interest" in some aspect(s) of the inquiry's terms of reference. But commission counsel responsible for marshalling the evidence and managing the hearings represents the public interest with respect to all aspects. No other person has the same comprehensive and intimate knowledge of all of the evidence and witnesses and their interrelationships. Her written submissions can provide a blueprint for the commissioner's final report, subject of course to contrary or modifying submissions made by parties with more specific interests. The latter provide a useful counterbalance for the commissioner in weighing the former. Hearings counsel has considerable freedom and latitude to suggest specific findings and conclusions. However, as one of the commission counsel, the objectivity of the commission will be enhanced if such submissions are not "urged" upon the commissioner. Instead, potential conclusions should be identified together with alternatives and the relative merits of each.

A final role for hearings counsel is in relation to the notices of potential findings of misconduct required by section 13 of the *Inquiries Act*, comparable provisions in the other jurisdictions, or the principle of fairness. This subject is discussed in greater detail in Chapter 9, but the bifurcation of commission counsel roles provides a further opportunity for the commissioner to distance himself from perceptions of pre-judgment. These notices should be initiated by hearings counsel rather than the commissioner. The commissioner's role would be limited to approving them as bearing a "reasonable possibility" of adverse findings. Hearings counsel would then distribute them to the parties, possibly in a form revised by the commissioner with the assistance of advisory counsel. Ordinarily, the parties receiving such notices will have received "actual notice" during the course of the interviews and hearings, as occurred in the *Kingsclear* case. If so, any further opportunity to be heard normally could be restricted to further written submissions on the specific allegations and supporting basis for them.

---

60 Discussed in Section A(3), above in this chapter.

## C. OTHER COUNSEL

Apart from actual notice of potential findings of misconduct, the Ontario Act is the most direct in establishing the procedural rights of parties to a commission of inquiry. Section 5(1) provides:

> A commission shall accord to any person who satisfies it that the person has a substantial and direct interest in the subject-matter of its inquiry an opportunity during the inquiry to give evidence and to call and examine or to cross-examine witnesses personally or by counsel on evidence relevant to the person's interest.

In contrast, the *Inquiries Act* does not refer to standing, restricts procedural rights to the right to counsel, and limits that to persons whose conduct is investigated. Representation by counsel is discretionary unless the party is actually subject to a "charge" of misconduct. Section 12 provides:

> The commissioners may allow any person whose conduct is being investigated under this Act, and shall allow any person against whom any charge is made in the course of an investigation, to be represented by counsel.

Comparable legislation in other jurisdictions varies greatly. Some jurisdictions are silent on procedural rights. The British Columbia Act provides greater detail but leaves much discretion in the commissioner.

Apart from the legislation, the principle of fairness would establish some procedural rights for everyone with a "direct and substantial interest" and for some witnesses as well. The extent of the right to participate depends on the extent to which their interest might be affected. The right to be heard does not necessarily include the right to call or cross-examine witnesses or to be represented by counsel. The principle of fairness is discussed further in Chapter 7, Section D.

The general practice, supported by the rules of procedure of investigative commissions of inquiry, inevitably permits parties to be represented by counsel and to participate in the hearings. It is still the commissioner's inquiry and witnesses. But, through hearings counsel, a party's counsel is permitted to arrange to question witnesses and to suggest additional witnesses who should be called in the interests of fairness. Witnesses who are not parties are usually entitled to have counsel present when they testify. Such counsel are entitled to intervene on behalf of their clients and, where circumstances warrant, may be permitted to lead the evidence of their client.[61]

The Walkerton Inquiry's Report listed the procedural rights of parties with standing, in addition to the right to counsel, as follows:

- access to documents collected by the Commission subject to the Rules of Procedure and Practice;
- advance notice of documents that were proposed to be introduced into evidence ;
- advance provision of witness statements of anticipated evidence that were prepared by the Commission;
- a place at counsel table;
- the opportunity to suggest witnesses to be called by Commission counsel, or alternatively, an opportunity to apply to the Commissioner to lead the evidence of a particular witness;
- the opportunity to cross-examine witnesses on matters relevant to the basis upon which standing was granted; and
- the opportunity to make closing submissions.

In addition, they could apply for funding to support their participation. Witnesses were entitled to have counsel present during interviews and at the time of their testimony. Of course, there is also the right to receive notice of potential adverse findings.

Some counsel who are not familiar with the nature of commissions of inquiry attempt to protect the interests of their clients by adopting an adversarial strategy. That is a mistake. Few commissioners are likely to appreciate such an approach and some will not tolerate it. Moreover, it may be counter-productive for the client. In the glare of publicity and the likelihood that all relevant evidence will be presented, it is far better for counsel to project a positive image by being fair, open, and cooperative.

This requires that the nature of the process be understood by the client so that efforts to cooperate are not misunderstood as sacrificing his rights. He should also understand the importance of being realistic about accepting that he might have acted inappropriately. An honest effort to understand why that happened and to explain the circumstances surrounding it is likely to find its way into the final report. Attempts to

61 Above note 58.

deny misconduct or to blame others may result in a report that not only describes the misconduct but also notes the refusal to take responsibility for it.

The Royal Newfoundland Constabulary received high praise from Commissioner Lamer for admitting mistakes in past investigations and taking concrete steps to institute reforms even before the hearings were completed. In contrast, he was highly critical of a "Crown culture" that would not recognize how it contributed to wrongful convictions. This led to a consequent independent review of the Office of the Department of Public Prosecutions.

If the misconduct cannot be diminished through extenuating circumstances, it is better not to attempt to do so. This will simply invite extensive cross-examination and greater public scrutiny of the client. Sometimes an early and straightforward acknowledgment and drawing as little attention to it as possible is the best service counsel can provide to a client in this forum.

There also may be scope for protecting a client's best interests during informal discussions with hearings counsel. For example, she might be persuaded that both fairness and the public interest would best be served by reducing the number of possible allegations to be introduced against a party at the public hearings.

It is also important to be fair when acting for a victim or a victim's family. Not every tragedy means there is a responsible villain. Even where there is misconduct that contributed to a tragic result, there often is an important context of circumstances, including systemic factors. Efforts should be focused on assisting the commission to gain a full understanding of what happened so that effective recommendations can be made for the future. There is little to be gained in seeking some form of "revenge" by attempting to "beat up" those responsible through cross-examination. There is much more to be gained by assisting the commissioner in fulfilling her mandate as fully, fairly, and expeditiously as possible. Counsel for parties should also assist the commissioner by ensuring that their clients understand why they are not allowed to comment to the media on the evidence that is being presented.[62]

---

62 Discussed in Chapter 5, Section D(3).

CHAPTER SEVEN

# *The Legal Framework*

In previous chapters, the relevant legal issues have been raised and sometimes analyzed in the context of specific topics or in describing the work of particular commissions of inquiry. In this chapter, they are laid out more broadly to demonstrate their interrelationship. There are some cross-references to the previous and subsequent discussions and analysis, and some additional issues are discussed and analyzed.

In describing any legal "framework," the starting point is the *Constitutional basis* for the laws that follow. In Canada, that includes asking whether the authority for making such laws falls within federal or provincial jurisdiction. It also requires a recognition that some laws may be invalid because of the *Canadian Charter of Rights and Freedoms* or some other organic constitutional constraints. For example, the provincial governments cannot create superior courts and the federal government cannot abolish them. At the federal level, additional constraints may also be imposed by the *Canadian Bill of Rights*.

The laws that flow from this constitutional foundation are found in the *Inquiries Act* and the corresponding provincial and territorial Acts. The constitutional validity of these statutes is neutral on their face. They are simply "enabling." But each level of government is prevented from going beyond its jurisdiction by attempting to use its statute to invade a subject area that has not been allocated to it under the constitution. That subject area is defined by the *terms of reference* given to each commission of inquiry when it is created. These terms are expressed through an order in council of the government. Since the order in council is made under the authority of the *Inquiries Act*, it is a statutory instrument with the same force of law as a statute (provided it passes constitutional muster).

In carrying out its mandate, a commission of inquiry is bound by the *principle of fairness*. This principle constrains the manner in which it must treat people when exercising its legal powers. It also has the force of law, but that arises from common law rather than statute. This means that procedural rights protected by the principle of fairness may be qualified or eliminated if a statutory law speaks clearly to that effect.

It has become common practice in recent years for each commission to create its own *rules of procedure*. The legal status of such rules may best be described as an "institutional policy" of the commission. They are not legally binding and a commissioner is entitled to depart from them when there is good reason to do so. Indeed, they are usually drafted explicitly to authorize the commissioner to do so. To some extent, they "codify" the rights that are already protected by the principle of fairness but explain how those requirements will be satisfied in the context of a particular inquiry. It is possible they could generate additional legal, procedural rights by creating "legitimate expectations" under the principle of fairness.

The "legal framework" is an appropriate context within which to examine the interrelationship of commissions of inquiry to *parallel legal proceedings*. This is of special importance when the conduct of an individual is under criminal investigation or prosecution yet is also an important subject of an inquiry.

Finally, this chapter examines *judicial interim review*. This is the vehicle by which the legal constraints upon a commission of inquiry are enforced during its operation.

## A. CONSTITUTIONAL BASIS

### 1) Division of Powers

The most frequent constitutional challenges to provincial commissions of inquiry allege encroachment on the federal criminal law power. The case-law development of the dividing line between federal and provincial jurisdiction in this respect was described in Chapter 3, Section E.[1] Initially, *Keable* and *Di Iorio* appeared to give broad authority to provincial commissions of inquiry to investigate specific crimes. The Supreme Court of Canada faced the issue squarely in *O'Hara*, where it found that the subject of the inquiry did fall within the federal power to investigate criminal offences. But it also fell within the provincial responsibility for the administration of justice, arising out of its authority over policing and jails. The Court concluded that the core purpose of the inquiry related directly to this provincial responsibility. Accordingly, it was valid, even though it might investigate events involving criminal conduct.

In *Starr*, the issue also was whether the "pith and substance" of the terms of reference served a valid provincial purpose. Here the Supreme Court held that there was no broader, provincial policy basis for the inquiry. Upon analysis, it was merely a "substitute police investigation" to determine whether there was a *prima facie* case that named individuals had committed a specific criminal offence. This purpose went beyond provincial jurisdiction.

Apart from the extreme situation in *Starr*, the courts seem, generally, receptive to permitting inquiries to proceed where there is a valid provincial purpose even though criminal conduct may also be involved. In *Phillips*, the Supreme Court accepted this characterization of the dominant purpose and effect of the Westray Inquiry's terms of reference:

> The pith and substance of the Westray inquiry is firmly anchored to the province's power to regulate coal mines within the province . . . . Neither the fact that part of this task would involve the investigation of the conduct of the mine managers nor the possibility that criminal charges might ensue once the report was made were fatal to the validity of the terms of reference.[2]

---

1 This line of cases includes: *Di Iorio v. Warden of the Montreal Jail*, [1978] 1 S.C.R. 152 [*Di Iorio*]; *Quebec (Attorney General) v. Canada (Attorney General)*, [1979] 1 S.C.R. 218 [*Keable*]; *Re Nelles and Grange* (1984), 46 O.R. (2d) 210 (C.A.) [*Nelles*]; *O'Hara v. British Columbia*, [1987] 2 S.C.R. 591 [*O'Hara*]; *Starr v. Houlden*, [1990] 1 S.C.R. 1366 [*Starr*].

2 *Phillips v. Nova Scotia (Commission of Inquiry into the Westray Mine Tragedy)*, [1995] 2 S.C.R. 97 at para. 53 [*Phillips*].

More commonly, where criminal conduct is involved, the provincial power that is most likely to be engaged is the "administration of justice" under section 92(14) of the *Constitution Act, 1867*. That was the situation in *O'Hara* and it arose again in the Stonechild Inquiry, where the Saskatchewan Court of Appeal adopted the "same line of analysis" as in *O'Hara*:

> Mr. Stonechild's death, particularly when seen in the context of other situations where aboriginal men had apparently been abandoned in remote areas, was a source of significant and justifiable concern. The situation was highly corrosive of public faith in the Saskatoon Police Service. The Government had every right to establish a commission for the purpose of investigating the conduct of police officers within provincial jurisdiction and attempting to restore public confidence.[3]

Similarly, the Taman Inquiry sought to restore public confidence in relation to the investigation and prosecution of a police officer. It reported that both had been improperly influenced by his status as a police officer and made a series of related recommendations, which subsequently were adopted.

It is clear from all of these cases that, for the purpose of establishing provincial commissions of inquiry, section 92(14) includes the administration of "criminal" justice and that includes "law enforcement."[4] In this respect, the conduct of RCMP officers may be examined when they provide policing services to a province. This is subject to the caveat that such examination cannot extend to the actual management or operation of the federal institution involved (here the RCMP).[5]

This boundary was underlined in a recent decision arising out of the Milgaard Inquiry in Saskatchewan. The attorney general of Canada became concerned about proposed lines of questioning of two lawyers from the federal Department of Justice who had been involved in Milgaard's unsuccessful application for a review of his conviction. There was no objection to them being questioned about factual matters related to the application but the attorney general objected to them being questioned

---

3 *Hartwig v. Saskatoon (City) Police Assn.*, 2008 SKCA 81 at para. 57 [*Stonechild*].

4 *O'Hara*, above note 1 at para. 14.

5 *Ibid.* at para. 16. See also *MacKeigan v. Hickman* (1989), 61 D.L.R. (4th) 688 at 724 (S.C.C.), McLachlin J. [*Hickman*].

about legal discussions among the lawyers and advice provided to the minister in this respect. The commissioner ruled that the lawyers could not be questioned about "the administration or management of a federal institution" but this did not limit questioning about the advice they provided. This ruling was set aside on judicial review, with Chief Justice Robert Laing rejecting the notion that the limitation upon probing a federal institution extended only to "governance":

> The advice lawyers working on Mr. Milgaard's applications offered to each other within the Department of Justice or to their Minister, or why they did certain things and did not do other things while engaged in this activity, as counsel for the applicant puts it, is within the core area of operation of the Department of Justice. (*Vide: Department of Justice Act*, R.S.C. 1985, c. J-2, ss. 2, 4 and 5). In addition such inquiries would be inquiring into the federal employee's performance of his duties, or conduct.[6]

For both of these reasons, the commissioner had crossed the constitutional boundary that prevents a provincial commission of inquiry from investigating a federal institution.

Former Commissioner Lamer articulated the boundary between the criminal law power and the provincial responsibility for the administration of justice in the context of commissions of inquiry into wrongful convictions:

> Such a commission may review the same subject matter as that of a criminal investigation and trial, but it must do so for a different and legitimate provincial purpose. It examines what mistakes or congruence of circumstances may have led to the results in question. It tells the Government what happened and why and it may make recommendations to avoid pitfalls in future cases. It may review the conduct of police officers, prosecutors and defence counsel, but it does not do so as a disciplinary body. A Commission may review the findings of a trial judge, but it does not do so as an appellate court. As one of the parties stated, a court of appeal does not ask, "what went wrong"? A Commission may do these things for the public purpose described above.[7]

6 *Canada (Attorney General) v. Saskatchewan (Commission of Inquiry into the Investigation of the Death of Gail Miller and the Wrongful Conviction of David Edgar Milgaard)*, 2006 SKQB 385 at para. 26 [*Milgaard*].

7 Lamer Inquiry, "Ruling on Terms of Reference," Report Annex 3 at 342.

Such an inquiry is not bound by rules of criminal procedure and evidence and may take into account matters inadmissible at the criminal trial or that became known only afterwards. However, it is subject to constitutional and other legal limitations.

In the same ruling, Commissioner Lamer held that his terms of reference did not authorize him to make a determination of factual innocence. But then he asked the constitutional question of whether a provincial commission of inquiry could be authorized to investigate and report on whether a person, who has been tried in a criminal court, is factually innocent. This would not merely involve reporting on what occurred in the previous investigation and prosecution. The commission would also have to examine the same evidence as well as many of the identical issues as those at the previous criminal trial.

> However, there are important differences. The most fundamental is that a criminal trial does not address "factual innocence." The criminal trial is to determine whether the Crown has proven its case beyond a reasonable doubt. If so, the accused is guilty. If not, the accused is found not guilty. There is no finding of factual innocence since it would not fall within the ambit or purpose of the criminal law.[8]

In contrast, a commission of inquiry provides advice. A provincial government may decide to make an *ex gratia* payment to a person who has been wrongfully convicted. In doing so, it must rely on the advice of someone who has reviewed the proceedings and all other relevant factors. Why can it not rely on a commission of inquiry as the vehicle to investigate and provide appropriate advice on this issue? Compensating someone who was wrongfully convicted falls within provincial responsibility for the administration of justice. A commission of inquiry simply would be assisting in fulfilling that responsibility.

Such proceedings before a commission of inquiry might have the appearance of a "re-trial" but they would be for a completely different purpose. That purpose would be to determine an issue that the criminal process cannot determine, namely, factual innocence. But, if the commissioner concludes that the person is not factually innocent, she would not be permitted to go further and conclude that the person was

---

8 These comments were adopted by the Ontario Court of Appeal in *R. v. Mullins-Johnson* (2007), 87 O.R. (3d) 425 at 432. See also, generally, Chapter 3, Section D.

"factually guilty." That is the very issue that only a criminal court may determine.

## 2) Other Limitations

Another constitutional limitation upon commissions of inquiry was upheld by the Supreme Court of Canada in *Hickman*.[9] The Marshall Inquiry sought to compel the attendance as witnesses of the appellate judges who acquitted Marshall but blamed him for his wrongful conviction. The Court held that the principle of judicial independence required absolute immunity for these judges from testifying about the grounds for their decision. This principle does not flow from the federal-provincial distribution of powers but is an organic feature of our constitution that would apply to federal as well as provincial inquiries. The Court held that this immunity also extended to protect the chief justice from being required to testify as to the assignment of judges to cases, even though this was an administrative function. Different views were expressed on this issue. Justices Wilson and Cory would have required such testimony in limited circumstances.

The *Canadian Charter of Rights and Freedoms* applies to both federal and provincial commissions of inquiry. However, the circumstances in which that application could arise are very limited. Section 13 is operative in protecting inquiry witnesses from having their testimony used against them in most future criminal proceedings. Section 7 might also protect against the use of derivative evidence, but there are few examples where the *Charter* has been successfully invoked in relation to commissions of inquiry. In *Phillips*, the majority of the Supreme Court decided the case on other grounds, but Justice Cory discussed the application of the *Charter*.[10] The issue was whether the *Charter* required that the Westray Inquiry be halted until the disposition of the outstanding criminal charges against two former managers of the Westray Mine.

Justice Cory pointed out the concern that, even if a commission of inquiry is established for a legitimate purpose, an attempt could be made

9 Above note 5. See also Chapter 3, Section D(1).

10 Above note 2. Sopinka wrote for the majority (Lamer C.J., La Forest, Gonthier, and McLachlin JJ.). Cory wrote for himself, Iacobucci, and Major JJ. L'Heureux-Dubé delivered a separate judgment.

to call a particular witness for the specific purpose of obtaining incriminating evidence. Where that is identified as the real purpose of compelling the testimony, section 7 of the *Charter* would exempt the witness from testifying. Even where that is not found to be the real purpose, a person accused of a crime may not be compelled to testify if significant prejudice to the criminal trial can be demonstrated. If such a witness is compelled to testify at the inquiry, there still may be grounds for objecting to individual questions that go beyond the purpose of the inquiry. In this case, the strong public interest to have the inquiry proceed as quickly as possible, and the limited demonstration of potential prejudice, required that the accused be compelled to testify at the inquiry.

Section 7 of the *Charter* provides that:

> Everyone has the right to life, liberty and security of the person and the right not to be deprived thereof except in accordance with the principles of fundamental justice.

Apart from the previous example, there is no authority to support the application of section 7 to a commission of inquiry. The threshold requirement is some infringement on a person's "life, liberty or security of the person." The exposure of a person to publicity at the hearings of an inquiry or to adverse findings in the final report may have dire consequences for a person's reputation. But this does not appear to pose a threat to "life, liberty or security of the person" that would trigger the protection of this section.

In *Blencoe*,[11] the majority of the Supreme Court of Canada provided an expansive exposition of "liberty" and "security of the person" in section 7 of the *Charter*. In the majority of the British Columbia Court of Appeal, Chief Justice Allan McEachern had concluded that these threshold requirements protected individual "privacy and human dignity." However, the majority in the Supreme Court held that notions such as privacy, dignity, and reputation represented only underlying values protected by the *Charter*. An intrusion on them directly would not generate the protection of section 7. The majority said that liberty extends beyond

---

11 *Blencoe v. British Columbia (Human Rights Commission)*, [2000] 2 S.C.R. 307 [*Blencoe*]. Bastarache wrote for the majority (McLachlin C.J., L'Heureux-Dubé, Gonthier, and Major JJ.). LeBel J. wrote for the minority (Iacobucci, Binnie, and Arbour JJ.), dissenting in part.

freedom from physical constraint to encompass personal autonomy in making important decisions. Security of the person also includes "serious state-imposed psychological stress." But they found that none of these standards was met as a result of the delay in dealing with the human-rights allegations against the respondent in this case. Moreover, the most prejudicial impact upon his personal life was occasioned not by the actions of the human rights commission but by the sexual-harassment claims themselves.

Section 2(e) of the *Canadian Bill of Rights* might be easier to engage because it refers to depriving a person:

> of a right to a fair hearing in accordance with the principles of fundamental justice for the determination of his rights and obligations.

However, it is limited to the construction of federal laws (rather than actions) and would have no application to provincial inquiries. It could also be rejected on the basis that a commission of inquiry does not "determine" any "rights and obligations."

In any event, the common law principle of fairness would appear to address most concerns that would fall under section 7 of the *Charter* or section 2(e) of the *Bill of Rights.* The need for these constitutional provisions would arise only if a government sought to override the common law protection, for example, through a commission's terms of reference.

## B. INQUIRIES ACTS

### 1) Overview

Only the federal and New Brunswick statutes use the name "Inquiries Act." British Columbia uses "Public Inquiry Act" and Quebec uses "Public Inquiry Commissions." The Manitoba provisions are contained in Part V of the *Manitoba Evidence Act.* The remaining six provinces and three territories use "Public Inquiries Act."[12] The criteria that authorize when a commission of inquiry may be established vary with each jurisdiction. They are all broad in scope, referring to such matters as "good government," "conduct of the public business," "public interest," "pub-

12 See the Table of Authorizing Statutes at the front of this book. The *Nunavut Act,* S.C. 1993, c. 28 provides for the *Public Inquiries Act* of the Northwest Territories to apply to Nunavut.

lic concern," "sufficient public importance," "administration of justice," "elections," "public health," and "welfare." Section 83(4) of the Manitoba Act contains a unique provision authorizing every commission to:

> include an inquiry into and concerning the conduct, character, and motives, of any person by whom a demand for the inquiry was made . . .

In each jurisdiction, the Cabinet is also given a subjective discretion to determine when any of these threshold criteria are met so that a challenge to the validity of a commission of inquiry on this basis would be almost impossible.

The central substantive feature of every Act is that it gives the government the power to establish the subject and scope of each inquiry through terms of reference, which have the force of law. The central procedural feature of each is to authorize commissioners to compel testimony and the production of evidence. These statutes then elaborate, in various ways and to varying degrees, on the authority and powers given in each jurisdiction.[13] The British Columbia Act is the most elaborate and requires that each commission be designated as "a study commission, hearing commission or both." Newfoundland and Labrador adopted a new Act in 2006 that, while shorter and more traditional than British Columbia's, reflects a thorough canvassing of all of the other statutes and includes some new features as well. Some jurisdictions have made piecemeal amendments over the years. For example, Saskatchewan added an immunity provision for commissioners in 2004.

It is, of course, necessary to pay close attention to the Act that is applicable in the jurisdiction of a particular commission of inquiry. It may have some specific provisions not contained in corresponding legislation in other jurisdictions. However, differences between jurisdictions are often more apparent than real. For example, the Ontario Act requires that anyone with a substantial and direct interest be given a full opportunity to participate in the hearings in relation to that interest.[14] The *Inquiries Act* is silent in this respect. But the terms of reference of recent federal inquiries permit such participation in almost identical language to Ontario's. Reference was also made in that earlier discussion to the

---

13 See the general survey of provincial legislation in Chapter 5.5 of the Ontario Law Reform Commission, *Report on Public Inquiries* (Toronto: The Commission, 1992). The Ontario Act is discussed in Chapter 2 of the Report.

14 See Chapter 5, Section C(3).

Milgaard Inquiry, where standing was determined on the very same criteria. Yet the Saskatchewan Act is completely silent on the right to participate through standing.

The Newfoundland and Labrador Act is the only one that authorizes the commissioner to recommend funding for participants. Yet the terms of reference in almost every jurisdiction tend to authorize recommendations as to funding. These often authorize such recommendations only if the party otherwise would be unable to participate. The Newfoundland and Labrador Act contains no such restriction. The North Battleford Inquiry authorized the commissioner, himself, to grant and set the levels of funding for counsel.

The principle of fairness also contributes to the uniformity of procedures at commissions of inquiry. For example, the *Inquiries Act* forbids a finding of misconduct against any person unless it is preceded by reasonable notice and an opportunity to be heard. Most of the Acts contain comparable provisions but some are silent in this respect. That was the situation in Newfoundland and Labrador at the time of the Lamer Inquiry, but he reported: "In my view, such an opportunity to be heard is required by the Administrative Law principle of fairness, even if it is not mandated by legislation. I adopted a specific procedural rule for this Inquiry and incorporated this practice into my proceedings."[15] As discussed above, Newfoundland and Labrador has since adopted a new and comprehensive Act.

Section 3 of the Ontario Act gives a commission "control and direction" of the "conduct of and procedure to be followed on an inquiry." Other Acts provide little guidance. The latitude given to commissions when operating under a sparse Act may be expanded by provisions, such as the following taken from the federal *Interpretation Act*:[16]

> 12. Every enactment is deemed remedial and shall be given such fair large and liberal construction as best ensures the attainment of its objectives.
>
> 31. (2) Where power is given to a person, officer or functionary to do or enforce the doing of any act or thing, all such powers as are

15 See also *Consortium Developments (Clearwater) Ltd. v. Sarnia (City)*, [1998] 3 S.C.R. 3 at para. 31 [*Consortium*]. Justice Binnie delivered the judgment of the Court.

16 R.S.C. 1985, c. I-23.

> necessary to enable the person office or functionary to do or enforce the doing of the act or thing are deemed to be also given.

The case law also contains judicial observations such as the following from Justice Cory in *Phillips*:

> In my view, the nature and the purpose of public inquiries require courts to give a generous interpretation to a commissioner's powers to control their own proceedings under the Nova Scotia Act.[17]

However, such latitude does not extend to the standard of review applicable to the commissioner in relation to the issues of procedural fairness[18] or jurisdiction arising from the terms of reference.[19] In both cases, the standard is correctness.

## 2) Specific Provisions

Section 3 of the *Inquiries Act* states that an inquiry may be established only where the subject "is not regulated by any special law." Most of the other Acts contain similar provisions. The purpose of this restraint appears to be to avoid duplication where the machinery of government already has established a vehicle for dealing with the specific problem.[20] In *Pitura*, the Ontario Court of Appeal upheld the validity of a commission of inquiry into the safety of using certain toxins and contrasted its mandate to the process under another statute:

> The present inquiry is a plain inquiry to obtain information and recommendations, and nothing more. The hearing provided for under the *Environmental Assessment Act, 1975* . . . is clearly part of an adjudicative process, a process leading to a decision affecting rights or interests. In our view, s. 2 of the *Public Inquiries Act, 1971* should not be interpreted as preventing the Lieutenant-Governor in Council from causing an inquiry to be made into matters of public concern where the inquiry does not duplicate, or substantially duplicate, the legal process relating to the

17 Above note 2 at para. 175.

18 *Chrétien v. Canada (Commission of Inquiry into the Sponsorship Program and Advertising Activities, Gomery Commission)*, 2008 FC 802 at para. 66 [*Chrétien*].

19 *Ontario (Provincial Police) v. Cornwall (Public Inquiry)*, [2008] ONCA 33 at para. 24 [*Cornwall*], Moldaver J.A., Doherty and Gillese JJ.A. agreeing.

20 Referred to in Chapter 4, Section B(3).

> inquiry regulated by the alleged special law so that the purpose of the special law would be frustrated.[21]

In its analysis of this case, the Law Reform Commission of Ontario stressed the differences in the two processes. The mere fact the report of the commission of inquiry could influence the granting of a permit did not replace the permit process itself.[22]

Another comment on this case would narrow even further the scope of the phrase "not regulated by any special law." In this view, "it is not enough that statutes other than the inquiries statutes potentially apply; there must be some action, such as an application, or particular circumstances to engage proceedings under the other statutes."[23]

This suggests that it would not be enough for a special law to authorize a public inquiry into the exact same subject matter as the proposed commission of inquiry. That special law would have to be actually invoked. Such an interpretation raises practical difficulties. To overstep an established statutory process to achieve exactly the same purpose through a commission of inquiry would undermine such a process. This would seem to defeat the objective of this restriction. And what would happen if that process were invoked after the commission of inquiry was under way? Would the commission of inquiry become *functus*?

A good illustration is the process established under the *Judges Act* for inquiring into the conduct of a superior court judge.[24] Even if that process were not invoked, surely the government would not be able to establish a commission of inquiry for the same purpose. Indeed, the whole impetus for establishing such a process was the failure of a commission of inquiry to deal properly with such a matter. If the government attempted to proceed with such a commission of inquiry, the restriction in section 3 should be applied. To do otherwise would defeat the purpose of the *Judges Act* process. In this example, the constitutional principle of judicial independence might well reinforce this conclusion but it should prevail even without such support.

---

21 *Re Canadian Environmental Law Association and Pitura* (1981), 122 D.L.R. (3d) 492 at 497 (Ont. C.A.) [*Pitura*].

22 Ontario Law Reform Commission, *Report on Public Inquiries*, above note 13 at 31.

23 "Public Inquiries" in *Canadian Encyclopedic Digest, Ontario*, 3d ed., vol. 29 (Agincourt, ON: Carswell, 1982) Title 22 at 38.

24 See Chapter 3, Section F(1).

Unlike the other Acts, the *Inquiries Act* also provides for departmental investigations under Part II.[25] These may be appointed by a minister (rather than the Cabinet) to investigate the business and conduct of officials within her department. Even where the scope of an inquiry could be accommodated under a Part II Inquiry, the government is free to proceed under Part I if it so chooses.[26]

There are provisions for similar inquiries in various statutes in the other jurisdictions. In Manitoba, the primary authority to initiate these is given to the minister of justice. *The Department of Justice Act*[27] states:

> 4(1) the Lieutenant Governor in Council may, by order in council, appoint such committees as may be required
>
> (a) to inquire into, investigate, report, and advise on *any matter referred to any such committee by the minister*; and
>
> (b) to perform such other duties as may be prescribed by the Lieutenant Governor in Council. [Emphasis added.]
>
> . . .
>
> 4(4) A committee appointed under subsection (1) shall report to the minister within such period as he may direct, or may report to him periodically or from time to time as he may require.

Such committees may be granted some or all of the powers given to a commission of inquiry under the Manitoba Act.

The Arar Inquiry met an interesting challenge based on the Part I and Part II distinction under the *Inquiries Act*. The applicant claimed that the commission was improperly constituted on the basis that the Act contemplated a public inquiry under Part I or a departmental investigation under Part II but not a hybrid of the two. The commission had been established under Part I but was required "to investigate and report on" the actions of Canadian officials. This was said to track the language of "the conduct of any person in the service" of a specific department. However, Commissioner O'Connor ruled that

> the Commission's terms of reference are not limited to investigating and reporting on the state and management of the business of any particu-

25 See Chapter 4, Section B(4).

26 McDonald Inquiry.

27 C.C.S.M. c. J35.

> lar department of the federal government, nor even to federal government employees. A departmental investigation could not be convened in relation to the Prime Minister's office, the offices of ministers of the Crown or the Privy Council Office, because these parts of the executive branch of government are not departments.

To confine the commission's terms of reference to a departmental investigation would undermine the very mandate that was given.[28]

Other specific provisions in the various Acts, which are discussed above and below, include the following:

- immunity: Chapter 5, Section B(1)
- standing and funding: Chapter 5, Section C(3)
- rights of parties: Chapter 6, Section C
- interim judicial review: Chapter 7, Section G
- compelling testimony and production: Chapter 8, Section B
- controlling proceedings: Chapter 8, Section C
- findings of misconduct: Chapter 9, Section B
- notices of misconduct: Chapter 9, Section C

### 3) Fundamental Nature

The Somalia Inquiry provides an excellent illustration of the fundamental nature of a commission of inquiry as a legal, governmental, and political institution. No matter how important its contributions may be to Canadian society, and how important its independence may be to achieving those goals, it is ultimately an "appendage" of the executive branch of government.

The Somalia Inquiry provided a valuable context for examining this issue because it brought together so many of the potential dynamics involved, in such an intense way. The inquiry was established for the usual reasons: public concern over shocking stories about the conduct of members of an important public institution. But it became apparent at the outset that there was little enthusiasm among senior officials for a thorough process. The time for reporting was impossibly short. As the inquiry proceeded, officials took considerable liberties in delaying and withholding the production of documents. Time limits were extended,

---

28 Arar Inquiry, Ruling on Jurisdictional Issue (3 January 2006).

but never to the degree necessary to complete the task. As the hearings proceeded in full public view, they were perceived as overly legalistic and adversarial. The public began to tire of the bad news, particularly since it involved an institution—the military—to which Canadians are conditioned to be loyal and supportive.

The commissioners were diligent and conscientious but did not appreciate the political situation that was evolving. Reference was made to the commission's frustration in dealing with lack of cooperation and obstruction by officials.[29] The commissioners decided to suspend their substantive hearings to confront this problem directly by holding a public investigation into alleged document tampering and document destruction in the Directorate, General Public Affairs. This investigation consumed forty hearing days, from 15 April 1996 to 30 August 1996. The commissioners may have had little choice, but this led to opening up another front of confrontation and bad news. It also encouraged critics, including the government, to emphasize the increasing delay and expense.

Six months later, with an election on the horizon, the government took the bold step of simply shutting down the inquiry. It was a political gamble but an accurate reading of public opinion. It did not become a significant issue in the election and the government was returned with another majority. But the commissioners felt betrayed. Following the government's decision to require completion of the hearings within the previously allocated time frame, they held a press conference. One of the commissioners said:

> When I was asked to serve on this inquiry . . . I accepted the government's assurances that what was wanted was a full and fair investigation . . . . Now the government has unilaterally broken the contract that it had made with myself and my fellow commissioners . . . a public inquiry like ours does stand outside the system . . . .

He described the government's action as being "alien to our political tradition" and endangering "principles of accountability."[30] Do these observations have any legal implications or are they merely hortatory?

---

29 See Chapter 3, Section B(5) and Chapter 5, Section B(3)

30 Somalia Inquiry, Press Conference (13 January 1997), reproduced in volume 5 of the report.

John Dixon was a special advisor to the minister of national defence at the time of some of the events relevant to the Somalia Inquiry. He was directly involved in communications between the Canadian Forces and the minister and a controversy arose as to when the minister's office was informed of the murder of a Somali youth by Canadian soldiers. Dixon had been scheduled for a long time to be a witness at the inquiry but the commissioners determined that the truncated hearings prevented them from examining whether there was a cover-up of this murder. Since he had been publicly implicated in such a possible cover-up, he was anxious to testify and have his personal account placed on the public record.

Dixon applied to the Federal Court to strike down the government's order in council terminating the hearings and to require the commissioners to fulfill their mandate. His argument was as follows. The original broad mandate continued to exist but was impossible to complete within the prescribed deadline. This made it impossible for the commissioners to comply with the law. The government was without jurisdiction in attempting to impose a legal mandate that could not be fulfilled. Its order in council was a "sham."

Justice Sandra Simpson essentially accepted this argument.[31] In doing so, she held that the initial and subsequent reporting dates in the terms of reference were never intended to be final. Rather they were "target" dates which served the useful purpose of encouraging reasonable projections and related diligence in working to meet them. They also encouraged accountability by requiring the commission to justify its requests for extensions. Yet the government did ultimately become frustrated with the delay in completion. This raised the issue of whether it is the government or the commissioners who have the authority to decide "when the investigation has been adequate." In Justice Simpson's view, a commission of inquiry must be independent in deciding "the manner in which it will carry out its mandate." Accordingly, it was for the commissioners to decide when their fact finding was sufficient to enable them to report in the manner required by their mandate. And they must provide a full report rather than "simply a list of unanswered questions." As a result, the order in council breached the rule of law by impinging on

---

31 *Dixon v. Canada (Commission of Inquiry into the Deployment of Canadian Forces to Somalia)*, [1997] 2 F.C. 391 [*Dixon* (T.D.)].

their independence to determine the sufficiency of their investigation. It also breached the rule of law by making it impossible for them to obey the law, that is, to fulfil their legal mandate.

Justice Simpson acknowledged that the government did have authority to curtail the commission's mandate. But she found that authority in the *Interpretation Act*,[32] which provides that such variations must be made "in the same manner" as that of the original order. This meant that the government would have to specifically delete items in the original mandate to allow the remaining mandate to be addressed in full. The order in council to terminate the hearings was declared *ultra vires* as beyond the government's jurisdiction.

The government responded by enacting a new order in council limiting the remaining terms as prescribed by Justice Simpson. Although the issue had been resolved, the government of Canada urged the Federal Court of Appeal to hear the appeal as an important issue of public law not likely to arise again in the near future. The court agreed, stating that the decision on appeal

> goes to an issue which lies at the heart of the division of responsibilities between the Judiciary and the Executive. Indeed, the case involves the extent to which a court, exercising its proper adjudicative role, should be entitled to interfere with discretionary decisions made by the Governor in Council.[33]

The Court of Appeal answered emphatically that, when the executive makes a discretionary decision within its legal authority, the courts have no supervisory role.

The legal authority of the government for its "discretionary decisions" in this case was the *Inquiries Act*. It authorized the government to create a new administrative body to assist in carrying out specified executive functions. This new body was entirely a creature of the executive and its mandate could be established only by the executive under the same authority of the *Inquiries Act*. The court asked:

---

32 Above note 16, s. 31(4).

33 *Dixon v. Canada (Commission of Inquiry into the Deployment of Canadian Forces to Somalia)* (1997), 149 D.L.R. (4th) 269 at 272 (Fed. C.A.). Marceau J.A. delivered the judgment of the court (Isaac C.J. and McDonald J.A.) [*Dixon (C.A.)*].

> By what principle of public law can a commission of inquiry acquire, once created, the independence and autonomy necessary to allow it to prevail over the will of the Governor in Council as to its structure and its existence?[34]

That same legal authority, under the *Inquiries Act*, also permits the government to express its "will" by changing this body's mandate or by simply putting it out of existence.

The court below had misinterpreted section 31(4) of the *Interpretation Act* which states:

> Where a power is conferred to make regulations, the power shall be construed as including a power, exercisable in the same manner and subject to the same consent and conditions, if any, to repeal, amend or vary the regulations and make others.

The power to change or revoke the mandate of a commission of inquiry does not come from that Act. It comes from the *Inquiries Act*. The *Interpretation Act* is merely saying that the power to create a commission under the *Inquiries Act* includes the power to "repeal" it under the same Act. That power cannot be modified by the content of the regulations previously created. It is a statutory authority, subject to any statutory "manner . . . consent and conditions" that may exist (and none existed here). That statutory power to create and repeal cannot be modified by the subordinate regulations or terms of reference, which are the very things being created and repealed.

It was also an error to conclude that it was for the commissioners rather than the government to decide the stage at which the investigation was "sufficient." That decision already had been made by the terms of reference. There was no legal foundation for the time deadlines to be interpreted as "target dates," no matter how often they had been extended. Unlike the courts, the findings of commissions of inquiry are not "determinative":

> It is the legal duty of the commissioners to report, but that report is limited to explaining what they have done, what they were able to draw from their investigations (in terms of findings of fact) and what

34 *Ibid.* at 277.

> advice they are in a position to give to the Executive in light of those findings.[35]

They were required to explain the results of their work and related opinions but only to the extent permitted by "the time and resources available to them." The implication is that, if the government wants a superficial or shoddy report and a commissioner is willing to accept a corresponding mandate, that is the end of the matter. Such a commissioner has no guaranty of independence to conduct a thorough inquiry.

The court made this general observation about the independence of commissions of inquiry:

> No one disputes the necessity of preserving the independence of commissions of inquiry as to the manner in which they may exercise their powers, conduct their investigations, organize their deliberations and prepare their reports. The role they play in our democracy has become much too vital to accept that the manner in which they investigate matters and formulate the conclusions and recommendations that they arrive at, can be freely tampered with or influenced by anyone within or outside the government of the day.[36]

In my view, the breadth of this observation is inconsistent with the central thrust and analysis of the court's decision. According to that decision, the government is prevented from interfering with such independence only to the extent that it is specifically constrained by the authorizing legislation. For example, the *Inquiries Act* gives commissioners the independence to compel testimony and the production of documents. The government could not interfere with that authority in the terms of reference. But other aspects of independence are not protected in the Act. And, in the absence of statutory constraints, a government is free to run roughshod over commission independence.

To take some extreme examples, the terms of reference could require that an advisor of the minister be permitted to participate in all deliberations of the commissioners. A commissioner could be required to submit the report in draft form, subject to such revisions as the government might see fit. And the commissioner could be forbidden from disclosing the content of such a draft. Budgetary restrictions could be imposed

35 *Ibid.* at 278.

36 *Ibid.* at 277.

that severely limit the independence of the inquiry. On the basis of *Dixon (C.A.)*, the government would be answerable only politically for such infringements on independence. They would not be "the business of the Court." Such political accountability normally will be adequate to ensure an independent commission of inquiry, but it was not in the Somalia Inquiry and the courts could offer no relief.[37]

The fundamental legal nature of a commission of inquiry is simply that it is a temporary appendage of the executive branch of government, created and potentially extinguished at its will or whim.

## C. TERMS OF REFERENCE

The terms of reference are the defining feature of each commission of inquiry. Extensive commentary on them is made throughout this book and they were discussed more collectively in Chapter 4, Section C. The emphasis here is on their legal significance.

Their legal character is that of "subordinate legislation." Parliament makes laws by approving statutes. But those statutes may also delegate to some other body the authority to create "statutory instruments" which have the same legal force as a statute. The *Inquiries Act* delegates to the executive the authority to create commissions of inquiry and to define the unique legal jurisdiction of each one.

We have seen that the terms of reference may grant additional powers beyond those specified in the Act. Such additional powers are considered to be authorized by the Act. They are complementary or supportive of the Act in fulfilling its purpose. But the terms of reference cannot limit or be inconsistent with any of the powers granted by the Act. The terms of reference gain their authority from the Act and are subordinate to it. They cannot derogate from what Parliament has established.

The legal authority or jurisdiction of a commission is both granted and limited by its terms of reference (as well as by constitutional and statutory limitations). The terms of reference may be subject to interpretation as to their breadth. A government may change the terms of

---

37 See the detailed analysis of this general issue, as well as the *Dixon* decisions, in Tamar Witelson, "Declaration of Independence" in A. Manson & D. Mullan, eds., *Commissions of Inquiry: Praise or Reappraise?* (Toronto: Irwin Law. 2003) 301.

reference, as we have seen in the previous section, but cannot tell a commissioner how to interpret her terms of reference.[38] That is the responsibility of the commissioner although such an interpretation is a legal decision that can be reviewed by the courts. The courts will give a commissioner generous latitude in determining whether evidence to be explored is reasonably relevant to the subject matter of the inquiry. But the definition of that subject matter goes to jurisdiction and, in making this interpretation, the commissioner must be correct.[39] Moreover, an error related to jurisdiction cannot be cured by consent of the parties: "A person either has jurisdiction or does not have jurisdiction."[40]

In addition to the erroneous ruling of the commissioner in the Cornwall Inquiry,[41] other examples include the *Landreville* and *Stevens* cases.[42] In *Landreville*, the subject of the inquiry had been found guilty of judicial misconduct through "gross contempt" of other legal tribunals. But nowhere in the terms of reference could authorization be found for such a finding. In *Stevens*, the commissioner also made an erroneous finding of misconduct by adopting a definition of conflict of interest that was not authorized by his terms of reference.

## D. PRINCIPLE OF FAIRNESS

### 1) General

The common law principle of procedural fairness had its origins in England in the nineteenth century. It was a time of rapid industrialization accompanied by extensive legislative regulation which formed the genesis of what is now commonly known as administrative law. Prior to this time, it was the practice and expectation that the adjudication of individual rights would be done by the courts. But, increasingly, statutory powers of decision making that affected the rights of individuals were being assigned to government officials and government-appointed committees and tribunals.

---

38 Chapter 4, Section C(4).

39 *Ibid.* and below note 41.

40 *Stevens v. Canada (Attorney General)*, [2005] 2 F.C.R. 629 at para. 34 (Fed. Ct.).

41 *Cornwall*, above note 19. Discussed in Chapter 5, Section D(2).

42 Chapter 3, Sections B(1) & (2).

The courts became concerned about the potential arbitrariness and unfairness of such decision making and established judicial precedents that gave them a supervisory role. They did this by utilizing two concepts, jurisdiction and statutory interpretation. This approach allowed them to give apparent deference throughout to parliamentary supremacy. The concept of jurisdiction permitted the courts to find that a statutory body attempted to act beyond the authority granted by Parliament. The concept of statutory interpretation allowed them to determine the limits of that authority. By striking down such administrative actions, the courts were merely confirming the will of Parliament by keeping these bodies within the mandates Parliament had assigned to them.

But they extended this concept of limited jurisdiction to procedural as well as substantive jurisdiction. Take this example. A property owner is taken aback one day when construction workers appear to install sewer lines through her property. The owner objects but the foreman shows her a decision of the sewer commissioners that authorized the construction. Her lawyer then examines the authorizing legislation and discovers that the commissioners were simply given *carte blanche* to make such an order on a simple application to them by the municipality.

When she goes to court to try to halt the construction, there is no legal argument except to say that it was unfair. If she had been consulted, she could have demonstrated that her soil made such construction hazardous, that a better route would have avoided interference with any property rights, and that it would have provided a great saving to all taxpayers. The court looks at the statute and sees no procedural rights whatsoever. But the court "interprets" the statute by reading into it the unspoken will of Parliament: in granting such a decision-making power, surely Parliament intended that it would be exercised only with procedural fairness.

This means that the commissioners were expected to follow procedural rules similar to those applied by the courts when they adjudicate legal rights. Here the owner's property could be diminished in value. She should have a right to be heard, as she would in court. Since no code of procedure existed for these statutory tribunals, the courts created one. It was described as the rules of natural justice and was cobbled together through precedents developed in successive cases.

In subsequent cases, the analysis went like this. Was the statutory body acting in a "judicial" manner? This was determined by ascertaining whether the body was given authority to make legally binding decisions about a person's rights; many factors were taken into account but financial or proprietary consequences were the predominant consideration. If the body did have this authority, did it act like a court? Was the decision maker impartial? Was the person affected given a fair hearing? These procedural rules were flexible and could be satisfied in different ways. But, if they were not satisfied, the decision maker acted contrary to the will of Parliament and without jurisdiction. The decision could be quashed and, if the process was not complete, the decision maker could be prohibited from acting further.

As the processes evolved, Parliament began to establish procedures in the statutes themselves that would meet some of these requirements. But many situations still required judicial review. A lingering problem was the determination of the threshold question: Was the body acting judicially? The answer led to an "all or nothing" result. If it was a decision affecting rights, it was judicial and the procedural rules were necessary. If not, there were no procedural constraints.

This problem was finally resolved in Canada by the *Nicholson* case,[43] which held that a general duty of procedural fairness applied to administrative decisions, even if they could not be classified as "judicial." What became more important in imposing procedural requirements was the nature of the issues and how seriously the "interests" of an individual were affected. If the decision were straightforward and the consequences minor, fairness might be satisfied by inviting a written comment from the individual. If the consequences were serious and the process required fact finding and issues of credibility, a full oral hearing with the opportunity to cross-examine might be required to satisfy the principle of fairness.

The concept of "interests" affected is much broader than legal "rights." Such rights could include monetary or proprietary interests or legal status. "Interests" extend to broader entitlements that might be legally classified as legal "privileges" rather than rights. And "interests" include a public report which has no legal consequences but which may adversely affect reputation. In *Krever*, the Supreme Court clearly stated:

---

43 *Nicholson v. Haldimand-Norfolk (Regional) Police Commissioners*, [1979] 1 S.C.R. 311 [*Nicholson*].

> The findings of fact and the conclusions of the commissioner may well have an adverse effect upon a witness or a party to the inquiry. . . . It is true that the findings of a commissioner cannot result in either penal or civil consequences for a witness. . . . . Nonetheless, procedural fairness is essential for the findings of commissions may damage the reputation of a witness. For most, a good reputation is their most highly prized attribute. It follows that it is essential that procedural fairness be demonstrated in the hearings of the commission.[44]

The court below had suggested that procedural fairness was not as important for a commission of inquiry since such a body made only a report rather than a "decision."[45] In spite of this clear statement to the contrary by a unanimous Supreme Court in *Krever*, doubts continue to be expressed about the applicability of the fairness principle to commissions of inquiry.[46] Such doubts are misplaced and the distinction between a recommending and a decision-making body for this purpose should be treated as historical.

In *Baker*, Justice Claire L'Heureux-Dubé stressed that the duty of fairness is flexible and variable but there are a number of contextual factors to be considered.[47] In the context of commissions of inquiry, the most relevant are the importance of the potential findings to the individual affected and the need for deference to the commissioner in choosing the manner in which fairness was sought to be satisfied. But fulfilling that objective need not be unduly complicated. As then Justice Brian Dickson stated:

---

44 *Canada (Attorney General) v. Canada (Commission of Inquiry on the Blood System in Canada—Krever Commission)*, [1997] 3 S.C.R. 440 at para. 55, Cory J. delivering the judgment of the Court [*Krever*].

45 *Canada (Attorney General) v. Canada (Commission of Inquiry on the Blood System—Krever Commission)*, [1997] F.C.J. No. 17 at para. 102 (C.A.), Décary J.A., Strayer and MacGuigan JJ.A. agreeing. Referred to in Chapter 6, Section A(2).

46 See, for example, Tamar Witelson, above note 37 at 343 and Grant Huscroft, "The Duty of Fairness" in Lorne Sossin & Colleen Flood, *Administrative Law in Context* (Toronto: Emond Montgomery, 2008) 123. Where there is both an investigative and a hearing stage, limited procedural protections may be necessary at an earlier stage if a full opportunity to be heard is provided later.

47 *Baker v. Canada (Minister of Citizenship and Immigration)*, [1999] 2 S.C.R. 817 at para. 22 writing for the Court on this issue [*Baker*].

> In the final analysis, the simple question to be answered is this: Did the tribunal on the facts of the particular case act fairly toward the person claiming to be aggrieved? It seems to me that this is the underlying question which the courts have sought to answer in all of the cases dealing with natural justice and with fairness.[48]

The following points have already been made but should be emphasized. If fairness is denied, any related findings will be a nullity. Since fairness is a jurisdictional requirement, it cannot be satisfied by consent of the parties but that could be a factor in determining fairness. The principle may be supplemented by statutory procedures but cannot detract from such procedures. Since the principle of fairness arises from common law, it may be reduced or eliminated by statute but only where the statute speaks very clearly to that effect.[49] When speaking of a statute here, the terms of reference are included as a statutory instrument.

### 2) Fair Tribunal

The requirement of an independent and impartial tribunal is often expressed in the negative as the absence of bias. In considering this issue, there seldom will be evidence of an actual bias. To protect both the interests of affected parties and the public view of the legitimacy of the process, the courts have adopted a test related to a "perception" or "apprehension" of bias. The Supreme Court of Canada[50] recently confirmed that "one standard" has emerged for determining whether there is a reasonable apprehension of bias. This test was established by Justice L.-P. de Grandpré in the National Energy Board case, as follows:

> [T]he apprehension of bias must be a reasonable one, held by reasonable and right minded persons, applying themselves to the question and obtaining thereon the required information. In the words of the Court of Appeal, that test is "what would an informed person, viewing the matter realistically and practically—and having thought the matter through—

---

48 *Martineau v. Matsqui Institution Disciplinary Board (No. 2)*, [1980] 1 S.C.R. 602 at 630–31 [*Martineau*].

49 *Ocean Port Hotel Ltd. v. British Columbia (General Manager, Liquor Control and Licensing Branch)*, [2001] 2 S.C.R. 781.

50 *Wewaykum Indian Band v. Canada*, [2003] 2 S.C.R. 259 at para. 60 [*Wewaykum*].

conclude. Would he think that it is more likely than not that [the decision maker], whether consciously or unconsciously, would not decide fairly."[51]

These "right minded persons," in effect, represent whether or not public confidence in the process would be adversely affected. The test attempts to impose a practical and objective assessment rather than one based on speculation. In *Wewaykum*, the Supreme Court also emphasized that there is a strong presumption of judicial impartiality.[52] This presumption probably extends to a commissioner in the sense that a person who agrees to fulfill an important public service can be expected to do so fairly and in good faith.

The issue of bias already has been discussed in various situations. Reference was made to one of the original commissioners resigning from the Somalia Inquiry. A perception of bias existed because of her association with senior officials of the Department of National Defence who were potential subjects of the inquiry.[53] The circumstances that led to a finding of bias against Commissioner Létourneau with respect to Brigadier-General Beno and the Federal Court of Appeal decision overruling that finding were described.[54] The same section contains a discussion of the circumstances leading to a finding of bias on the part of Commissioner Gomery against former prime minister Chrétien also were discussed. This case also confirmed that issues of procedural fairness are reviewed as questions of law subject to the standard of correctness.[55] The Beno and Chrétien judgments provide a full analysis of the application of the concept of bias to commissioners. For a broader canvassing of this subject, see the hundreds of Canadian precedents collected and classified in the book simply entitled *Bias*.[56] Ultimately, the determination of a reasonable apprehension of bias will simply rest on a judicial perception of the thinking of "right minded persons."

---

51 *Committee for Justice and Liberty v. National Energy Board*, [1978] 1 S.C.R. 369 at 394 [*Energy Board*].

52 Above note 50 at para. 76.

53 See Chapter 3, Section B(5).

54 *Beno v. Canada (Commission of Inquiry into the Deployment of Canadian Forces in Somalia—Létourneau Commission)*, [1997] 2 F.C. 527 (C.A.). See discussion in Chapter 5, Section B(3).

55 *Chrétien*, above note 18 at para. 66 citing *Dunsmuir v. New Brunswick*, [2002] 1 S.C.R. 249 [*Dunsmuir*]. Also discussed in Chapter 5, Section B(3).

56 Robert D. Kligman, *Bias* (Toronto: Butterworths, 1998).

### 3) Fair Process

In *Chrétien*, Justice Teitlebaum quoted the following passage from *Baker* which, again, simplifies the basic objective of the principle of fairness:

> underlying all these factors is the notion that the purpose of the participatory rights contained within the duty of procedural fairness is to ensure that administrative decisions are made using a fair and open procedure, appropriate to the decision being made and its statutory, institutional, and social context, with an opportunity for those affected by the decision to put forward their views and evidence fully and have them considered by the decision-maker.[57]

In assessing whether a commissioner has met the principle of fairness, one need ask only whether this broad objective has been met. It is simply an elaboration of the question asked above by Justice Dickson: Did the tribunal treat the person affected fairly? However, Justice Teitlebaum went on to address the "five non-exhaustive factors" articulated in *Baker* for determining the extent of the procedural fairness required in any particular context. The following is a summary of his analysis:

1) *The decision and decision-making process*: The more that a commission resembles a court, the greater is the degree of formal procedural protections required. The hearings of an investigative commission closely resemble those of a court: testimony, counsel, cross-examinations, procedural motions. But, unlike trials, commissions of inquiry are inquisitorial, with "wide-ranging investigative powers" to achieve their objectives. The role of fact finding and recommending is also different from the decision making of courts. These differences suggest that a lower level of procedural fairness is required, according to Justice Teitlebaum.

   In my view, this analysis places too much emphasis on "form." The reality is that when reputation is at stake, the principle of fairness results in a hearing that is indistinguishable from a judicial hearing. Also, a "finding" of misconduct affecting reputation really amounts to an adjudication about conduct, quite apart from any recommendation.
2) *The statutory scheme and statutory provisions*: The *Inquiries Act* requires notice and an opportunity to be heard before findings of mis-

57 Above note 47 at para. 22.

conduct can be made. Although the report does not involve a legal determination of issues, it is determinative as the final "say" on what has been investigated within this inquiry. It has a finality in the sense of an absence of any appeal. This suggests that a high degree of fairness is owed.

3) *The importance of the decision to those affected*: The potential impact on a person's reputation may be serious and, as the Supreme Court sated in *Krever*, a good reputation may be a person's "most highly prized attribute." Here, Commissioner Gomery acknowledged that, for this reason, the inquiry's process had to be "scrupulously fair." This factor also warrants a high degree of procedural fairness.
4) *The legitimate expectations of the parties*: Chrétien had a legitimate expectation arising out of the Opening Statement assuring a "scrupulously fair" process. A similar expectation arose that the commissioner would comply with all of his rules of procedure and practice. This justified a strong expectation of a fair process.
5) *The tribunal's choices of procedure*: Here the commissioner is authorized to adopt whatever procedures "that he may consider expedient." This broad discretionary authority regarding procedure suggests the requirement of a lower standard of procedure. Again, this conclusion may not recognize the reality that such a broad authorization is subordinate to the requirements of the principle of fairness when reputation is at stake.

Justice Teitlebaum concluded that, considering all of these factors, Chrétien was entitled to a "high level of procedural fairness." This was not the same level as required at a judicial trial. However, it fell within the upper end of the spectrum required for administrative tribunals. This appears to be an appropriate assessment applicable to most investigative commissions of inquiry and, as suggested, an even higher standard may be justified when findings of misconduct involving reputation may be made.

One way of looking at the procedures required for a commission of inquiry to satisfy the principle of fairness is to start with the most complete protection possible. That then can be scrutinized by asking what is the underlying purpose of that protection. The great procedural flexibility of commissions of inquiry then permits a further exploration. How can that underlying purpose be achieved in the most simple, direct, and expeditious manner possible? If the underlying purpose is met, fairness will have been achieved. Examples were provided in Chapter 6, Section B(2) above of expeditious yet fair procedures adopted by recent commissions of inquiry that did not simply follow judicial models. A survey of the gamut of procedural protections that a commission must satisfy could be characterized as generally falling within three broad stages.

At the pre-hearing stage, the emphasis is on *notice* to the affected parties. This includes information about the purpose of the hearing that will be held, including the time and place. It must provide an adequate opportunity to prepare yet avoid undue delay. The Supreme Court of Canada recently discussed delay in the context of procedural fairness in *Blencoe*.[58] Notice of the purpose should convey the issues to be addressed and the potential consequences for the party. Adequate notice might also extend to disclosure of the evidence that will be called, including the names and anticipated testimony of witnesses. The disclosure of evidence as an aspect of the fairness of "notice" was discussed fully in *Kingsclear*.[59] Such disclosure could extend to the extreme of an opportunity to explore the actual evidence to be given by witnesses, as occurs during examination for discovery in civil procedure or the preliminary inquiry in criminal procedure. The necessity for such an opportunity under the principle of fairness was rejected recently in *Clifford*.[60]

At the hearing stage, the requirement of notice continues since a party is normally entitled to hear the evidence that may be adverse in interest, the "case to meet," before responding. But the emphasis here is on *participation*.[61] That may include the opportunity to be represented by legal counsel. It permits submissions to exclude evidence that may be irrelevant or marginally relevant but overly prejudicial. It includes the opportunity to test the evidence of witnesses who are adverse in interest through rigorous questioning. Fairness also extends to procedural rulings such as reasonable adjournments. Finally, there is an opportunity to make written and/or oral submissions as to how the evidence should

---

58 *Blencoe*, above note 11. Discussed in Section A(2), above in this chapter.

59 *Richards v. New Brunswick (Commission of Inquiry into the Kingsclear Youth Training Centre* (1996), 180 N.B.R. (2d) 1 (Q.B.) [*Kingsclear*]. Discussed in Chapter 6, Section B(2).

60 *Clifford v. Ontario (Attorney General)* (2008), 90 O.R. (3d) 742 (Div. Ct.) [*Clifford*]. See also Chapter 6, Section B(3) and Chapter 9, Section C(1).

61 See, generally, Chapter 6, Section C.

be assessed and the findings that should be made. If there is any ambiguity as to notice of potential adverse findings, they should be explained to the party so that further submissions and even the calling of further evidence may be directed to these.

At the post-hearing stage, the emphasis is on a *fair result*. A party is entitled to a report within a reasonable time, as an aspect of the "result." But this aspect of fairness also has implications for how the evidence is assessed and expressed, including the sufficiency of reasons and remaining within jurisdiction.[62]

## E. RULES OF PROCEDURE

The rules of practice and procedure[63] are not legally binding but may best be described as having the status of a "policy" adopted by a commission of inquiry to assist in carrying out its work. An important purpose is to explain in greater detail how it will satisfy the legal requirements imposed by the principle of fairness. These rules of procedure could generate increased legal requirements under the principle of fairness by creating a "legitimate expectation."[64]

In *Krever*, the Supreme Court of Canada described the procedural protections under the rules of that inquiry to be "extensive and exemplary." The Court provided the following examples of their "commendably wide range of protections":[65]

> all parties with standing and all witnesses appearing before the Inquiry had the right to counsel, both at the Inquiry and during their pre-testimony interviews;
>
> each party had the right to have its counsel cross-examine any witness who testified, and counsel for a witness who did not have standing was afforded the right to examine that witness;
>
> all parties had the right to apply to the Commissioner to have any witness called whom Commission counsel had elected not to call;

62 These aspects are discussed in Chapter 9, Sections A(3) and D(2).

63 Introduced in Chapter 5, Section C(4).

64 See the discussion of *Chrétien*, above note 18, in the previous section.

65 Above note 44 at para. 67.

all parties had the right to receive copies of all documents entered into evidence and the right to introduce their own documentary evidence;

all hearings would be held in public unless application was made to preserve the confidentiality of information; and

although evidence could be received by the Commissioner that might not be admissible in a court of law, the Commissioner would be mindful of the dangers of such evidence and, in particular, its possible effect on reputation.

These rules were made pursuant to the terms of reference authorizing the commissioner to adopt such procedures "as he may consider expedient for the proper conduct of the inquiry." Where such authorization is not contained in the terms of reference, it can be found in the wide latitude given by some inquiries Acts, the *Interpretation Act*, and judicial precedents.[66]

As occurred in the Krever Inquiry, it has become common practice for commissions of inquiry to circulate draft rules for input from the parties.[67] This participation could reduce any later complaints that legitimate expectations were created by implication since there was an opportunity to request they be specified. In *Krever*, the Court took such consultation into account in rejecting any objections to the process that had been adopted.[68] In the Arar Inquiry, Commissioner O'Connor noted that he had incorporated "many of the suggested changes" into the rules which he adopted. But he also drew a line: "A number of intervenors made submissions requesting very detailed Rules to address what they see as a possibility of unfairness arising from circumstances that may or may not occur. For the most part I have not revised the rules to reflect these types of concerns." Instead, they could be addressed if and when they arose under his overriding discretion to conduct the inquiry in a fair and expeditious manner. Such an overriding discretion is often explicitly included in the rules to authorize a departure from them, or their amendment, when fairness and expedition require. Of course, Commis-

66 Discussed in Section B(1), above in this chapter and Chapter 8, Section A.

67 See Chapter 5, Section C(4).

68 Above note 44.

sioner O'Connor also rejected some submissions that would result in him altering or expanding the terms of reference.[69]

These rules now frequently include a "deemed undertaking" of the parties such as these provisions from the Goudge Inquiry:

> All parties, witnesses and their counsel will be deemed to undertake to adhere to these Rules, and may raise any issue of non-compliance with the Commissioner.
>
> The Commissioner may deal with any non-compliance with these Rules as may be appropriate, including by revoking the standing of a party or imposing restrictions on a party or person in attendance at a hearing.

In imposing any such sanctions, a commissioner must be conscious of any statutory rights of participation. Section 3 of the Ontario Act provides that

> the conduct of and the procedure to be followed on an inquiry is under the control and direction of the commission . . . .

However, this authority is subject to the right of parties with a substantial and direct interest to call evidence and examine or cross-examine witnesses personally or by counsel. Any attempt to revoke standing would have to take into account any such statutory provisions and the principle of fairness as well as the rules of procedure.

Commissioner Goudge reported that "[c]ommissioners and their counsel often begin their work by reviewing the rules and procedures developed by preceding inquiries: they select those they think are most appropriate for their own purposes. That too is how my counsel and I spent our first weeks." An examination of the rules of practice and procedure adopted by previous commissions clearly demonstrates the value of past precedents. They also reflect an evolution in adopting new and expeditious approaches.[70] Yet there are a number of recurring issues that could be usefully addressed but seldom are. One area that could be included in the rules of procedure is a prohibition against the parties or counsel commenting publicly on the evidence presented at hearings.[71]

---

69 Ruling (15 June 2004).

70 See Chapter 6, Section B(2)

71 See Chapter 5, Section D(3)

Another would be to specify the procedure that will be followed in providing notices of potential misconduct and opportunities to respond.[72]

## F. PARALLEL PROCEEDINGS

In discussing the "legal framework" of commissions of inquiry, it is important to consider other legal processes that may be related to them by the same subject matter. For example, a civil action for damages may be commenced separately against parties to an inquiry into a tragedy such as the contamination of the blood supply. Professional disciplinary proceedings may have been commenced against police officers or lawyers who are also parties to an inquiry into a miscarriage of justice. A coroner may be investigating deaths that were caused by a disaster that is also the subject of a commission of inquiry. Human-rights complaints may have been filed in relation to a serious racial incident that is also the subject of an inquiry. But the relationship usually is most significant where an important party to a commission of inquiry is also the subject of a criminal investigation or already has been charged.

We have seen attempts by provincial governments to use the coercive powers of commissions of inquiry to investigate crimes in Chapter 3, Section E and the constitutional issues and prohibition were revisited in Section A(1), above in this chapter. Reference was also made to the potential application of the *Charter* to protect a criminal accused who may be called as a witness before a commission with a valid provincial purpose. But, apart from constitutional constraints, there is no legal barrier to prevent a number of these processes from proceeding simultaneously. For example, a police officer could be subject to criminal charges and disciplinary proceedings for professional misconduct in relation to a prisoner, whose death in custody is the subject of a coroner's investigation and whose family has sued the officer and the police force for damages arising out of the death. And the entire incident could be the subject of a commission of inquiry.

In this respect, there are two seminal authorities that have stood the test of time. The first is *Stickney v. Trusz*, in which then High Court Justice Thomas Zuber said:

---

72 This subject was raised in Chapter 6, Section B(3) and is discussed more fully in Chapter 9, Section B(2).

> [I]t is my opinion that the mere fact that there are both criminal and civil proceedings pending against a person arising out of the same facts is not a sufficient ground to qualify as an exceptional case in which the civil proceedings should be stayed. It is incumbent upon the applicant to show some specific or particular way in which he will be prejudiced in his criminal trial.[73]

Although the passage has been cited frequently and adopted by the Supreme Court of Canada, the judgment of Justice Lieff in the Divisional Court is highly recommended for its keen appreciation of scholarly analysis and exposition.[74] The second case is *R. v. Wigglesworth*,[75] which upheld the criminal prosecution of an RCMP officer for assault even though he had been convicted of a "major service offence" under the *Royal Canadian Mounted Police Act*[76] for the same assault. The disciplinary offence was characterized as regulatory, protective, and corrective rather than penal in nature. Therefore, the double-jeopardy protection in section 11(h) of the *Charter* did not apply.

The Westray Inquiry was faced with the problem of commencing its hearings when key witnesses, former managers of the mine, were facing charges under the *Occupational Health and Safety Act*.[77] They were also under criminal investigation. The Nova Scotia Court of Appeal upheld the constitutional validity of the inquiry by finding that its dominant purpose was related to the regulation of coal mining rather than criminal investigation. However, it held that the fair trial interests of the managers would be violated if their conduct became the subject of the inquiry hearings. This was true, whether or not the accused managers were required to testify, because of the inevitable news coverage of the hearings. The public hearings of the inquiry were stayed pending resolution of the existing charges, criminal investigation, and any consequent criminal charges. Before the case reached the Supreme Court, the charges under the above Act were quashed and two of the managers

---

73 *Stickney v. Trusz* (1973), 2 O.R. (2d) 469 at 472 (H.C.J.).

74 *Ibid.*, aff'd (1974), 3 O.R. (2d) 538 (Div. Ct.), aff'd (1974), 3 O.R. (2d) 539 (C.A.), leave to appeal to S.C.C. refused, [1974] S.C.R. xii.

75 [1987] 2 S.C.R. 541.

76 R.S.C. 1985 c. R-10.

77 R.S.N.S. 1989, c. 37, s. 5.

were charged with manslaughter and criminal negligence causing death under the *Criminal Code*.

The central concern of the Court of Appeal was the potential prejudice of jurors through adverse publicity if the hearings were allowed to proceed. It was expected that the accused would be tried by judge and jury. However, following argument before the Supreme Court, the accused elected trial by judge alone. As a result, the central issue had become moot and the majority in *Phillips* simply held that there no longer was any foundation for the stay of the inquiry's hearings.[78]

But Justice Cory[79] fully addressed the issues that were raised and provided a valuable exposition of the relationship between validly constituted commissions of inquiry and the rights of a criminal accused who may be called as a witness at the hearings of such an inquiry. Although his reasons are *obiter*, they are likely to be treated as authoritative unless and until they are modified by future rulings of the Supreme Court.

The first issue is the compellability of an accused person to testify at a commission of inquiry about the same subject matter that forms the basis for the criminal charges. The principle against self-incrimination protects compelled testimony at the criminal trial. Since the inquiry hearings are not a criminal trial, the starting point is that an accused is compellable, provided the inquiry serves a valid provincial purpose and is not a disguised criminal investigation.

The question then is whether that principle is indirectly offended by compelling such testimony in parallel proceedings. The principle against self-incrimination is now protected by sections 11(c) and 13 of the *Charter* together with the "residual protections" in section 7. Justice Cory based his analysis of this extended issue on the Court's decisions in *R. v. R.J.S.*[80] and *British Columbia (Securities Commission) v. Branch*.[81] This analysis requires a balancing of the rights of the individual accused against the interest of the state in receiving the compelled testimony. In receiving such testimony, all of the requirements of the *Charter* must be upheld. In

78 Above note 2. Sopinka writing for Lamer C.J. and La Forest, Sopinka, Gonthier, and McLachlin JJ. This case was discussed in Chapter 3, Section B(3) and Section A(2), above in this chapter.

79 *Ibid.*, writing for himself, Iacobucci, and Major JJ. L'Heureux-Dubé wrote separate reasons.

80 [1995] 1 S.C.R. 451 [*R.J.S.*].

81 [1995] 2 S.C.R. 3 [*Branch*].

this respect, the witness will be protected against any derivative use of the testimony. Moreover, if any other significant prejudice to a fair trial can be shown, the witness should not be compellable.

In the case of the Westray Inquiry, its purposes were of very significant public importance. The scale of the disaster, its widespread impact, and extensive publicity indicated an exceptional community interest. In this respect, access to the testimony of the two accused was crucial:

> First, to conduct the inquiry without full access to the information which will be provided by the testimony of the two most senior mine managers would severely impair the effectiveness of the Inquiry. More importantly, it would aggravate rather than assuage the public cynicism concerning the ability of government to protect industrial laborers adequately or to investigate the circumstances surrounding this tragedy properly.[82]

The threat to individual rights that had to be fairly balanced against this strong public interest was the crucial importance of a fair criminal trial.

Section 13 of the *Charter* greatly diminishes such a threat by providing "use immunity" to any testimony given at the inquiry hearings. This means that, while a witness may be compelled to testify, the testimony cannot be used to incriminate the witness in any subsequent proceedings (apart from a prosecution for giving false evidence). This protection extends beyond use of the actual testimony to exclude "derivative evidence." In *R.J.S.*, the test for such evidence derived from testimony was expressed as:

> evidence which could not have been obtained or the significance of which could not have been appreciated, but for the testimony of a witness.[83]

This exclusion falls under the residual protection against self-incrimination contained in section 7 of the *Charter*.

Another factor considered by Justice Cory in allowing the inquiry hearings to proceed was the role of the government in the circumstances of this case. It was responsible for both the criminal charges and the inquiry process. The government, itself, would run the risk of the criminal prosecution being jeopardized by the inquiry if excessive

---

82 Above note 2 at para. 91.

83 Above note 80 at 561, Iacobucci J.

publicity rendered a fair trial impossible or for other reasons. However, in oral argument before the Court, the attorney general:

> acknowledged the risk in proceeding immediately with a full inquiry. He nonetheless stated that his government considered the immediate resumption of the Inquiry to be of such overriding importance to the community that it is willing to accept the risk that the criminal prosecutions may be adversely affected or even stayed as a result of the Inquiry proceedings.[84]

Justice Cory concluded that the government was in a better position than the courts to weigh the "risks and benefits" of proceeding with the public hearings. He concluded that the accused managers were compellable witnesses before the inquiry but their status in relation to criminal charges also could be taken into account in relation to how they were treated as witnesses at the inquiry hearings.

Although the issue of the effect of pre-trial publicity upon potential jurors was moot, Justice Cory decided to address it. To begin with, there is a heavy burden in attempting to obtain *Charter* relief for an "anticipated breach":

> Because it is an exercise in speculation, it will be difficult for the applicant to demonstrate the high degree of probability that a *Charter* breach will occur which is required to warrant relief being granted.[85]

For this reason, the right to a fair trial is best determined by the trial judge at the trial itself. Similar considerations apply to imposing publicity bans, *in camera* hearings, and other protective measures upon a commissioner, who is in a better position to make such determinations.

Justice Cory disagreed with the view of the Court of Appeal that it would be possible and practical to conduct the inquiry hearings only with "full and unrestricted publicity." But even if this were the case, the prejudicial effects of the publication of the evidence would not be as serious as findings of misconduct in a final report. One approach might be to proceed with the hearings but delay publication of such a final report until the criminal proceedings have been completed. It must also be kept in mind that negative publicity, in itself, does not preclude a fair

84 Above note 2 at para. 98.

85 *Ibid.* at para. 112.

trial. A link must be demonstrated between such publicity and adverse consequences for the trial. There are also safeguards such as a change of venue, jury selection, the juror's oath, and the innate goodwill and good sense of jurors.

*Phillips* gives broad latitude to commissions of inquiry to compel testimony even though the witness may be facing criminal charges. It is now "standard" for terms of reference to preclude findings of criminal or civil liability.[86] The Goudge Inquiry was prohibited from reporting on any specific cases "that are, have been, or may be subject to a criminal investigation or proceeding." The Air India Inquiry was instructed not to jeopardize "any ongoing criminal investigation or proceeding." Even where such guidance is not provided in the terms of reference, commissioners should conduct inquiries in a manner that is sensitive to parallel processes.

In the Gomery Inquiry, commission counsel undertook not to adduce evidence of the government contracts that were the subject of criminal charges. As suggested in *Phillips*, the questioning of witnesses who are also subject to criminal charges should be carefully circumscribed to remain within the legitimate purpose of the inquiry.

Publication bans or *in camera* hearings may be appropriate for some aspects of such testimony. In some circumstances, it may be possible to schedule the testimony of such witnesses only after the completion of the criminal proceedings.

The terms of reference for the Driskell Inquiry directly linked it to other legal processes by requiring the commissioner

> [t]o give advice about whether the conduct of Crown Counsel or members of the Winnipeg Police Service should be referred to the Law Society of Manitoba, or to the Law Enforcement Review Agency or an appropriate independent police service, for review and possible investigation by those bodies.

Even without such an explicit mandate, it would be open to most commissioners to make recommendations along these lines in their reports. But what of cooperation with parallel processes during the course of an inquiry?

86 Chapter 3, Section C(3) and see, generally, Chapter 3, Section E.

The late Justice Archie Campbell strongly warned against "mixing" investigations:

> It often happens, when a problem is immense enough to require an inquiry, that there are other investigations underway of the same problem. During the Bernardo review there were many parallel reviews, debriefings, and investigations . . . . It was important not to mix up the different investigations conducted for different purposes, particularly the ongoing criminal investigation by the OPP. It was important to maintain a completely arm's-length relationship with the other investigations, particularly the criminal investigation of Bernardo's lawyer. It was also important to avoid any suggestion that information gathered for one purpose was improperly shared or used for another purposes. The short-term gain of sharing information or pooling investigative results is not worth the long-term pain of defending against allegations of improper sharing or use of information.[87]

This approach was probably justified in the *Bernardo* case, which was highly volatile, complex, and involved many potential findings of misconduct. In contrast, the Westray Inquiry worked in close cooperation with the RCMP in gathering evidence, as described in *Phillips*:

> The staff indexed and summarized all the documents and provided the indices and summaries to the RCMP. The police in turn used these materials to obtain search warrants for the documents in the Commissioner's possession. These warrants were executed in September and December of 1992. The RCMP in turn provided the Commissioner with witness statements taken during the police investigation and cooperated with him in the development of a plan to re-enter the mine to gather evidence.[88]

Justice Cory found no "unwelcome complicity" in this cooperation but rather deemed it to be efficient, sensible, and necessary to deal with the "enormous investigative tasks required." In "Lessons from Walkerton," Allan Manson and David Mullan describe the cooperation between the commissioner and the coroner's process:

---

87 "The Bernardo Investigation Review" in Manson & Mullan, eds., above note 37 at 394–95.

88 Above note 2 at para. 44.

> Justice O'Connor recognized the parallel nature of much of his work and that of the Coroner's Office. While the coroner was required to investigate the deaths, whether to conduct a formal inquest was a discretionary decision. Not only was the Office of the Chief Coroner designated as a party with standing, but also arrangements were made for ongoing consultation at various stages of the process including a general discussion of the substance of the Commission's conclusions in advance of publication of the report.[89]

Where both bodies have statutory responsibility for aspects of the same events, such cooperation is eminently desirable but must be exercised with due regard for the duty of fairness to any persons who might be affected.

## G. INTERIM JUDICIAL REVIEW

Judicial review is mentioned here as the vehicle for patrolling and enforcing the boundaries of the legal framework. It may be invoked by the parties on an interim basis, during the course of the inquiry proceedings. Or it may be brought after the commission has completed its work, to attack findings in the final report, as discussed in Chapter 9. The standard of review is deferential to a commissioner's determination of the relevance of evidence but strict (correctness) in the determination of jurisdiction.[90] The standard for applying the principle of fairness is also correctness.[91] Both *Cornwall* and *Chrétien* have already been discussed with respect to their categories.

The Ontario Court of Appeal provided an excellent exposition of the analysis of the appropriate standard of judicial review in *Episcopal*.[92] The commissioner in the Cornwall Inquiry had declined to order a publication ban and the court had to determine whether to apply the deferen-

---

89 Allan Manson & David Mullan, "Lessons from Walkerton" in Manson & Mullan, eds., above note 37 at 507.

90 Section C, note 39, above in this chapter.

91 Section D(2), note 55, above in this chapter.

92 *Episcopal Corporation of the Diocese of Alexandria-Cornwall v. Cornwall Public Inquiry*, 2007 ONCA 20 [*Episcopal*], MacPherson and Blair JJ.A. agreeing. Although *Episcopal* preceded the decision in *Dunsmuir*, above note 55, it appears to be perfectly compatible with it. See Chapter 9, Section D(2).

tial standard of reasonableness or the strict standard of correctness. In rendering the judgment of the court, Justice Robert Sharpe referred to the need for a "pragmatic and functional" balancing of the four factors established by the Supreme Court in *Pushpanathan*,[93] namely:

- whether there was a right of appeal or privative clause;
- the expertise of the tribunal;
- the purpose of the legislation in general and the particular provision;
- the nature of the issue before the tribunal.

The absence of an appeal or privative clause in the Ontario Act rendered this first factor neutral.

The question of expertise was less relevant when dealing with specialized boards or tribunals but Justice Sharpe identified aspects that warranted deference. These included the commissioner's familiarity with his mandate, operations, and the community. He was familiar with the "tone and quality of the media's coverage" and already had made rulings on requests for publication bans and similar relief. These indicia suggest it is appropriate to take into account expertise not necessarily "brought to the table" at the outset but acquired by becoming immersed in the terms of reference and the subject matter and understanding the impact of the inquiry on the community.

Justice Sharpe's characterization of the general legislation in the third factor is particularly helpful. It is obvious that "legislation" encompasses the terms of reference in this respect:

> This Commission is not asked to resolve a bi-polar dispute over a specific legal or factual issue. The Commissioner is not entitled to make findings of criminal or civil liability. He is faced, rather, with a broad issue of policy affecting the public at large. His mandate concerns, in the words adopted in *Pushpanathan, supra*, a "polycentric issue" involving "a large number of interlocking and interacting interests and consideration." In formulating his recommendations, the Commissioner will be required to take into account a wide variety of factors and considerations of a kind not ordinarily encountered by a court of law.[94]

---

93 *Pushpanathan v. Canada (Minister of Citizenship and Immigration*, [1998] 1 S.C.R. 982 [*Pushpanathan*].

94 *Episcopal*, above note 92 at para. 26.

The particular provision here was section 3 of the Ontario Act that requires all hearings to be in public with limited exceptions. The terms of reference also required a discretionary balancing of the general principle of openness against specific privacy interests. Both aspects of this third factor warranted the deferential standard of reasonableness.

The fourth factor was the specific issue of whether or not to order a publication ban. This required a "discretionary balancing exercise" under the test established by the Supreme Court.[95] Again, this feature supported a more deferential standard than the one of correctness, leading to the conclusion that the standard of review was simply reasonableness. This in turn required only a reasonable line of analysis that proceeded from the evidence to the tribunal's conclusion and a tenable explanation for that conclusion that could withstand "a somewhat probing scrutiny."[96] The subsequent Supreme Court decision in *Dunsmuir*[97] does not diminish the value of *Episcopal* as a precedent on this issue.

The courts appear generally reluctant to interfere with a commission's work while it is proceeding. In *Krever*, a number of parties sought to quash notices of potential findings of misconduct but Justice Cory stated:

> As a general rule, a challenge such as this should not be brought before the publication of the report, unless there are reasonable grounds to believe that the Commissioner is likely to exceed his or her jurisdiction.[98]

He refused to speculate as to the possible findings the commissioner might make and characterized the challenges as premature. One commentator expressed regret that leave to appeal had even been granted by the Supreme Court. This delayed the inquiry by a further nine months, causing hardship for the victims of the contaminated blood, who were dying before their compensation could be addressed.[99]

---

95 In *Dagenais v. Canadian Broadcasting Corp.*, [1994] 3 S.C.R. 835 [*Dagenais*] and *R. v. Mentuck*, [2001] 3 S.C.R. 442 [*Mentuck*]. Discussed in Chapter 8, Section D.

96 *Law Society of New Brunswick v. Ryan*, [2003] 1 S.C.R. 247 at para. 55.

97 Above note 55. See discussion in Chapter 9, Section D(2).

98 *Krever*, above note 44 at para. 60.

99 Andrew J. Roman, "Public Inquiries: A Brief Review of the Recent Cases Involving Contaminated Blood and the Canadian Armed Forces in Somalia" (1998) 3 Admin. L.R. (3d) 319.

In *Consortium*, the Supreme Court gave the commissioner some latitude in proceeding without providing detailed notice of the issues to the parties:

> If the municipality had a sufficient grip on the relevant facts to give detailed particulars there might be no need for an inquiry . . . . Aspects of procedural fairness, such as the need for particulars, should not defeat an inquiry at the outset . . . the inquiry should be allowed to proceed, and procedural objections dealt with at a later stage . . . .[100]

This was subject to a situation where a mandate is so unclear that "a fair inquiry simply cannot be had." The Court also gave short shrift to another argument based on procedural fairness. The commissioner had explained the manner in which he would proceed with the hearings even though a judicial-review application had been filed. The parties did not request an adjournment but later attempted to characterize the commissioner's explanation of how he would proceed as a ruling that denied them fairness. Justice Binnie would have none of it:

> In the absence of any notification that an adjournment would be sought, the Commissioner cannot be faulted for outlining his proposal to proceed with the inquiry in an expeditious way, nor can he be faulted for declining to consider a possible adjournment in circumstances where the appellants themselves refused, in apparent umbrage, or for tactical reasons, to make submissions in support of that relief.[101]

The parties were not denied a hearing and the commissioner's conduct did not disclose any bias.

Following Commissioner Gomery's press interviews prior to the Christmas break in 2004, counsel for Jean Chrétien brought a motion for him to recuse himself as commissioner. On 1 February 2005 he dismissed this motion. Chrétien then sought judicial review of this decision but discontinued the application before it was heard. However, counsel for Gomery argued that it should proceed. The prothonotary agreed with Chrétien that he had followed the proper course in withdrawing the application for judicial review. An allegation of bias must be raised at the first reasonable opportunity. But if the decision maker refuses to recuse himself, judicial

---

100 Above note 15 at para. 30.

101 *Ibid*. at para. 56.

review should ordinarily await the final decision, which, in this case, was the issuing of the report. Once the report was issued, judicial review proceeded and was successful, although that decision is under appeal.[102]

In some circumstances, a commissioner may be in a position to make an initial ruling on the constitutionality of aspects of the terms of reference. A statutory tribunal may be given jurisdiction to consider and rule on *Charter* issues. However, a formal declaration of the invalidity of an enabling statute can be made only by a court. While such a situation would be rare, a commissioner could decide that one of the terms of reference contravened the *Charter*. Since these terms have legal status, they could be subject to review under section 52 of the *Charter*, and the offending term simply could be ignored.[103]

The *Inquiries Act* contains no reference to judicial review and that is true of most of the provincial and the territorial Acts. In these jurisdictions, judicial review simply proceeds in the same manner as review of any administrative tribunals. At the federal level, such judicial review is governed by the *Federal Courts Act*.[104]

Section 6(1) of the Ontario Act authorizes the commission to "state a case in writing to the Divisional Court" either on its own initiative or at the request of "a person affected." If the commissioner declines, the court may direct the commission to do so, under section 6(2). Under section 6(3), the court then "shall hear and determine in a summary manner the question raised." Under section 6(4), the commission's proceedings are stayed pending the court's decision, but only with respect to the subject matter before the court. The earlier Ontario legislation had authorized a case to be stated as to the "validity of any decision, order, direction or other act of a commissioner." But it is now clearly established that the court's role is confined to ensuring the commission does not exceed its jurisdiction.[105]

---

102 Chapter 5, Section B(3).

103 *Nova Scotia (Workers Compensation Board) v. Martin and Laseur*, [2003] 2 S.C.R. 504, overruling *Cooper v. Canada (Canadian Human Rights Commission)*, [1996] 3 S.C.R. 854. See, generally, the recent discussion and authorities cited in *Kelly v. Ontario* (2008), 91 O.R. (3d) 100 (S.C.J.).

104 R.S.C. 1985, c. F-7.

105 Above note 19 at paras. 18–21. This conclusion does not restrict judicial review on other grounds as illustrated by the discussion of *Episcopal* above.

Section 95(1) of the Manitoba Act provides for a stated case to the Court of Appeal and retains the language of the earlier Ontario legislation. Such review appears to extend well beyond the supervision of jurisdiction. Section 95(3) also goes further than Ontario by providing that "no further proceedings shall be taken by the commission" pending the court's decision. This prohibition is not restricted to the subject matter of the stated case. Section 15(1) of the Newfoundland and Labrador Act authorizes a commission to apply to the Trial Division for direction on a question of law or jurisdiction. Section 15(2) provides that there is no right of appeal from a decision made by the Trial Division judge.

CHAPTER EIGHT

# *The Conduct of Hearings*

## A. CONTROLLING PROCEEDINGS

This chapter is a more specific response to the criticism that the hearings conducted by commissions of inquiry sometimes appear to be "out of control." This probably was the perception of the Canadian government when it shut down the Somalia Inquiry and of the Ontario government when it imposed a comparable time deadline on the Cornwall Inquiry. Reference was made to the "circus" atmosphere ascribed to some inquiries and to the frustrations expressed by one commissioner.[1] He spoke of the "bitter confrontational approach" some parties took to each other as they were "at each other's throats." He felt the inquiry was "forced . . . to chase down many blind alleys."

The following passage was quoted in Chapter 1: "At trials, strict rules of evidence exclude unreliable sources of information, such as hearsay, speculation, or opinion evidence by non-experts. At public inquiries, witnesses are relatively free to trash the reputation of others in front of a large television audience."[2] These comments may describe how some hearings have unfolded in the past. They are not an accurate description of how hearings should be conducted.

---

1 See Chapter 5, Section D(1).

2 Bryan Schwartz, "Public Inquiries" in Allan Manson & David Mullan, eds., *Commissions of Inquiry, Praise or Reappraise?* (Toronto: Irwin Law, 2003) at 445.

There are a number of reasons why a commission of inquiry may fail to control its hearings. The terms of reference may be broad and not adequately broken down into manageable subjects for the purpose of the hearings.[3] A commissioner who resolves to "hear everything" may allow the proceedings to drift into aimless meandering. Since the process is not adversarial, there are no applicable rules of civil procedure and the strict rules of criminal evidence do not apply. At the same time, there often are parties who are adverse in interest, so that adversarial attitudes and instincts may lurk beneath the surface. Most commissions adopt their own rules of procedure but these seldom provide much assistance to the commissioner in controlling the proceedings. The challenge is to impose discipline on the hearings both in structure and in execution. The commissions' hearings counsel has an important role to play in this respect but ultimately the responsibility lies with the commissioner.

Commissions of inquiry have broad powers to conduct and control their proceedings. Section 3 of the Ontario Act states:

> the conduct of and procedures to be followed on an inquiry is under the control and direction of the commission conducting the inquiry.

The Act specifically states that this authority is subject to the rights of parties and the general requirement that hearings be open to the public. Most Acts do not have comparable provisions but section 5 of the Nova Scotia Act provides:

> The commissioner or commissioners shall have the same power to enforce the attendance of persons as witnesses and to compel them to give evidence and produce documents and things as is vested in the Supreme Court or a judge thereof in civil cases, and the same privileges and immunities as a judge of the Supreme Court.

Justice Cory interpreted this provision as suggesting that:

> commissions of inquiry have a general power to control their proceedings and are not tied to a narrow interpretation of the enabling statute.[4]

---

3 Consider the unfortunate consequences for the Erebus Inquiry discussed in Chapter 6, Section B(3).

4 *Phillips v. Nova Scotia (Commission of Inquiry into the Westray Mine Tragedy)* [1995] 2 S.C.R. 97 at para. 174 [*Phillips*].

Since this general power probably arises out of the power to compel testimony and production, it is equally applicable to all of these Acts. In any event, Justice Cory added that the "nature and purpose of public inquiries" required the courts "to give a generous interpretation" to the general power of commissioners to control their proceedings.[5] In addition to the statutory authority, the terms of reference may authorize the commissioner "to adopt any procedures and methods that he may consider expedient for the proper conduct of the inquiry." This phrase has become standard in recent federal terms of reference.

Commissions of inquiry are not bound by the rules of evidence, with some exceptions. For example, section 11 of the Ontario Act provides:

> Nothing is admissible in evidence at an inquiry that would be inadmissible in a court by reason of any privilege under the law of evidence.

Exclusion based on privilege is canvassed in Section E below.

However, the inapplicability of most rules of evidence does not mean that "anything goes." A commission's hearings are still restricted in scope by relevance to the terms of reference. It is not able "to 'define its own terms of reference under the guise of evidential rulings or admissibility' and consequently to govern its jurisdiction."[6] The Ontario Court of Appeal added that to reject reasonably relevant evidence or to accept evidence that is not reasonably relevant is jurisdictional error.

A commission of inquiry is also bound by the principle of fairness when considering evidentiary issues. The rejection of relevant evidence may have such an impact on the fairness of the proceeding as to constitute a breach of that principle.[7] Although many specific rules of evidence are not binding, they may provide a helpful frame of reference for assessing fairness in a particular situation. Assessing the admissibil-

---

5 *Ibid.* at para. 175.

6 *Bortolotti v. Ontario (Ministry of Housing)* (1977), 76 D.L.R. (3d) 408 at 417 (Ont. C.A.) quoting Morden J. in *Re Royal Commission into Metropolitan Toronto Police Practices and Ashton* (1975), 64 D.L.R. (3d) 477 at 485 (Div. Ct.) [*Ashton*].

7 *Université de Québec à Trois Rivières v. Larocque*, [1993] 1 S.C.R. 471 at 491, Lamer C.J. writing for himself and La Forest, Gonthier, and Iacobucci JJ., L'Heureux-Dubé J. delivering separate reasons. Here the arbitrator lost jurisdiction in spite of a very broad private clause. See also *Bond v. New Brunswick (Board of Management)* (1992), 95 D.L.R. (4th) 733 (N.B.C.A.), where an arbitrator lost jurisdiction by relying on hearsay for a serious finding of misconduct.

ity of evidence from the perspective of evidentiary principles provides some structure for determining fairness.[8]

If a commissioner is faced with evidence that is not admissible according to an exclusionary rule of evidence, that should be a warning that the evidence might be unreliable to some degree. This warrants the further examination as to whether it would be unfair to receive that evidence. And that examination must take into account the context in which the evidence is tendered. If it is submitted in support of an allegation of serious misconduct against an individual, then special care must be given as to whether or not to receive it.

Most exclusionary rules are based on the suspicion that the human processes of drawing conclusions from what one hears or sees are often unreliable. Unlike a judge, a commissioner is able to look beyond the "rule" itself and apply the underlying "rationale" for the rule. For example, hearsay evidence is excluded as a rule. The rationale for the rule is that the statement may not have been given under formal circumstances and the party affected by the evidence has no opportunity to cross-examine the maker of the statement. If a commissioner receives an objection to relevant hearsay evidence, she does not merely apply the hearsay exclusionary rule. She must ask further: "Even though it is hearsay, why is it unfair to consider this evidence in the circumstances before us?" The circumstances in which the statement was made might strongly support its reliability and cross-examination might serve little value in the actual context. Indeed, the courts have been moving to a more "principled" approach towards admitting hearsay evidence, generally, but they still do not simply ask the direct question as to whether it is fair to consider the evidence.

A distinction must also be drawn between the admissibility of evidence and the weight to be given to it. A commissioner may simply decide to receive the evidence but take any objections into account when deciding what, if any, weight to give it. Such an approach may help to expedite the proceedings rather than spending time on the issue of admissibility. But it may also introduce a lack of rigour that other parties may try to exploit. It also might be unfair to individual reputations if the evidence is highly critical but also unreliable. Often such matters can be

---

8 See, generally, Ed Ratushny, "Rules of Evidence and Procedural Problems before Administrative Tribunals" (1989) 2 Can. J. Admin. L. & Prac. 157.

sorted out by hearings counsel prior to the hearing but they may have to be resolved by the commissioner and may arise spontaneously during the hearing itself.

Reference has been made to facilitating the presentation of evidence in various ways before commissions of inquiry.[9] It is not always necessary to rely on traditional witness testimony and primary documents, particularly where potential findings of misconduct are not at stake. Many of the approaches discussed in Chapter 6 would not be acceptable at a trial but, in their inquiry context, they were expeditious, effective, and accepted by the parties. In such circumstances, the principle of fairness was not a concern. Another example is provided in a ruling from the Arar Inquiry. Two of the parties sought to file chronologies of events related to their detention in Syria as part of the inquiry's public record. They were not submitted as proof of the facts they set out nor of any pattern of complicity. Rather, they were to be background or contextual information relevant to the parties' reputational interests. They might also help the commissioner in making recommendations. They were accepted as exhibits but marked as "for reference purposes only" and not for proof of the truth of their contents. This allowed the parties to refer to the chronologies in their submissions and the commissioner to do so in his report if he so decided.[10]

## B. COMPELLING TESTIMONY AND PRODUCTION

The central feature of each commission of inquiry is its power to compel the testimony of witnesses and the production of documents related to its terms of reference. The *Inquiries Act* provides:

> 4. The commissioners have the power of summoning before them any witnesses, and of requiring them to
> (a) give evidence, orally or in writing, and on oath or, if they are persons entitled to affirm in civil matters on solemn affirmation; and
> (b) produce such documents and things as the commissioners deem requisite to the full investigation of the matters into which they are appointed to examine.

9 Discussed in Chapter 6, Section B(2)(c).

10 Arar Inquiry, Rulings (7 September 2005).

> 5. The commissioners have the same power to enforce the attendance of witnesses and to compel them to give evidence as is vested in any court of record in civil cases.

No distinction is made or special notice required for a witness who also may be a party and against whom findings of misconduct might be made. Notice of potential adverse findings usually occurs informally at first and then culminates in a formal notice as required under section 13 of the Act.

What is the enforcement power of "any court of record in civil cases"? In the absence of specific language granting the power of a superior court, a court of record is deemed to be an inferior court. This means that the power to punish for contempt is limited to contempt "in the face of the tribunal." This would enable a commissioner to fine or imprison (or both) a witness who attends but refuses to testify. Does this power extend to a witness who refuses to attend? In *Diamond*, the Ontario Court of Appeal stated that it does.[11] The authorities are not entirely clear but *Diamond* appears to have been approved by the Supreme Court of Canada.[12] Moreover, it would make little sense to authorize a commissioner to compel testimony but not attendance for the purpose of giving that testimony.

The provincial and territorial Acts contain identical or analogous provisions. The Manitoba and New Brunswick Acts specifically authorize the commissioner to issue a warrant and commit the uncooperative witness to jail. British Columbia, Newfoundland, and Ontario authorize the commissioner, in effect, to refer the contempt issue to the courts. There are a number of variations in the Acts. The British Columbia Act is the only one that provides for pre-hearing "disclosure." However, a witness who refuses to be interviewed probably could be compelled to testify prior to the hearing for that purpose.[13]

A commissioner will not always seek to punish a recalcitrant witness. There may be compassionate reasons to decide not to call a witness even

---

11 *Re Diamond and Ontario Municipal Board*, [1962] O.R. 328 at 332 [*Diamond*].

12 *Canadian Broadcasting Corp. et al. v. Quebec Police Commission*, [1979] 2 S.C.R. 618. See also Harry R. Johnson, *Federal Part I Commissions of Inquiry: A Study of Certain of Their Rights, Obligations and Privileges* (LL.M. Thesis , University of Ottawa, 1984) [unpublished].

13 See Chapter 6, Section B(3).

though the potential testimony is highly relevant. Reference was made to the "fact finder" appointed by Commissioner O'Connor in the Arar Inquiry.[14] In a related ruling, he said that one potential witness refused to cooperate: "El Maati alleges that he was tortured in Syria. I do not intend, nor have I been asked, to compel anyone who alleges torture to give evidence or otherwise become involved in this Inquiry. Thus, I will not direct the fact-finder to include Mr. El Maati in his investigation."[15] In the same ruling, he deferred the decision whether Arar should be compelled to testify until the release of the commission's interim report. This would allow him to receive disclosure of the maximum amount of information about the matters about which he could testify, prior to his potential testimony.

On the other hand, the commissioner may find it necessary to take enforcement proceedings, either to attempt to force the witness to testify or to punish the witness as a deterrent to others. The Ontario Act provides that a commission may require any person by summons to give evidence under oath or affirmation. Where, without lawful excuse, the person refuses to attend, take an oath, or make an affirmation or to answer any question, the commission may state a case to the Divisional Court. The court may then "punish or take steps for the punishment" of the witness as if the witness were in contempt of court.

Perry Dunlop is a former police officer who refused to testify before the Cornwall Inquiry. He had played a central role in the subject matter of the inquiry. He was the initial "whistle-blower," who interviewed alleged victims and collected information on an alleged conspiracy to obstruct justice in the original police investigation. He attended at the hearings and provided a "Will State" document outlining his evidence. However, he refused to answer questions on the basis that he had no faith in the justice system or the commission of inquiry. He claimed that the process was a cover-up and that he would be made a scapegoat. He made a number of these allegations in media interviews after having ample opportunities to testify and refusing to reconsider his position.

The Ontario Divisional Court found him guilty of civil contempt on 6 December 2007 and ordered him to attend before the commission on 14 January 2008 to testify. Sentencing for the civil contempt was postponed, presumably to take into account whether he would testify on

---

14 See Chapter 6, Section A(4).

15 Arar Inquiry, Rulings (9 May 2005).

that date. The refusal to testify, in itself, constituted the civil contempt. Criminal contempt occurs when the conduct tends to interfere with the due course of justice or bring the administration of justice into scorn. In this case, Dunlop defied the court order through continued media interviews and orchestrated publicity. On 5 March 2008 the court imprisoned him for six months for the civil contempt. If he purged his contempt by testifying during that period, he could apply for immediate release from custody. If not, upon completion of his sentence, he would be brought before the court again for sentencing on the criminal contempt. On 19 September 2008, after serving the full six months, he was sentenced to an additional thirty days for the criminal contempt. The court stated that the seriousness of his disobedience was not diminished because the proceedings were before a commission of inquiry rather than a court.[16]

The commissioner may have to make a ruling on the capacity of a witness to testify. This occurred in the Morin Inquiry when a former police sergeant claimed he was too ill to be called as a witness. His medical records were available but Commission Kaufman "considered his potential testimony to be of sufficient importance to have an independent expert examine him and provide the Commission with an assessment of his capability to appear as a witness." The expert reported that neither he nor the treating cardiologist "can be certain whether or not Mr. Michalowsky would suffer an acute myocardial ischemic event while testifying. There is evidence that is likely because he is a very anxious man who is quite depressed and who has myocardial ischemia with very little provocation." Counsel for Morin argued that the witness should be compelled to testify, referring to an earlier witness's opinion that he was "faking" and to the timing of the assertions of illness. The commissioner ruled that this was simply "not a risk we can impose" and declined to compel the testimony.[17]

It is usually not necessary for parties granted standing to be served with a summons or subpoena unless they are not represented by counsel. Other witnesses normally should receive a summons or subpoena.

---

16 *Cornwall Public Inquiry v. Dunlop*, 2008 CanLII 10382 (Ont. S.C.J.); *Cornwall Public Inquiry v. Dunlop*, 2008 CanLII 47729 (Ont. Div. Ct.), Ferrier and Swinton JJ.

17 Morin Inquiry, "Inquiry Ruling on Mr. Michalowsky's Appearance as a Witness before This Commission," Appendix O.

Broad latitude is given to compel the testimony of a person charged with a criminal offence, provided there is a legitimate purpose beyond simply investigating the offence in question.[18] Judges are immune from compelled testimony about their judicial conduct.[19] Ministers of the Crown and even government officials may be protected by Crown immunity although voluntary attendance may be a practical necessity. But the compellability of witnesses must also take into account constitutional limitations.

A witness called before the Somalia Inquiry had full standing and participation through counsel at the hearings. He challenged his compellability as a witness without "full disclosure of the issues with which he would be faced as a witness, and the facts and evidence and specific documents with which he is to be confronted at hearings before the Commission." The reviewing court simply held that "reasonable disclosure" had been provided and that further detail and particulars were not required prior to testifying.[20] Another witness declined to testify before the Niagara Inquiry unless he received standing and the assistance of counsel. The Ontario Divisional Court held that, as a mere witness, he faced no adverse findings and was required to testify.[21]

When a witness refuses to testify, it is reasonable to take that position into account when making findings. The commissioner in the Westray Inquiry stated his intention, at the end of the hearings, to draw adverse inferences against such witnesses.[22] It would be better to express such intentions in neutral terms. In other words, the commissioner should draw any inferences that are reasonable in the circumstances and not necessarily "adverse" inferences. Full notice of potential adverse findings also should be given, even if the person affected is not a party or witness. For example, section 13 of the *Inquiries Act* applies to "any person" and the principle of fairness would require such notice in any event. It is better to address potentially "adverse" findings in this more specific context than as a general conclusion. Otherwise, that could be

---

18 See Chapter 7, Section F.

19 See Chapter 7, Section A(2).

20 *Labbé v. Canada (Commission of Inquiry into the Deployment of Canadian Forces in Somalia—Létourneau Commission)* (1997), 146 D.L.R. (4th) 180 (F.C.T.D.), MacKay J.

21 *Royal Commission (Niagara Regional Police Force Inquiry) v. DeMarco* (1990), 36 O.A.C. 387 (Div. Ct.).

22 Documented in Wayne Mackay & Monica G. McQueen, "Public Inquiries and the Legality of Blaming" in Manson & Mullan, eds., above note 2 at 264 n. 36.

interpreted as a "punishment" for not testifying rather than a reasonable inference to be drawn from the facts and circumstances.

Section 4(1) of the *Inquiries Act* gives commissioners authority to require production of such documents as they "deem requisite to the full investigation" of the matters described in their terms of reference. This is a broad and subjective discretion that is probably reviewable only when exercised in bad faith. The production of documents, to a large extent, will occur through requests and dialogue at the pre-hearing stage. Claims of privilege may be settled informally by hearings counsel and, if necessary, resolved by adjudication, as discussed in Chapter 6.

Part II of the *Inquiries Act*, which is restricted to "departmental investigations," authorizes a commissioner to enter into any public premises to examine documents and records. Some of the provincial Acts have similar powers but are restricted in various ways. The Manitoba Act authorizes the entry into public or private premises for a "view." British Columbia authorizes the inspection and copying of records in a public place but requires a court warrant for doing so in a "private place." Newfoundland authorizes entry and copying for both public and private premises. A court warrant also may be obtained for that purpose. Part III powers under the Ontario Act must be specifically included in the terms of reference. Where they are, the commissioner may obtain a search warrant for public or private premises and for the removal of documents. The Alberta Act also requires that the "entry" power in section 7 be specified in the terms of reference. Where it is, and where the commissioner is also a superior court judge, she may issue an order to enter and remove documents. If section 7 is applicable but the commissioner is not a superior court judge, she must apply to such a judge for such an order. These powers are seldom invoked but may be helpful in encouraging cooperation.

## C. QUESTIONING WITNESSES

### 1) Introduction

The manner in which witnesses are questioned is probably the most important factor in conveying to the public how effectively the hearings are being conducted. Questioning must be substantive in its relevance to the terms of reference. It must be focused in getting to the point and then moving on to the next point. It also must be fair to the witnesses. Hearings counsel can contribute greatly to the effectiveness of the hearings by setting the stage. This includes full exploration of the evidence in advance and preparation of the witnesses and other counsel through disclosure.

Where there are many counsel, their roles should be allocated in advance, including the order in which they will question, if at all. Their questions should be confined to the interests of their clients on which their standing was based. Where a number of counsel represent the same interest, only one of them should question a particular witness.[23] Such questioning might be rotated among those counsel for future witnesses. Allowing every counsel automatically to question each witness leads, inevitably, to a great loss of time, focus, and momentum.

Hearings counsel can also contribute to a spirit of cooperation among counsel through complete openness and fairness. Frequent meetings, especially among those opposed in interest, can often lead to agreements as to matters that need not be explored or that can be adequately explored in a limited way. Counsel should come to understand that there is little to be gained for their clients by being "at each other's throats."

But the tone ultimately must be set by the commissioner, in the hearing room. Complete civility must be demanded of counsel. A factual basis may have to be established for a potential finding of misconduct. The consequences for the affected party are to be found in such a finding itself, however, and not through opposing counsel berating the witness about that conduct. Conducting hearings in a business-like manner requires great concentration on the subject matter in order to make appropriate rulings. As in conducting trials, attempts at humour are seldom helpful. They may invite similar attempts by counsel and may detract from the perceived seriousness of the task at hand.

The topics that follow are familiar to lawyers and judges but a review of them, by both the commissioner and counsel, prior to the hearings may be helpful as a "refresher." They are the evidentiary issues that arise most frequently in the examination and cross-examination of witnesses. While a commissioner has flexibility in the extent to which these rules are applied, having them in mind can contribute to the fair and expeditious conduct of hearings. Where testimony relates to issues of crucial

---

23 See also Chapter 5, Section C(3) and Chapter 6, Section B(3).

importance to the commissioner's mandate, and particularly where potential findings of misconduct are engaged, a stricter assessment of the relevance and fairness of receiving evidence should occur. Issues related to legal privilege are discussed separately in Section E, below in this chapter.

### 2) Relevance and Repetition

The foremost requirement in conducting hearings is to ensure that the evidence adduced is relevant to the terms of reference. Does it relate to some issue arising out of those terms and does it help to reach some conclusion about that issue? This is not a legal question but must be answered simply on the basis of logic and common sense. The legal standard for judicial review is "reasonably" relevant,[24] but that seems inherent in the word "relevant" itself. Still, it is a reminder that it does not mean remotely relevant or potentially relevant through speculation. It may be tempting at the early stages of hearings to be lax in this respect. But, if hearings counsel has done the necessary preparation in advance to define the issues, the standard of relevance can be strictly applied from the outset.

In this respect, the concept of "proportionality" may also be helpful. Even though the proposed line of questioning can be "associated" with an issue, to what extent does it really assist in understanding or resolving the issue? If it contributes only marginally and there is better evidence to serve the same purpose, it should be avoided.

Repetition may occur, not only by many counsel asking the same witness the same questions, but also by one counsel asking the same witness the same questions. This sometimes is more difficult to control and hearings counsel may be reluctant to object out of concern for causing even further delay. This often is a situation that invites direct intervention by the commissioner but it requires concentration and focus. The intervention is most effective when the commissioner can accurately state that a similar question already has been asked or the line of questioning has no apparent objective. Requests by counsel for patience in waiting for the matter to unfold should be treated with some scepticism.

---

24 Above note 6.

Sometimes the reason counsel is not getting anywhere is that there simply is no place to go.[25]

Repetition may not always be the fault of counsel. Occasionally, witnesses may be evasive, requiring counsel to be given some leeway. This was the concern of the commission chairperson in the Somalia Inquiry when he suggested that the witness stop "fiddling around."[26] Such interventions can be counterproductive, as in this case. It would have been preferable to have the question repeated and, if the same answer were given, to point out specifically how it did not answer the question. Of course, witnesses cannot be required to give a "Yes-No" answer to every question. A qualification may be justified.

Some commissions have imposed time limits but they are a blunt instrument. Commissioner O'Connor reported that in the Walkerton Inquiry:

> I considered, but did not impose, time limits on cross-examinations. Before cross-examinations began, I routinely asked counsel for estimates of time and generally held them to their estimates. Counsel for the parties kept their cross-examinations focused, thus avoiding considerable duplication and delay.

Commissioner Goudge adopted the norm of allocating no more than the same amount of time to all cross-examinations as was allocated to commission counsel for examination-in-chief. Time limits may be appropriate for systemic inquiries (such as Goudge) and for intervenors. However, when cross-examining on an allegation of personal misconduct, imposing a time limit may be unfair.

The courts have commented unfavourably on the imposition of time limits on cross-examination in criminal cases. The Ontario Court of Appeal stated:

> The right and indeed the responsibility of the trial Judge to control the proceedings before him to prevent conduct which may well be or become an abuse of the process of the Court is unquestioned. It must, however, be exercised with caution so as to leave unfettered the right

---

25 Consider again the immortal words of Yogi Berra cited at the end of Chapter 5, Section B(2), to the effect that if you don't know where you are going you might never get there.

26 Discussed in Chapter 5, Section B(3).

> of the defendant, through his counsel, to subject any witness's testimony to the test of cross-examination. The disallowance of questions ruled improper, as inviting the introduction of hearsay evidence, or as being irrelevant or for the protection of a witness from unwarranted harassment falls within the scope of the trial Judge's authority. We do not consider that it is allowable, in advance, to place any restriction on the length of time to be consumed by cross-examination. The rulings of the trial Judge should be made when questions are put or about to be put and should be confined to the propriety of the question or questions in issue.[27]

A finding of serious misconduct by a commission of inquiry could be struck down as a breach of the principle of fairness through denial of adequate cross-examination. Controlling improper questioning by addressing the problem raised by a specific question is the fair way to impose limits although it does place much higher demands on the commissioner.

### 3) Examining and Cross-Examining

Generally speaking, in our adversary system, a witness is considered to be a witness for one side or the other. When examining your own witness, he is considered to be "favourable" so restrictions are placed on questioning. Leading questions are not permitted and the "agenda" of the testimony may be guided but not the substance. When examining a witness for the other side, or "cross" examining, the witness is considered to be "unfavourable." As a result, wider latitude is given in order to question the credibility of the witness and the reliability of his testimony. There are three broad avenues for doing this:

(1) Testing how the witness obtained the information including how it was observed, perceived, evaluated and recollected;
(2) Exposing errors, omissions, contradictions and improbabilities in his testimony;

---

27 *R. v. Bradbury* (1973), 14 C.C.C. (2d) 139 (Ont. C.A.), Kelly J.A. delivering the judgment of the court. See also, for example, *R. v. Makow* (1973), 13 C.C.C. (2d) 167 (B.C.C.A.) and *R. v. Roulette* (1972), 7 C.C.C. (2d) 244 (Man. Q.B.).

(3) Attacking how truthful he is likely to be through exposing bad character, personal bias in relation to the parties and previous statements contradictory to his testimony.[28]

Since a commission of inquiry is inquisitorial rather than adversarial, there is not such a clear demarcation of "sides." But opposing "interests" are inevitable in investigative inquiries. It is the challenge of hearings counsel to sort out these interests and arrange the questioning by counsel accordingly. Ordinarily, hearings counsel will conduct the "examination" of the witness unless the witness is facing potential, serious adverse findings, in which case the witness's counsel may "lead" his evidence.[29] Normally, only one counsel should be designated to conduct the cross-examination, and, of necessity, this may be hearings counsel. Other counsel may have limited questions for the witness, affecting their own clients. Counsel who conducted the initial examination should be permitted to re-examine the witness, but only in relation to any new matters raised in the questioning following the initial examination. Cross-examination by successive parties should not be permitted. Nor should "sweetheart" questioning, where parties with similar interests attempt to place the witness in a more favourable light.[30]

### 4) Evidentiary Issues

#### a) Leading Questions

Witnesses are asked questions during their examination to ensure that their testimony is presented in a logical manner, often in chronological sequence. The questions also ensure that the witness does not forget to include all relevant information. But the examiner must not influence the substance of that information by asking "leading" questions. There are two kinds of leading questions. The first simply suggests the desired answer, for example, "Did the defendant punch you in the nose?" The second requires the concession of a fact if it is to be answered, for example, "When did you stop beating your wife?" The rule applies only to examination and not to cross-examination.

---

28 *R. v. Mulvihill* (1914), 18 D.L.R. 189 (B.C.C.A.), quoting from *Phipson on Evidence*.

29 *Re Shulman*, [1967] 2 O.R. 375 (C.A.) and see Chapter 6, Section B(3).

30 See, generally, C. Kemm Yates, "Whither the Woodshed?: Counsel/Witness Relations in Regulatory Proceedings" (1987–88) 1 Can. J. Admin. L. & Prac. 183.

The rationale for the rule is that witnesses often may assent to questions that, on further reflection or on cross-examination, they will qualify significantly. They may be led, unthinkingly, simply to agree with questions that are really statements of fact. There is also a danger of collusion between the examiner and the witness. Adducing testimony through leading questions reduces its weight or value since the information is coming from the examiner rather than the witness.

Leading questions are permissible and, indeed, desirable when the subject matter is not in dispute. They allow introductory and preliminary matters to be addressed quickly before the witness gets to matters that may be contentious. At that point, leading questions should stop and the witness be permitted to recount the evidence in his own way. Where the evidence relates to potential misconduct, for example, great care should be taken to avoid using leading questions.

Leading questions are also permissible when it is difficult or impossible to ask the question another way. For example, if a witness is to be asked if he knows a certain person, it is necessary to name that person. Where the witness is a child, has difficulty hearing, or has poor understanding of the language, it may be necessary to simplify the questions by leading. The subject matter might be complicated and require a leading explanation before the relevant question can be asked. Finally, the witness may have simply forgotten some aspect of his expected testimony and can be reminded only by a leading question.

Leading questions are permissible and expected during cross-examination. Here the witness is opposed in interest to the questioner and is not as likely to be swayed by the form of the questions. The strength of the witness's testimony during examination may be tested by posing directly contrary assertions during cross-examination. However, if the witness should appear to be too willing to aid the interest of the person purporting to cross-examine, leading questions may be curtailed. This also may be taken into account later in assessing the value of the witness's testimony.

### b) Opinion

A witness is expected to testify as to facts and not to draw inferences, opinions, or beliefs from those facts. That is the role of the commissioner. For example, a witness may have come upon a car with a crumpled fender resting against a lamp post. The witness should testify as to the position and condition of the vehicle but leave it to the commissioner to draw the inference that it had been driven into the post. But some latitude is necessary since the presentation of evidence would be tortuous if minor and obvious inferences were not occasionally allowed.

There are also a number of recognized exceptions where witnesses may offer opinions. These are described as "matters of common experience" such as estimates of distance, the speed of a vehicle, or the age of a person.[31] It is not permissible to ask a witness whether he thinks a previous witness was lying or mistaken.[32] It is the responsibility of the commissioner, and not the witness, to form an opinion about the credibility and reliability of other witnesses.

The major exception, however, is "expert opinion." Persons who are qualified by some special skill, training, or experience may give opinions on matters within their expertise. Usually, it is a combination of such qualifications. It is usually desirable that commissions of inquiry follow the rules of evidence when dealing with expert testimony. This means that the subject matter of the opinion truly requires expertise, that it is within a recognized discipline, and not within the "common stock of knowledge" of the public. Nor should an expert opinion be given directly as to the key findings the commissioner must make. That could be seen as abandoning the role of commissioner in favour of the expert.

The qualification of the expert to give an opinion in a defined subject area should be presented and an opportunity given to the parties to test the strength and scope of that expertise. Usually, it will be acknowledged without question and the expert's report disclosed in advance. The factual basis on which the opinion rests should be clearly established. The commissioner should take the same precautions as the courts to confine expert opinion to the boundaries of the expertise established and not to be unduly influenced by the "expertise."

### c) Hearsay

The essence of the hearsay rule is that a witness must be called who can testify directly as to the fact to be proven. It cannot be proven by a witness relating "second hand" what another person said. If John sees a red car and tells Mary, John should be called to testify as to what he

---

31 *R. v. German*, [1947] O.R. 395 at 409–10 (C.A.).

32 *R. v. Markadonis*, [1935] S.C.R. 657.

saw. Mary cannot be called to prove the car was red simply by relating what John told her. However, Mary could testify as to what John told her if that was for some relevant purpose other than establishing that the car was red. For example, it might have prompted her to recall that she also saw a red car on a similar occasion. Here, the reference to John's statement is not to establish its truth—i.e., that he saw a red car—but merely to establish the fact it was said. That mere fact is relevant to Mary's recollection (assuming her sighting of a red car was also relevant to an issue before the commissioner).

The rationale for excluding such "second hand" evidence is twofold. First of all, the circumstances under which John made the statement may have been casual. It likely was not made with the same care and accuracy as would occur under oath in the course of a hearing. Secondly, the opposing party is denied the opportunity of testing the accuracy of the evidence. Was it dark outside? How good is John's eyesight? How far away was the car? Mary is unlikely to be able to provide much assistance in assessing the reliability of the evidence.

Such a statement would be admissible to prove the truth of its content if it fell within one of the established exceptions to the hearsay rule. These are highly technical and not completely rational. And. even if the statement does not fall within one of these exceptions, it still may be admitted if it meets the "principled approach" by satisfying the standards of "necessity and reliability." A commission of inquiry need not go through these gymnastics in dealing with hearsay evidence. It may simply ask what the value of the evidence is and how fair would it be to consider it. Unless there are compelling reasons for considering hearsay statements, it often will be better not to clutter the record with them. Where they are accepted, the parties will have the opportunity to make final submissions on the weight, if any, to be given to them.

### d) Consistent Statements

Previous statements made by a person who takes the stand as a witness are, generally, not admissible. A party may wish to introduce such statements to enhance the credibility of the witness by demonstrating that the earlier statements were identical to the testimony now given. But they are superfluous since the testimony can stand on its own. The earlier statements really add nothing and can be time-consuming at the hearings. They should be rejected, with one exception. That is where, for example, an opposing party says to the witness: "You just made that up for this hearing, didn't you?" The witness should be allowed to reply: "No, I told my neighbour exactly the same thing six months ago." This is simply a fair and reasonable response to an allegation that the testimony was fabricated subsequent to the events in question. But the commissioner should avoid any further inquiry into the details of what might have been said on earlier occasions. It also should be noted that a general attack on the credibility of a witness should not be allowed to trigger this exception.

A previous statement of a witness may be used to "refresh" his memory, subject to certain conditions. The statement, often in the form of his notes, must have been made at a time when the event was fresh in the witness's mind. If the statement is in the form of notes, the witness must be able to testify that these notes represent an accurate portrayal of what occurred. If the witness did not actually take the notes, he must have "adopted" them, just as, for example, a police officer who, shortly after the event, reads over the notes made by his partner and decides they are accurate. Such notes are not the evidence but are used merely to stimulate memory. If they are used by an opposing party to test the witness's credibility, they should be made an exhibit, simply to assist in assessing credibility.

In some circumstances, an earlier statement or record may be introduced as evidence even though it does not trigger a recollection by the maker. For example, a witness could introduce a chequebook to prove a cheque was written for a certain amount of money even though the witness does not remember doing so. The evidence is reliable if the witness testifies, for example, that she is always careful in making such entries and reconciles her record with the bank's monthly statements.

### 5) Credibility

Generally speaking, when a witness is called to testify, her credibility is assumed. It is not permissible to adduce evidence to attempt to enhance the credibility of a witness. That is another reason for rejecting the previous consistent statements of a witness. However, evidence of good character may be helpful in assessing both the credibility and the conduct of parties against whom adverse findings might be made. In the Morin Inquiry, Commissioner Kaufman reported:

> The good reputations of parties against whom misconduct is alleged have been considered by me both in relation to their credibility and to the unlikelihood that the alleged misconduct would be committed by them. A number of parties led character evidence during the Inquiry, either through witnesses otherwise testifying on relevant issues, or through character witnesses or letters . . . . I have considered the excellent prior reputations of various parties against whom allegations of misconduct have been made in assessing the evidence.

The character and reputation of witnesses also may be presented when they are introduced as witnesses at the hearings. For example, their professional qualifications, careers, experience, and achievements may be adduced, and may be helpful to the commissioner.

However, as indicated in Section C(3), above in this chapter, the credibility of an unfavourable witness may be attacked through exposing bad character, personal bias, or previous inconsistent statements.

#### a) Bad Character

On cross-examination, a witness may be asked about his past misconduct, unsavory associations, and other aspects of his past life that could reflect badly on his character. The commissioner then may take the answers into account in weighing the likely truthfulness of the witness. However, such questioning is "collateral." The response of the witness must stand and cannot be contradicted by rebuttal evidence.[33] The rule was established to avoid trials becoming bogged down in collateral issues that are only incidental to the issues in the case, including the issue of credibility. If the witness denies the allegation, the trier of fact still is entitled to disbelieve that denial.[34]

Questions that are only marginally relevant in this respect should not be permitted, such as improprieties of a remote date or that are not serious. Counsel asking such questions have an ethical obligation to be satisfied that the imputation has a "good faith basis."[35] Of course, the denial of such allegations always may be contradicted if they are rel-

---

33 *R. v. Krause*, [1986] 2 S.C.R. 466.

34 *Ibid.* at para. 17, McIntyre J. delivering the judgment of the Court.

35 *R. v. Lyttle*, [2004] 1 S.C.R. 193 [*Lyttle*]; *R. v. Bencardino and De Carlo* (1973), 15 C.C.C. (2d) 342 (Ont. C.A.).

evant beyond mere credibility to another issue arising out of the terms of reference.

Another avenue of introducing evidence of the bad character of a witness is to cross-examine the witness as to previous criminal convictions or penal convictions under other statutes.[36] The *Canada Evidence Act*[37] and comparable provincial legislation specifically authorize such convictions to be proven if the witness denies the allegation or refuses to answer. Commissioner Kaufman also reported that he had taken into account the "criminal records or discreditable conduct of some witnesses" in assessing credibility.

### b) Bias

A witness may be asked on cross-examination about facts that suggest the witness is biased or partial. This could arise from personal relationships, personal interests that might be affected, or prejudices. The issue arose at the Ipperwash Inquiry when the lawyer for the Chiefs of Ontario sought to question the former executive assistant to the premier about her political involvement, work history, and remuneration over the previous ten years: "The issue is whether or not she has a motive to protect Premier Harris, whether or not she has been rewarded by the relationships she has had with Mr. Harris and the Progressive Conservative Party." The questioning was allowed and revealed extensive political associations.[38] The issue of the former premier's credibility was an important issue and she was an important witness on this issue. Ultimately, Commissioner Sidney Linden concluded that Harris had made a racist statement in spite of his denials.

Unlike the collateral-issue rule related to character, contradictory evidence may be introduced to refute a denial of bias. In most situations, a commissioner should exercise a discretion not to permit a separate evidentiary inquiry into the issue of bias. The rationale of not getting bogged down in collateral issues should be equally applicable here unless the issue of bias is of significant proportion.

---

36 *Ashton*, above note 6.

37 R.S.C. 1985, c. C-5, s. 12.

38 Kate Harries, "Gloves Come Off at Ipperwash Probe" *Globe & Mail* (24 November 2005).

### c) Inconsistent Statements

The *Canada Evidence Act*[39] and comparable provincial legislation specifically addresses this situation. The cross-examiner normally will begin by establishing clearly the specific testimony the witness is giving on the same matters that are contained in the previous written statement. The nature and circumstances of the earlier statement must then be clearly identified and the inconsistent parts brought to his attention. The statement may then be proven and the witness cross-examined on the inconsistencies.

## 6) Notice Issues

Some constitutional protections and the requirements of the principle of fairness can be traced to evidentiary rules established at common law. For example, the rule in *Brown v. Dunne* was stated by Lord Herschel well over one hundred years ago as follows:

> My Lords, I have always understood that if you intend to impeach a witness you are bound, whilst he is in the box, to give him an opportunity of making any explanation which is open to him; and, as it seems to me, that is not only a rule of professional practice in the conduct of a case, but is essential to fair play and fair dealing with witnesses.[40]

This concept is one aspect of the broader constitutional law principle of the "case to meet."[41] The commission of inquiry context was expressed in *Kingsclear* as follows:

> [T]he fact-finding function of an inquiry is an important feature of any investigatory and advisory commission and a commissioner's discretion to make findings on the credibility of witnesses and express his reasons for doing so is part and parcel of the necessary decision-making process of such an inquiry. Finally, it should be noted that a judge sitting alone at a

---

39 Above note 37, ss. 11 & 12.

40 (1893), 6 R. 67 at 70 (H.L.). Quoted in *Lyttle*, above note 35 at para. 64.

41 *R. v. Dubois*, [1985] 2 S.C.R. 350, adopting Ed Ratushny in "The Role of the Accused in the Criminal Process" in Walter S. Tarnopolsky & Gérald A. Beaudoin, eds., *The Canadian Charter of Rights and Freedoms* (Toronto: Carswell, 1982) at 358–59 and in Ed Ratushny, *Self-Incrimination in the Canadian Criminal Process* (Toronto: Carswell, 1979) at 180.

> trial is not required to forewarn a witness likely to be disbelieved what he has in mind. He must ensure, however, that a witness whose credibility is suspected has a fair opportunity of rebutting contradictory evidence.[42]

While notice of matters such as this may be given informally in meetings with commission counsel, it is important that they also be addressed on the record at the hearings.

Another category of evidence that should be placed on the record is judicial notice. The rule itself is relatively narrow, permitting notice of facts to be taken without proof only where they are:

(1) so notorious or generally accepted as not to be the subject of dispute among reasonable persons; or
(2) capable of immediate and accurate demonstration through readily accessible sources of indisputable accuracy.[43]

Thus, it is notorious that Toronto is a city in Canada or that it is extremely difficult to terminate a heroin addition. Other facts, such as the chemical formula for water or salt, may not be notorious but they are easily ascertainable in textbooks and are indisputable. It is important that the issue of potential judicial notice be raised so that parties may make representations and, if there is a dispute as to facts to be judicially noticed, call contrary evidence. In addition, it is important to place on the record factual issues that have been resolved by consent of all the parties. Also, since the process is not exclusive to the parties, the commissioner should be in a position to explain why that was an acceptable basis for resolving the factual issues in the public interest.

## D. RESTRICTIONS ON PUBLICITY

### 1) *In Camera* and Non-Publication

The process of conducting open and public hearings is one of the essential features of commissions of inquiry that enhance public confidence.

---

42 *Richards v. New Brunswick (Commission of Inquiry into the Kingslcear Youth Training Centre* (1996), 180 N.B.R. (2d) 1 at para. 30 (Q.B.) [*Kingsclear*] and see the discussion in Chapter 6, Section B(2)(b).

43 *R. v. Krymowski*, [2005] 1 S.C.R. 101. Commissioner Gomery took judicial notice of media coverage and the public reaction in ruling on an application for a publication ban, discussed in the next section.

Lord Justice Salmon elaborated on the importance of transparency in this respect:

> It is . . . of the greatest importance that hearings before a Tribunal of Inquiry should be held in public. It is only when the public is present that the public will have complete confidence that everything possible has been done for the purpose of arriving at the truth . . . .
>
> When there is crisis of public confidence abut the alleged misconduct of persons in high places, the public naturally distrusts any investigation carried out behind closed doors. Investigations so conducted will always tend to promote the suspicion, however unjustified, that they are not being conducted sufficiently vigorously and thoroughly or that something is being hushed up. Publicity enables the public to see for itself how the investigation is being carried out and accordingly dispels suspicion. Unless these inquiries are held in public, they are unlikely to achieve their main purpose, namely, that of restoring the confidence of the public in the integrity of our public life. And without this confidence no democracy can long survive.[44]

Justice Cory spoke of the therapeutic value of open hearings when the inquiry relates to a tragedy in the local community:

> Open hearings function as a means of restoring the public confidence in the affected industry and in the regulations pertaining to it and their enforcement. As well, it can serve as a type of healing therapy for a community shocked and angered by a tragedy. It can channel the natural desire to assign recommendations for reform and improvement.[45]

The basic underlying premise, therefore, is that these hearings should be conducted in public so that all relevant information can be made available to the public.

However, some information may not be accessible because of the law of privilege. Some of the Acts specifically exclude evidence that would be inadmissible by reason of any privilege under the law of evidence.[46] In

---

44 Great Britain, Royal Commission on Tribunals of Inquiry, *Report of the Commission under the Chairmanship of the Rt. Hon. Lord Justice Salmon* (London: H.M.S.O., 1966) Cmnd 3121.

45 Above note 4 at para. 117.

46 Ontario, s. 11; Alberta, s. 9(1); British Columbia, s. 22(2); Newfoundland and Labrador, s. 12(1).

the other jurisdictions, the common law exclusionary rules would apply even if there were no statutory adoption of them. Privilege is discussed in the next section.

Some of the Acts also specifically provide that hearings are to be conducted in public, but where they do, they also authorize hearings in the absence of the public in certain circumstances.[47] These circumstances relate to public security and privacy rights such as financial or personal matters and must be balanced against the importance of public hearings. Newfoundland and Labrador also specifies the right "to a fair trial" as one of these circumstances. Where no such provision exists, it is simply assumed that hearings will be held in public. But the commissioner would also have the same discretion to proceed in private under the general power to control proceedings, discussed in Section A, above in this chapter.

Restricting public access to information placed before the commissioner can be done in two ways. The first is to hold a portion of the hearings *in camera*. The public and some or all of the parties may be precluded from attending these proceedings. The second manner of limiting public access is through an order of the commissioner banning publication of specified information.

The Supreme Court of Canada established the test for when a publication ban may be ordered in *Dagenais*[48] and *Mentuck*.[49] The party seeking the ban must overcome the strong presumption of openness in relation to the administration of justice, which has been reinforced by the principle of freedom of expression under the *Charter*. The very nature and purpose of a commission of inquiry lends even greater weight to that presumption when applied to this forum. The party seeking the ban must provide a convincing evidentiary basis to overcome the principle of openness in the courts which "is so strong and so highly valued in our society."[50]

The *Dagenais* case involved balancing freedom of expression against the right to a fair trial. In *Mentuck*, the ban was sought to protect the safety of police officers and the mode of certain undercover police oper-

---

47 Ontario, s. 4; British Columbia, s. 15(1); Newfoundland and Labrador, s. 6(2).

48 *Dagenais v. Canadian Broadcasting Corp.*, [1994] 3 S.C.R. 835 [*Dagenais*].

49 *R. v. Mentuck*, [2001] 3 S.C.R. 442 [*Mentuck*].

50 *Ibid.* at para. 39, Iacobucci J. delivering the judgment of the Court.

ations. As a result, the *Dagenais* test was reconfigured more broadly to encompass other aspects of the administration of justice, as follows:

> A publication ban should only be ordered when:
> (a) such an order is necessary in order to prevent a serious risk to the proper administration of justice because reasonably alternative measures will not prevent the risk; and
> (b) the salutary effects of the publication ban outweigh the deleterious effects on the rights and interests of the parties and the public, including the effects on the right to free expression, the right of the accused to a fair and public trial, and the efficacy of the administration of justice.[51]

The test for ordering *in camera* proceedings is essentially the same.[52] In applying this test, it must be kept in mind that:

> the relevant rights and interests will be aligned differently in different cases, and the purposes and effects invoked by the parties must be taken into account in a case-specific manner.[53]

In *Toronto Star*,[54] the Court also emphasized the need to apply the *Dagenais/Mentuck* test in a "flexible and contextual manner." Justice Morris Fish gave the example of granting a sealing order for a search-warrant application at an early investigative stage but only for a brief period. As a general principle, bans should be removed immediately when their purpose has passed.

In the same case, the Ontario Court of Appeal had ruled that the judge below had exceeded her jurisdiction by denying a brief adjournment to allow counsel for the media to attend and make submissions. Justice Fish did not address this issue but referred to the "guidelines on notice to the media and media standing."[55] The implications of these for a commission of inquiry are that notice should be given to the media of

---

51 *Ibid.* at para. 32.

52 *Canadian Broadcasting Corp. v. New Brunswick (Attorney General)*, [1996] 3 S.C.R. 480 [*New Brunswick*], La Forest J. delivering the judgment of the Court, discussed in *Mentuck*, above note 49 at paras. 24–27, 36, and 38.

53 *Mentuck, ibid.* at para. 37.

54 *Toronto Star Newspapers Ltd. v. Ontario*, [2005] 2 S.C.R. 188 at para. 8, Fish, J. delivering the judgment of the Court [*Toronto Star*].

55 *Ibid.* at para. 13, referring to *Dagenais*.

motions for publication bans. It is in the discretion of the commissioner to whom and how notice should be given. The media-relations officer will know what journalists, publications, or stations have been covering the proceedings and may suggest others as well. The granting and extent of their standing on the motion is also discretionary but could include some or all of these opportunities: to cross-examine witnesses, call *viva voce* evidence, file affidavit evidence, and present other written evidence. A publication ban should be placed on the hearing of the motion itself but restricted or removed if the motion is (partially) denied.

The decision in *Episcopal*[56] provides a good illustration of the application of the *Dagenais/Mentuck* test. The commissioner denied a publication ban to a witness in the Cornwall Inquiry. The witness had been acquitted of sexual-abuse charges over fifteen years previously but the complainant was also to be called as witness at the inquiry to testify about the same allegations. The applicant sought to protect his privacy and reputational interests but the commissioner held that the allegations already had received widespread publicity. The public would be reminded of the acquittal and the mandate "to clear the air" would override any interest of the applicant that would be protected by the ban.

The Court agreed that protection of the reputation of innocent persons was a highly significant factor to be weighed against openness and freedom of expression. But the commissioner had weighed several factors that mitigated the risk to reputation. The commission could not "re-try" the allegations of sexual abuse. As well, counsel for the applicant could be expected to ensure that evidence of the acquittal was made clear. The Court was also able to take into account the complainant's evidence that actually was taken at the hearings. A publication ban was placed on the details of the alleged sexual abuse. It was emphasized that the witness was testifying about allegations and not the truth of those allegations. The acquittal was introduced by commission counsel. When the complainant testified that the acquittal was due to a reasonable doubt, the commissioner intervened to point out that the trial judge had given reasons stating he believed the accused's denial. The Court

---

56 *Episcopal Corporation of the Diocese of Alexandria-Cornwall v. Cornwall Public Inquiry*, 2007 ONCA 20, Sharpe J.A. delivering the reasons of himself, MacPherson, and Blair JJ.A. [*Episcopal*].

concluded that the commissioner had acted reasonably in protecting the applicant's innocence.

The applicant also argued that the requested ban would not affect the commission in fulfilling its mandate. But the Court pointed to the purpose of the inquiry as a response to allegations of a pedophile ring, conspiracy, collusion, and cover-up. It had to examine whether the allegations of this complainant and others were properly investigated. In this context, the commissioner also acted reasonably in concluding that the applicant's name was relevant to the interrelationship of the persons involved. The applicant's prosecution and acquittal were widely reported and his identity was germane to clearing the air in the community. It was an important element of the broad objective of this commission of inquiry to inform, educate, and "heal" members of the public.

Taking all these facts into account, the Court upheld the commissioner's decision. He had applied the correct test and acted reasonably in concluding that the applicant had not satisfied its burden.

The Goudge Inquiry also faced motions to restrict publication of the names of some individuals. Notice was given to the parties and media and published on the inquiry's website. Redactions were required for the names of those who had been investigated and prosecuted under the *Youth Criminal Justice Act* but the actual physical redactions would have taken "many months." Instead, access to the unredacted documents was restricted to counsel for the parties and to the media, who were expected to comply with the non-publication order with respect to the names.

The order also required that certain persons be identified by first name only in some circumstances and, when required by this Act, by initials only. This allowed them to be referred to at the hearings without their names being revealed. On the "rare occasion" where a name was mentioned inadvertently, the time delay in the webcast allowed it to be removed. The transcript also was corrected.

The issue of a publication ban often arises where a witness is facing criminal investigation or already has been charged. In Walkerton, a key witness was the subject of an ongoing criminal investigation. Commission counsel took the initiative to inform the witness's counsel that a publication ban might be appropriate, but none was requested.

In *Phillips*, Justice Cory expressed the view that findings of misconduct in a commissioner's final report would be a much greater risk to a fair trial than merely testifying at the hearings:

> the potential for lasting impartiality is much less when what is published are the carefully reasoned conclusions of a judge who has heard all of the testimony and examined all of the evidence relevant to the inquiry mandate. The publication of these findings of facts and conclusions will create a much greater risk of prejudice to fair trial rights.[57]

In his view, the publication of such a report should be delayed until those facing trial have an opportunity to review it and consider an application for a publication ban until the disposal of the criminal charges.[58] The publication of the Mount Cashel Inquiry's Report was delayed until the completion of the trials of all the former brothers of the institution who had been charged.

A publication ban was sought for the testimony of three witnesses who were subpoenaed and scheduled to testify before the Gomery Inquiry in April 2005. They were also scheduled to be tried before courts composed of a judge and jury commencing on 2 May 2005, and the trials were expected to last from four to six weeks. The charges involved multiple counts of fraud and conspiracy under the *Criminal Code*. The witnesses sought the ban not only for their own testimony but also for the testimony of other witnesses that related to the criminal charges they were facing.

One of the applicants requested, as an alternative remedy, that his testimony before the commission be postponed until after the completion of his criminal trial. This was rejected since a publication ban would provide equivalent relief. Also, to postpone his testimony would "disrupt the orderly presentation of the evidence and unduly delay" the completion of the hearings and the report, which was urgently required.[59]

The commissioner pointed out that commission counsel had undertaken not to adduce evidence or to question the applicants on any of the matters underlying the criminal charges they were facing. He also noted that the primary responsibility for ensuring a fair trial rested with the trial judge, through means such as jury selection and instructions. However, he also took judicial notice of the great public interest in his hearings, as "evidenced by extensive media and broadcast coverage and commentary." This coverage had intensified in recent months and the

---

57 Above note 4 at para. 124.

58 *Ibid.* at para. 163.

59 Gomery Inquiry, Ruling (29 March 2005).

commissioner was aware of media reports of "a high degree of public indignation" in response to "recent revelations" at the hearings. The problem was exacerbated by the timing of the testimony at the hearings, which would be only a few weeks or days before the start of the criminal trials.

He also took into account the difficulty an applicant has in satisfying the *Dagenais/Mentuck* test when the consequences of future testimony have to be assessed: "I cannot imagine how one is to assess the effect that revelations will have upon the public consciousness, particularly when one does not know what the revelations will be, the extent to which they will be reported by the media and in what terms." The prejudicial effect of future testimony "can only be guessed." He concluded that a publication ban was required "as a precaution" to prevent a serious risk to the proper administration of justice. It was not certain that alternative measures could prevent that risk.

In order to restrict only minimally the freedom of expression of the press, a publication ban should be limited in "duration, content and scope." In the case of the Gomery Inquiry, it was imposed "only until the moment at the end of the criminal trial of the applicant concerned when jurors are sequestered to deliberate." In addition, the commissioner invited representations from the media at the end of the testimony of each of the applicants as to whether some or all of it should be released from the publication ban. As a result, further rulings were made following the testimony of each of the applicants, on 7 April, 27 April, and 4 May, respectively. The publication bans were lifted for all three applicants with the exception of specifically identified portions of the testimony of each.

In another ruling, Commissioner Gomery referred to "a kind of no-publication order"[60] that was requested for certain documents. These related to the financial statements for a trust and corporations of the applicant. He sought an order that the documents be kept confidential and not disclosed to anyone unless a confidentiality agreement was signed. The commissioner had no doubt that disclosure of this financial information would have a negative effect on the applicant's business interests and would constitute an invasion of his privacy. But he applied

60 *Ibid.*, Ruling (13 April 2005).

Justice Iacobucci's test for granting such an order in civil litigation. According to this test, it should be granted when:

- such an order is necessary to prevent a serious risk to an important interest, including a commercial interest, in the context of litigation because reasonably alternative measures will not prevent the risk; and
- the salutary effects of the confidentiality order, including the effects on the right of civil litigants to a fair trial, outweigh its deleterious effects, including the effects on the right to free expression, which in this context includes the public interest in open and accessible court proceedings.[61]

Justice Iacobucci elaborated that the risk must be solidly substantiated by evidence and pose a "serious threat to the commercial interest" in question. Commissioner Gomery ruled that the strictly commercial private interest here had to give way to freedom of expression. Unless all of the details were disclosed, Canadians would be denied important information about where the sponsorship money "went."

Inquiries are increasingly addressing non-publicity issues in their rules of procedure or in separate "protocols." See, for example the "Media Protocol for Confidentiality Issues" of the Cornwall Inquiry, which refers to "*In Camera* Hearings, Non-Identifying Initials and Non-Publication."

### 2) National Security Confidentiality

Reference was made to the problem faced by the Air India Inquiry when the government claimed National Security Confidentiality (NSC) over large portions of the documents before the commissioner. The terms of reference required him to prevent disclosure of information that could be injurious to international relations, national defence, or national security. A process was established whereby the commissioner would receive *in camera* any such information so identified by the government. The commissioner would then make a ruling and give notice to the government. The difficulty was that the government could then institute a court challenge, as it had done in the previous Arar Inquiry.

---

61 *Sierra Club of Canada v. Canada (Minister of Finance)*, [2002] 2 S.C.R. 522 at para. 53 delivering the judgment of the Court.

As a practical matter, this left Commissioner Major in the position of having to announce that it simply would be impossible for him to continue if the government continued to refuse to allow so much relevant information to be made public. The prime minister intervened and arrangements were made with counsel for the attorney general that allowed the hearings to be completed.[62]

The terms of reference of the previous Arar Inquiry contained similar provisions with respect to NSC claims. However, they presented even greater challenges since the events in question were more recent and these terms of reference had a more specific investigation component in relation to "the actions of Canadian officials." Commissioner O'Connor adopted rules that reflected the process for dealing with NSC claims that was established by his terms of reference. He would convene *in camera* hearings to address such claims and periodically rule on them. He would also prepare summaries of the *in camera* evidence that could be disclosed publicly. This would keep the public informed, to some extent, as to what was happening behind closed doors. It would also assist parties who were excluded from the *in camera* hearings but were participating in the public hearings.[63]

However, the government challenged the content of the first summary of *in camera* evidence. Following unsuccessful negotiations, an *in camera* hearing was held to hear the government's evidence and submissions on the disputed summary. A ruling was issued with reasons for rejecting some of the government's NSC claims. The government then challenged this ruling in the Federal Court. The commissioner was forced to reconsider his approach to these claims: "The nature of the disagreements over what could be disclosed was such that I believed that trying to resolve them, most likely through litigation, would result in considerable delay and might seriously impair the Inquiry's work, if not bring it to a complete halt." After hearing submissions from the parties, he decided to discontinue issuing summaries of the *in camera* hearings and to defer any further rulings on NSC claims. He would proceed to hear all of the RCMP and CSIS evidence *in camera* and then conduct

---

62 Discussed in Chapter 5, Section D(4).

63 The following discussion is taken from the Arar Inquiry, *The Factual Inquiry Report*, Part One, c. 8, dealing with the process. See also Ruling on Summaries (7 April 2005).

whatever public hearings that were possible. He would then issue his report, including his view of what parts of the report could be made public: "If there were to be disagreements with the Government about its NSC claims, I thought it best to address these in the context of a report, rather than in a series of protracted and costly interlocutory proceedings." As a result, the public hearings would proceed without any challenge to the government's NSC claims, even when the commissioner disagreed with them. This was a bold but effective decision.

It was a challenge to conduct public hearings when so much of the evidence could not be disclosed because of these claims. But at least the commissioner and his counsel had seen all of this information. Also, once these hearings commenced, the government began to reconsider and provide publicly some of the information it previously had withheld. In the end, the hearings went as well as could be expected in the circumstances and the commissioner was satisfied that he was able to fulfill his mandate. He had access to all of the relevant material in spite of all of the NSC claims and prepared a full report without regard for them. He also prepared a shorter factual summary based on the comprehensive report but including only information that could properly be disclosed publicly without being injurious to international relations, national defence, or national security.

However, in some concluding observations, the commissioner raised disturbing issues about the role of the government in this commission of inquiry. The public was deprived of a full hearing process by the government "over claiming" NSC at the outset. That these claims were excessive is proven by the fact that the government ultimately released much of the information. The government also reneged on its assurance at the start of the inquiry that its claims would be carefully considered to ensure maximal public disclosure. The commissioner could understand the responsible officials initially choosing to "err on the side of caution." But this lack of transparency "promotes public suspicion and cynicism" about how legitimate these claims may be, as well as exacerbating problems of procedural fairness for the parties.

Other motives on the part of government may also be engaged: "Although government agencies may be tempted to make NSC claims to shield certain information from public scrutiny and avoid potential embarrassment, that temptation should always be resisted." Without making specific allegations in this respect, two examples certainly raise strong suspicions that such motives led to the manipulation of the timing in making embarrassing information available. The first involved "border lookout" request letters to the United States that contained a "highly inflammatory and unfounded description" of Arar and his wife as Islamic extremists. This was made available when the public hearings were virtually complete. The second involved a letter from the RCMP to Syrian military intelligence offering to share information about its investigation involving Arar, who was in their custody at the time. This was very troubling in light of the Syrian practice of torturing prisoners during interrogation. The letter was made available only after the hearings were complete.

What is impressive is that, with all of the NSC hurdles it faced, this seemingly "Co-Mission Impossible" was able to complete its mission as successfully as it did.[64]

## E. PRIVILEGE

### 1) Introduction

It was pointed out in Section D(1), above in this chapter, that some of the Acts specifically exclude evidence that would be inadmissible by reasons of any privilege under the law of evidence.[65] Some privileges exist by virtue of common law and others were established or adopted by statute. Even where the Act governing commissions of inquiry does not specifically adopt the laws related to privilege, they would be applicable by such common law or statutory provisions.

What follows is a "checklist" of most of the various privileges that could be encountered by a commission of inquiry together with a "thumbnail sketch" of each. As with the topics addresses under the heading "Questioning Witnesses" in Section C, above in this chapter, they are familiar to lawyers but a review of them may be helpful as a "refresher."

Unlike many of the evidentiary issues that may arise when questioning witnesses, issues related to privilege are usually identified and addressed prior to the hearings stage. Merely having them in mind may help to identify at the outset some of the issues that have to be addressed. Even if the law of privilege is not applicable, some of the underlying issues raised may invite the discretion of the commissioner in terms of

---

64 See also Chapter 9, Section D(1).

65 Above note 46.

whether certain evidence should be adduced and, if so, whether limits should be placed on its publicity.

Hearings counsel often may resolve issues of privilege informally with the parties. Portions of documents may be excluded and others may not be of sufficient importance to the commission's mandate to warrant insistence on their introduction into evidence. A process for obtaining rulings on privilege, independent of the commissioner, was described in Chapter 6, Section B(2).

The person who is entitled to claim a privilege often may waive the claim and agree to the protected information being introduced in evidence. It is, therefore, important to identify the holder of the privilege. For example, in solicitor-client privilege, it is the client who has complete control of the decision to waive and may do so, in spite of objections from the lawyer. But the client cannot be selective and disclose only part of the communications on a subject. A partial waiver can be treated as an "implied" waiver of the entire communication as well as requiring the production of documents that relate to the communication. Normally, a waiver must be explicit but there are many examples of an implied waiver through conduct as well as expression. Where the holder inadvertently discloses privileged information to another, the claim to privilege is lost and the information, once "out of the bag," may be introduced.

A claim to privilege is most clearly available when it falls within one of a number of well-recognized categories. However, the Supreme Court of Canada has accepted that a privilege also may be established for specific situations, beyond any of those categories, on a case-by-case basis. This requires that four conditions be satisfied by the person making the claim, namely:

(1) The communications must originate in a *confidence* that they will not be disclosed.
(2) This element of *confidentiality must be essential* to the full and satisfactory maintenance of the relation between the parties.
(3) The *relation* must be one which in the opinion of the community ought to be sedulously *fostered*.
(4) The *injury* that would inure to the relation by the disclosure of the communications must be *greater than the benefit* thereby gained for the correct disposal of litigation.[66]

66 *Slavutych v. Baker*, [1976] 1 S.C.R. 254 [*Slavutych*].

These are often referred to as the "Wigmore criteria" after the author from whom they were adopted. Although this approach has been recognized and applied in a number of Supreme Court decisions,[67] it almost inevitably falls short in establishing a privilege beyond the pre-existing categories.

### 2) Solicitor-Client

This privilege applies to communications made between a lawyer and a client in the course of obtaining legal advice. Even though there is a lawyer-client relationship between them, the privilege does not apply to communications beyond the scope of legal advice. Once disclosed to a third party, the client no longer has control of their use. Nor does the privilege apply to communications that have as their purpose the facilitation of commission of a crime. Nor does it apply to documents or other articles merely placed with the lawyer since these are not communications.

The communications need not to be made directly to the lawyer to be protected. They may be given to staff acting under the supervision of the lawyer. The information remains privileged even though the client may change lawyers or even die (with very limited exceptions). The Supreme Court recently developed two extreme situations in which narrow exceptions would be made to solicitor-client privileged information. These are where the information is absolutely necessary to establish innocence in a criminal case[68] or to avoid a clear and imminent danger of a risk of death or serious bodily harm.[69]

As mentioned in the previous section, the solicitor-client privilege belongs to the client and only the client may waive it. The commissioner who conducted the Toronto Leasing Inquiry spoke of her experiences at the Canadian Bar Association's annual meeting in 2007. Justice Bellamy said that five lawyers had appeared before her as witnesses and were subjected to "rigorous questioning." She reminded the lawyers that any

---

67 Affirmed in *R. v. Gruenke*, [1991] 3 S.C.R. 263 [*Gruenke*]; *M.(A.) v. Ryan*, [1997] 1 S.C.R. 157 [*Ryan*].

68 *R. v. Brown*, [2002] 2 S.C.R. 185; *R. v. McClure*, [2001] 1 S.C.R. 445 [*McClure*]; *Goodis v. Ontario (Ministry of Correctional Services)*, [2006] 2 S.C.R. 32.

69 *Smith v. Jones*, [1999] 1 S.C.R. 455.

of them who provided legal advice could end up as such a witness. She added: "If you think you're going to be protected by solicitor-client privilege, think again. The reality is that most clients waived solicitor-client privilege, and if the government is the one calling for the public inquiry in the first place, they're very likely going to be waiving solicitor-client privilege."[70] Parties may often place themselves in a better light in the eyes of the commissioner by waiving this privilege. The nature of the legal advice they received may also help them to explain their conduct.

### 3) Other Relationships

Section 4(3) of the *Canada Evidence Act*[71] provides:

> No husband is compellable to disclose any communication made to him by his wife during their marriage, and no wife is compellable to disclose any communication made to her by her husband during their marriage.

The provincial evidence Acts contain similar provisions and the Alberta Act extends the relationship to "adult interdependent partners."[72] The other Acts do not extend beyond marriage to common law unions but they could be protected by an application of the Wigmore criteria.[73]

As with solicitor-client privilege, this privilege does not extend to marital communications overheard by a third party. But, in contrast, the privilege for marital communications ends with the relationship, including the death of a spouse.

Other professional relationships, such as priest-penitent, doctor-patient, and journalist-source, have been denied privilege as a class, even though they may create strong expectations of confidentiality. And these may carry with them some societal justification for legal protection as privileged communications. Attempts have been made to have them recognized as engaging such a privilege under the Wigmore criteria. These attempts have been only marginally successful. But they have been treated seriously enough to raise an expectation that, in

---

70 Helen Burnett, "Ethical Culture Can't Be Left to Evolution" *Law Times* (27 August/3 September 2007).

71 Above note 37.

72 *Alberta Evidence Act*, R.S.A. 1980, c. A-21, s. 8.

73 As in *Letourneau v. Clearbrook Iron Works Ltd.*, [2004] F.C.J. No. 1796 (Fed. Ct.).

the right circumstances, such communications could be fully excluded under the legal privilege.

The term priest-pertinent refers to the classic example of a priest who hears a confession of a serious crime. It always has been expected that such a priest would simply go to jail, if necessary, rather than reveal such a serious confidence. In these circumstances, the courts in both England and Canada have not, as a matter of practice, compelled members of the clergy to disclose confidential religious communication.[74]

The Supreme Court in *Gruenke*[75] held that the religious communications there did not meet the first Wigmore criterion of originating in a confidence that they would not be disclosed. The communications in question were from the accused to a lay counsellor and a pastor of a fundamentalist Christian church. On hearing of the victim's death, the lay counsellor visited the accused who began speaking of her involvement in the murder. The pastor was called and the conversation continued, which resulted in admissions that directly supported the Crown's theory. The majority held that the purpose of the communications were to relieve the accused's emotional stress rather than to give effect to a religious or spiritual purpose.[76] The minority agreed that the first criterion was not satisfied but placed a high value on the "human need for a spiritual counselor." It was important to the members of religious organizations, was supported by religious freedom under the *Charter*, and would promote the special values of privacy. This discussion might provide some guidance for commissions of inquiry in dealing with religious communications even in the absence of a legal privilege.[77]

In *Ryan*,[78] the Supreme Court held that psychiatrist-patient records could be privileged in appropriate circumstances. The plaintiff sued a psychiatrist who had treated her when she was seventeen and had sexual relations with her in the course of treatment. As a result, she had

---

74 Although police have not been beyond creating a "fake" priest and confessional in a criminal investigation. See *R. v. Clot (No. 1)* (1982), 69 C.C.C. (2d) 349 (Que. S.C.), *R. v. Clot (No. 2)* (1982), 69 C.C.C. (2d) 365 (Que. S.C.), *R. v. Clot (No. 3)* (1982), 69 C.C.C. (2d) 367 (Que. S.C.).

75 Above note 67.

76 Lamer C.J. delivering the judgment of himself, La Forest, Sopinka, Cory, McLachlin, Stevenson, and Iacobucci JJ.

77 L'Heureux-Dubé J for herself and Gonthier J.

78 Above note 67.

sought further treatment from a second psychiatrist and obtained assurances that their communications would be confidential. The defendant sought disclosure of the second psychiatrist's reporting letters and notes of her discussions with the plaintiff. The Court upheld disclosure but applied the privilege to support the stringent conditions imposed on such disclosures.

The first three Wigmore criteria were satisfied in support of the privilege. The communications were confidential, that confidence was essential to the psychiatrist-patient relationship, and that relationship and its purpose in providing treatment were of transcendent public importance. This left the fourth requirement of balancing the interests of confidentiality against getting at the truth and avoiding injustice in the litigation. In this case, a partial privilege was the best answer to serving the compelling privacy interest of the plaintiff. The conditions imposed were that the defendant could not inspect the notes; only his solicitors and expert witnesses could. Those who saw the documents could not disclose their contents to anyone not entitled to inspect them and they were to be used only for the purposes of the litigation. Only one copy of the notes could be made and would have to be circulated among those entitled to see them.

Protecting confidential information in this way makes sense. Imposing conditions sensitive to privacy interests is an approach open to commissions of inquiry for information beyond such relationships. A variety of considerations may be balanced, including the privacy interest, the importance of the information to the inquiry, and fairness to parties who might be adversely affected.

Journalists often may have written on issues related to the controversies that form the subject of commissions of inquiry. In the course of gathering information for their articles, they may give undertakings of confidentiality to persons who are the source of information not otherwise available. Freedom of the media is an important value in Canadian society and a central feature of any true democracy. Investigative journalism, which has made significant contributions to public understanding of noteworthy events, often is based on such sources. But the identification of such sources, or documents that would identify them, may also be essential to getting at the truth in the courts or other forums. The Supreme Court has confirmed the applicability of the Wigmore test to determining whether a journalist should be protected in law from disclosing such sources.[79]

The *St. Elizabeth* case[80] contains an excellent exposition of related principles and issues. Justice Sharpe of the Ontario Court of Appeal noted the direct bearing that freedom of expression and of the media have on a journalist's claim to confidentiality. In his view:

> There can be no doubt that when applying the four-part Wigmore test to journalist-informant confidentiality and assessing the weight to be given to protecting confidentiality, courts must take into account relevant *Charter* values, even though the *Charter* does not directly apply.[81]

He rejected the contention that there was insufficient evidence to support the concern that forcing disclosure of sources would have a "chilling effect" on news gathering. He referred to other legal rules based on experience of human behaviour rather than empirical evidence and to recognition of this concern in our Supreme Court and in other jurisdictions. It is apparent that the need for some sources to conceal their identity would otherwise discourage their cooperation.

In this case, the reporter had obtained documents and other information from a confidential source that led to a series of three articles critical of the health and safety practices of a senior citizens' home. These revealed detailed investigations by municipal authorities and led to the nursing home suing the municipality. The trial judge directed that the examination of the journalist proceed in three stages. The first would question him as to what documents he received pursuant to his undertaking to the source. The second would cover communications with employees of the municipality, but without identifying the source. The scope of the third stage would be determined by the trial judge, depending on the results of the first two. This was an attempt to limit encroachment on the journalist-source relationship only to the extent necessary for the trial. If sufficient information could be obtained by proceeding incrementally, it might not be necessary to require disclosure of the source.

---

79 *McClure*, above note 68.

80 *St. Elizabeth Home Society v. Hamilton (City)* (2008), 89 O.R. (3d) 81 (C.A.) [*St. Elizabeth*], Sharpe J.A. delivering the judgment of the court (Cronk and Gillese JJ.A.).

81 *Ibid.* at para. 30.

However, the journalist felt unable to answer the questions put to him without revealing the source and he was cited for contempt. Prior to the contempt hearing, a former city official came forward and testified that he was the confidential source and that he released the journalist from his undertaking. The trial judge proceeded with the contempt hearing anyway, and ordered the journalist to pay over $30,000 to the parties in costs flowing from his "improper" refusal to testify.

Justice Sharpe held that the trial judge had erred in requiring the journalist to answer questions that would reveal his source. The trial judge had not taken the required preliminary step of determining whether or not the privilege applied to this situation. The journalist was entitled "to have his claim for privilege tested" through the application of the Wigmore criteria.

He also held that it was a mistake to cite the journalist for contempt immediately. Other means of proceeding that are less intrusive to the confidential relationship should have been explored first. A court should proceed carefully and incrementally to preserve confidentiality to the extent possible. Justice Sharpe added this sage advice:

> To these legal considerations I would add a practical concern. Precipitous resort to the contempt power may be in the end counter-productive. By raising the stakes and presenting the journalist with an immediate all-or-nothing choice, there is a risk that the court's actions will foreclose the exploration of alternative means of securing the information. This does not assist the litigant who seeks the information and runs the risk of making a martyr of the defiant journalist, all to the detriment of the integrity of the courts and the administration of justice.[82]

Restraint in exercising the contempt power is generally inherent but "particularly apt" in its application to journalist-source confidentiality.

Justice Sharpe also adopted the suggestion that the *Dagenais/Mentuck* test, discussed in the previous section, provided a "useful analogy" in this context. While that test was developed in the context of publication bans, it is helpful whenever a balancing is required involving freedom of expression and freedom of the media. This is because

---

82 *Ibid.* at para. 45.

> courts are required to explore alternative measures and to minimize the impact upon the rights and values affected, essentially incorporating the proportionality and minimal impairment principles enshrined in s. 1 of the *Charter*.[83]

Here, the confidential source came forward and disclosed his identity. Had the trial judge exercised more restraint, the disputed information still would have become available while entirely avoiding the issue of contempt.

Finally, there was no justification for continuing with the contempt proceedings after the disputed information had become available. The journalist's refusal to answer was not in defiance of the court's authority. It was a respectful position taken out of deference to the undertaking he had given to his source and the ethics of his profession. The problem that posed for the court was how best to obtain the necessary evidence. Once the evidence became available, there was no need to continue any contempt proceedings.

These observations provide valuable guidance for commissioners and commission counsel. Often journalists are instrumental in exposing information that leads to the appointment of a commission of inquiry. Great deference should be given to the protection of their sources. Compelling journalist testimony should not be simply an alternative to a commission's own thorough investigation.

In *National Post*, the same court held that the privilege did not apply to a document that achieved prominence in relation to the "Shawinigate" investigation. Alleged bank documents and an envelope were provided by a confidential informant to a *National Post* reporter in connection with a loan from the Canadian Business Development Bank and a hotel in then Prime Minister Chrétien's riding. The Ontario Superior Court had ruled that the document was privileged under the Wigmore criteria and quashed an RCMP search warrant.[84] The Court of Appeal took issue with the lower court's balancing of freedom of expression against the law-enforcement interest. It concluded that the law-enforcement issue in disclosure was "overwhelming" so that the fourth criterion had not been satisfied and the documents had to be produced.[85] The Supreme

83 *Ibid.* at para. 47.

84 *R. v. National Post* (2004), 69 O.R. (3d) 427 (S.C.J.), Benotto J.

85 *R. v. National Post*, 2008 ONCA 139, Laskin and Simmons JJ.A., Gillese J.A. agreeing.

Court of Canada heard the appeal from this decision on 22 May 2009 but, at the time of writing, its ruling on this and other cases involving journalist privilege remain outstanding.

### 4) Litigation-Related

The Supreme Court recently explained the nature and application of "litigation privilege" in the *Blank* case.[86] Its purpose is to create a "zone of privacy" in relation to existing or anticipated litigation by protecting communications with third parties in preparation for trial. It also covers documents made in preparation for trial. Unlike solicitor-client privilege, it is not driven by a confidential relationship but by the exclusive "ownership" of a work product in the course of adversary proceedings.

Since the purpose of litigation privilege is entirely related to specific litigation, it loses that purpose and, therefore, its application once that litigation has ended. However, it does extend to "closely related" litigation that has not ended. Justice Fish elaborated upon this extended definition as including:

> separate proceedings that involve the same or related parties and arise from the same or related course of action (or "juridical source"). Proceedings that raise issues common to the initial action and share its essential purpose would in my view qualify as well.[87]

He added that it is not necessary that the documents in question be prepared for the sole purpose of litigation. Litigation privilege will also apply if that is their dominant purpose. It is also accepted that "litigation" applies to criminal proceedings.

The application of this privilege arose in the Goudge Inquiry when the Kingston Police Service objected to the production of documents related to a criminal prosecution. One of the documents was a memorandum from an investigating officer to the Crown attorneys prosecuting the case. The other document was a note of a meeting between officers and the Crown attorneys relating to matters required in prep-

---

86 *Blank v. Canada (Minister of Justice)*, [2006] 2 S.C.R. 319, Fish J. delivering the judgment of himself, McLachlin C.J., and Binnie, Deschamps, and Abella JJ.; Bastarache J. delivering the separate judgment of himself and Charron J. [*Blank*].

87 *Ibid.* at para. 39.

aration for the trial. The Crown subsequently withdrew the charge and the issue was whether the litigation privilege, which clearly existed, had survived the termination of the criminal proceedings. In accordance with his rules of procedure, Commissioner Goudge directed the issue to be resolved by the associate chief justice of Ontario.

The police argued that the litigation had not ended since there was no adjudication and the charge could be relaid in future. But Associate Chief Justice O'Connor held that the "theoretical possibility of a future charge," in place of the one that was withdrawn almost seven years previously, was not sufficient to support a claim that the litigation privilege continued. The police also argued that the Kingston Police Service was a party to "closely related proceedings" as a defendant by way of cross-claim in a lawsuit brought by the former accused arising out of her prosecution. But she had dropped her lawsuit against the police and provided a full and final release. While the police still would have to participate in discovery and testify at trial, they were not subject to liability. This did not constitute "closely related proceedings" that would support continuation of the litigation privilege arising from the prosecution.[88]

While the litigation privilege allows adversaries in litigation to keep certain cards "close to the vest," a separate privilege encourages them to talk. Communications between parties to a dispute are privileged when their purpose is to attempt to settle that dispute without resort to litigation or in the course of litigation. This settlement-negotiation privilege encourages settlement by respecting the intention of the parties that any admissions made during such discussions not be used against them if the litigation is inferred in the absence of evidence to the contrary.

This privilege does extend beyond the dispute in question to other proceedings that might arise subsequently. It also applies to criminal plea negations. Exceptions to the privilege may arise, for example, where the communications contain unlawful threats or the existence or nature of an alleged settlement, itself, is disputed.

88 Goudge Inquiry, Ruling (20 November 2007).

## 5) Police Informer

In *Leipert*, then Justice Beverley McLachlin described informer privilege as:

> an ancient and hallowed protection which plays a vital role in law enforcement.[89]

It allows a witness to decline to provide information that could disclose the identity of a confidential informant. Often such informants have access to information valuable to the police because they are marginally involved in criminal activities themselves. This permits police officers to establish personal relationships with them, sometimes through lenient treatment in law enforcement. In turn, the informants may provide information obtained through their criminal associations that will assist in important investigations. However, if they are exposed as police informers, they are at risk of retribution, including death.

Justice McLachlin explained the essential features of this privilege. The courts have no discretion to reject it in the circumstances of any particular case, with one exception. That is where there is a basis on the evidence for concluding that disclosure of the informer's identity is necessary to demonstrate the innocence of the accused. Mere speculation that the information might assist the defence is insufficient. But circumstances where the informer was a material witness to the crime or acted as an agent provocateur could establish a basis for the exception. Where that should occur, the Crown normally would stay the proceedings or elect not to call further evidence, with the result of an acquittal, rather than reveal the identity.

The privilege belongs to the Crown but the Crown may not waive it without the informer's consent. It applies in civil as well as criminal proceedings and protects a witness from having to answer a question as to whether she is a police informer. The privilege extends beyond the actual name of the informer to any information that might lead to revealing identity. This raises difficult problems for the Crown in determining how much evidence can be introduced without encountering that danger. It also creates difficulties for the trial judge in attempting

---

89 *R. v. Leipert*, [1997] 1 S.C.R. 281 at para. 9 [*Leipert*], delivering the judgment of herself, Lamer C.J., and La Forest, Sopinka, Gonthier, Cory, McLachlin, Iacobucci, and Major JJ. L'Heureux-Dubé J. delivered separate reasons.

to "edit" information to assist the accused. Justice McLachlin noted that there may be cases where the court can be certain that an edited document will not reveal the informer's identity. But, in this case, that was not possible since it was an anonymous tip sheet and the informer could not be consulted. In such circumstances, none of the details should be disclosed, subject only to the "innocence at stake" exception.

If the exception is asserted by the accused, the following steps should follow:

- The accused must show some basis to support the conclusion that without disclosure his innocence is at stake.
- If the court finds such a basis, only as much information should be revealed as is essential to permit proof of innocence.
- The Crown should first be given the option of staying proceedings.
- If the Crown chooses to proceed, the essential information should be disclosed to the accused.

It should be kept in mind that, while the public interest in law enforcement underlies this privilege, there is no balancing of that public interest in its application to specific situations. It must be applied as rule of law.

### 6) Public-Interest Immunity

At common law, where the government seeks to withhold its documents or information from the courts, a judicial discretion exists to weigh the public interest in protecting them against that of disclosing them in the courts.[90] This discretion still exists throughout Canada but at the federal level it has been emasculated by superimposed statutory provisions in the *Canada Evidence Act*.[91]

Section 39 applies to Cabinet-related documents and is cast very broadly. A minister or the clerk of the Privy Council simply files a certificate that the information in question is covered by this section and the protection is absolute. Reference was made in Chapter 5, Section A

---

90 The nature and exercise of discretion was addressed in *Carey v. Ontario*, [1986] 2 S.C.R. 637.

91 Above note 37.

to the circumstances in which Commissioner Gomery was able to gain access to the secret Cabinet documents relevant to his mandate, but this was highly unusual. There is no legal avenue by which such access can be obtained.

Section 38 is equally restrictive with respect to National Security Confidentiality but in a more convoluted way. There is no provision for judicial balancing of the public interest in disclosure against potential injury to international relations, national defence, or national security. The extent of government resistance to disclosure on these grounds was demonstrated in both the Arar and Air India inquiries.[92] In Arar, the commissioner essentially abandoned any attempt to obtain disclosure on a claim-by-claim basis in favour of writing the entire report as his vehicle for expressing his views on these issues. In Air India, Commissioner Major used the threat of his resignation to gain sufficient ground in the war of attrition to allow his hearings to be completed. Under section 38, the attorney general may overturn the judge's decision requiring disclosure by simply filing a certificate.

Section 37 applies to the protection or disclosure of government information on grounds other than Cabinet or NSC immunity. The ground of public interest for claiming immunity must be specified by the government in each situation. The court then may order disclosure where the public interest in disclosure is more important than the specified public interest. The form and conditions of disclosure may be directed to limit encroachment on the specified public interest. The forum for adjudicating the government objection is the Federal Court or the provincial superior court, depending on the jurisdiction under which the commission of inquiry is established.

### 7) Official Functions

A number of privileges and immunities arise out of the functions performed in a variety of public roles. These include the absolute immunity of judges from testifying about the grounds for their decisions, based on the principle of judicial independence.[93] Closely related is the quali-

---

92 Section D(2), above in this chapter.

93 Chapter 7, Section A(2).

fied privilege for deliberative secrecy that arose in litigation out of the Stevens Inquiry.[94]

The secrecy of jury deliberations is specifically protected by the *Criminal Code*. This protection goes beyond a privilege not to disclose. It makes it a criminal offence for a juror to disclose any information relating to private jury proceedings.[95] This issue has arisen in the wrongful-conviction inquiries, where commissioners have been urged (unsuccessfully) to examine aspects of jury deliberations to shed light on the causes of wrongful convictions.

Finally, the issue of parliamentary privilege arose in the Gomery Inquiry's hearings. One of the parties sought to cross-examine a witness on statements made earlier before a parliamentary committee that were dramatically different from the witness's testimony at the inquiry hearings. In a comprehensive decision analyzing the privilege in this context, Justice Danièle Tremblay-Lamer upheld the exclusion of the use of the earlier testimony at the subsequent inquiry hearings.[96]

---

94 Chapter 6, Section A(2).

95 R.S.C. 1985, c. C-46, s. 649.

96 *Gagliano v. Canada (House of Commons)*, [2005] 3 F.C.R. 555 (Fed. Ct.). See also the Arar Inquiry, Ruling on Parliamentary Privilege (30 May 2005).

CHAPTER NINE

# *Final Report*

## A. WRITING THE REPORT

### 1) General Considerations

Completion of the final report is the ultimate goal of a commission of inquiry. The manner in which the journey is conducted will help to demonstrate how effectively the commission has fulfilled its purpose. That includes acting independently, effectively, and transparently in using its powers to fulfill its mandate. This in turn will be reflected in how the commissioner, counsel, and other staff have carried out their roles and how they have dealt with the parties, the media, and the public. The journey will be especially reflected in the public hearings. But the ultimate contribution and standard for judging a commission of inquiry is its final report. This report, itself, will be the main basis on which the recommendations it contains will be assessed.

The late Justice Archie Campbell established his own standards which he "plastered" on his office walls "on large posters" when writing the report of his Bernardo Inquiry:

- Does it give the public the significant facts?
- Does it identify the significant issues?
- Are all the problems covered?
- Are the recommendations doable?
- Would they prevent another *Bernardo* case?

- Is it accurate?
- Is it clear?
- Is it fair?[1]

One of the commissioners in the Somalia Inquiry wanted no part in writing the report:

> Assembling, writing, and editing a royal commission report is perhaps the most unrewarding task in the world. This is a job for technicians who have the skills needed to absorb mountains of data, sort it into neat piles, and process it into something recognizable and meaningful.
>
> I'm not saying that I don't admire people who can do this. It's a special ability that is in high demand in Ottawa, where the production of speeches, manuals, press releases, studies, and reports of every size and description provides employment for a small army of anonymous writers. But better them than me.[2]

Such an approach is appropriate when dealing with technical information, which is generally descriptive and not contentious. But where potential findings of misconduct or other controversial issues are involved, the commissioner will want to engage in the drafting personally, or at least be in ongoing dialogue with the drafter. This is important, not only for actual findings, but also for how they are expressed.

The foundation for making recommendations has two broad components. The first is to analyze the evidence and determine the relevant factual basis for the report. The second is to draw inferences and conclusions from those findings of fact. Both aspects are dictated and constrained by the terms of reference. In the context of potential findings of misconduct in *Krever*, it was argued that findings of fact were permissible but not the evaluation of those facts "according to a standard of conduct." This argument was rejected, since "it simply would not make sense for the government to appoint a commissioner who necessarily becomes very knowledgeable about all aspects of the events under investigation, and then prevent the commissioner from relying upon this

1 "The Bernardo Investigation Review" in Allan Manson & David Mullan, eds., *Commissions of Inquiry, Praise or Reappraise?* (Toronto: Irwin Law, 2003) at 402.

2 Peter Desbarats, *Somalia Cover-Up: A Commissioner's Journal* (Toronto: McClelland & Stewart, 1997) at 296.

knowledge to make informed evaluations of the evidence presented."[3] These two steps then place the commissioner in a unique position to make recommendations for the future.[4]

The terms of reference will provide initial guidance as to what should be placed on the factual record. They will inform the commissioner's initial "game plan" and the manner in which commission counsel organizes the hearings and calls evidence. It is important not to make factual assumptions and to anticipate all evidence that will be required for writing the report, so that it may be adduced and tested. Where there appears to be a consensus among the parties about some important facts and there are no other relevant interests, that consensus should be placed on the record so there can be no objection after the report is written. Reference has been made to the role of the commissioner in assessing the facts individually and collectively, including their interrelationships.[5]

In Walkerton, Commissioner O'Connor qualified the factual basis on which he reached certain conclusions: "Instead of making findings of fact, in some instances I have set out my conclusions by expressing them in terms of the probability or likelihood of something happening or not happening . . . . Several of my conclusions are qualified by rather remote possibilities."[6] Precision and clarity in expressing the extent of reliance on facts will contribute to the accuracy of the report. In turn, that should lead to a better understanding of the nature of the inferences drawn from them.

In some circumstances, especially when an inquiry continues over an extended period, it may be important to verify whether further developments have occurred since the time when particular issues were addressed at the hearings. Praise has been given to a police force, in a commission report, for reforms adopted even before hearings were completed.[7] Where

---

3 *Canada (Attorney General) v. Canada (Commission of Inquiry on the Blood System in Canada—Krever Commission)*, [1997] 3 S.C.R. 440 at para. 40, Cory J. delivering the judgment of the Court [*Krever*].

4 In *Morneault*, Justice Reed identified three steps in making findings but her last two can be subsumed under "evaluations," as used in the above quote from *Krever*. See *Morneault v. Canada (Attorney General)* (1998), 150 F.T.R. 28 at para. 61 (T.D.) [*Morneault*].

5 See Chapter 5, Section B(2).

6 Walkerton Inquiry, Part One at 37.

7 See Chapter 3, Section D(4) and Chapter 6, Section C.

such positive changes occur, the parties responsible are likely to take the initiative to inform the commission. But changes could also occur in a negative direction or otherwise cause the report to appear "outdated." Such circumstances are not likely to arise frequently but should be covered off as a matter of "good housekeeping."

Once facts have been determined, inferences must then be drawn from the primary facts as to what happened, how, and why. At this stage, there should be some context or criteria for evaluating or explaining the consequences that follow. In *Krever*, it was argued that the use of words such as "failure" would imply a finding of civil liability. But Justice Cory rejected this notion:

> As the Court of Appeal pointed out, there are many different types of normative standards, including moral, scientific and professional-ethical. To state that a person "failed" to do something that should have been done does not necessarily mean that the person breached a criminal or civil standard of conduct. The same is true of the word responsible.[8]

The specific issue of findings of misconduct is discussed in the next section. The point here is simply that, where the commissioner reaches a conclusion about matters based on some criteria, those criteria should be articulated.

The actual form the report takes will depend on a variety of factors but its structure and organization will contribute to how well it is understood. Often the terms of reference, game plan, and organization of the hearings will provide guidance. But not always, since the same topic may emerge in different stages of the hearings. Often final submissions will be helpful since the relative significance of evidence and related issues may change over the course of the hearings. Time and effort spent on the organization and structure of the report will be worth the investment, as with any massive and complex writing challenge.

Efforts should be made to achieve a writing style that is friendly to members of the public, who do not have legal or other expertise that may be engaged. Usually, there is a story or stories to tell. Often they can be told in an interesting as well as an informative way. Even if most members of the public won't actually read the report, it will be quoted by the media. The quotes that are used are likely to be those that suc-

---

8 Above note 3 at para. 62.

cinctly, clearly, and directly summarize particular issues of importance to the public.

In making the report readable, it also helps to strive for expression in "plain English." Like the rules of natural justice, the rules of natural English are not codified. They both reflect the underlying principle of fairness . . . to a party and to a reader. They are flexible but have some guidelines. In the case of natural English, some examples are:

- use short and direct sentences;
- use active rather than passive voice;
- move thoughts in logical sequence;
- show the links in that movement;
- use small words when they suffice;
- avoid double negatives; and
- avoid a cliché unless it is really necessary.

Especially when massive detail is available, it is important to avoid the clutter of marginal and trivial information. Technical detail that is considered necessary often can be included as an appendix rather than in the text.

The late Charles Dubin conducted the commission of inquiry into the Ben Johnson doping scandal. The former Chief Justice of Ontario was fond of recounting his experience when first appointed directly from the bar to the Ontario Court of Appeal. He attended an international judges conference and was required to submit a judgment-writing assignment as part of the program. His assignment was returned with many passages underlined in red, with the initials "wgas" handwritten in the margins. He was puzzled but the instructor subsequently explained that they stood for "who gives a shit?"

I fully realize that, in offering these suggestions, I am exposing myself to standards that may not have been met in this book. If so, I apologize to you, the reader, for any pain I have inflicted. My only explanation is that it just seemed right at the time.

### 2) Critical Analysis

Writing imposes a valuable discipline on analysis and reasoning. If it just doesn't "write," it may well be wrong or incomplete or deficient for some other reason. Writing encourages self-questioning by requiring logical connections and accurate descriptions. It may reveal inappropriate assumptions. It engages a dialogue with oneself. That dialogue can be enhanced by introducing a second mind that represents a "sounding board" for the commissioner. This was one of the six broad functions of commission counsel identified by former commissioner O'Connor. It was recommended earlier that this function should be removed from hearings counsel and assigned to advisory counsel, who would play no role in the hearings.[9] This bifurcation of roles has the added advantage of allowing hearings counsel to take on an adversary role, when appropriate, and to make comprehensive final submissions.

The ongoing dialogue between the commissioner and advisory counsel allows the exploration of ideas that may be "half-baked." At times it may lead nowhere but it also may reveal unsound assumptions, put preliminary findings in perspective, and identify alternative findings or avenues of pursuit. The commissioner may then advise hearings counsel of additional areas that should be explored in the hearings. The dialogue between the commissioner and advisory counsel will be most extensive in the process of writing the final report but will be subject to deliberative secrecy throughout.[10]

Lord Justice Salmon identified one of the pitfalls that a commissioner may face:

> Every experienced judge must know that sometimes he starts with the hope that he may be able to reach a certain conclusion, either because to him it seems just or sensible or even in the national interest. He knows too that there is a subconscious tendency or temptation to mould the facts to accord with that conclusion. This is a tendency to temptation against which every experienced judge of intellectual integrity is always on his guard . . . .[11]

A sounding board is particularly valuable when a commissioner becomes too quickly or too deeply enamored with a result. As suggested above, that predisposition may affect fact finding (including credibility). It may

9 Above Chapter 6, Sections A(3) & (4).

10 *Stevens v. Canada (Attorney General)* (2002), 215 F.T.R. 228 at paras. 37 and following (T.D.). Heneghan J. acknowledged the privilege but characterized it as qualified.

11 Sir Cyril Salmon, *Tribunals of Inquiry*, Lionel Cohen Lectures, The Hebrew University of Jerusalem, Fourteenth Series—1967 (Jerusalem: Magnes Press, Hebrew University, 1967) at 10.

also contaminate other findings. Critical thinking is often enhanced by the expression and elaboration of "contrarian" views. As with circumstantial evidence, it is important to give adequate prominence to the few parts that "don't fit" in the context of the many that do. This was demonstrated in the analysis of police and prosecutorial conduct that led to a number of wrongful convictions. Tunnel vision was identified as a subconscious "locking in" to a particular theory of the case, aggrandizing supporting evidence, and ignoring or rationalizing contradictory evidence, as well as adopting related questionable attitudes and practices.[12]

It is not always easy to sort out the relative weight that should be given to the various factors that are at play. One commentator on the Westray Inquiry, Eric Tucker, observes:

> While it is not true that everything causes everything else, a large number of events and actions are, in some sense, causally connected to a particular outcome. Thus, while there may be agreement that some factors can be eliminated because they are not causal in any sense, there is room for substantial disagreement about the relative significance of the many events that are causal in some sense.[13]

Tucker points out that various criteria may be invoked to assign relative significance to multiple causes. The choice of criteria may depend on the purpose of the analysis. For example, if the goal is occupational safety, the analysis may be different than if the purpose is to assign responsibility. Commissions of inquiry often must approach the same facts for a variety of purposes, requiring corresponding perspectives. Often both an individual and a systemic analysis will be most helpful.

A series of individual actions sometimes may be connected to reveal a broader picture. The commissioner in Westray observed:

> This Report has been written with the benefit of hindsight, which, as the saying goes, provides 20/20 vision. Many of the incidents that now appear to fit into the mosaic might at the time, and of themselves, have seemed trivial. Viewed in context, these seemingly isolated incidents

---

12 Discussed in Chapter 3, Section D(4).

13 Eric Tucker, "The Westray Mine Disaster and Its Aftermath: The Politics of Causation" (1995) 10 C.J.L.S. 91 at 94–95.

> constitute a mind-set or operating philosophy that appears to favour expediency over intelligent planning and that trivializes safety concerns.[14]

But inappropriate reliance on hindsight also may drive findings out of perspective and may be unfair when assessing individual conduct.

Justice Campbell described hindsight as the "most insidious" of all of a commissioner's temptations.[15] In conducting his review, and knowing that Bernardo was the rapist and killer, it would have been easy to focus on the many references to his name in the documentation of the police investigations. But he was only one name among thousands of potential suspects and many were much stronger suspects than him. It was easy in hindsight to ask why the police did not identify him as the murderer when interviewing him several times. But the context of serial-predator investigations had to be considered:

> It is surprisingly common . . . for the police to interview the killer several times without connecting him to the deaths. Predatory psychopathic killers can be very plausible and appear innocent. They do not typically reveal themselves during police interviews. It is a commonplace of such investigations that the Yorkshire Ripper was interviewed by the police at least nine times during the course of his six-year series of seven attacks and thirteen murders.[16]

Moreover, the investigating officers were fully aware of this phenomenon and lived with the fear that they would interview the killer and not know it.

Justice Campbell drew a distinction between formulating recommendations, where hindsight is essential, and assessing past conduct, where hindsight is unfair:

> The only fair way to review past conduct is to avoid hindsight. The only fair way is to put yourself in the shoes of the person who had to make the decision. What did they know when they decided to quit a particular line of investigation? What did they know and what did they think when they failed to report a particular incident?[17]

---

14 Westray Inquiry, "Executive Summary" at ix.

15 Above note 1 at 395.

16 *Ibid.* at 396.

17 *Ibid.*

He added that, even when conscious of the temptation of hindsight, it is difficult for a commissioner to avoid since it may be attractive to the public and those critical of the individuals and organizations involved.

The importance of fairness and impartiality on the part of the commissioner is worth emphasizing in the context of writing the final report.[18] The danger of "crusading zeal" must be avoided. There may be an appropriate place for blunt and scathing comments in a report, but a commissioner, and even a judge in a criminal trial, may get carried away. Examples include the Erebus Inquiry in New Zealand and the conduct of the judge in the *Elliott* case. A report does not have to scream to be heard and often a calm, rational, and fair presentation will be powerful on its merits.

Another example of a commission of inquiry getting "off track" was described in *Peters v. Davison*.[19] The plaintiff made allegations against law-enforcement bodies in relation to the investigation of transactions said to be fraudulent. As a result, a commission of inquiry was established to inquire into how these bodies carried out their functions in relation to the transactions in question. But, instead of inquiring into the transactions and how they were investigated, the commission focused entirely on the plaintiff. It insisted that he produce complete evidence in support of his allegations. When he could not, the commission lambasted both him and his counsel in its report. The court held that it was not within the plaintiff's intention or ability to act as a prosecutor before the commission. It was for the commission to make its own inquiries and, in failing to do so, it committed errors of law which were reviewable.

### 3) Expressing Reasons

The effectiveness of a commission of inquiry will often depend on the strength of the commissioner's reasoning and that will be judged by how it is expressed in the final report. There is considerable case law and legal literature on the duty of trial judges and administrative tribunals to give reasons for their decisions. Written reasons may be a legal requirement of the principle of fairness:

---

18 See discussion in Chapter 5, Section B(3).

19 [1999] 2 N.Z.L.R. 164 (C.A.) [*Peters*]. This decision cites Canadian cases arising out of the Landreville, Krever, and Somalia inquiries.

> [I]n certain circumstances, the duty of procedural fairness will require the provision of a written explanation for a decision. The strong arguments demonstrating the advantages of written reasons suggest that, in cases such as this where the decision has important significance for the individual, where there is a statutory right of appeal, or in other circumstances, some form of reasons should be required.[20]

There is no issue about whether or not a commission of inquiry must provide written reasons. Its findings and reasoned conclusions are the very purpose for its existence.

But the principle of fairness may come into play in challenging the adequacy of a commissioner's reasoning. A finding of misconduct may have "important significance" for the reputation of an individual. Such a finding would be a denial of fairness if there were no adequate explanation to support such a conclusion. The Supreme Court in *Baker* indicated that this requirement had to be applied flexibly, with consideration given to the variety of administrative agencies and processes that might be affected.[21] Even so, the application of the principle of fairness to findings of misconduct by commissions of inquiry[22] strongly suggests that adequate reasons would be required in these circumstances.

The case law related to the requirement of reasons in civil and criminal cases is not directly applicable to the reports of commissions of inquiry. However, some of the discussions in those cases provide guidance as to the importance of supporting conclusions by articulating the underlying analysis and reasoning. The following passages[23] illustrate the problem:

> [R]easons that, for page after page, describe the facts, but never refer to them again, detail the parties' submissions, state the law, and leap straight to the conclusion, are not helpful. When the section of the reasons headed, "Analysis," is shorter than the others, there is something wrong.[24]

---

20 *Baker v. Canada (Ministry of Citizenship and Immigration)*, [1999] 2 S.C.R. 817 at para. 43, L'Heureux-Dubé J. writing for the Court on this issue [*Baker*].

21 *Ibid.* at paras. 23–27 and 44.

22 Above note 3 at para. 55. Quoted in Chapter 7, Section D(1).

23 Quoted in Phillip Bryden, "Standards of Review and Sufficiency of Reasons: Some Practical Considerations" (2006) 19 Can. J. Admin. L. & Prac. 191 at 216 & 217.

24 J. Evans, "Writing Effective Tribunal Decisions and Reasons" (2002) 19 Can. J. Admin. L. & Prac. 95 at 102.

> The obligation to provide adequate reasons is not satisfied by merely reciting the submissions and evidence of the parties and stating a conclusion. Rather, the decision-maker must set out its findings of fact and the principal evidence upon which those findings were based. The reasons must address the major points in issue. The reasoning process followed by the decision-maker must be set out and must reflect consideration of the main relevant factors.[25]

In other words, mere recitation of the facts and arguments does not constitute analysis and reasoning. In effect, it amounts to no reasons.

The leading case on reasons for judgment in criminal cases is *Sheppard*, where Justice Binnie delivered the judgment of the Supreme Court of Canada.[26] He characterized the obligation to provide reasons as the vehicle for making the decision maker accountable. This obligation is owed to the parties but also "to the public at large." He added that accountability "seeks basic fairness, not perfection." This characterization is analogous to the accountability of a commissioner for the content of her final report.

In *Sheppard*, the sum total of the trial judge's reasons was as follows:

> Having considered all of the testimony in this case, and reminding myself of the burden on the Crown and the credibility of witnesses, and how this is to be assessed, I find the defendant guilty as charged.

Such "generic" reasons amounted to no reasons at all and, as the court below observed, the circumstances of the case "cried out for some explanatory analysis."[27] Justice Binnie adopted the following passage from an earlier case:

> Where the record, including the reasons for judgment, discloses a lack of appreciation of relevant evidence and more particularly the complete disregard of such evidence, then it falls upon the reviewing tribunal to intercede.[28]

---

25 *VIA Rail Canada Inc. v. Canada (National Transportation Agency)*, [2001] 2 F.C. 25 at para. 22 (C.A.), Sexton J.

26 *R. v. Sheppard*, [2002] 1 S.C.R. 869 [*Sheppard*]. See also: *R. v. Gagnon*, [2006] 1 S.C.R. 621; *R. v. Dinardo*, 2008 SCC 24 [*Dinardo*]; *R. v. Walker*, 2008 SCC 34.

27 *Sheppard, ibid.* at para. 1 (Newfoundland Court of Appeal).

28 *Harper v. The Queen*, [1982] 1 S.C.R. 2 at 14, Estey J. delivering the judgment of himself and Martland, Dickson, Betz, McIntyre, and Lamer JJ., Ritchie J. dissenting.

Reasons may demonstrate a failure to grasp an important point or complete disregard for it. In *Sheppard* there were no reasons, but there were important issues that should have been addressed. The evidence revealed significant inconsistencies or conflicts and the "confused and contradictory evidence" related to key issues in the case. Justice Binnie also provided this example from another case:

> The trial judge made no comment on the frailty of the identification evidence other than the general statement that she found L.'s evidence credible and accepted it. No reference is made to the fact that the appellant was not identified in court and that no explanation for failure to ask L. to do so was given. No reference is made to the erroneous identification made by T. using the photograph of the appellant.[29]

These problems were not even acknowledged by the trial judge, which leads to the reasonable inference that she was oblivious to them.

In *Dinardo*,[30] the Court said that the sufficiency of reasons turns on whether they respond to the "live issues" in the case, having regard to all of the evidence and the submissions of counsel. Identifying and addressing the "live issues" is at the heart of the work of a commission of inquiry. In the *Dinardo* case the central issue again was credibility. There were numerous inconsistencies in the complainant's testimony and she admitted that she sometimes "invented stories." On cross-examination, she admitted she made up the story of the sexual assault in question because she did not like the accused. She said she was afraid of him because of his tattoos. On re-examination, she said she did not make up this story. In questioning by the judge she said she did not know what it meant to "make something up."

The Court acknowledged the difficulties in assessing credibility and the deference due to the trial judge on this issue. But here the reasons for judgment failed to explain how he could find the complainant to be a credible witness in the circumstances. Reasons must attempt to resolve confused and contradictory evidence on a key issue. Factors detracting from credibility cannot simply be ignored. The requirement "to

29 *R. v. Burke*, [1996] 1 S.C.R. 474 at para. 53, Sopinka J. delivering the judgment of the Court.

30 Above note 26, Charron J. delivering the judgment of the Court.

give reasons itself concentrates the judicial mind on the difficulties that are presented."[31]

In developing reasons, it is often helpful to have in mind the audience at whom the reasons are directed. In writing judicial reasons, it is sometimes said that the most important audience is the losing party:

> It is the loser and his representative, colleagues, friends and relatives who must be especially assisted in understanding the basis for the tribunal's conclusion. Failure to provide an adequate explanation of the tribunal's reasons can only leave an impression of arbitrariness and unfairness and a legacy of bitterness and alienation.[32]

There often are many audiences for a commission's report: government, parties, victims, a local community, professional communities, the media, the general public, and others. The focus and emphasis on particular audiences may shift for reasons given on different subjects or aspects of a particular report.

### 4) Making Recommendations

It is difficult to generalize about the process a commission of inquiry should follow in making recommendations. They often arise out of specific problems expressed in the terms of reference, which may also identify specific solutions that should be investigated. For example, the Cornwall Inquiry was directed to "inquire into and report on processes, services or programs that would encourage community healing and reconciliation in Cornwall." Recent federal terms of reference direct the commissioner "to make any recommendations that he considers advisable" related to the subject matter of the inquiry. Almost all commissions of inquiry receive a comparable open-ended invitation.

It is ideal if the entire community that is the subject of an inquiry will "buy in" to a commission's recommendations. That is most likely when those recommendations arise from within that community itself. When that happens, there is also a stronger likelihood that the recommendations will be implemented. To quote the late Justice Archie Campbell:

---

31 *Sheppard*, above note 26 at para. 23.

32 S. Ronald Ellis, Carole Trethewey, & Frederika Rotter, "Tribunals—Reasons, and Reasons for Reasons" (1990–91) 4 Can. J. Admin. L. & Prac. 105 at 109.

> Our good fortune in the Bernardo review was that the police and public safety and forensic communities, from the top down, realized that changes were needed. It was clear from our soundings of those communities that there was a will to change. Our recommendations came from within those communities, were welcomed, and are now either fully implemented or in the final stages of implementation.[33]

The inquiry process can be fertile ground for consensus building about solutions. Those who most directly experienced the problems, and perhaps were a part of those problems, are often best situated to generate solutions that are practical and effective. When these solutions coalesce into a commissioner's recommendations, there is added credibility and momentum for implementation.

The evolution of consensus over the course of some recent inquiries is reflected in the prompt and positive government responses to their reports. The Ontario government agreed to all of the recommendations of Part One of the Walkerton Report when it was released and subsequently adopted all of the recommendations in Part Two. Upon release of the Lamer Report, the government of Newfoundland and Labrador announced that it would implement every one of its recommendations. The report of the Taman Inquiry received the same complete endorsement from the government of Manitoba. Within a month of the Goudge Report, the Ontario government presented legislation to address all of Goudge's recommended legislative changes.[34]

Even when consensus is not possible, it is important to expose potential recommendations to public scrutiny. For investigative commissions, this may generate some opposing views from affected interests and parties. The objective of finding common ground rather than polarizing will be important but there also are broader interests than the parties most directly affected. These essentially involve the public and the government. The government's interest in recommendations will impose a different set of criteria for implementation, such as budgetary implications, government priorities, and political ramifications. The public reaction, in turn, will influence that of the government, and a range of more narrow interests beyond the parties also may come into play.

---

33 Above note 1 at 400.

34 Robert Todd, "Measures Unveiled to Address Goudge Report" *Law Times* (27 October 2008).

The identification, exploration, and evaluation of broad policy choices is more characteristic (by definition) of policy/advisory commissions, discussed in the next chapter. But policy considerations may also arise in investigative commissions. Their terms of reference often have two aspects. The first is investigative or fact finding and the second is to make recommendations for broader changes to avoid similar problems in future. Systemic aspects arising out of investigative commissions of inquiry are discussed in Section B(4) below.

## B. FINDINGS OF MISCONDUCT

### 1) Reputation

In "Public Inquiries and the Legality of Blaming," Wayne MacKay and Monica G. McQueen state:

> An integral part of this growing demand for accountability is the concept of blaming. When things go wrong, people want to know whom to blame for the state of affairs. This is particularly true in respect to commissions of inquiry where the government or one of its agencies is the most likely candidate for blame and accountability.[35]

They argue that the purpose of attributing blame cannot be justified as remedial since public and media interest dissipates as soon as "names have been named." There is often little public pressure to implement the report's recommendations. For some inquiries, the interest in blame may relate to human curiosity or to the desire to deflect blame to a particular individual to avoid broader responsibility. Finally, MacKay and McQueen suggest, there may be a desire for retribution.

Findings of misconduct should be kept in perspective as merely a necessary part of telling the story of what happened. In some inquiries, they may be the central theme of the story. But the parties as well as the commissioner should always be mindful of the serious consequences they may have. In *Peters*,[36] the court frequently referred to the "devastating" effect a report may have on individual reputations. In *Krever*, Justice

35 Wayne MacKay & Monica G. McQueen, "Public Inquiries and the Legality of Blaming: Truth, Justice, and the Canadian Way" in Manson & Mullan, eds., above note 1 at 250.

36 Above note 19.

Cory agreed with the following passage from the judgment of the court below:

> a public inquiry would be quite pointless if it did not lead to identification of the causes and players for fear of harming reputations . . . . I doubt it would be possible to meet the need for public inquiries whose aim is to shed light on a particular incident without in some way interfering with the reputations of the individuals involved.[37]

He added that damaged reputations might simply be "the price which must be paid."

Later, Justice Cory stressed the need for fairness in dealing with reputation:

> [P]rocedural fairness is essential, for the findings of commissions may damage the reputation of a witness. *For most, a good reputation is their most highly prized attribute*.[38]

Fairness requires advanced notice and the opportunity to respond to potential findings of misconduct. It also requires fairness at the hearings where parties should not be permitted to use cross-examination simply to "beat up" witnesses for their past conduct.[39]

The importance of reputation to individuals is demonstrated in the successful applications for judicial review in the *Landreville, Stevens*, and *Chrétien* cases. It took former Cabinet minister Stevens almost twenty years to establish, judicially, that he had been unfairly treated. But he was satisfied it was worth it.[40]

Guy Pratte is currently acting as counsel to former prime minister Brian Mulroney in the Mulroney-Schreiber Inquiry. In an interview some time before the hearings, he spoke of the devastating effect of the Air Canada Inquiry on his father's reputation, more than thirty years earlier.[41] Yves Pratte was a prominent Quebec corporate lawyer, and a former dean

---

37 Above note 3 at para. 39, quoting from Décary J.A. who delivered the judgment of the Federal Court of Appeal. *Canada (Attorney General) v. Canada (Commission of Inquiry on the Blood System in Canada—Krever Commission)*, [1997] F.C.J. No. 17 (C.A.), Strayer and MacGuigan JJ. agreeing.

38 *Ibid*. at para. 55 [emphasis added].

39 See Chapter 6, Section C.

40 Chapter 3, Section B(2).

41 Richard Cleroux, "Pratte-à-porter" *Canadian Lawyer* (July 2008).

of the Laval law school, when he was appointed as head of Air Canada by newly elected Prime Minister Pierre Trudeau in 1968. He led a corporate makeover that adopted aggressive marketing practices in the early 1970s, including arrangements with travel agencies and resorts. The vice-president responsible for marketing, Yves Ménard, resigned in the wake of revelations of a $100,000 payment to a travel agency. A commission of inquiry was established to inquire into the Crown corporation's practices and Commissioner Willard Estey's report in 1975 was critical of Pratte. His son, Guy Pratte, recalled seeing the letter from the minister of transport dismissing his father and his subsequent futile attempts to gain employment: "People would say 'oh no, we don't want him; he's tainted goods. He's been fired from Air Canada.' I don't think he ever really recovered from that. It was a hurt that was always there because he had loved Air Canada, and although he was a lawyer, he would have gladly left law forever for the business world." Many felt that he had been unfairly treated and Trudeau appointed him to the Supreme Court of Canada in 1977 but his heart wasn't in it and he returned to Montreal within two years. He died nine years later at the age of sixty-three.

Rather ironically, or perhaps appropriately, Guy Pratte has frequently represented clients before commissions of inquiry and parliamentary committees. He has strong feelings about their potential for unfairness: "Those public inquiries are very, very crude instruments . . . . I've seen first-hand the harm they can do to people's reputations . . . . I think we fail to see how hurtful these things can be for people in the public eye." His experience in appearing with Mulroney before the House of Commons Ethics Committee left him even more critical: "At a parliamentary committee there are absolutely no rules. Zero rules. At least at inquiry commissions some rules of fairness apply."[42] The principle of fairness must be applied with meticulous care when potential findings of misconduct arise.

### 2) Civil and Criminal Liability

The terms of reference of almost every investigative commission of inquiry specifically direct the commissioner "to perform his duties with-

---

42 See the account of the performance of the House of Commons Standing Committee on Access to Information, Privacy and Ethics, in relation to the Mulroney-Schreiber affair in Chapter 4, Section B(1).

out expressing any conclusions or recommendation regarding the civil or criminal liability of any person or organization."[43] Even where such a prohibition is not expressed, it probably exists as a matter of law. In *Nelles*, the Ontario Court of Appeal stated:

> This inquiry should not be permitted to become that *which it could not have legally been constituted to be*, an inquiry to determine who was civilly or criminally responsible for the death of the children . . . .[44]

In this case, a finding of criminal liability would have offended the federal government's constitutional jurisdiction over criminal law. The terms of reference in *Starr*[45] were struck down on this basis, and with the approval of the decision in *Nelles*. Additionally, a finding of civil liability likely would impinge on the jurisdiction of a superior court under section 96 of the *Constitution Act, 1867*, while a finding of criminal responsibility by a federally constituted commission likely would offend section 7 of the *Charter* by using coercive investigative powers to purport to render a finding of criminal guilt.

The *Nelles* court faced squarely the question of what would constitute a finding of civil or criminal responsibility and said:

> In our opinion, such a conclusion may be expressed by findings of fact which without more, when found against a named person, constitute a conclusion of criminal or civil responsibility. In the circumstances, if in carrying out the direction in the Order in Council the commissioner, in determining the cause of death makes such findings, then he is by this specific limitation precluded from naming the persons whose act caused or contributed to the death or deaths of the children.[46]

The court saw no problem with the commissioner hearing all of the evidence relating to the cause of death of the children. This included evidence tending to show that some died as a result of unlawful or negligent acts. It said that he should analyze and report on all of the evidence

43 The Gomery, Arar, Air India, Iacobucci, and Mulroney-Schreiber inquiries all have this exact wording in their terms of reference. Almost identical language is found in those of provincial commissions of inquiry.

44 *Re Nelles and Grange* (1984), 46 O.R. (2d) 210 at 217 (C.A.) [*Nelles*], discussed in Chapter 3, Section E(3) [emphasis added].

45 *Starr v. Houlden*, [1990] 1 S.C.R. 1366, discussed in Chapter 3, Section E(5) [*Starr*].

46 Above note 44 at 219.

related to the circumstances of each death and could make recommendations on such evidence. But he could not identify an individual as being responsible for a death. Findings of fact that a deliberate action of a named person caused a death would amount to a conclusion that death was intended. This would amount to a conclusion of law as to civil or criminal responsibility. What is important is that the public would consider it a determination, which would be "seriously prejudicial" in subsequent criminal proceedings.

In *Kingsclear*, the applicant sought to quash findings of misconduct against him arising out of an inquiry into allegations of sexual abuse of students in a training school. The applicant, Richards, was the supervisor of programs at the time of the alleged abuse. Chief Justice Daigle was faced with determining whether the findings amounted to a conclusion of civil or criminal liability under the limitation established in *Nelles*. He stated that this limitation:

> precludes a commissioner from making findings of fact which, without more, amount to a conclusion of law of civil or criminal responsibility of a named person.[47]

He interpreted *Nelles* as prohibiting the association of an individual with findings of fact that meet all of the essential elements of a crime or tort (or some other basis for civil liability).

The commissioner in the Kingsclear Inquiry had included this finding in his report: "[T]he bitter truth is that the officers and employees responsible for the care and safety of the boys of the Training School failed to take any realistically appropriate action and thereby failed and dishonoured the boys." It is obvious from the report that Richards was one of those "officers and employees" since he is specifically named in this context and his conduct is scrutinized. Chief Justice Daigle concluded that the factual findings in the report satisfied the four essential elements of the tort of negligence, namely: duty of care, breach of the standard of care, injury, and causation. Therefore, they amounted to a legal conclusion of civil responsibility on the part of Richards and had to be quashed.[48]

---

47 *Richards v. New Brunswick (Commission of Inquiry into the Kingsclear Youth Training Centre)* (1996), 180 N.B.R. (2d) 1 at para. 68 (Q.B.) [*Kingsclear*].

48 *Ibid.* at paras. 87 & 88.

The extent of the limitation imposed by *Nelles* on findings of misconduct was revisited by the Supreme Court of Canada in *Krever*. Justice Cory rejected the contention that a commissioner could not make findings which would appear to the public to be determinations of legal liability. He distinguished *Nelles* and *Starr* as being applicable only to commissions investigating the circumstances of a particular crime. They do not apply when findings of misconduct arise out of a wider investigation such as the commission before him involving the nation's blood supply, the Westray Inquiry into a mining disaster, or the inquiry involved in *O'Hara* to ensure the proper treatment by police officers of persons in custody.[49] Otherwise, he said:

> if the comments made in *Nelles* were taken as a principle of law applicable to every inquiry, the task of many if not most commissions of inquiry would be rendered impossible.[50]

In distinguishing *Nelles* and *Starr*, he added:

> Clearly, those two inquiries were unique. They dealt with specific incidents and specific individuals, during the course of criminal investigations. Their findings would inevitably reflect adversely on individuals or parties and could well be interpreted as findings of liability by some members of the public. In those circumstances, it was appropriate to adopt a strict test to protect those who might be the subject of criminal investigations.[51]

That was very different from the situation facing the Krever Inquiry or the other two referred to above.

What, then, is the limit imposed on commissions of inquiry when making findings of misconduct that could involve civil or criminal liability? Justice Cory concluded:

> From the findings of fact the commissioner may draw appropriate conclusions as to whether there has been misconduct and who appears to be responsible for it. However, the conclusions of a commissioner should not duplicate the wording of the Code defining a specific offence.

---

49 *O'Hara v. British Columbia*, [1987] 2 S.C.R. 591 discussed in Chapter 3, Section E(4) [*O'Hara*].

50 Above note 3 at para. 44.

51 *Ibid.* at para. 47.

> If this were done it could be taken that a commissioner was finding a person guilty of a crime. This might well indicate that the commission was, in reality, a criminal investigation carried out under the guise of a commission of inquiry. Similarly, commissioners should endeavour to avoid making evaluations of their findings of fact in terms that are the same as those used by courts to express findings of civil liability . . . . Despite these words of caution, however, commissioners should not be expected to perform linguistic contortions to avoid language that might conceivably be interpreted as importing a legal finding.[52]

He later offered this further guidance:

> a commissioner may make a finding that there has been a failure to comply with a certain standard of conduct, so long as it is clear that the standard is not a legally binding one such that the finding amounts to a conclusion of law pertaining to criminal or civil liability.[53]

In other words, the misconduct must not be characterized by measuring it against legal standards of civil or criminal liability.

This aspect of *Krever* is important in permitting commissions of inquiry to fulfill their roles. The limitations imposed by *Nelles* or *Starr* are still necessary but should be confined to the need to prevent an inquiry from becoming a criminal investigation. Indeed, the Court in *Nelles* was fully conscious of the difficulty in reconciling the broad purposes of the inquiry with the restriction against allowing it to become a criminal investigation. It described this problem as "one of extreme difficulty, at times approaching the impossible."

The *Kingsclear* case was not cited before the Supreme Court in *Krever* but it was referred to before the Federal Court of Appeal, where Justice Décary was critical of its approach:

> With respect, I would say that this confirms the danger of setting up the test stated in *Nelles* as a principle of general application, and clearly illustrates the impasse to which a literal application of that principle would inevitably lead.[54]

52 *Ibid.* at para. 52.

53 *Ibid.* at para. 57.

54 Above note 37 at para. 53.

In light of the Supreme Court decision in *Krever*, the approach taken in *Kingsclear* is no longer valid. Justice Robert Richards of the Saskatchewan Court of Appeal provides an excellent and recent illustration of the proper application of *Krever* to a challenge alleging a finding of criminal or civil liability.[55]

In addition to the "civil or criminal liability" prohibition, the Goudge Inquiry's terms of reference prohibited the expression of "any conclusion or recommendation regarding professional discipline matters involving any person." This might be interpreted as referring to discipline matters already in progress or it could be interpreted more broadly as precluding findings that a disciplinary standard had been breached. It seems reasonable to preclude such matters that fall within the statutory jurisdiction of other bodies for analogous reasons to excluding findings of civil liability. Civil liability might also be interpreted broadly to include professional misconduct. According to *Krever*, there generally would be no objection to finding fault on the part of a professional provided that it is not measured against legal standards.

The terms of reference of the Driskell Inquiry expressly directed Commissioner LeSage "[t]o inquire into the conduct of Crown Counsel . . . and consider whether that conduct fell below the professional and ethical standards expected of lawyers and agents of the Attorney General conducting prosecutions at the time." They also asked for advice as to whether such conduct should be referred to the law society or a law-enforcement agency. And there was, again, the normal exclusion for "civil or criminal liability." This suggests that professional misconduct was not viewed as falling within "civil liability," if this was even considered. Section 83(1) of the Manitoba Act authorizes inquiries "if the inquiry is not otherwise regulated."[56] However, this did not appear to be an issue and the commissioner did find that the conduct of three Crown counsel fell below their existing professional standards.

---

55 *Hartwig v. Saskatoon (City) Police Assn.*, 2008 SKCA 81, Klebuc C.J.S. and Hunter J.A. concurring [*Stonechild*].

56 This provision is comparable to section 3 of the *Inquiries Act*, discussed in Chapter 7, Section B(2).

### 3) Actual Findings

Findings of misconduct should be viewed in the context of the commissioner's broader role. Justice Cory did so, in what he described as an "overly simplified" summary in *Krever*:[57]

- A commissioner has the power to make all relevant findings of fact necessary to explain the recommendations, even if these findings reflect adversely upon individuals;
- A commissioner may make findings of misconduct based on the factual findings, provided they are necessary to fulfill the purpose of the inquiry as it is described in the terms of reference;
- Such findings must not be based on the application of legal standards that would amount to a finding of civil or criminal liability but other standards of conduct may be applied;
- Such findings should not be couched in the specific language of criminal culpability or civil liability.

What is the nature of the misconduct that may be found? How should it be characterized or described? What standards of conduct may be applied in making such findings? What standard of proof should be applied? How should the credibility of witnesses be determined? When are such findings "necessary" to fulfill the inquiry's purpose?

The nature of a finding of misconduct is important since it allows the identification of those findings for which notice is required, either by legislation or by the principle of fairness. Section 13 of the *Inquiries Act* refers to a "charge of misconduct." Prince Edward Island and Newfoundland and Labrador use the same phrase. British Columbia, Ontario, New Brunswick, and the Northwest Territories refer to "findings of misconduct" and Alberta refers to a "report that alleges misconduct." The remaining jurisdictions do not contain a notice requirement so that the requirement there arises from the common law principle of fairness.

The *Inquiries Act* is the most formal of all in contemplating "a charge" being "made in the course of an investigation." This suggests a formal or explicit accusation. In the Stevens Inquiry, it was explicit in the terms of reference that asked whether he "was in real or apparent conflict of interest." Usually the misconduct will become more apparent during

---

57 Above note 3 at para. 57.

the investigation and preparation stage and more developed during the hearings. It is discovered or understood in the course of addressing the broader question of "what happened and why."

In *Krever*, Justice Cory freely used the word "misconduct" but also referred to findings that "reflect adversely" on individuals. In *Kingsclear*, Chief Justice Daigle sought a definition of misconduct but noted that

> I was unable to find a definition in the statutes of the other Canadian provinces or any judicial interpretation of the term in a context similar to that of our legislation. I am prepared to adopt, however, the definition suggested in the reports of the Ontario Law Reform Commission and of the Alberta Law Reform Institute (supra) as "any findings or conclusion that could reasonably be construed as bringing discredit on an individual."[58]

In my view, there is not much difference between "reflect adversely" and "bring discredit" but they both appear to be broader than "misconduct." It seems that "misconduct" moves closer to a more specific act judged by more specific criteria.

Justice Campbell drew a distinction between the two but had a difficult time identifying the boundary between them. He made the following suggestion: "It may be that the problem of adverse findings and findings of misconduct can be avoided by simply saying what happened; instead of characterizing it legalistically."[59] It certainly should not be characterized "legalistically" since to apply legal standards would run afoul of the prohibition against findings of civil or criminal responsibility. But "simply saying what happened" is not enough since, as noted above,[60] the government and the public should be entitled to know the inferences and opinions the commissioner draws from "what happened."

The best approach is simply to apply the broader definition of any findings that could "reflect adversely" on an individual. This would encompass misconduct but also extend to inferences about such things as "incompetence" or "an attitude of callous disregard." Of course, these would have to be supported by a factual foundation and the dangers of

58 Above note 48 at para. 29.

59 Above note 1 at 394.

60 Above note 3.

subjectivity avoided. But they might be obvious from the findings of what happened and they could well "reflect adversely" on an individual.

In *Kingsclear*, Chief Justice Daigle concluded that findings of lack of credibility do not amount to misconduct:

> I think that an alleged misconduct of a witness, or some other person, must relate to discreditable conduct by that person with respect to incidents or matters under investigation. "Misconduct" cannot refer to a commissioner's observation or conclusion regarding a witness' demeanour or lack of candour during his or her testimony before the inquiry except perhaps, under certain circumstances, a conclusion that a witness has committed perjury.[61]

This may be true with respect to a finding of "misconduct" but most findings of lack of credibility would "reflect adversely" on the person who is not believed. Nothing is lost if this broader "nature" of misconduct is adopted for the purpose of identifying when notice should be given. And it may generate helpful explanations or qualifications from the person affected. It also may be required by the principle of fairness, even where the legislation, such as the *Inquiries Act*, may contemplate a more narrow definition.

The nature of "misconduct" for our purposes, then, is any finding that would reflect adversely on someone. This could be the result of a mere finding of fact. For example, "Company X knew the product was unsafe but failed to withdraw it." Or the commissioner could go further and characterize the failure to act as "unacceptable conduct."[62] Each would be an "adverse finding."

Sometimes the adverse inference may not be apparent from the description of a fact (or facts) in itself. But the commissioner may still characterize the conduct related to those facts in a critical or adverse manner. This may result from the analysis and evaluation of those facts:

> According to the Concise Oxford Dictionary (8th ed. 1990), misconduct is "improper or unprofessional behaviour" or "bad management." Without the power to evaluate and weigh testimony, it would be impossible for a commissioner to determine whether behaviour was "improper" as opposed to "proper," or what constituted "bad management" as opposed to

61 Above note 48 at para. 30.

62 This example was used in *Krever*, above note 3 at para. 41.

> "good management." The authority to make these evaluations of the facts established during an inquiry must, by necessary implication, be included in the authorization to make findings of misconduct contained in s. 13.[63]

In the course of that evaluation, standards of conduct may be invoked, quite apart from standards of civil or criminal liability. As Justice Cory pointed out, there are many different types of normative standards. He referred to "moral, legal, scientific, social or political" and "professional ethical" standards as examples.[64]

Sometimes, the applicable standard will be established by the terms of reference. The Stevens Inquiry was directed to determine whether he "was in real or apparent conflict of interest" as established by a written code and a letter from the prime minister[65] (although these "standards" proved to be elusive). The Taman Inquiry was required to determine whether the services provided to the family of the victim were sufficient with respect to the Manitoba *Victim's Bill of Rights*. The Arar Inquiry was required to address "the actions of Canadian officials" in relation to his treatment. No standard was expressed for assessing that conduct. Counsel for some officials and RCMP officers argued that no adverse findings should be made about them unless it could be found as a fact that their actions "caused or contributed to" that treatment. Commissioner O'Connor rejected that argument and provided this example:

> in this Report I have pointed out that some information provided to American agencies by the RCMP was inaccurate and unfair to Mr. Arar and that the RCMP did not follow its established information-sharing policies. In order to properly report on these actions, I have set out how and why they took place and, importantly, why they were unacceptable, creating unfair risks for Mr. Arar. . . . In several places in the Report, I comment on the actions of Canadian officials that created or increased a risk that Mr. Arar would be subjected to unacceptable treatment. While creating or increasing an unacceptable risk may sometimes fall short of establishing causation as that term is used in a strictly legal sense, creating an unacceptable risk is still something that should be avoided.[66]

---

63 *Ibid.* at para. 40.

64 *Ibid.* at paras. 19 and 62.

65 See Chapter 3, Section B(2).

66 Arar Inquiry, "Analysis and Recommendations" at 288. See also the reference to "standards" in Section C(1), below in this chapter.

In the case of the RCMP, they had failed to comply with their own policies. But both the RCMP and the officials had created or increased an "unacceptable risk" and the commissioner explained why he considered this to be unacceptable.

The terms of reference for the Mulroney-Schreiber Inquiry included the following questions:

> 11. Were these business and financial dealings appropriate considering the position of Mr. Mulroney . . . ?
> 12. Was there appropriate disclosure and reporting . . . ?
> 13. Were there ethical rules or guidelines . . . ? Were they followed?

Commissioner Oliphant conducted a special hearing to address the standards that he should apply in determining these questions. The subsequent ruling provides an excellent analysis for the guidance of future commissioners.[67]

The standard for Question 13 did not pose much difficulty since the 1985 Ethics Code[68] and the *Guidance for Ministers*[69] were both applicable at the relevant times. But these did not resolve the issue of what was "appropriate" in Questions 11 and 12. Even if the conduct were not in breach of the Code, it did not necessarily follow that the conduct was appropriate. The ruling elaborates on why Canadians were entitled to expect the conduct of public office holders to be "exemplary" whether in their official or personal capacity. It concludes that Mulroney's conduct would be assessed by whether it conformed to the "highest standards of conduct . . . so scrupulous that it can bear the closest possible scrutiny." But this standard also would be applied on an "objective basis."

In discussing the problem of standards for scientific assessment,[70] the "determination of risk" was described as much more complex when applied to such matters as nuclear safety. When assessing the risk of

---

67 Mulroney-Schreiber Inquiry, Ruling on Standards of Conduct (25 February 2009). This analysis also includes a discussion of the approach taken by Commissioner Iacobucci in determining the standard he would apply to whether the actions of certain Canadian officials "were deficient in the circumstances" of his terms of reference.

68 *Conflict of Interest and Post-employment Code for Public Office Holders* (Ottawa: Office of the Prime Minister, 1985).

69 (Ottawa: Privy Council Office, 1988).

70 See Chapter 4, Section A(2).

exposing a Canadian citizen to torture in Syria, it should not take much to reach the standard of "unacceptable."

The characterization of conduct that may reflect adversely can be described in various ways:

- mistaken;
- unfortunate; inappropriate; ill-advised;
- irresponsible; failure to act; wilful blindness;
- improper; negligent; bad judgment; or
- grossly negligent; malicious; corrupt.

Of course, these may overlap and a myriad of additional characterizations can be found simply by reference to a thesaurus. The description will depend on the factual circumstances and how the commissioner assesses them and often a simple characterization may require qualification. For example, a mistake may be simple, honest, and not unusual (there but for the grace of God go I). Or it may amount to negligence or gross negligence. The "corruption" may be "noble cause corruption," often identified as a companion of "tunnel vision" in the wrongful-conviction cases.[71]

Commissioner Kaufman explained that the standards he adopted in assessing credibility were analogous to those used by a trial judge in a criminal case: "These include the demeanour of witnesses, the plausibility of evidence measured both internally and in relation to other evidence, prior statements or testimony, and the motivations and possible unconscious biases of parties." He also took into account criminal records or other discreditable conduct as well as evidence of good character.[72]

Is there a standard of proof that should be applied to the findings of a commission of inquiry? Does that standard vary when the finding may reflect adversely on an individual? In *Erebus*, the Privy Council contrasted the role of a commissioner with that of a trial judge:

> Where facts are in dispute in civil litigation . . . the Judge has to decide where, on a balance of probabilities, he thinks the truth lies as between the evidence which the parties . . . adduce before him. He has no right to travel outside that evidence . . . and if the parties' evidence is so in-

71 See generally Chapter 3, Section D.

72 See also Chapter 8, Section C(5).

> conclusive as to leave him uncertain . . . he must decide the case by applying the rules as to onus of proof.[73]

In contrast, a commissioner may take the initiative to go where the evidence leads and pursue new lines of investigation. There is no legal onus of proof on the parties to a commission of inquiry and no standard of proof by which evidence must be evaluated.

This gives the commissioner freedom to report her findings on the basis of whatever standard she considers most appropriate. Commissioner O'Connor reached various conclusions with a range of qualifications from "probability" to "remote possibilities."[74] Reporting on "remote possibilities" still may help to shed light on what happened without determinative conclusions.

These observations do not apply when the findings reflect adversely on an individual. Such findings must be made in accordance with the principle of fairness. Where adverse findings potentially affect professional reputations, the standard of proof in a civil case should be applied. This is the standard of proof on a balance of probabilities. The evidence must be clear, convincing, and cogent and must be scrutinized with care, taking into account the seriousness of the potential findings.[75] This civil standard should be appropriate to withstand scrutiny under the principle of fairness on judicial review.[76]

*Krever* said that findings of misconduct may be made provided they are "necessary to fulfill the purpose of the inquiry."[77] In her inquiry into a riot at the Kingston Prison for Women, Commissioner Louise Arbour simply declined to make any such findings:

> I have concluded that it would not be fair for me to embark upon personal attribution of responsibility, for many reasons. Many persons were not called to testify and had therefore no opportunity to address allegations that might have been made against them. The witnesses who were called were not meant to be singled out as blameworthy, but were called for the sake of expediency, as the ones who had the most to contribute to the

---

73 *Re Erebus Royal Commission: Air New Zealand Ltd. v. Mahon*, [1983] N.Z.L.R. 662 at 666 (P.C.) [*Erebus*].

74 Described in Section A(1), above in this chapter.

75 *F.H. v. McDougall*, 2008 SCC 53.

76 The relevant considerations are discussed in Chapter 7, Section D(3).

77 Above note 3 at paras. 53 and 57.

> unfolding of the narrative. Many individuals who, by their own account, made errors, or whose actions I found did not meet a legal or policy standard or expectation, are otherwise persons greatly committed to correctional ideals for women prisoners.[78]

The terms of reference contemplated the usual investigative commission that would include the investigation of individual conduct. It referred to certain "incidents" and the response of Correctional Services to them. They also included reference to:

- actions and decisions taken;
- deployment of an all-male emergency response team;
- the team's conduct;
- the circumstances of segregation confinement; and
- the treatment of inmates in segregation.

The commissioner did make findings, including the conclusion that the treatment of inmates was "cruel, inhumane and degrading." But those responsible for individual acts were not named.

The commissioner chose to focus mainly on broader systemic issues. In the context of polarized and conflicting accounts of what occurred, that may have been a reasonable, strategic decision. The failure to identify individual responsibility for the treatment of prisoners did not seem to attract criticism.

The report of the Iacobucci Inquiry also declined to make specific findings of personal misconduct. The commissioner did detail a series of investigatory and diplomatic failures with respect to three Canadians tortured in Syria and Egypt: "However, the judge did not single out any individual for blame. Instead, he said the officials involved conscientiously carried out their duties at a time—post 9/11 –when there was 'intense pressure' on intelligence and law enforcement agencies."[79] While his terms of reference referred to "actions of Canadian officials," he tended to refer to actions generally rather than of individuals. This omission was the subject of strong criticism from human-rights activists

78 Canada, *Commission of Inquiry into Certain Events at the Prison for Women in Kingston*, (Ottawa: Public Works and Government Services Canada, 1996) at xiii (Chair: Louise Arbour).

79 Alexander Duffy, "Critics Demand Review of 'Culture of Impunity' in Security" *Ottawa Citizen* (24 October 2008).

such as author Kerry Pither, Amnesty International Canada head Alex Neve, and former solicitor general Warren Allmand.[80]

There is a danger in making sweeping generalizations about misconduct without specifying the individuals involved, so that proper notice and an opportunity to respond may be given to those who might be affected. The Somalia Inquiry made a "blanket statement" about "individuals who blamed others for their actions, who failed to question the appropriateness of the commands they received and who failed in their duty to advise against improper actions." Another "blanket statement" condemned many senior officers who testified because they "exhibited a pattern of evasion and deception, betrayed the public trust and . . . if they still remained in the military, they should have their status reviewed." In *Morneault*, the applicant argued that this characterized unnamed individuals as liars, who lacked personal and moral integrity. This blackened everybody's reputation without regard to individual conduct. Justice Barbara Reed granted a declaration that the record of the commission did not support a finding that the applicant's own conduct fell within the scope of these general statements.[81]

### 4) Systemic Explanations

Justice Campbell provides an excellent exposition of the importance of systemic explanations and the need for systemic solutions.[82] He found that, although the Bernardo investigation had its share of human errors, it also reflected great skill and dedication. But more was required:

> The *Bernardo* case shows that motivation, investigative skill, and dedication are not enough. The work of the most dedicated, skillful, and highly motivated investigators, supervisors, and forensic scientists can be defeated by the lack of effective case management systems and the lack of systems to ensure communication and co-operation among law enforcement agencies.

He provided this advice to commissioners:

---

80 *Ibid.*

81 Above note 4 at paras. 21, 22, and 29. Upheld on this issue in *Morneault v. Canada (Attorney General)*, [2001] 1 F.C. 30 (C.A).

82 Above note 1 at 399.

> It is often the case that systemic failures, as opposed to individual mistakes, are the real cause of public disasters and the most appropriate focus of public inquiries. The public identification of individual mistakes or wrongdoing, while important, does not necessarily address the underlying problem. And unless the underlying problem is addressed, the same mistakes or wrongdoing will likely occur again if the system that permitted them is not fixed.
>
> It is a mistake for a Royal Commissioner or public inquiry to focus exclusively on the search for scapegoats when the failure is really an institutional failure in the sense of a lack of appropriate systems, a lack of reasonable resources, a flawed institutional culture, or a breakdown in the machinery of accountability.

He added that commissioners should not conclude that the basic problem is solved by identifying human error or unprofessional conduct. That may well be important, "but these problems do not go away simply because individuals have been implicated. These problems only go away when people change their systems, their attitudes, and the way that they do business."

The investigative aspects and findings of misconduct are often important in informing the public what happened. But often that conduct, itself, is influenced or even cased by systemic factors. The greatest potential for effective recommendations and related change lies in addressing systemic issues. No doubt this was a significant consideration in limiting the Goudge Inquiry to a systemic review.

It was recommended earlier that the drafters of terms of reference for investigative commissions include an examination of systemic issues.[83] While such issues may seem intangible at first, they often emerge in issues such as leadership, relationships, morale, past practices, and institutional "culture." They are, essentially, any factors that transcend individual conduct but influence events, including individual conduct. They may impose rigidity in dealing with problems, or create "gaps" by discouraging cooperation and coordination. They may generate insensitivity and create barriers. They often do not appear to be offensive on their face but only upon understanding their influence on consequences.

---

83 Chapter 4, Section C(2).

In the context of the Arbour and Iacobucci inquiries, they could be characterized as "institutional misconduct."[84]

The term "culture" is sometimes used as shorthand for describing a cluster of attitudes that can be a positive or negative force upon individual conduct. Former commissioner Bellamy stressed the importance of leadership in providing ethical guidance for both public and private institutions: "Within organizations . . . history makes it clear that scrutiny alone is not enough to prevent ethical lapses and the first thing to do is take a look at the culture of an organization." She added that "ethical culture" is so important that no organization should leave its evolution "simply to chance."[85] The idea of "cultural" attitudes is a recurring theme in commission reports, as an explanation of events. For example: "[M]anagement at Westray displayed a certain disdain for safety and appeared to regard safety-conscious workers as the wimps in the organization." This attitude lost sight of the basic principle that "safe mining is good business" owing to the high cost of accidents, as was amply demonstrated by the Westray disaster.

In the wrongful-conviction cases, there is frequent reference to a "police culture" that encouraged tunnel vision and "noble cause corruption." In the Lamer Inquiry, that description was extended to Crown prosecutors when reviewing the various steps taken by them: "What is disturbing is their cumulative effect. It reflects a Crown 'culture' that is not objective but over-reaches." It also was affected by tunnel vision and contributed to the unjust consequences reviewed by Lamer.

The terms of reference may dictate the need to plan the inquiry's work by including a systemic stage or phase. Even where that does not appear as a requirement at the outset, it should be kept open as an option that could emerge as being desirable over the course of the hearings. Such a phase invites complete informality of proceedings and a "seminar" rather than a "hearings" approach. It could be enhanced by background study papers, although these should be "commissioned" as early as possible since time will be required for their completion. The Driskell Inquiry provides an excellent illustration of the value of such studies in addressing systemic issues. There, a background study

---

84 This phrase was used in *Kingsclear*, above note 48 at para. 87.

85 Helen Burnett, "Ethical Culture Can't Be Left to Evolution" *Law Times* (27 August/3 September 2007).

brought together and analyzed the relevant knowledge and experience on the subject. It was then subjected to critical analysis and discussion by a panel of experts with their own backgrounds of experience and expertise.[86]

## C. NOTICE OF MISCONDUCT

### 1) Notice Requirement

In the criminal process, a person is formally accused of committing a specific offence defined in the *Criminal Code*. In addition to specifying the criminal offence, the alleged conduct that constituted the crime is also specified, including the date, place, time, and victim, if any. The accused may request further particulars of the allegation. Prior to the trial, the accused is entitled to full disclosure of the evidence the prosecutor will rely upon to prove the charge. The prosecutor must also disclose evidence in her knowledge that would assist the accused in his defence. But the accused has no general obligation to disclose.

At the trial, the prosecutor has the burden of presenting all of the evidence against the accused first. The accused may challenge each witness through cross-examination. At the end of the prosecution case, the accused is entitled simply to argue that the case against him does not meet the standard of proof beyond a reasonable doubt. If the trier of fact agrees, he is acquitted. Or the accused may postpone this argument and first present evidence in his defence, including his own testimony, if he chooses.

Civil litigation has analogous features since it is also adversarial. The plaintiff must plead and prove her case but on a lower standard of proof. There is full disclosure prior to the trial but the defendant, as well as the plaintiff, must disclose his case. As in a criminal trial, the judge plays a passive role and leaves the presentation of the case to the parties.

In contrast, a commission of inquiry is inquisitorial rather than adversarial. It begins with the terms of reference rather than allegations by one party against another. The commissioner does not wait for the parties to present the evidence but directs commission counsel to do so. A commission of inquiry may adopt "rules of procedure" but they are

86 Described in Chapter 5, Section A(2).

informal and flexible. There is no decision—only findings and recommendations.

But those findings may reflect adversely on an individual and, when that possibility arises, the principle of fairness must be satisfied.[87] It does not require that any technical rules be followed. Provided it is "substantially" satisfied, fairness may be achieved informally. If a commissioner may possibly make a finding that reflects adversely on your reputation, what would you expect as fair treatment? Probably:

- that you be told what conduct of yours is being called into question;
- that you know what facts will be relied upon and have an opportunity to challenge their reliability;
- that you have an opportunity to introduce additional facts in response to the "case" against you, and those could include your own explanation;
- that you know the basis or standard by which that conduct will be assessed and have an opportunity to challenge whether that is appropriate or whether other factors should be considered; and
- after all of the evidence has been presented and tested, that you have an opportunity to hear any arguments that may be made against you and to make any arguments of your own to the commissioner who might make the adverse findings.

These would provide protections against a finding that otherwise could be arbitrary, unduly influenced, or simply wrong. The hearings of a commission of inquiry usually involve many parties and a variety of events so the satisfaction of these requirements may not occur in a compact or linear fashion. But they must be substantially satisfied.

Section 13 of the *Inquiries Act* states:

> No report shall be made against any person until reasonable notice has been given to the person of the charge and the person has been allowed full opportunity to be heard in person or by counsel.

The principle of fairness must be met even where there is no such statutory requirement in the jurisdiction of a commission of inquiry. Where such provisions do exist, they are "informed" by the principle of fairness.

---

87 See, generally, Chapter 7, Section D(3).

David Scott, a veteran of a number of prominent federal commissions of inquiry, has made this observation:

> The difficulty with section 13 relates to its administration. How can a commission fairly and at the same time procedurally comply with this provision? If reasonable notice is given during the inquiry, either by specifics in its terms of reference or by allegations during its course, then if the persons affected responded and met the allegations during the course of the inquiry, no special notice need be given under section 13 thereafter. However, if no such notice of allegations of misconduct was given before or during the course of the inquiry, then section 13 must specifically be complied with before the commission's report is delivered. If notice is given literally before the report is released, the opportunity to be heard would be somewhat illusory because the commission would have identified allegations of misconduct in the course of arriving at its conclusion and thus might be said to have effectively made up its mind before notice was given. In such circumstances, one might be forgiven for concluding that the opportunity to be heard was somewhat of a sham. If the commission gives notice after hearing the argument of counsel, the same sort of problem may arise . . . . In any event, there is a universal plea for amendment to this clumsy statutory arrangement.[88]

In my view, these difficulties can be largely resolved by providing actual notice over the course of the investigation and hearings. This would include full disclosure, prior to the hearings, of the evidence to be called in order to permit adequate preparation. At the hearings, it would involve hearing adverse testimony so that it can be challenged before testifying and calling other evidence in response. Potential findings of misconduct can then be identified by commission hearings counsel in the final submissions. At that point, the formal notices should be largely redundant but a useful "safety net" to ensure complete fairness. Presumably, Scott's concerns were born of experiences with commissioners and commission counsel who did not practise "substantive" fairness.

---

88 David W. Scott, Q.C., "The Rights and Obligations of Those Subject to Inquiry and of Witnesses", in A.P. Pross, I. Christie, and J.A. Yogis, eds., *Commissions of Inquiry* (Toronto: Carswell, 1990) at 144–45.

The procedural protections of pre-hearing disclosure, and the evidentiary "case to meet"[89] at hearings, might be interpreted as a part of the "full opportunity to be heard" that is required by section 13. Even if it is not, they should be treated as aspects of fairness to be respected. As suggested previously, the bifurcation of the roles of commission counsel permits hearings counsel to take a greater adversarial role by cross-examining in relation to potential misconduct and by identifying and elaborating on it in final submissions. It also permits a more defined role for hearings counsel in the process of providing formal "notice" of possible adverse findings.

The related provision under the New Brunswick Act is similar to section 13 and uses the identical words "allowed full opportunity . . . to be heard in person or by counsel." In *Kingsclear*, Chief Justice Daigle found that this notice provision

> does not provide for pre-hearing disclosure, and does not provide explicitly that a person must have an opportunity to know and meet the case against him or her . . . it does not codify or exhaust all of the procedural rights of a person whose reputation or interests might be affected.[90]

However, he held that the requirements of fairness "supplement" the statutory notice requirement. He had no doubt that the duty of fairness "requires compliance with pre-hearing disclosure" but it did not require advance notice of "proposed adverse findings."[91] Often such potential findings become apparent only over the evidentiary evolution of the investigation and hearings:

> In the course of such an investigation facts turn up giving rise to allegations asserted during the course of the hearing. Moreover, it is only as the story unfolds that the significance of given pieces of evidence is realized. That which appeared to be of no significance during the third month may become important six months later in light of other evidence.[92]

---

89 See the comments of commissioner and former chief justice Lamer in the Lamer Inquiry's Report, c. 3 at 160.

90 Above note 48 at para. 23. See also the discussion in Chapter 6, Section B(2)(b).

91 *Ibid.* at para. 49.

92 *Ibid.* at para. 52 quoting *Re First Investors Corp. Ltd.* (1988), 54 D.L.R. (4th) 730 at 738 (Alta. C.A.). See also *Krever*, above note 3 at para. 69.

In this case, the pre-hearing interviews and questioning of the party while he gave testimony provided "actual notice of the substance of the misconduct alleged against him" and the party had a full opportunity to be heard.

The Ontario Divisional Court also upheld a similar finding of actual notice and observed

> that the applicants and their counsel were well aware from the outset of the possible allegations against them and that they had every opportunity during the course of the inquiry to respond to those allegations, that they took the opportunities and responded to the allegations, that they had witnesses called specifically to deal with the allegations . . . .[93]

Justice Reed acknowledged that notice can be "constructive as well as express" but full participation by someone in the inquiry

> does not necessarily lessen the duty to give specific notice of what it is that is causing the Commissioners to think that his conduct may deserve the label misconduct.[94]

For most inquiries, it makes sense to provide disclosure during the investigation stage and an opportunity to respond to adverse evidence at the hearings and to allegations of potential adverse findings during closing submissions. In other words, the entire process should set the stage for ultimate formal notice of potential findings of misconduct.

In *Krever*, Justice Cory had no problem with the notices being given at the end of hearings:

> I see no objection in principle to a commissioner waiting until the end of the hearings, when he or she has all the information that is required, to give notices, rather than taking a day to day approach to it, with the uncertainty and inconvenience that this might involve.[95]

The Somalia Inquiry sent out notices, at a very early stage and without much focus, that Justice Reed described as "boiler plate." They were

---

93 *VanderMeer v. Royal Commission of Inquiry into the Niagara Regional Police Force* (1992), 90 D.L.R. (4th) 409 at 417 (Ont. Div. Ct.).

94 *Morneault*, above note 4 at para. 45.

95 Above note 3 at para. 70 quoting Décary J. who gave the judgment of the court below, above note 37.

"in no way sufficiently detailed "to satisfy the section 13 requirement, but she thought they might serve a useful purpose in giving general notice to participants that adverse findings were a possibility.

In my view, such early and general notices can be counterproductive and are undesirable. Preliminary notice can be better provided with reference to identified evidence relating to a potential witness. General notices suggest superficial prejudgment and can cause unnecessary concern to many of those who receive them.

As we have seen, Justice Cory also established that adverse findings must be "necessary to fulfill the purpose of the inquiry." They may not be findings of civil or criminal conduct but they may adversely characterize individual conduct. Since the notices are issued to parties in confidence, greater latitude is given to their content. They will not be strictly judged for overreaching the terms of reference since greater detail is in the interests of the party receiving the notice. The notices should be as detailed as possible and concerns about exceeding jurisdiction can await the actual final report. Justice Reed provided the helpful elaboration that reasonable notice can be assessed "by asking whether a reasonable person, who thinks he or she has acted without fault, has been given enough information to know what aspects of his or her conduct the decision-maker is considering might ripen into, or support, a finding of misconduct."[96] What will be reasonable notice will vary with the circumstances. Where the inquiry has a very narrow focus, the conduct in question may be obvious. Where the subject matter is extensive and "scattered," the commissioner should identify what evidence raises adverse inferences that are a real possibility.

In the Arar Inquiry, Commissioner O'Connor rejected the argument that section 13 notices had to be based on "articulated or published standards or guidelines." He distinguished *Stevens*[97] as relating to the specific terms of reference that referred to a set of conflict-of-interest guidelines. He then referred to *Krever* as the basis for the following guidance on the need for section 15 notices to articulate specific standards:

> In my view, a proper statement of the law is that, in reaching conclusions, a Commissioner should rely upon standards of conduct that could reasonably have been expected of an individual at the time when the

96 Above note 4 at para. 46.

97 *Stevens v. Canada (Attorney General)*, [2004] F.C.J. No. 2116 (Fed. Ct.) [*Stevens*].

> conduct under consideration occurred. *It may be that in some instances such standards will be articulated or published. In other instances, the standards may be obvious, based on reasonable expectations or, indeed, common sense.* Whatever the case, the notice should make clear what conduct was expected of the individual and the actions or conduct for which the Commissioner may be making a finding of misconduct.[98]

At the same time, detailed particulars or reasoning need not and probably should not be included. They may give the impression that the commissioner is really giving reasons for a decision already taken. They might also impose unnecessary constraints on findings to be made or the wording used to describe them. Exact details of what findings may be made and in what manner may not emerge until well into the deliberative stage. There is no reason why all notices must go out at the same time. Some potential adverse findings will be clear at the end of closing submissions. Others may emerge and notice given in the course of analysis and deliberations.

### 2) Process

The process for dealing with section 13 or comparable notices has been conspicuously absent from the rules of procedure adopted by commissions of inquiry. An appropriate process might be expressed as follows:

1) After closing submissions have been completed, commission hearings counsel will prepare draft letters giving notice to parties against whom adverse findings might possibly be made by the commissioner.
2) The commissioner will review the draft letters and may receive advice from commission advisory counsel in order to determine whether there is a reasonable *possibility* that she might make a finding as suggested by hearings counsel.
3) The commissioner may adopt, revise, reject, or hold in abeyance any such draft letters.
4) Where the commissioner adopts or revises any such draft letters, she will direct commission hearings counsel to send the (revised) draft letter to the proposed recipients in the form of a notice letter.

---

98 Arar Inquiry, "Decision on Section 13 Notices," vol. 2, Appendix 5(c) at 667 [emphasis in original]. See also the discussion of "standards" in Section B(3), above in this chapter.

5) Any such notice letter will not represent any conclusions reached by the commissioner nor even "tentative" findings but only possible findings that she will consider in the context of any further response from the recipient, further analysis, and deliberation.
6) Every recipient is invited to write directly to the commissioner (with a copy to commission hearings counsel) and to provide written submissions in response to the notice letter.
7) Commission hearings counsel may respond in writing to the commissioner with a copy to the recipient in question, who may reply.
8) If the recipient wishes to make oral submissions or introduce further evidence, full justification for doing so must be provided in the light of the opportunity already provided for full participation in the hearings and related "actual notice."
9) Notice letters will be treated in strict confidence and not provided to the other parties, unless disclosure is required by considerations of fairness.
10) The commissioner will make findings that reflect adversely on individuals only when they are necessary to fulfill the purposes established by the terms of reference.
11) The commissioner will not make any findings of civil or criminal responsibility and, in assessing conduct, will not apply legal criteria that would lead to such a conclusion.

The content of the notice letters will be specific to the facts of the particular inquiry. However, it might not hurt to paraphrase the gist of items 2 ("reasonable possibility"), 5 (not even "tentative" findings), 10 ("necessary"), and 11 ("not civil or criminal") in these letters as a general assurance to the recipients. In *Krever*, Justice Cory said:

> The potential findings as set out in the notices may imply civil liability but the Commissioner has stated that he will not make a finding of legal liability, and I am sure he will not.[99]

In other words, even apart from assurances to the parties, it may not hurt to have a record of good intentions when faced with subsequent judicial review!

99 Above note 3 at para. 63.

In the Krever Inquiry, the commissioner invited the parties to make confidential submissions as to what findings of misconduct he should consider for the purpose of providing section 13 notices. In my view, such a practice is undesirable. Any such allegations against a party by another party should be made openly, during the investigative stage, at the hearings, in closing submissions, or at all three stages. There is an appearance of unfairness in receiving confidential allegations. It is the responsibility of the commissioner, with the assistance of her counsel, to identify any possible adverse findings and to provide notice accordingly. In this respect, care should also be taken to provide notice where generalizations could apply to individuals even though they are not named.[100]

Sometimes a lawyer's response to any form of an allegation is to demand an exhaustive list of particulars. Such demands must always be given careful consideration since it may be necessary to provide greater detail in the section 13 (or equivalent) notices to achieve fairness. They might also cause the commissioner to consider whether the notices should be given at all. However, occasionally such demands are merely designed to create battlegrounds. The idea is to generate as many side issues as possible and, through relentless engagement, to create procedural deficiencies. These might include alleged inconsistencies or erroneous subfindings. Such engagement often can be avoided by bearing in mind that fairness need only be met substantially and this permits flexibility and informality. The party need only know what aspects of his conduct are being considered that might lead to an adverse finding.

In the Walkerton Inquiry, an environmental officer received a notice under the Ontario Act. It said that the commissioner "may find" that her review of daily chlorine levels was "cursory" and as a result she failed to identify suspicious entries. The officer brought a motion before the commissioner to quash the notice on the basis that there was "no evidence to causally connect" her conduct with the events in question. Commissioner O'Connor ruled that this argument was premature since it could be made during the forthcoming closing submissions. Moreover, the officer was offered the opportunity to testify further but declined to do so. The commissioner added that it was not desirable to engage in a separate hearing and related adjudication arising out of the notices

100 See, generally, *Morneault*, above note 4 at paras. 21, 22, and 29, discussed in Section B(3), above in this chapter.

themselves: "[I]t is not in the best interests of the inquiry to inject a new level of decision-making of the nature proposed, prior to hearing final arguments and before the issuance of my report." It was imperative that procedural fairness be given to anyone who could be the subject of a potential adverse finding. However, "this can be done without putting in place a procedure for the screening of potential findings prior to final argument. To establish such a procedure would be in my view add an unnecessary layer of complexity, expense and potential delay."[101] The applicant had received details of possible allegations, full disclosure of all adverse evidence, and the opportunity to cross-examine other witnesses, to testify herself, and to call other evidence in relation to the possible allegations. Here the notices were issued prior to closing submissions but the above observations are just as applicable to notices issued after closing submissions have been made.

Justice Cory took a similar approach to section 13 notices in *Krever*, stating:

> As a general rule, a challenge such as this should not be brought before the publication of the report, unless there are reasonable grounds to believe the Commissioner is likely to exceed his or her jurisdiction.[102]

As stated above, broad scope should be given to a commissioner in relation to such notices since greater detail benefits the recipients. Accordingly, the courts will not lightly conclude that a commissioner is likely to exceed her jurisdiction because of the wording of such notices.

### 3) Opportunity to Respond

The opportunity to respond to a section 13 (or equivalent) notice is one aspect of the general right of parties to procedural fairness throughout the commission's proceedings. Justice L'Heureux-Dubé observed that

> the concept of procedural fairness is eminently variable and its content is to be decided in the specific context of each case.[103]

---

101 Walkerton Inquiry, "Ruling on the Motion and Supplementary Motion on Behalf of Michelle Zillenger" (4 July 2001), Part One at 159.

102 Above note 3 at para. 60.

103 *Knight v. Indian Head School Division No. 19*, [1990] 1 S.C.R. 653 at 682.

She added that

> the aim is not to create "procedural perfection," but to achieve a certain balance between the need for fairness, efficiency and predictability of outcome.[104]

In my view, this means that the nature of the opportunity to respond to a notice must be assessed in the context of the events preceding the notice.

Section 12 of the *Inquiries Act* states that

> The commissioners may allow any person whose conduct is being investigated under this Act, and shall allow any person against whom any charge is made in the course of an investigation, to be represented by counsel.

Section 13 then requires that reasonable notice be given of the "charge of misconduct" and a "full opportunity to be heard." These provisions suggest a sequence of events: an investigation; a charge; notice of the charge; a full opportunity to be heard on the charge. And this in turn suggests that a full hearing should be conducted on the charge following the earlier investigation.

This approach does not take into account the manner in which investigative inquiries are currently conducted. Any suggestion of possible adverse findings is now drawn to the attention of the party affected at an early opportunity prior to the hearings. Evidence in support of such findings is also disclosed prior to the hearings. At the hearings, efforts are made to present all adverse evidence before the affected party testifies. If that is not possible, he is given a chance to testify again after such additional evidence is presented. He then has a full opportunity to make submissions to the commissioner as to the inferences that should be drawn from the evidence, particularly any that might reflect adversely on him. In other words, substantive fairness and a full opportunity to be heard often is achieved prior to formal "notice" being given. That is the ideal situation and this objective has been assumed in describing the role of the commissioner and her counsel throughout.

However, as suggested above, these notices provide a useful "safety net" to ensure that no adverse findings are made without notice. In this

104 *Ibid.* at 685.

context, where a party wishes to make further submissions, usually fairness can be met by limiting these to written submissions. Occasionally, it may be necessary to call or re-call witnesses when areas that were not explored at the hearings are subsequently recognized as relevant and may require findings of credibility. A party seeking an oral hearing to have further witnesses called should be required to justify why that is required by fairness. If it is necessary, the commissioner may impose limitations on the scope of such a further hearing, again subject to fairness. In *Addy*, Justice Teitlebaum upheld the commissioner's decision to limit the number of witnesses to be called in response to section 13 notices and to require affidavits rather than oral testimony for some witnesses.[105]

Written responses to confidential notices of potential adverse findings should also be treated as confidential. It should not be necessary to disclose them to other parties unless they are so directly affected that fairness also requires that they have a further opportunity to be heard. This is another reason not to elaborate beyond what is necessary in such notices.

On rare occasions, it may be necessary for a commissioner to reconvene hearings. This should have occurred, for example, in *Stevens*, when the commissioner developed a new standard for conflict of interest. The report was set aside after the commissioner applied this new standard without providing Stevens any opportunity to be heard as to its applicability.[106] Similarly, in *Landreville*:

> the Commission should have been reconvened. The substance of the proposed allegations of misconduct . . . should have been made known to the plaintiff in accordance with s. 13. The plaintiff should have been given the opportunity to meet those specific charges.[107]

A declaration was granted that the report was void and should be quashed.

---

105 *Addy v. Canada (Commission of Inquiry into the Deployment of Canadian Forces in Somalia)*, [1997] 3 F.C. 784 (T.D.) [*Addy*].

106 Above note 97.

107 *Landreville v. The Queen (No. 2)* (1997), 75 D.L.R. (3d) 380 at 405 (F.C.T.D.) Collier J. [*Landreville*]. Discussed in Chapter 3, Section B(1).

## D. RELEASE AND CONSEQUENCES

### 1) Release

There is no inherent authority in a commissioner to publish her final report. Its legal status is that of a memorandum presenting recommendations to the Governor in Council and, therefore, "a confidence of the Queen's Privy Council" under the *Canada Evidence Act*.[108] Once received, the report belongs to the government, which has complete power whether, when, and to what extent to make it public.[109]

The Ontario government has, in effect, adopted a policy of legal undertakings to make public the reports of its commissions of inquiry. The Walkerton, Ipperwash, and Goudge inquiries, like the ongoing Cornwall Inquiry, all had in their terms of reference the requirement that the attorney general "shall make the report available to the public." This is a welcome development.

The terms of reference at the federal level tend to direct only that the commissioner report in both official languages by a certain date. Of course, there may be political consequences for not making such a report public but there is no legal requirement to do so. Still, if the government can find a legal justification for failing to disclose, that may soften the political fallout.

The difficulties faced by the Arar Inquiry in relation to National Security Confidentiality were discussedabove.[110] The commissioner decided not to risk aborting the inquiry through ongoing legal challenges but to hear most of the evidence *in camera*. He then wrote a confidential report with reference to all of the evidence for the benefit of the government. Finally, he edited this report to remove portions he thought would be subject to NSC so that the edited report could be made public.

However, the government redacted large portions of the summary of the testimony he heard *in camera*. Although only some 1,500 words were blacked out, the summary already had been reduced to twelve pages by the commissioner and involved secret testimony from nine members of

---

108 R.S.C. 1985, c. C-5, s. 39(2)(a).

109 *Canada (Attorney General) v. Canada (Commission of Inquiry into the Actions of Canadian Officials in Relation to Maher Arar—O'Connor Commission)*, [2007] FC 766 at para. 34, Noel J. [*Arar*].

110 See Chapter 8, Section D(2).

CSIS. The government then applied to the Federal Court for an order prohibiting disclosure of the redacted passages on the basis of NSC. Commission counsel Paul Cavaluzzo strongly opposed the claim on the basis that the censored passages were crucial for both Arar and the public to know and that Commissioner O'Connor already had weighed the potential dangers related to NSC. Justice Simon Noel welcomed the participation of a party who opposed the government's position but who also was familiar with the evidence in question.[111] That is not usually the case in applications under section 38 of the *Canada Evidence Act*.

The court upheld the NSC claim for approximately one-third of the redactions but permitted disclosure for the balance. The disclosures revealed that the government censoring was more related to the potential for embarrassment than to valid concerns about injury to national security. For example, it revealed a "post-9/11 trend" to render suspects to countries where they could be tortured: "The deputy director of Canadian Security Intelligence Service, Jack Hooper, wrote a memo on Oct. 10, 2002, saying: 'I think the U.S. would like to get Arar to Jordan where they can have their way with him.'"[112] When the Arar Inquiry's Report had been released, prior to the judicial decision and subject to all of the redactions, it included this prominent disclaimer: "The decision to omit this material is made by the Government of Canada and does not represent the views of the Commission of Inquiry."

Following the Noel judgment, the commission issued a press release in which Cavaluzzo noted that the government had released a great deal of information it had initially resisted disclosing. He expressed the view of the commission that "the public interest would be adequately served" by all parties simply accepting the decision. The government did not appeal the decision and the additional information referred to above was released.

The issue of releasing a commission's report also arose in *Phillips*. Two former managers of the Westray Coal Mine were facing criminal charges and were likely also to be called as witnesses before the commission of inquiry looking into the tragedy. The Nova Scotia Court of Appeal stayed the public hearings of the inquiry pending resolution of the criminal charges. The Supreme Court held that the hearings could proceed and Jus-

---

111 *Ibid.* at para. 36.

112 Colin Freeze, "Court Lifts Lid on Secret Arar Details" *Globe & Mail* (10 August 2007).

tice Cory noted that the prejudicial effects of the publication of evidence would not be as serious as findings of misconduct in the final report. Such findings could well influence the jury's deliberations. In his view:

> The publication of the report should be delayed until such time as Parry and Phillips have had an opportunity to review it and, if so advised, to bring an application to ban its publication until such time as the criminal charges had been disposed of after trial or stayed.[113]

He noted, for example, that publication of the final report of the Hughes Inquiry was withheld until completion of the criminal trials of all of the former brothers of Mount Cashel.[114]

In addition to his judgment in *Phillips* and the landmark decision in *Krever*, Justice Cory conducted the Sophonow Inquiry following his retirement from the Court.[115] After his "retirement," he also took on an important assignment for the British and Irish governments in May 2002, involving eight controversial killings. Four of these were committed by the Irish Republican Army, with allegations of collusion by Irish security forces. There were allegations that the British army and security forces colluded in the other four. Justice Cory's mandate was to conduct an investigation and report to both governments as to whether there was sufficient evidence of state collusion to warrant a full public inquiry in each case. The British and Irish governments both agreed that they would establish full public inquiries if recommended by him. He reported to both governments on 7 October 2003.

The Irish government accepted his recommendations and established a tribunal of inquiry into the killing of two members of the Royal Ulster Constabulary. Justice Cory did not find sufficient evidence of collusion to warrant such an inquiry into the killing of Lord Justice Gibson and his wife, Cecily. A roadside bomb had blown up their car on their return from a holiday. In December, the Irish government published redacted versions of Justice Cory's reports on the four Irish killings. The minister for justice stated publicly that the redactions were performed

---

113 *Phillips v. Nova Scotia (Commission of Inquiry into the Westray Mine Tragedy)*, [1995] 2 S.C.R. 97 at para. 163 [*Phillips*]. Also discussed in Chapter 3, Section B(3) and Chapter 7, Sections A(2) and F.

114 *Ibid.* at para. 124.

115 Discussed in Chapter 3, Section D(3).

"with the explicit consent and approval of Judge Cory." The British government was not so forthcoming.

In spite of pleas from the families of the other four victims, these reports were not disclosed. Justice Cory considered this a breach of an undertaking made to him and to the families and asked the government at least to release the "bottom line" of his reports. Finally, in early February 2004, he took the initiative personally to telephone the families of the four victims. He told them that he had found sufficient evidence of state collusion to warrant a full public inquiry in each case. Justice reporter Kirk Makin called this "an extraordinary move that the British media are calling a humiliating direct challenge to Mr. [Tony] Blair . . . . The 78-year-old judge is being widely hailed in Britain as a courageous figure who refused to stand by while the Blair government defied his terms of reference by suppressing the report."[116] Justice Cory's reports on all four cases were finally tabled in the House of Commons on 1 April 2004 and the Northern Ireland secretary announced that full public inquiries would be held into three of the cases.

The fourth case involved the murdered Patrick Finucane, a lawyer who defended a number of IRA members. He was having dinner with his wife and three children in the kitchen of their home when they heard a noise at the front door. He opened the kitchen door and they saw a masked man walking down the hall towards them. He closed the door and a flurry of shots were fired. His wife landed on the floor with her hands over her head. She then heard more shots "very slow and deliberate." When the shots stopped, she got up and the intruder was gone but her husband lay dead on his back. The autopsy revealed that he had been shot six times in the head, three times in the neck, and three times in the torso. Any of the wounds would have been fatal. Although the report found "strong evidence" of collusion in this case, the minister said that his inquiry would be delayed because of a pending criminal trial. In response, "Mr. Finucane's widow expressed anger that there would be a delay in investigating the death of her husband . . . . 'The British government continues to cover up the truth about the death of my husband with their delaying tactics,' Geraldine Finucane said."[117] In his report, Justice Cory

116 Kirk Makin, "Canadian Judge Hailed in U.K. for Defying Blair" *Globe & Mail* (4 February 2004).

117 Caroline Alphonso, "N. Ireland Killings To Be Probed" *Globe & Mail* (2 April 2004).

had noted that the case "may be one of the rare situations where a public inquiry will be of greater benefit to community than prosecutions." Indeed, if Justice Cory's reasons in *Phillips* had been adopted, the public inquiry could have proceeded in spite of the criminal trial.

In another irony, the British government created a new *Inquiries Act 2005* to replace the *Tribunals of Inquiry (Evidence) Act 1921*, under which the other three public inquiries were being conducted. In a press release posted on 20 April 2005, the United Kingdom branch of Amnesty International said:

> Amnesty International supports the call of Geraldine Finucane, Patrick Finucane's widow[,] to all senior judges in England, Wales and Scotland not to serve on an inquiry into her husband's case under the new legislation . . . . "Any judge sitting on such an inquiry would be presiding over a sham."

The new Act would allow crucial evidence to be omitted "at the executive's discretion, 'in the public interest.'" The press release was highly critical of the new Act and quoted Justice Cory as stating that it "would make a meaningful inquiry impossible." Lord Saville, who chaired the Bloody Sunday Tribunal of Inquiry, said that he would not accept an appointment under the Act.[118]

### 2) Judicial Review

The New Zealand Court of Appeal pointed out that *Landreville*[119] was the first case in Canada, Australia, New Zealand, or the United Kingdom to review the final report of a commission of inquiry and

> to make a declaration which, though devoid of any legal effect, would from a practical point of view, serve some useful purpose.[120]

In *Landreville*, the findings were quashed even though the events were largely historical. The judge had long since resigned from the

---

118 Amnesty International United Kingdom, News Release, "UK: Amnesty Urges Judges Not to Be a Part of Finucane Inquiry" (20 April 2005).

119 Above note 107.

120 *Peters*, above note 19 at 1884, quoting from *Landreville v. the Queen* (1973), 41 D.L.R. (3d) 574 at 581 (F.C.T.D.).

bench and in that sense the declaration would serve no practical purpose. But it still would be useful to make it "a matter of public record" that he did not have full opportunity to refute the finding that he had committed "gross contempt" as a judge when testifying before certain tribunals. The declaration could also assist him in seeking the judicial pension he had been denied.

The New Zealand Court noted that, since *Landreville*,

> the situation has changed, with a number of the reports of commissions being reviewed after the completion of the commission process, with the Court in some cases issuing relevant relief.[121]

A number of New Zealand and Australian examples are provided.

Reference has been made in the preceding chapters to a variety of Canadian cases in which parties have been successful in striking down findings in a final report. In *Kingsclear*, the basis was that they amounted to findings of civil liability.[122] *Stevens*[123] was similar to *Landreville* in failing to provide adequate notice of the basis on which findings of misconduct were made. Former prime minister Chrétien was denied an impartial commissioner, contrary to the principle of fairness.[124] In *Morneault*, the declaration excluded the applicant from sweeping generalizations alleging misconduct against unnamed persons.[125]

The Supreme Court of Canada revisited the law governing standards of judicial review in *Dunsmuir* in three concurring but very different judgments. The majority was troubled by the recent history of judicial review in Canada, which, they said, was

> marked by ebbs and flows of deference, confounding tests and new words for old problems, but no solutions that provide guidance . . . . The time has arrived for a reassessment of the question.[126]

---

121 *Ibid.* at 184.

122 Above note 47.

123 Above note 97.

124 *Chrétien v. Canada (Commission of Inquiry into the Sponsorship Program and Advertising Activities, Gomery Commission)*, 2008 FC 802 [*Chrétien*].

125 See above note 4.

126 *Dunsmuir v. New Brunswick*, 2008 SCC 9 at para. 1 with Bastarache and LeBel delivering the judgment of themselves, McLachlin C.J., and Fish, and Abella JJ. [*Dunsmuir*].

They set about to address the entire "structure and characteristics" of judicial review in order to develop a "more coherent and workable" framework.

The majority reaffirmed that the courts are to apply the standard of correctness to administrative decisions in relation to constitutional questions, issues of jurisdiction, and general questions of law. The word "general" is used to exclude specific questions of law related to the expertise of tribunal members, their statutory and regulatory laws, and probably the surrounding "culture" that has evolved. The latter might include, for example, "how things are done" and why they should continue to be done that way. General questions of law include statutory and common law rules of broader application that require uniform and consistent determination.

The most apparent change adopted by the majority was to collapse the "patent unreasonableness" and "reasonableness *simpliciter*" standards into a single standard of "reasonableness." This standard is deferential in permitting tribunals to select from within a range of solutions that are "acceptable and rational." Judicial review is concerned with

> the existence of justification, transparency and intelligibility within the decision-making process. But it is also concerned with whether the decision falls within the range of possible, acceptable outcomes which are defensible in respect of the facts and law.[127]

The majority also confirmed that the analysis on review must be "contextual" and listed the following factors: Privative clause? Purpose of the tribunal legislation? Expertise? Nature of the issue under consideration? These are essentially the same factors established by *Pushpanathan* as requiring a "pragmatic and functional" balancing to determine which of the previous two standards of reasonableness should be adopted.[128] The majority not only collapsed the two standards but also seemed to merge "deference" into the new standard of reasonableness.

Justice Binnie had no problem with the new single standard or abandoning the "pragmatic and functional" terminology. But he pointed out

---

127 *Ibid.* at para 47.

128 *Pushpanathan v. Canada (Minister of Citizenship and Immigration)*, [1998] 1 S.C.R. 982 applied in *Episcopal Corporation of the Diocese of Alexandria-Cornwall v. Cornwall Public Inquiry*, 2007 ONCA 20 and discussed in Chapter 7, Section G [*Episcopal*].

that this did nothing to resolve the "level of deference" that would have to be found within the standard of reasonableness in each case:

> The Court's adoption in this case of a single "reasonableness" standard that covers both the degree of deference assessment and the reviewing court's evaluation, in light of the appropriate degree of deference, of whether the decision falls within a range of reasonable administrative choices will require a reviewing court to juggle a number of variables that are necessarily to be considered together.[129]

He saw no problem with this, either, since there are "ample precedents" to guide the courts in when to intervene in "different administrative situations" no matter how the analysis is characterized.

The remaining judgment essentially says that it's not all that complicated and improvement can be made simply by clearing the law "of superfluous discussion and processes":

> This area of the law can be simplified by examining the *substance* of the work courts are called upon to do when reviewing any case, whether it be in the context of administrative or of appellate review.[130]

The word "reasonableness" should be applied to the decision while "deference" shapes the "contours of reasonableness" by assessing the decision maker. Just as with appellate review, what emerges will be "more like a rainbow than a black and white situation" but

> [t]he process of stepping back and taking an *ex post facto* look at the decision to determine whether there is an error justifying intervention should not be more complex in the administrative law context than in the criminal and civil law contexts.[131]

In the end, the application of the standard of correctness has not changed. Where it does not apply, the standard of reasonableness must be applied. The four factors previously used to select the proper standard of reasonableness will now be used to determine the degree of deference to be given to the decision maker.

---

129 *Dunsmuir*, above note 126 at para. 153.

130 *Ibid.* at para. 158, Deschamps J. for herself, Charron, and Rothstein JJ.

131 *Ibid.* at para. 167.

With respect to commissions of inquiry, we have seen the standard of correctness applied to jurisdiction in the Cornwall Inquiry.[132] The commissioner must be correct in interpreting his terms of reference. The majority in *Dunsmuir* elaborated on the role of the courts in such a situation:

> When applying the correctness standard, a reviewing court will not show deference to the decision maker's reasoning process; it will rather undertake its own analysis of the question. The analysis will bring the court to decide whether it agrees with the determination of the decision maker; if not, the court will substitute its own view and provide the correct answer.[133]

A denial of the principle of fairness is also a breach of jurisdiction and will be reviewed on a standard of correctness. But there are two considerations. First is the degree of procedural fairness required. We have seen this determined in *Chrétien*[134] through the application of the criteria established in *Baker*.[135] Second is whether the procedures adopted were sufficient to meet that requirement. In this respect, there is flexibility in how fairness is satisfied so long as it is substantively met.

We have also seen the application of the "reasonableness" standard in *Episcopal*.[136] Although this decision was rendered prior to *Dunsmuir*, it provides an excellent illustration of the substantive application of *Dunsmuir*. *Episcopal* applied the standard of reasonableness *simpliciter* as a result of its analysis of the issue of deference. But it was implicit that the degree of deference should also influence the standard of deference, even before *Dunsmuir*.

It is clear from *Dunsmuir* that findings of fact are normally reviewed on the standard of reasonableness and are accorded considerable deference. Even greater deference is appropriate where the fact finding also has required findings of credibility. This point was well illustrated by the application of *Dunsmuir* by Justice Richards in *Stonechild*:

> It is simply not appropriate for this Court, in the context of a judicial review application, to be drawn into a fundamental reassessment of the

---

132 See Chapter 5, Section D(2).

133 *Ibid.* at para. 50.

134 Above note 124, discussed in Chapter 7, Section D(3).

135 Above note 20.

136 Above note 128.

> evidence. That is particularly so when the Commissioner's findings of fact are so deeply connected to his assessment of the credibility of the key witnesses who appeared before him.[137]

There may, however, be exceptional circumstances where findings of fact may constitute a denial of procedural fairness and, therefore, constitute jurisdictional error. In such circumstances, a detailed review of the evidence may be necessary.

This situation arose in *Erebus* where the commissioner made findings of a conspiracy to commit perjury. The following finding was contained in the final report:

> [I]n this case, the palpably false sections of evidence which I heard could not have been the result of mistake, or faulty recollection. They originated, I am compelled to say, in a pre-determined plan of deception. They were very clearly part of an attempt to conceal a series of disastrous administrative blunders and so, in regard to the particular items of evidence to which I have referred, I am forced reluctantly to say that I had to listen to an orchestrated litany of lies.[138]

The Judicial Committee of the Privy Council identified the limited boundaries of judicial review it faced as follows:

> As Courts whose functions in the instant case have been restricted to those of judicial review, both the Court of Appeal and this Board are disentitled to disturb findings of fact by the decision-maker whose decision is the subject of review, unless (1) the procedure by which such findings were reached was unlawful (*in casu* by failure to observe the rule of *audi alteram partem*) or (2) primary facts were found that were not supported by any probative evidence or (3) the reasoning by which the decision-maker justified inferences of fact that he had drawn is self-contradictory or otherwise based upon an evident logical fallacy.[139]

All three of these categories clearly go to jurisdiction. The first is explicitly a denial of procedural fairness. A finding of fact for which there is no evidentiary basis and a drawing of inferences that make no sense also would

---

137 Above note 56 at para. 103. See also the application of *Dunsmuir* in *Canada (Citizenship and Immigration) v. Khosa*, 2009 SCC 12 [*Khosa*].

138 Above note 73 at 669.

139 *Ibid.* at 681.

be denials of fairness. And the degree of potential unfairness was underlined in this case by the aggressive and devastating nature of the findings.

After a detailed review and analysis of the evidence, the Committee concluded there was no evidence of any probative value on which to base such findings. It also provided this succinct guidance for judicial review of factual findings in such circumstances:

> What is required . . . is that the decision to make the finding must be based upon some material that tends logically to show the existence of facts consistent with the finding and that the reasoning supportive of the finding, if it be disclosed, is not logically self-contradictory.[140]

In this case, the principle of fairness also was breached by the failure to provide any notice of the dramatic findings that ultimately were made. There was a denial of any opportunity to respond, as discussed under Section C(3), above in this chapter.

### 3) Other Consequences

The recommendations contained in the reports of commissions of inquiry have had a profound effect on Canadian society. The contributions of policy/advisory commissions, the wrongful-conviction inquiries, and others have been described above.[141]

Governments are in a position to study a final report prior to making it public and to provide a response shortly after its release. The governments of Ontario, Manitoba, and Newfoundland and Labrador each announced, within a matter of days, that they would implement all of the recommendations of the Walkerton, Goudge, Taman, and Lamer inquiries. Policy/advisory recommendations often take longer to be adopted. They engage more public discussion and their impact is often incremental but also catalytic. Occasionally, massive reports such as that of the Aboriginal Peoples Commission seem to be too overwhelming for a government to embrace, at least at the outset.[142]

The reaction of the government to the report of the Somalia Inquiry was simply hostile. On 4 February 1997 the government directed the commission to finish its public hearings by 31 March and to file its final

---

140 *Ibid.* at 671.

141 Chapter 2, Section C and, generally, Chapter 3.

142 Mentioned in Chapter 3, Section C(2) and discussed further in Chapter 10, Section E.

report three months later.[143] On 2 June the government was re-elected with a majority, and on 2 July it released the report. Defence Minister Art Eggleton was in full attack mode.[144] He called the report a "blanket condemnation of our military" that was "unfair and unjust." It was an "insult. The commissioners made accusations without proof'" and they were "wrong." He stressed that there was no evidence of any conspiracy or cover-up, that the events in question had occurred four years earlier, and that "the time for finger pointing is past." He also attacked the integrity of Commissioner Desbarats for signing a contract to write a book about the inquiry. Of course, he also stated that the commissioners were supposed to report in nine months and received three extensions.

Reference already has been made to the massive terms of reference, the ridiculous original deadline of nine months, and the public optics of three extensions, even though each was inadequate.[145] But terminating the commission was not an issue in the election. No doubt the government also had polls to reinforce its earlier assessment that the public generally had lost interest in the commission's work. The government could be seen as defending Canada's military while the commissioners were portrayed as indiscriminately and unfairly attacking it. They were vulnerable and, apart from their press conference on the same day to reiterate their findings, they were in no position to engage in debate or to sustain any defence of their report.

Similarly, Justice Estey was critical of Emmett Hall for "promoting" his report, which was the precursor of Medicare: "I am a strong believer that silence is golden on the part of a commissioner and a judge . . . . He is *functus officio* when he is done and he should keep quiet."[146] In these particular circumstances, however, there may have been greater leeway. Emmett Hall was no longer a judge at the time and his report was entirely of a policy/advisory nature. He was in a position to enrich the public discussion as a result of his knowledge and experience and that was not a bad thing. Of course, restraint should be exercised to avoid "muddying" the content of any report and it would be unseemly to lobby the

---

143 Chapter 3, Section B(5).

144 See, for example, online: http://archives.cbc.ca/war_conflict/peacekeeping/clips/4322.

145 Chapter 3, Section B, Chapter 5, Section A(1), and Chapter 7, Section B(3).

146 Willard Estey, "The Use and Abuse of Inquiries: Do They Serve a Policy Purpose?" in Pross, Christie, & Yogis, eds., above note 88.

government for implementation of an inquiry's recommendations. Still, enlightening as opposed to lobbying may be a difficult line to draw.

Associate Chief Justice O'Connor offered this observation:

> As a final note, I observe that an inquiry commissioner should play no role in the implementation of the recommendations contained in the inquiry report. Implementation of a commission report is a matter for the political process. In my view, once a commissioner delivers a report, that should be the end of his or her involvement. This is particularly the case when a sitting judge has served as commissioner. Commissioners should give reasons for their conclusions in the reports and leave it to others to debate questions relating to implementation.[147]

Perhaps that is always the safest course to follow. It certainly would have been better if former commissioner Gomery had followed this advice.

The Gomery Commission reported in two parts. The first report involved fact finding arising out of the creation, operation, and management of the sponsorship program and advertising activities. It was a response to the terms of reference based on questions raised directly or indirectly by the auditor general. The second report was to make broader recommendations for governmental changes that would avoid such problems in future. This report was made public on 1 February 2006.

A letter dated 3 March 2006 was sent to the prime minister and signed by sixty-one persons described in the letter as "private sector leaders, representatives of the voluntary sector, former senior officials in provincial and federal governments, and former political leaders of different partisan stripes from across the country." They included, for example, Allan Blakeney, Dominic D'Alessandro, Yves Fortier, Arthur Kroeger, Harry Swain, Marc Lalonde, Barbara McDougall, John Manley, Bob Rae, and Paul Tellier. The letter described some recommendations in the report as "useful." It expressed strong concern about others because they would radically transform our parliamentary system and the doctrine of ministerial responsibility. It opposed the recommendations that would increase the powers of unelected officials at the expense of ministers, transfer the prime minister's authority to appoint deputy ministers to

147 Associate Chief Justice Dennis K. O'Connor & Freya Kristjanson, "Some Observations on Public Inquiries" (Paper presented to the Canadian Institute for the Administration of Justice, Annual Conference, 10 October 2007, Halifax, Nova Scotia).

their ministers, and modify the role of the clerk of the Privy Council. The prime minister responded by letter dated 14 December 2006 and essentially agreed. He explained that he had delayed responding pending Royal Assent of the *Federal Accountability Act*.[148]

In a separate development, a round table was held in September of the same year to discuss the Gomery Commission. It was attended by leading Canadian academics in the field of public policy and public administration, who concluded that the public-policy value of the report was weakened by "[a]n apparently heavy reliance on the advice of one or two known experts in the field of public administration, whose views on how the system of government should be fixed were already well known, raising the question of whether the conclusions were known before the evidence was weighed completely." A number of those attending the round table had been asked to contribute ideas to Gomery and to prepare papers with recommendations. But they were not made aware of what recommendations were ultimately considered. Nor were they invited to any group discussions where the recommendations that were adopted could first be discussed and debated.[149]

But these informed criticisms from such diverse, experienced, and expert sources did not deter the former commissioner, and now retired judge, from expressing his indignation:

> Mr. Gomery also admitted he was annoyed, even hurt, by an "ungrateful" Conservative government . . . . "I think they owe the fact they are in office to the work of the commission. That wasn't the objective, but it was the consequence and I think they are ungrateful to treat me that way . . . when recommendations are made, they don't even tell you they received them . . . My feelings are hurt, if you must know, all that effort, thought and good intentions . . . . I have a sense that my report was disregarded."[150]

On 13 March 2008 he made similar comments before a parliamentary committee. He argued that the *Federal Accountability Act* passed by

148 Online: www.pm.gc.ca/eng/media.asp?category=1&id=1473.

149 Peter Larson, Larson Associates (September 2006), online: http://74.125.95.132/custom?q=cache:voozMx_5ddsJ:www.ipac.ca/documents/ExBrief3Commissions31.pdf+larson&cd=2&hl=en&ct=clnk&client=google-coopat www.ipac.ca. Discussed in Chapter 4, Section C(1) and Chapter 5, Section B(3).

150 Kathryn May, "Gomery: Canada on Road to 'One-Man Government'" *Ottawa Citizen* (12 March 2008).

the government did not go far enough and urged that his recommendations be adopted.[151] In an editorial the next day, the *Globe and Mail* acknowledged that he made a valuable contribution in his fact-finding report. However, "[h]e should now accept that it is not his place to tell the government to reshape itself."[152] The doctrine of legitimate expectations certainly transfers no entitlement to a *functus* commissioner in this situation.

In addition to requiring the submission of the report, the federal terms of reference usually include a clause that "[t]he Commissioner be directed to file the papers and records of the inquiry with the Clerk of the Privy Council as soon as reasonably possible after the conclusion of the inquiry." The MacDonald Commission was able to obtain a provision in its terms of reference authorizing it to publish its research papers. As a policy/advisory commission on a massive scale, it generated a wealth of research. The Somalia Inquiry was able to negotiate with the Privy Council Office its right to publish all of its studies. Its "leverage" arose from the government's desire to obtain one detailed study that it required for another purpose.[153] Of course, a commission may also decide to publish some or all of its studies in the course of its operations. The Abella Commission simply included its main studies in a separate volume accompanying the report.

Another consequence of the report of a commission of inquiry may be to generate an unreasonable expectation of criminal prosecutions. This appeared to be what happened in *Armour*,[154] where the five accused were not only acquitted but described as innocent. The prosecutions arose out of the tainted-blood tragedy that was the subject of the Krever Inquiry. Justice Mary Lou Benotto said that "to assign blame where none exists is to compound the tragedy" and characterized the charges as "disproved." One defence counsel, Earl Levy, said: "The charges were clearly ill advised, but the trial went ahead anyway because of political pressure . . . the government . . . was under a microscope." The report of the Krever Inquiry had created expectations within the hemophiliac

151 Kathryn May, "Cut Number of Political Aids in PMO: Gomery" *Ottawa Citizen* (14 March 2008) A4.

152 "Gomery's Aftermath," Editorial, *Globe & Mail* (14 March 2008).

153 Desbarats, above note 2 at 249.

154 *R. v. Armour Pharmaceutical Company* (2007), 226 C.C.C. (3d) 438 (Ont. S.C.J.) [*Armour*].

community and the acquittals left these people angry and disappointed, according to Levy.[155]

Another defence counsel, David Scott, added that public inquiries incite public compassion that generates pressure to lay charges: "Instead of making a decision based on the evidence that charges are not warranted, frequently charges are laid to assuage public outcry."[156] The criminal charges that were the focus of the Supreme Court decision in *Phillips*[157] raised similar concerns. The charges against the two managers were simply stayed. But internal Crown documents, revealed under freedom-of-information legislation, showed that the prosecutions were "unfair and doomed to failure." The Crown attorney who had reached that conclusion asked to be reassigned as a result.[158] It is in such situations that Crown discretion must be exercised with particular care, scrutiny, objectivity, and fairness.

---

155 Jennifer McPhee, "Public Review Called For in Tainted Blood Case" *Law Times* (15 October 2007).

156 *Ibid.*

157 Above note 113.

158 "Westray Investigation Was Botched, Former Prosecutor Argues in Memo" *Ottawa Citizen* (17 December 1998).

CHAPTER TEN

# Policy/Advisory Commissions

## A. INTRODUCTION

Policy/advisory commissions were introduced in Chapter 3, Section C and the commissions described there provide illustrations of some of their features. They explore broad societal problems that require a governmental response. Unlike investigative commissions, their primary purpose is not to investigate specific events or related individual or institutional conduct. Specific events may be catalysts leading to their creation but their origins have much deeper roots, requiring more fundamental approaches and solutions.

Policy/advisory commissions provide the following examples:

- the tragedy of families being unable to afford medical treatment during the Great Depression, leading to a comprehensive system of public "medicare";
- the crisis in Confederation arising out of political developments in Quebec in the 1960s, leading to policies of bilingualism and multiculturalism;
- systemic discrimination in employment leading to policies of affirmative action in the form of "employment equity" and corresponding legislation;
- large-scale criminalization of younger Canadians for the non-medical use of drugs and the "calming" of inter-generational conflict

through a process of dialogue as well as the ultimate moderation of penalties and enforcement policies; and
- a deep economic recession leading to resolution of the perennial protectionist-liberalization trade debate in favour of free trade with the United States.

Many investigative commissions also have a policy component but these tend to be more narrow and more directly related to the specific events or conduct under investigation. For example, the Walkerton Inquiry investigated the tragic events in that community but was also directed to inquire into "any other relevant matters that the commission considers necessary to ensure the safety of Ontario's drinking water." The Gomery Commission was required to investigate the creation and management of the sponsorship and advertising programs, including specific problems identified by the auditor general. The second part of its mandate was to make general recommendations, arising out of its fact finding, to prevent future mismanagement of such programs. The Arar Inquiry had to investigate the detention, deportation, imprisonment, treatment, and return of Maher Arar to Canada. In addition, it was directed to conduct a policy review of oversight of the RCMP in national-security matters.

In many such investigative commissions, these broader components of the terms of reference essentially address "systemic" problems that are identified and informed by the more specific investigations. In contrast, the Goudge Inquiry was predominantly systemic. It was specifically directed not to report "on any individual cases" and to "conduct a systemic review." However, the review was very much grounded in the specific infant deaths that occurred, the conduct of Dr. Smith in relation to them, and the (non) leadership of the Office of the Chief Coroner in failing to prevent such conduct. In that respect, it could not be characterized as a pure policy/advisory commission. I would describe it as an investigative inquiry with a primarily systemic mandate. The Air India inquiry could be characterized in the same way.

Liora Salter has suggested that inquiries simply "can be arranged on a continuum in terms of how they balance policy-making and investigation."[1]

---

1 Liora Salter, "The Complex Relationship between Inquiries and Public Controversy" in Allan Manson & David Mullan, eds., *Commissions of Inquiry: Praise or Reappraise?* (Toronto: Irwin Law, 2003) at 186.

The idea of a "balance" between these functions does not seem helpful or accurate. The investigation of specific events and related conduct is, essentially, fact finding and often requires findings of credibility. It is analogous to the fact finding required in judicial or other adjudicative proceedings. A systemic or policy review may accompany this kind of investigation but it is normally treated as a distinct and separate phase. Another example is the Mulroney-Schreiber Inquiry, which is conducting its "Policy Review" parallel to its "Factual Inquiry." Unlike a "pure" policy/advisory commission, the policy issues here are relatively narrow. They are restricted to Canada's ethics rules, primarily as they apply to politicians, and the handling of correspondence by the Privy Council Office. While this policy review is proceeding separately, the related recommendations are likely to be informed by broader inferences drawn from the fact-finding stage as well.

John McCamus has expressed his impressions as to why policy inquiries seem to be less frequent in recent decades:

> First, it is obvious that there are many more players in the policy field than they were as recently as a few decades ago. We have seen in many ministries and departments the growth of policy branches—some of them rather large in size—that have developed an in-house capacity for policy work that was previously lacking.[2]

He adds that they have been successful, not only in developing policy, but also in "managing policy processes." This includes consultation with stakeholders and moving policy through government processes to implementation. McCamus also identifies the proliferation of non-governmental "research institutes both within and outside the academic community," and he notes, too, that "[t]he number and range of public interest groups, often single interest groups, have mushroomed in recent decades."[3] Many of these public-interest groups have at least some research capacity. Finally, McCamus cites the attempts to enhance the role of parliamentary committees in policy formulation over the years. However, he is hard-pressed to identify successes among these bodies, having to go back to the MacGuigan Committee on Statutory Instruments in 1975.

---

2 John McCamus, "The Policy Inquiry: An Endangered Species" in Manson & Mullan, eds., *ibid.* at 216.

3 *Ibid.* at 217.

On closer scrutiny of these alternatives, McCamus concludes that there is a "continuing and strong need for the type of policy-making" that can be achieved through policy/advisory commissions. Public-interest groups really tend to be advocacy groups for particular interests. Academic as well as private research centres often tend to be "animated by a particular ideological perspective" and frequently the research does not readily translate "into policy prescriptions" for current public problems. He acknowledges the shortcomings of parliamentary committees, which are often partisan and superficial. I believe he also accurately identifies the limitations of departmental policy branches:

> Government policy groups tend to be quite preoccupied by the urgent and short-term issues of the government of the day . . . policy branch budgets have been vulnerable to the winds of fiscal restraint. The range of expertise is likely to be limited . . . it may be that policy branch personnel have or are perceived to have fixed views . . .[4]

In contrast, a policy/advisory commission "can be structured to function independently . . . with greater transparency . . . engage in public education . . . float trial balloons . . ."[5] Perhaps most important, it also has the capacity to engage in comprehensive information gathering, research, and consultation with experts, interest groups, and the general public.

A policy/advisory commission can devise its own "game plan" and related structure and processes to define and attack the issues in a concentrated, focused, and relentless way that is not available to government officials. It must be kept in mind that government departments normally operate at close to full capacity. The kind of commitment and related resources that a major policy/advisory commission can make is simply not realistic within a departmental policy branch.

McCamus does seem to be correct in identifying a decline in the creation of policy/advisory commissions in recent decades. At the federal level, since 1990, there have been only three such major commission reports. They are the Royal Commission on New Reproductive Technologies (chaired by Baird, 1993), the Aboriginal Peoples Commission (1996), and the Commission on the Future of Health Care in Canada (chaired by Romanow, 2002). It is difficult to imagine how any of these reports could

---

4 *Ibid.* at 221.

5 *Ibid.*

have been produced without the status and resources of a commission of inquiry. Again the role of each fits the description of a "residual institution" of government.

## B. PURPOSE

Liora Salter and John McCamus, both cited above, provide some excellent insights into policy-advisory commissions. To quote Salter again:

> [I]nquiries are justified because they allow for a relatively independent assessment of complex issues that are deemed unsuitable for legislative or judicial scrutiny in the first instance. The issues that attract inquiries are those that have public significance, require open scrutiny, involve a complex determination of fact, and seem to require government action. Such issues are prone to controversy.[6]

She argues that these commissions are created because the issues are complex and conflicting pressures must be addressed but that often means they tend "to be all things to all people at once." As a result, "[b]ecause inquiries are shot through with controversy . . . and because a resolution of issues seems imposed in their final reports (often illusory), it would be tempting to believe that inquiries actually resolve controversies."[7] Salter maintains that they do not. Controversies may "dissipate" for a variety of reasons generated by these commissions:

> the value debates they spawn have no resolution; definition battles preoccupy protagonists so much that the public is repelled; the specificity of the issues at the heart of the controversy is lost to view; interest groups prefer to press their interests without public scrutiny; advocate groups run out of resources; and individuals find doors closed and their voices silenced.[8]

The mere exposure of controversies is a valuable contribution in itself. It brings problems to public attention. It encourages "whistle-blowing." It attracts people to the political process and broadens public discourse since controversies are "an essential element" of democracy.

---

6 Above note 1 at 185–86.

7 *Ibid.* at 207.

8 *Ibid.* at 208.

Still, policy/advisory commissions should be reserved for exceptional circumstances:

> Only when issues have broad public consequences, when complex information must be dealt with, when the justice-seeking is complex, when open public scrutiny is demanded, when new voices have the potential to reshape policy, and when policy recommendations are not obvious is the bother and cost of inquiries justified.[9]

Salter rejects the "popular wisdom" that the purpose of these commissions is mainly "to take the heat off politicians." In her view, they have produced many other benefits beyond the resolution of controversies through their recommendations.

McCamus argues that these commissions have surely "contributed" at least to the resolution of controversy, and "it is undeniable in my view that the policy inquiry has performed an important, indeed invaluable, role in public policy formulation in Canada, both at the federal and provincial levels of government."[10] Public education and debate has facilitated the emergence of consensus and underlined the obligation of commissions to make recommendations designed to resolve problems and identify common ground. Such commissions have often provided good advice as a stimulus for action. But "incremental and temporary solutions" are often the real path to progress in addressing controversial issues. And on the question of "heat":

> a properly conducted policy inquiry may well return the heat to the minister at a much lower degree. Perhaps I should add that I do not consider the use of a policy inquiry for the purpose of taking the heat off for a period of time to be a necessarily dishonourable or bad thing to do. Sidetracking an issue for a period of time may be an important part of a government strategy to deal with more pressing problems. The passage of some time may create better conditions for consensus building and taking action with respect to a particular issue. The passage of some time facilitates a period of study and reflection that may be crucial to developing sound policy. And so on. "Taking the heat off" is likely to be a continuing source of inspiration for the establishment of policy inquiries.[11]

---

9 *Ibid.* at 199.

10 Above note 2 at 212.

11 *Ibid.* at 222.

In my view, this is a very thoughtful and appropriate response to the cynicism often expressed about the purpose of policy/advisory commissions.

The decision to establish a commission of inquiry is inherently political because it is a Cabinet decision. There may be a number of tactical, political considerations at play. As Michael J. Trebilcock explains:

> [A]ll public inquiries offer to politicians the opportunity to demonstrate concern about a policy issue and to indicate that action is being taken upon it, while deferring the need to expend substantial resources in response to a perceived policy concern; to obtain advice, while maintaining some distance from the source of that advice, so as to be able to reject it where necessary; to generate, analyze, and exchange information, while informing and persuading the public of the merits of certain points of view; and to assess the public's tastes for proposed policy initiatives.[12]

A government is perfectly free to invoke this residual institution to serve any or all of these purposes. But there also may be risks. The recommendations may not be as expected and could generate pressure for the government to act in a way it does not want. It could identify previous government shortcomings in addressing the problems under consideration. It could make popular recommendations that interfere with the government's priorities. It could provide a public platform for government critics.

## C. DECISION TO ESTABLISH

Although the decision to establish every commission of inquiry is inherently political, the considerations related to policy/advisory commissions are usually very different from those applicable to investigative commissions. An investigative commission may be established in response to mounting political and public pressure arising from allegations of governmental wrongdoing.[13] It also may be a direct response to local disasters such as a deadly coal mine explosion or the deadly contamination

---

12 Economic Council of Canada, *The Choice of Governing Instruments* by Michael J. Trebilcock *et al.*(Ottawa: Canadian Government Publishing Centre, 1982) at 44.

13 See the discussion in relation to *Starr v. Houlden*, [1990] 1 S.C.R. 1366 in Chapter 4, Section A(1). Also discussed in Chapter 3, Section E(5).

of a drinking-water supply.[14] In contrast, policy/advisory commissions are more likely to be born of an "accumulation" of events combined with long-standing societal problems. Such problems often persist through unsuccessful government policies and programs to address them. Over the decades they manifest themselves in different ways and to varying degrees.

A good example is the Aboriginal Peoples Commission established in 1991.[15] The commissioners reported that their work began at a difficult time:

> It was a time of anger and upheaval. The country's leaders were arguing about the place of Aboriginal people in the constitution. Fist Nations were blockading roads and rail lines in Ontario and British Columbia. Innu families were encamped in protest of military installations in Labrador. A year earlier, armed conflict between Aboriginal and non-Aboriginal forces at Kanesatake (Oka) had tarnished Canada's reputation abroad—and in the minds of many citizens.[16]

The abysmal conditions in many Aboriginal communities persisted. High rates of poverty, ill health, and family breakdown continued to be prevalent. Media reports of suicide among children and youth were particularly disturbing.

Salter has expressed the view that the "bother and cost" of a policy/ advisory committee are justified only when the issues involve complex information with broad public consequences.[17] The process of "justice-seeking" must also be complex. This means that there are controversies or conflicting interests and demands with no agreement about the "standards of assessment" that should govern attempts at resolution. In these circumstances, the policy recommendations are not obvious but there may be "new voices" or approaches that have the "potential to reshape policy." Salter also points out the futility of attempting to resolve conflicting views about values:

---

14 See also the reference to the Westray and Walkerton inquiries in Chapter 4, Section A(1). Also discussed in Chapter 3, Sections B(3) & (4).

15 See the reference in Chapter 3, Section C(2) and discussion in Section F, below in this chapter.

16 Aboriginal Peoples Commission, "A Word from Commissioners."

17 Above note 9.

> Value debates are notoriously difficult to resolve .... A statement of principle on the part of one participant is simply a declaration of beliefs and opinions, seen from the perspective of others. Pointing out that, underlying discourse, are particular presumptions about the world or human activity is rarely persuasive to those who believe that such presumptions are indeed justified.[18]

A perceived consensus may be achieved by keeping discussion at a high level of generality which may disguise profound disagreement about specific policies. Former justice and commissioner Frank Iacobucci is of a similar view:

> A commission of inquiry will be less helpful in resolving an issue involving ethical or value choices. Neutrality lends little authority for the making of choices that clearly depend primarily on values. A Parliamentary committee, or in an extreme case, even a free vote in Parliament, will be of far greater utility and hence be far more effective in making such a choice.[19]

Also, as suggested earlier,[20] if the problem is essentially political, a commission of inquiry will have little to contribute. If the issues and options have been identified and are clearly understood, the political choice should be made by the government, with its ultimate accountability to the electorate.

Generally speaking, a policy/advisory commission will be established in response to long-standing social and economic problems that have not been ameliorated through previous governmental attempts. These problems seem to invite an independent and objective evaluation based on three interacting features: (1) the canvassing of all available and relevant information and, particularly, all relevant expertise; (2) the comprehensive synthesis, analysis, and evaluation of the information and alternative policy options; (3) a dialogue with experts, interest constituencies, stakeholders, and the general public to inform and to be informed. The political considerations and potential ramifications discussed at the end

---

18 Above note 1 at 196.

19 "Commissions of Inquiry and Public Policy in Canada" in A.P. Pross, I. Christie, and J.A. Yogis, eds, *Commissions of Inquiry* (Toronto: Carswell, 1990) at 25.

20 Chapter 4, Section A(2).

of the previous section are also bound to be part of the decision to establish a policy/advisory commission.

Alternative responses such as interdepartmental committees, task forces, and parliamentary committees are likely to be considered as well. However, by the time a policy/advisory commission is seriously being considered, they likely all will have had a "go" at the problem. Michael J. Trebilcock and L. Austin describe the far greater expense and length of the Krever Inquiry compared to an examination of the same subject matter in the United States by a medical subgroup of the National Academy of Sciences.[21] But, as McCamus observes, the two approaches were simply designed very differently and are, therefore, not really comparable.[22] Once the decision is made to establish a policy/advisory commission, the question of design moves from choice of response to the terms of reference and choice of commissioner(s).

The terms of reference for these commissions are necessarily cast in broad terms to ensure that the problems may be examined in a comprehensive manner. The commissioners of the Aboriginal Peoples Commissions summarized their mandate as being:

> possibly the broadest in the history of Canadian royal commissions. We were asked to look at virtually every aspect of the lives of the First Nations, Inuit and Métis peoples of Canada—their history, health and education; their aspirations for self-government and relations with Canadian governments; their land claims, treaties, economies and cultures; their living conditions in the North as well as in cities; their relationship with the justice system; the state of their languages; their spiritual well-being and, more generally, their situation in Canada relative to that of non-Aboriginal Canadians. As we discovered soon after embarking on our task, any of the sixteen points in our mandate could have been the subject of a royal commission.

Similarly, the Romanow Commission was directed to "undertake dialogue with Canadians" about the future of Canada's public health-care system and

---

21 M.J. Trebilcock & L. Austin, "The Limits of the Full Court Press: Of Blood and Mergers" (1998) 48 U.T.L.J. 1.

22 Above note 2 at 225.

> to recommend policies and measures respectful of the jurisdictions and powers in Canada required to ensure over the long term the sustainability of a universally accessible, publicly funded health system, that offers quality services to Canadians and strikes an appropriate balance between investments in prevention and health maintenance and those directed to care and treatment.

The Baird Commission likewise received a broad mandate:

> to inquire into and report on current and potential medical and scientific developments related to new reproductive technologies, considering in particular their social, ethical, health, research, legal and economic implications and the public interest, recommending what policies and safeguards should be applied and examining in particular . . .

Specific issues are then listed in a general way, such as: implications for women's reproductive health and well-being; infertility; reversals of sterilization, artificial insemination, and embryo transfers; social and legal arrangements as well as status and rights of participants in these procedures and processes; and economic ramifications. In spite of divergent societal views on many ethical implications, the commission's report led to the passing of the *Assisted Human Reproduction Act*[23] in 2004. It seeks to regulate assisted human reproduction by banning human cloning, "renting" of wombs, and the sale of human sperm and eggs. It also establishes rules for certain practices that are permitted and a regulatory agency to supervise the objectives of the Act.

It is difficult to attempt to impose constraints upon the scope of policy/advisory commission mandates. Reliance must be placed on the commissioners, to a large extent to sort out priorities for inclusion and emphasis. The standards applied by them for making choices and recommendations are not always articulated.

An interesting study for the Science Council of Canada examined six inquiries to determine their value in making a scientific assessment.[24] These were:

---

23 S.C. 2004, c. 2.

24 Liora Salter & Debra Slaco, *Public Inquiries in Canada* (Ottawa: Supply and Services Canada, 1981).

- the Environmental Assessment Review of the proposed Point Lepreau nuclear generating plant in New Brunswick;
- the Bayda Inquiry into balancing development and risk in uranium mining in northern Saskatchewan;
- the Porter Inquiry into electric-power planning in Ontario;
- the Wilson Inquiry into the potential problems of aluminum wiring in residential homes;
- the Le Dain Commission into the non-medical use of drugs; and
- the Canadian Radio-Television and Telecommunications Commission (CRTC) Inquiry into satellite communication systems.

To the layperson, a "scientific" inquiry suggests that the results will provide objective certainty. As with "expert" witnesses in court trials, however, the Science Council study demonstrates that such certainty is elusive in many respects.

These inquiries generally proceeded with the objective of "the determination of risk." This was done, for example, by studying different forms of energy production and comparing the level of risk with the consequences of other activities such as automobile accidents and assessing a variety of costs: financial, health, and social. But the determination of "acceptable" levels of risk in these situations is fraught with problems. What standard determines whether risks are "necessary" or "undesirable"? In measuring risk against other consequences, what is the causal link between them? Do the risks fall unevenly among those likely to be affected? Is the risk being assessed limited to "accidents," or does it weight the full nature of consequences over time? Does that risk involve "maximum possible or maximum practical protection"? These are important questions to consider and address when deciding to establish a commission of inquiry of this nature.

Unlike investigative commissioners,[25] policy/advisory commissioners normally require some familiarity or past association with the subject area under inquiry. It is also common for policy/advisory commissions to be composed of a panel of commissioners who bring a variety of backgrounds to the task.

The Aboriginal Peoples Commission was established following the report of then former chief justice Brian Dickson. He conducted con-

25 See Chapter 4, Section D. Although, for example, a wrongful conviction commissioner must have extensive knowledge about the general criminal justice system.

sultations with Aboriginal leaders throughout Canada, government officials, politicians, and academic and other experts. In addition to the broad terms of reference that were adopted, he recommended that the majority of commissioners be Aboriginal. The commission, established in 1991, consisted of two co-chairs and five additional commissioners. The co-chairs were George Erasmus, past chief (national) of the Assembly of First Nations (AFN), and René Dussault, then on the Quebec Court of Appeal and a legal expert in public law and government. The other Aboriginal members were: Viola Robinson, a past president of the Native Council of Canada; Mary Sillett, a past president of the national Inuit women's association and a vice-president of Inuit Tapirisat Canada; and Paul Chartrand, a Métis lawyer and academic. The other two commissioners were: Bertha Wilson, a retired judge of the Supreme Court of Canada; and Allan Blakeney, a former premier of Saskatchewan.

When Blakeney resigned two years later, he was replaced by Peter Meekison, a political science professor and former Alberta deputy minister. The replacement of a policy/advisory commissioner mid-stream does not pose the problems that would arise for an investigative commissioner. Where fact finding and potential findings of misconduct are involved, the principle of fairness normally would require continuity of the same commissioner from beginning to end.[26]

The New Reproductive Technologies Commission consisted of five women and was chaired by Patricia Baird, a paediatrician and professor in medical genetics. The other four commissioners included a theology philosopher, a law professor, a businessperson, and an anthropologist, Suzanne Scorsone, who was also the director of the Office of Catholic Life. She wrote dissenting opinions on six areas of disagreement, including termination as an appropriate response to the prenatal diagnosis of a disorder. She prefaced her dissenting views by relating the "free and wide-ranging" discussion among commissioners of "all concerns and perspectives" and added:

---

26 In Chapter 6, Section A(4), it was suggested that if the role of "advisory counsel" were established, he could be appointed as commissioner and continue, even in an investigative commission. Section 22(1)(c) of the *Interpretation Act*, R.S.C. 1985, c. I-21, provides that if a vacancy occurs the remaining commissioners could continue, provided there still is a quorum.

> The presence of these few supplementary differences of opinion as part of the unitary final report witnesses to the liberty given to the expression of viewpoints. That the areas of disagreement are serious should not be taken to reflect in any way on the rest of the report, since in other areas of similarly serious import we have been able to reach a mutual, collaborative view and common recommendations, if in a minority of instances out of different reasoning. These questions are matters of great debate in Canadian society at large; that there would be some degree of respectful difference of opinion on a Commission called together out of diverse backgrounds and expertise to examine these issues on behalf of Canadians is precisely what one would expect. The overall unanimity on all other recommendations witnesses to the fact that they arise out of genuinely achieved and viable agreement.[27]

Indeed, the areas of disagreement were remarkably few in the context of the controversial subject matter and massive report, including some 293 recommendations.

The variety of backgrounds that different commissioners bring can be valuable in strengthening the depth and scope of a commission's work. It can help to ensure that all relevant areas are explored and understood. Commissioners who are "representative" of important communities and interests can inspire confidence that those experiences and views will be understood. But the role of such commissioners should not be to "lobby" other commissioners in favour of such interests. They should be open to appreciating all perspectives and supporting recommendations that will achieve the objectives of their terms of reference.

Trebilcock[28] provides a good example of the extremes of a single impartial commissioner and a bipartisan (and polarized) panel with a neutral chair. Sole Commissioner Thomas Berger "announced a strong, uncompromising position on the MacKenzie Valley Pipeline, clearly choosing some interests (those of the native peoples, environmentalists, and others) over other interests (pro development), mainly those of white northerners and the project's proponents." In contrast, the Alaska Pipeline Inquiry had three commissioners: a representative of the Indian people of the Yukon, a representative of the white residents of the

---

27 Canada, New Reproductive Technologies Commission, *Final Report* (Ottawa: Research Branch, Library of Parliament, 1994) Annex IV, "Six Dissenting Opinions."

28 Above note 12 at 46.

Yukon, and neutral Chairperson Kenneth Lysyk. In contrast to the Berger Commission, "the Lysyk Inquiry, in reaching its unanimous report, issued recommendations based on compromise, attempting to promote common ground among the competing interests, thus avoiding the need to make more tough choices among the competing interests . . ."

Sometimes commissioners must choose between making compromises to achieve unanimity and forcefully expressing opposing views. Unanimity may enhance the likelihood of a commission's recommendations being adopted. But the sacrifices to achieve it may defeat some of the purpose of the policy/advisory commission. There certainly is ample opportunity for compromise at the implementation stage when political forces may require greater accommodation of diverse interests.

In appointing commissioners, the issue of expertise may be related to the representation of interests. Appointing an "expert" in the subject area under inquiry may lend credibility to a commission but it may also affect judgment because of strongly held views. There also may be a lack of consensus among experts in relation to relevant issues. The Law Reform Commission of Ontario observed:

> Even where the relevant field of expertise can be identified, uncertainty or disagreement within the community of experts is often one of the central foci of the inquiry, and the direct involvement of potentially "partisan" specialists might be considered inappropriate. Moreover, the means of resolving controversy might differ, ultimately, from professional practice within the field of expertise.[29]

It is preferable for commissioners to receive the views of experts through testimony from witnesses or advice from advisory panels rather than through a colleague. Serving as a source of expertise blurs the role of a commissioner and may obstruct the deliberative process.

While policy/advisory commissions ordinarily have some identification with the subject area under review, that need not be the case for a chairperson:

> It is sometimes forgotten by technical experts that in many fields it is possible for a lay chairman to learn quickly the essentials of the subject-matter, "to get up the brief." And this phrase reminds us that lawyers

29 Ontario Law Reform Commission, *Report on Public Inquiries* (Toronto: The Commission, 1992) at 145. See also above note 1 at 190–94.

> are often chosen as chairmen of committees of inquiry, for it is their profession to master the essentials of a problem, to know what use expert opinions can be, and to know how to extract what is relevant and needful from witnesses.[30]

As the deputy head to the appropriate minister, the chairperson is the chief executive for administrative and financial purposes. However, the chairperson has no authority beyond that of other commissioners in relation to the substantive work of the commission. The federal *Interpretation Act* provides that, when more than two persons receive authority to act, that authority may be exercised by a majority.[31] Even where the chairperson purports to make a ruling on the admissibility of evidence, she may be overruled by a majority of commissioners.[32] The Act also provides that at least one-half of the commissioners would be required for a quorum that would authorize them to act on behalf of the commission.

## D. PROCESS

In Chapters 5 and 6, the "game plan" for investigative commissions was described as requiring the exhaustive examination of documents and the interviewing of witnesses in preparation for hearings. The hearings provide the forum for the evidentiary base to be established and tested, particularly when the facts and inferences to be drawn are in dispute. In contrast, a policy/advisory commission is seldom involved in specific fact finding or related issues of credibility. It is highly unlikely that there will be any findings of "misconduct" requiring notice, as discussed above.[33] It will be engaged in broader social, economic, or scientific fact finding. As a result, its process essentially requires research and consultation. Rather than an evidentiary record, it requires an information base, which must be synthesized, analyzed, and assessed to identify the relevant issues and crystallize appropriate policy responses.

Establishing a "game plan" from the outset is equally as important as with investigative commissions but the requirements and features will be different. The role of legal counsel is not nearly as important

---

30 K.C. Wheare, *Government by Committee* (Oxford: Clarendon Press, 1995) at 85.

31 Above note 26, s. 22(1).

32 *Bortolotti v. Ontario (Ministry of Housing)* (1977), 76 D.L.R. (3d) 408 (Ont. C.A.).

33 Chapter 9, Section C.

and the "operational control centre" is more likely to be the executive director.[34] In addition to financial and general administration, there is a need for direction and coordination of the research and consultation in a progressive and timely manner. As the secretary to the Ocean Ranger Inquiry observed:

> A Commission of inquiry is a race against time from start to finish and there is very little opportunity to learn on the job as progression through each of its stages provides fresh challenges of a different kind . . .
>
> The role of the commission secretary is to orchestrate these diverse activities, to ensure that the commissioners are provided with an efficient organization able to provide them with sound advice and information on which good decisions can be based, and to produce a professional report. That way in which an inquiry is managed directly affects its credibility.[35]

The Secretary to the Macdonald Commission stressed the importance of establishing a strategy that is supported by the commissioners and senior staff "very early and then sticking to it."[36]

Many of the personnel and administrative requirements referred to in Chapter 5 are applicable here but with different emphasis. The role of the director of research is extremely important for a policy/advisory commission since it requires not only research skills and knowledge but also the management skills to validate, coordinate, and integrate research on a grand scale. A media-relations officer will be important in developing and executing a communications strategy, especially in relation to public consultations. Physical premises and a website are necessary but not necessarily a "hearings" room. A process for standing and funding will be required but that is not likely to be for legal representation at hearings. Rather, it will be to assist stakeholders, public-interest groups, and specialists in the subject area to conduct research and prepare "briefs" from their perspectives.

---

34 Also described as the chief administrative officer, executive officer, executive secretary, secretary, and registrar. See Chapter 5, Section C(1).

35 David M. Grenville, "The Role of the Commission Secretary" in Pross, Christie, & Yogis, eds., above note 19 at 70.

36 J.G. Godsoe, Q.C., "Comment on Inquiry Management," *ibid.* at 73. Quoted in Chapter 3, Section C(5).

Research is the foundation of a policy/advisory commission. Where the terms of reference are very broad, the challenge of establishing a comprehensive, integrated, and reliable information base is massive. Research usually begins with a canvassing of existing literature, including previous public reports, relevant legislation, regulations and policies, and parliamentary debates. This may be done by the commission's "in-house" research staff and will identify authors who can be retained to conduct specific studies of direct relevance to various aspects of the terms of reference.

Statistical surveys may be helpful but pose critical challenges for their design and administration to avoid challenges as to their validity. On the other hand, informal surveys of a general nature may be valuable:

> Abella had been given a very narrow mandate, but she chose to conduct a more extensive consultation on the promotion of equal employment opportunities for her four target groups. Shortly after her appointment as Commissioner to the RCEE, she sent a detailed letter to nearly three thousand individuals and organizations, asking their opinions not only on affirmative action, training, recruitment, promotion, employment equality, and pay equality, but also on the desirability of flexible work patterns, parental and maternity leave, child benefits, and child care.[37]

Although child care was not an issue identified in her terms of reference, the information she received helped her to conclude that "child care is the ramp that provides equal access to the work place for mothers. [And] . . . child care should be a public service to which every child has a right." Employment equity for women simply could not be addressed without including this crucial element.

Salter points out the difficulties that commissions may encounter when faced with "expertise":

> Scientific research always produces uncertain results, while inquiries attempt to achieve closure. In science, more research does not resolve issues, but muddies the waters and raises new questions to be addressed. Conflict is rife within scientific disciplines, where it is viewed

37 Annis May Timpson, "Challenging Policy Paradigms: Women, Royal Commissions, and the Public-Private Divide" in Manson & Mullan, above note 1 at 240.

> as normal: conflict within science can be confusing to the non-scientist and problematic for inquiries.[38]

This means that research must not only be gathered but also "tested." The secretary of the Ocean Ranger Inquiry explained how it dealt with expert studies that it commissioned:

> A small group of advisors reviewed and validated the study plan. This initial group was subsequently expanded into four advisory committees, composed of individuals with particular expertise in the key fields covered by the studies. These committees assisted in the selection of consultants, reviewed the work done and suggested how best to arrange for it to be checked independently by reference to other recognized experts.[39]

Thus, the commission's own experts reviewed the studies but also referred them to other experts for independent review. The product was then subjected to further critical scrutiny through a series of consultations. The objective was to ensure that the information assembled was credible so that the conclusions and recommendations ultimately reached would be "defensible and realistic."

The consultation process began in private with a seminar of a small number of government, industry, and academic experts, which led to the establishment of an Advisory Committee. Consultants and study teams were then engaged to provide a comprehensive review of the main subjects of concern:

> Twenty-four studies were undertaken over a two-year period in four principal areas: environment, design, safety and training and regulations. The views expressed and the conclusions reached in these study reports were those of the authors. They represented input to, rather than the output of, the Commission.[40]

Once the commission's advisers concluded that a report had reached a satisfactory standard, it was sent to another external expert for peer review. Submissions received from interested parties were subjected to a similar external review. It was only after all of the studies and submis-

38 Above note 1 at 191.

39 Above note 35 at 62.

40 *Ibid.* at 65.

sions were reviewed that they were made available to the public and public discussion began.

The commission was aware that there were ongoing developments in these areas. As a result, a series of seminars was conducted in the last stages before writing the final report. This focused the expert knowledge on key areas, filled gaps in the database, and updated the studies. Finally, an international consultative conference was held to stimulate debate by experts on the issues the commissioners had to address and the solutions available to them.

The consultations of the Macdonald Commission[41] also progressed from "private" to "focused" to "public" in the following stages:

- private meetings with provincial and territorial premiers;
- private consultations with representatives of business, manufacturing, labour, resources, agriculture, education, municipalities, volunteers, and Aboriginal communities;
- a series of seminars for many of these (invited) representatives;
- an invitation to the public to provide written responses to a widely distributed information booklet;
- twelve public workshops held at universities across the country; and
- public hearings in twenty-seven cities and five Arctic communities.

Unlike the Ocean Ranger Inquiry, this consultation process, even at the last stages, was not based primarily upon its research but proceeded simultaneously as the research progressed.

Allan Cairns, who was one of the three research directors for the Macdonald Commission, has written an excellent article documenting the massive challenge it faced.[42] The scale of the research undertaken is witnessed by the seventy volumes the commission published as supplements to the report itself. The value of that research is reflected in the 100,000 copies that have been sold, some of which have been used as university texts.[43] The thirteen commissioners and more than one

41 Chapter 3, Section C(5).

42 "Reflections on Commission Research" in Pross, Christie, & Yogis, eds,, above note 19 at 87.

43 *Ibid.* at 88.

hundred researchers created problems, not only in coordinating the research itself, but also in relating that research to the expectations and needs of the commissioners, who were focused on the ultimate recommendations they would have to make. And this was to happen, in the context of probably the broadest terms of reference ever established up to that time, within a three-year time limit.

Cairns describes the "pervasive uncertainty" over the first two years about the form or context of the report or who would write it. Most of the researchers were retained on a part-time contractual basis and continued with their regular (mostly academic) jobs. The commissioners also continued their regular professional lives apart from attending commission meetings or consultations. There was a value in this fluidity and uncertainty, however, since it prevented prejudgment on issues before results of the research and consultations were known.

Cairns identifies a number of consequences of the decision to publish the research studies, and his comments apply to other commissions as well. Publishing research studies prevents the commissioners from disguising weaknesses in the final report in its efforts to "sell" their conclusions and recommendations. The research can provide ammunition for the report's critics. But, from the public perspective, that adds to the transparency of the recommendations and the level of the debate. It can enhance the quality of the research when the authors know they will be subject to the scrutiny of their peers, but that also can be counterproductive. The writing may be strongly geared towards others within their academic discipline, with resistance to interdisciplinary aspects that might be of greater benefit to the commissioners. The presentation also may be subjected to every possible qualification in the desire for academic thoroughness and objectivity. This can detract from a more persuasive presentation that might be of greater value to commissioners, who are not experts in the field and are seeking policy advice. In the case of the Macdonald Commission, this tension between commissioners and researchers was exacerbated by their isolation from each other as a result of the "complex research mandate" coupled with "an exhausting hearings process."

Cairns found it "difficult to exaggerate the significance of limited time as a constraint on research." The actual time available for research was limited at the front end by start-up activities such as appointing staff, establishing a commission structure, and adopting a game plan.

The back end required writing, editing, translating, and publishing the final report. In effect, the three-year mandate allowed only about two years of research. The time constraints also meant that much of the research would have to be allocated to "the repackaging and dissemination of conventional wisdom" rather than exploring new frontiers. Similarly, interdisciplinary research, "much lauded and seldom effectively practiced," was elusive. The three research directors attempted to keep each other informed of their separate streams of research but the preoccupation with time pressures made greater collaboration difficult. The initial premise was that, upon completion of the work within each stream, the findings would be "synthesized and integrated" as they were applied to the various policy areas arising from the terms of reference.

> In retrospect, this was a utopian aspiration with its presupposition that integration would occur after the individual projects had been worked and reworked through the lens of particular disciplines. At this point, the assumptions, logic and analysis were no longer flexible and open to outside influence. They were embodied in finished products with their own internal symmetries resistant to modification. They had the characteristics of self-contained building blocks, not of the malleable clay they might have been at their onset.[44]

But this could mean only that the original expectation may have been unrealistic. The idea of "forging new models and methodologies for interdisciplinary work" simply may not be possible within the limited time frame of most commissions of inquiry.

These observations reinforce the importance of establishing research goals at the outset that will make a contribution to existing knowledge yet not overreach. The value of synthesis and analysis of existing information should not be undervalued, especially in its application to clearly identified problems. Consultation is the important partner of research for a policy/advisory commission. It encompasses a wide variety of opportunities to obtain advice and guidance, receive and test information, inform public opinion, identify policy alternatives, and test public reaction to them. The Macdonald Commission's consultations provide some examples of the formats that may be adopted but each commission may shape variations to respond to its own needs.

---

44 *Ibid.* at 101.

However, some general observations may be made. First, a gestation period prior to full public consultations is of great value. This allows a commission the opportunity to understand and clarify its terms of reference through private consultations identifying the issues and interests affected. Then, the publication of an "issues paper" in advance could help to focus and advance public consultations. Related to this is the enhancing of public discussion and debate through the process of public education and the identification of opposing views. The third consideration, flowing from the previous, is the importance of attempting to find common ground rather than fostering or intensifying the polarization of views and positions. A fourth aspect is to ensure that all potential policy choices are exposed in the course of both the private and public consultations. This was a fatal omission on the part of the Gomery Commission in both respects. Finally, it may also be fatal for a policy/advisory commission to fail adequately to consult with government. A full appreciation of its past positions and perceived interest may be of fundamental importance in understanding the basic nature of the issues and the viability of potential solutions. And, of course, it is the government that takes over at the implementation stage.

## E. RESULTS

Professor McCamus articulates the unreasonable expectations that a policy/advisory commission may create, not only for the public, but for the commission itself:

> It is an understandable conceit that, if only sufficient resources could be marshalled and enough time were permitted to gather all the relevant facts, examine experience in other jurisdictions, review the existing literature, conduct original research to fill in the gaps in the existing literature, consult the known experts in the field, consult with stakeholders and prepare, without undue haste, a lengthy and thoughtful final report, the issues assigned to the policy inquiry might be resolved for a very long time.[45]

It is, therefore, reasonable for the government establishing such an inquiry to impose resource and other limitations, even when the terms of

---

45 Above note 2 at 213.

reference are extremely broad. An important role for such a commission always will be to make choices about what is realistic. As the secretary to the Macdonald Commission observed: "[T]here is always a tremendous trade-off between speed and efficacy and, on the other hand, quality. Always your researchers will be telling you, 'For God's sake, if you only give us six more months or another year or even six more weeks, it can make a big difference on quality.'"[46] Similarly, in formulating recommendations, a commission should avoid the conceit of its reach exceeding its grasp.[47]

The example has been given of the strong, negative response that followed the Gomery policy recommendations in the form of the extraordinary initiative of a petition to the prime minister.[48] Many of the recommendations were condemned by an impressive "coalition" of Canadian leaders and the prime minister responded by expressing general agreement with their criticism. A commission should at least engage in extensive internal and external consultation before making recommendations that would be characterized as radical in their attempt to transform our parliamentary system and the doctrine of ministerial responsibility.

In addition to consultation, at various levels, the relationship of commissioners to their research staff was also identified above. The final stage of "relationships" is among the commissioners themselves, in the course of deliberations about their conclusions and recommendations. There is not the same concern about research staff participating in deliberations as would be the case for legal counsel, who had taken adversarial positions in the course of investigative hearings. At the same time, commissioners must be wary of becoming "captive" of the views of a limited range of internal "experts," as appeared to occur with Commissioner Gomery.[49] It is the experience, insights, and good judgment of the commissioners that ultimately are required.

---

46 Above note 36 at 71.

47 See, generally, Chapter 9, Section A(4).

48 Chapter 9, Section D(3). In these circumstances, it is difficult to appreciate the view of one author that the immediacy and specificity of the issues that led to the creation of the Gomery Inquiry created momentum for the "acceptance" of its policy recommendations. See Peter J. Carver, "Getting the Story Out: Accountability and the Law of Public Inquiries" in Colleen M. Flood & Lorne Sossin, eds., *Administrative Law in Context* (Toronto: Emond Montgomery, 2008) at 365.

49 *Ibid.*

Often there will be frequent interaction with research staff at earlier stages of the process, including the integration of the results of consultations. After the commissioners have been exposed to the subject matter and issues, they will develop their own views about inferences to be drawn and appropriate recommendations. As they engage in the final deliberative stages, staff researchers will not be required as participants, although they may be consulted for further directed research or for their views on specified issues. However, staff who will be responsible for drafting the report should be present during the deliberations to ensure that they capture the nuances of what the commissioners want the report to say.

Ideally, the commissioners will have an open mind and willingness to be persuaded during these deliberations. As with judges, they are likely to have personal preconceptions about the issues that must be addressed. But, like appellate judges, they must listen to each other and be open to modifying or abandoning such preconceptions and predilections. Additionally, some commissioners may be strongly drawn to firm and opposing positions. One participant described her experience after she decided she would represent the interests of a particular "constituency" during deliberations:

> I was engaged in a process of negotiation—I called it "horsetrading"—in which a great deal of "give and take" was necessary if the final report was to be written. As a result of these negotiations, the final reports of inquiries often contain seemingly contradictory recommendations. Ours was no exception.[50]

Such horse-trading may occur even where there is no polarization of positions by commissioners. Here the trade-off may be among the various interests affected. The commissioners may allocate recommendations to meet the concerns of each interest group without regard for overall cohesion or consistency. But these approaches are more likely to occur in more narrowly focused commissions.

Policy/advisory commissions with a broad policy mandate more often do provide vision, guidance, and a lasting contribution to society,

---

50 Liora Salter, "The Two Contradictions in Public Inquiries" in Pross, Christie, & Yogis, eds., above note 19 at 184.

as Canadian history has demonstrated. But their worth should not be measured merely by the adoption (or not) of their recommendations:

> Too frequently inquiries have been faulted because their specific recommendations are not accepted. We would do better if we understood that recommendations are important primarily because the pressure to produce them exerts a powerful control upon the commissioners and forces even the most radically inclined inquiries to be pragmatic and reformist in the final analysis. And even if none of their recommendations is accepted, inquiries are still important because they are the locus, and one of the very few occasions, for a public debate about the definition of public issues, including a debate about reformist and radical conceptions of these issues.[51]

This process provides an opportunity for the public to experience "direct democracy" through participation in the development of policies together with those who will be most directly affected by those policies.

With respect to a commission's substantive recommendations, often "incremental and temporary solutions to controversial issues are the more likely path of progress."[52] And the important question to ask is: "Did the work of the commission influence the course of public policy?"[53] It is the serving of a broader "social function" that may be the most important contribution of a policy/advisory commission:

> [A] commission . . . has certain things to say to government but it also has an effect on perceptions, attitudes and behaviour. Its general way of looking at things is probably more important in the long run than its specific recommendations. It is the general approach towards a social problem that determines the way in which a society responds to it. There is much more than law and governmental action involved in the social response to a problem. The attitudes and responses of individuals at the various places at which they effect the problem are of profound importance.
>
> What gives an inquiry of this kind its social function is that it becomes, whether it likes it or not, part of this ongoing social process. There is action and interaction . . . Thus this instrument, supposedly

51 *Ibid.* at 182.

52 Above note 2 at 213.

53 Above note 36.

> merely an extension of Parliament, may have a dimension which passes beyond the political process into the social sphere. The phenomenon is changing even while the inquiry is in progress. The decision to institute an inquiry of this kind is a decision not only to release an investigative technique but a form of social influence as well.[54]

## F. ABORIGINAL PEOPLES

Reference was made in Section C, above in this chapter, to the membership and extremely broad mandate of the Aboriginal Peoples Commission that was established in 1991. Its report, five years later, is important because it offers a comprehensive and integrated approach to a fundamental problem that has existed in Canada since before Confederation. That is the legal, political, economic, social, and cultural position of Inuit, Métis, and First Nations peoples in Canadian society.

Aboriginal peoples experience many manifestations of their disadvantaged position in comparison to other Canadians:

- lower life expectancy of seven to eight years owing to double the death rates of Aboriginal babies and higher rates for children, youth, and young adults through accident;
- higher rates of infections and other diseases;
- high rates of violence and self-destructive behaviour including substance abuse and suicide;
- conflict with the law and much higher rates of incarceration; and
- educational underachievement, unemployment, substandard housing, and poverty.

And, while many of these adverse consequences fall hardest on young people, the Aboriginal birth rate is rapidly outpacing that of other Canadians. The commission reported that 56 percent of the Aboriginal population was under twenty-four years of age, compared to 34 percent of the population at large.

---

54 Gerald E. Le Dain, "The Role of the Public Inquiry in our Constitutional System" in Jacob S. Ziegel, ed., *Law and Social Change* (Toronto: Osgoode Hall Law School, 1973) at 85. Quoted in full by Cory J. in *Phillips v. Nova Scotia (Commission of Inquiry into the Westray Mine Tragedy)*, [1995] 2 S.C.R. 97 at para. 64.

The commission saw as the underlying problem the forces of assimilation: it is the strong drive on the part of Aboriginal peoples for cultural survival that causes them to blockade roads, occupy sacred grounds, and engage in other protests. They seek recognition that their plight stems from the loss of their lands, resources, economic livelihood, and social institutions. The commissioners viewed their broad mandate as an advantage:

> For the first time, the problems confronting Aboriginal people could be approached not as single issues, to be dealt with in isolation and treated to *ad hoc* solutions, [but] as interrelated issues requiring the holistic approach that is fundamental to the Aboriginal view of the world: the sense that the many facets of human life and the natural world are interconnected, that problems arise from interrelated causes, not just a single cause, and that solutions must therefore be holistic and multifaceted as well.[55]

As with other policy/advisory commissions, the commission relied upon two basic sources: research and consultation. The consultation processes had many features similar to the other commissions described above. But they were also unique in some respects. Prior to attending for a public hearing, the commissioners often hired an "advance" person recommended by the community, who would identify the issues of greatest significance and interest to that community as well as local presenters. At each hearing, an elder or community leader would be invited to join the panel as a "commissioner for that day." These guest commissioners acted as animators to encourage the presenters to feel comfortable and speak their own languages. And they themselves were encouraged to ask questions and clarify issues as well as giving an opening and closing prayer at each hearing.

The commissioners visited ninety-six different communities and held 178 days of hearings. They heard from 2,067 persons speaking personally or representing groups. They also received close to 1,000 written submissions. The consultations additionally included brainstorming sessions with experts and a series of round tables on subject areas such as health, education, justice, and economic development.

---

55 See, generally, Aboriginal Peoples Commission, "Appendix C: How We Fulfilled Our Mandate."

Consultations also preceded the commission's extensive research program to identify areas where reliable research existed and where further research was required. The commission chose four major research themes: Governance, Lands and Economy, Social and Cultural Issues, and the North. The perspectives for approaching each of these included history, women, youth, and urban residence. They avoided single-discipline research by focusing on broader "themes" in order to achieve a more integrated approach to policy development. Most of the 330 completed studies have been made available to the public in a variety of formats, including CD-ROM. The remainder is available in the National Archives.

While this does not do justice to the detailed five-volume report, it may be of interest to sketch the broad nature of the report and its recommendations. In their "Last Words," the commissioners left no doubt that their recommendations were proposing a very dramatic change: "The changes we propose are not modest. We do not suggest tinkering with the *Indian Act* or launching shiny new programs. What we propose is fundamental, sweeping and perhaps disturbing—but also exciting, liberating, ripe with possibilities." Any proposals for dramatic change must have some core of validity if they are to have any credibility and hope of adoption. Here, the commissioners found that validity in Canadian history and the clear perspective they brought to the presentation of that history is valuable in itself.

The report points out that few Canadians know about the peaceful and cooperative relationship between Aboriginal peoples and the early European visitors. The Americas were inhabited by societies with a variety of languages, cultures, social traditions, and evolving systems of government. Nation-to-nation relations developed between the inhabitants and the newcomers based on barter and trade as well as military alliances, and, inevitably, personal bonds were created through friendship and intermarriage. Treaty making was common among Aboriginal peoples prior to the arrival of the Europeans. It was natural for both the previous inhabitants and newcomers to seal their cooperation and alliances in trade and defence through such treaties.

The Royal Proclamation of 1763 was a "defining document" in the relationship of Aboriginal and non-Aboriginal peoples. The preamble made it clear that Aboriginal peoples were entitled to enjoy the use of their lands; land treaties were to be negotiated properly and in public by the Crown and "assemblies of Indians"; and Aboriginal lands could be acquired only through purchase or treaty, by duly appointed representatives of the Crown, based on fair dealing. Indian nations, in short, were "autonomous political entities." But in the 1800s settlement increased dramatically, the economy moved away from the fur trade to timber, minerals, and agriculture, and military alliances no longer were necessary. The relationship also shifted from one of cooperation to European domination and then confinement on reserves, a process driven in part by a perceived need to "civilize" the Aboriginal peoples. Church and government leaders concluded that the goal of civilizing Natives could best be achieved by removing children from their homes at an early age and indoctrinating them during eight or nine years, and sometimes more, of residential schooling far from their families and communities.

The preoccupation with the need to "integrate" Aboriginal peoples into the "mainstream" of Canadian society through policies of assimilation found expression in the 1969 White Paper sponsored by then Indian Affairs Minister Jean Chrétien. The opposition by Aboriginal peoples was almost universal and the paper was withdrawn. And, at about the same time, a series of decisions by the Supreme Court of Canada began to force a re-examination of the rights arising from the spirit and intent of the earlier treaties, informed by the Royal Proclamation.

The commissioners saw, as the starting point for structuring their recommendations, the need for Canada to recognize Aboriginal peoples as nations. There is nothing in Canadian history to change that original status and it is reinforced by the historical treaty process. More fundamentally, Aboriginal peoples continue to be nations today "in their coherence, their distinctiveness and their understanding of themselves." Nor is there any justification for removing their right to self-government, which is now acknowledged and protected by the constitution. These nations should be recognized as a third order of government together with Canada and the provincial or territorial governments. Each should be autonomous in its own sphere to work in harmony and cooperation with the others. Once the status of self-governing nations is re-established, treaties should again be a vehicle for pursuing the ongoing relationship.

The report examines in greater detail the need to "rebuild" Aboriginal nations and the manner in which they can be recognized. It also analyzes some of the problems and flexible alternatives for achieving self-government. To achieve these objectives and give force to a new relationship of partnership to replace paternalism, a new Royal Proclamation should be adopted. While this would reinforce the foundation, companion legislation should be adopted to establish the laws and institutions that would authorize and enable Aboriginal peoples to pursue their own political, social, and economic future.

In addition to re-establishing this basic relationship, the report calls for a process to renegotiate the distribution of lands and resources. This should be governed by the spirit as well as the letter of previous treaties and with fairness to the requirements of Aboriginal peoples. Additional recommendations relate to: economic development; education and training; strengthening the family; health and healing; housing; and culture and language. The commissioners proposed a twenty-year agenda for change that would revitalize many self-reliant Aboriginal nations and reverse the "staggering human and financial cost" that continues to be paid.

The government of the day did not seem impressed: "Prime Minister Jean Chrétien has shown no taste for a more thoroughgoing approach, saying aboriginal issues will be addressed 'not in a grand scheme' but rather 'one solution at a time.'"[56] The government did not establish a First Ministers Conference within six months, as the report recommended, but it did suggest some other initiatives it would pursue. In contrast, Chrétien's successor demonstrated a strong commitment to addressing many of the issues identified by the report.

Then Prime Minister Paul Martin became the driving force behind the Kelowna Accord. Following eighteen months of consultations, a First Ministers Conference was convened in Kelowna, British Columbia, in November 2005. Together with the leaders of five national organizations of Aboriginal peoples, the first ministers undertook to make an immediate and concerted assault on the problems related to education, health, housing, and education. The federal government committed the expenditure of $5.1 billion over the next ten years for this purpose. The Martin government was defeated shortly afterwards and the cooperative goals of this unique agreement still have not been achieved. The larger structural changes that were proposed seem even more beyond

56 Howard Schneider, "Indians Impatient for Canada to Tackle Oldest Cultural Issues" *Washington Post* (18 April 1997). Prime Minister Chrétien might well have been influenced by the scars left from the total rejection of his White Paper, as minister of Indian and northern affairs, in 1969.

reach. However, the federal government is negotiating self-government agreements with interested first nations on an *ad hoc* basis.

The Aboriginal Peoples Commission illustrates the potential of a policy/advisory commission to provide a fundamental response to a fundamental societal problem. It came close to achieving a major breakthrough with the Kelowna Accord. But its grand scale ultimately seemed too overwhelming for political digestion. Its future contribution remains to be seen.

## G. TRUTH AND RECONCILIATION

Truth and reconciliation commissions do not really "fit" under the heading of policy/advisory commissions. Nor are they investigative inquiries of the kind discussed through most of this book. They are included here as a closing topic merely to introduce them to readers who are not already familiar with their role. This is of particular interest because of the creation of the Indian Residential Schools Truth and Reconciliation Commission in Canada in May, 2006, as part of the Indian Residential Schools Settlement Agreement.[57] Before this commission could commence its work, the chairperson and then the remaining two commissioners all resigned. It is a topic of ongoing interest and concern.

Although more than twenty truth and reconciliation commissions have been created throughout the world, the classic example is that established by President Mandela following the overthrow of the apartheid regime in South Africa. The South African Truth and Reconciliation Commission[58] was established under the *Promotion of National Unity and Reconciliation Act, 1995*,[59] The preamble lists the following purposes for this commission:

- to establish as complete a picture as possible of the gross violations of human rights that occurred under the previous regime;

---

57 The entire context of this commission, including the contribution of the Aboriginal Peoples Commission to this settlement, is presented in an excellent article by Professor Bradford W. Morse, "Government Responses to the Indian Residential Schools Settlement in Canada: Implications for Australia" (2008) 12(1) Australian Indigenous Law Review 41.

58 Online: www.doj.gov.za/trc.

59 *Ibid.*

- to determine the fate or whereabouts of the victims of such violations;
- to grant amnesty to persons who make full disclosures;
- to afford victims an opportunity to relate the violations they suffered;
- to grant reparation to victims and rehabilitation and restoration of their human and civil dignity; and
- to make recommendations to prevent such gross violations in future.

This process was bound to be accepted because of the heroic stature of Mandela and the commission's chairman, Archbishop Desmond Tutu in the fight against apartheid. But there were negative repercussions. Criminal acts escaped prosecution, the vast majority of victims were never compensated, and economic hardship continued as a way of life for most of them.

Truth and reconciliation commissions can be viewed as one component of "transitional justice." There is now a considerable volume of scholarly literature on this broader subject and a good introduction is the website of the International Center for Transitional Justice, which has its headquarters in New York and offices throughout the world. It offers this explanation:

> Transitional justice is a response to systematic or widespread violations of human rights. It seeks recognition for victims and to promote possibilities for peace, reconciliation and democracy. Transitional justice is not a special form of justice but justice adapted to societies transforming themselves after a period of pervasive human rights abuse.

There is a frank discussion of the limitations of some individual components and the need for a "holistic" approach. While there is a fundamental belief in universal human rights as the foundation, each society must tailor its approach to transitional justice to its own experience.[60]

In creating the Canadian Truth and Reconciliation Commission (TRC), the Indian Residential Schools Settlement Agreement observed that:

---

60 Online: www.ictj.org. See also Mark Freeman, *Truth Commissions and Procedural Fairness* (New York: Cambridge University Press, 2006). The author, a former senior associate at the Center, provides a comprehensive exposition of the processes and experiences of such commissions throughout the world.

> The truth telling and reconciliation process as part of an overall holistic and comprehensive response to the Indian Residential School legacy is a sincere indication and acknowledgment of the injustices and harms experienced by Aboriginal people and the need for continued healing.

The mandate for this commission is set out in great detail in Schedule "N" to the agreement.[61] The detail far surpasses that of the terms of reference for any commission established under the *Inquiries Act*. The actual order in council merely:

> establishes the Indian Residential Schools Truth and Reconciliation Commission, which is to consist of three Commissioners, including one Chairperson, to be appointed by the Governor in Council, to hold office during good behaviour for a term of five years . . .

It then specifies that the mandate is to be that set out in Schedule "N" to the agreement.

Unlike the situation in South Africa, at least the Aboriginal victims in Canada are being compensated. But also the design of the Canadian commission is entirely "victim-centred." The mandate stresses acknowledgment, bearing witness, promoting awareness, establishing the historical record ("and the ongoing legacy"), and commemorating both the former students and their families as victims. The mandate includes "former school employees" and "religious entities" in the groups between whom reconciliation may occur. But formal hearings, a public inquiry, or a formal legal process are expressly prohibited. No new findings of misconduct are to be made. There are no powers to compel testimony and any participation in the commission is "entirely voluntary." The issue of amnesty does not even arise. Instead, there will be community events and opportunities for victims to tell their stories in an informal setting.

The order in council took effect on 1 June 2008, as did the appointment of the three commissioners. Justice Harry LaForme, of the Ontario Court of Appeal, was selected as chairperson. A distinguished jurist, he had served as a judge of the Superior Court for ten years before going to the Court of Appeal in 2004 as Canada's first Aboriginal appellate judge. He practised Aboriginal law prior to becoming a judge and received many honours from Aboriginal communities. The other two commissioners also were highly qualified for the task. Claudette Dumont-Smith

---

61 See online: www.trc-cvr.ca.

had been involved in the Aboriginal health field since 1974. She held positions with organizations related to domestic violence, child care, and community health and has academic and professional qualifications in nursing and public administration. Jane Morley is a lawyer who had served as Child and Youth Officer for British Columbia where she collaborated with Aboriginal organizations to address problems of child abuse and suicide. On the commission's website, she described herself as "a lawyer, a facilitator, a mediator, an arbitrator and a public policy advisor." The three commissioners had all of the right qualifications.

On 20 October, less than five months after commencing operations, chairperson LaForme abruptly resigned. His letter of resignation spoke of an "incurable problem" in that he had lost confidence in his two colleagues:

> "The two commissioners are unprepared to accept that the structure of the Commission requires that the TRC's course is to be charted, and its objectives are to be shaped, ultimately through the authority and leadership of its chair," Justice LaForme said. "Challenging the reality that they were appointed as providers of advice and assistance to the chair, the two have chosen to compete for control of the commission by insisting that it is to be run on the basis of simply majority rule. They even retained legal counsel to formally demand that I change the structure of the Commission by agreeing to their majority rule."[62]

Of course, it is ideal if commissioners can work out a consensus and speak as one voice. But, as we have seen, the *Interpretation Act* dictates that differences are to be resolved in favour of the majority, and the chairperson has the same number of votes as any other member.[63] Justice LaForme may well have been misled by assurances given to him that it would be him and his "vision that would chart, lead and direct the course" of this important mission. In a speech scheduled long before his resignation but given three weeks afterwards, he drew attention to the selection criteria for his appointment, namely, to:

> Provide leadership; hold responsibility for the integrity of the commission and authorship of the report; lead and promote public awareness . . . ;

62 Cristin Schmitz, "Judge Resigns from Truth Commission, Slams Colleagues" *The Lawyers Weekly* (31 October 2008).

63 Above notes 31 & 32.

> exercise leadership internally and externally; set strategy, objectives and direction and supervise and direct the work of the commissioners.[64]

In contrast, he pointed out the commissioners would be expected to "support the leadership of the chair."[65]

In retrospect, Justice LaForme did not seem to anticipate the potentially political environment to which he was being exposed. And he did not anticipate that his high aspirations for this commission and his strong commitment to the vision of the Aboriginal Peoples Commission (including the plight of the victims) were not enough. All of that, together with the selection committee criteria, was no match for the legal hurdle of the *Interpretation Act* that a simple majority prevails. The mandate could have been structured differently. It could have provided that the actual decisions would be taken solely by the chairperson. That would leave no room for "interpretation." But there is nothing in Schedule "N" that would give complete authority to the chairperson.

The full nature of this misunderstanding is not clear but an underlying issue appeared to be the role of the Assembly of First Nations (AFN) and its leader, Phil Fontaine. Fontaine showed great political leadership in resolving the compensation issues and as a catalyst for the Kelowna Accord. In his first speech after being appointed as chairperson, Justice LaForme said:

> National Chief Phil Fontaine, my Friend, all I can say to you is well done. You have risen above your childhood experiences and have chosen to avoid the corrosive acid of hate. As such you have set yourself, your people and all Canadians upon the life-affirming path of truth, healing and reconciliation.[66]

On the same day, Chief Fontaine said of Justice LaForme:

> Not only is he a proud First Nations citizen, he is an outstanding jurist and compassionate and understanding person . . . [H]e will bring the

64 Joe Friesen, LaForme Quit Schools Commission to Satisfy 'Moral Code'" *Globe and Mail* (14 November 2008).

65 *Ibid.*

66 Speech by Justice Harry S. LaForme on his appointment (28 April 2008), online: www.trc-cvr.ca/pdfs/SpeechbyJusticeHarryE.pdf.

> grace and compassion required in the truth commission's work so necessary for healing to begin.[67]

But tensions soon appeared, and there was speculation that LaForme had concerns about the role the AFN might expect to play in the process. In September, LaForme declined an invitation for the commissioners to meet with the AFN and asked his colleagues to do the same. They disregarded him.[68]

Chairperson LaForme had concerns abut the commission's independence from the outset. In his inaugural speech, referred to above, he said: "Let us be clear at the outset: The Commission will operate independent from Government, the Church and First Nations and other Canadians." He took great pains to elaborate on the foundation for that independence and the need to protect it in subsequent speeches.[69] But his colleagues did not share his concerns. Commissioner Morley stressed the nature of this commission's mandate, which, in her view, provided a different context for the notion of "independence":

> We are not a court of law or a public inquiry. Part of our role is to facilitate others to engage in reconciliation. We can only do that if we work with partners and that includes the AFN, the churches and the government, the parties to the settlement agreement. We will need to meet with them separately and to listen to what they have to say. The impartiality that is required when one is adjudicating is not applicable to this process. We are told by our mandate to put the survivors at the centre of our process—that means to be partial towards them.[70]

This is understandable when viewing the features of the mandate described above. Schedule "N," adopted by the order in council, takes great pains to preclude any formality or adversarial hearings or "judicialization" that would require formal independence.

But Justice LaForme may have been concerned about a broader kind of independence, related to the general direction the commission would

---

67 Maritas S. Sison, "Justice LaForme Chosen to Chair Truth and Reconciliation Commission" *Anglican Journal* (28 April 2008).

68 Kevin Libin, "Chairman's Exit Leaves Panel in Disarray" *National Post* (28 October 2008).

69 Speeches delivered 15 and 23 July 2008, the latter online: www.trc-cvr.ca/pdfs.

70 Above note 62.

take. In explaining his resignation, he contrasted the emphasis of his colleagues on "truth" with the goal of "reconciliation." They responded that both were important.

Former Supreme Court justice and commissioner Frank Iacobucci was retained to meet with the parties and attempt to agree on a process to find a new chairperson.[71] However, in January 2009, the remaining two commissioners also resigned. This will allow the new commissioners to distance themselves from the previous controversy and start afresh. A six-person selection committee was established, including Fontaine and chaired by Iacobucci.[72] A call was issued for applications or nominations by 20 March 2009, for a chairperson and two commissioners.

On 10 June 2009, just over a year after the commission was created, the new commissioners were announced by Indian Affairs Minister Chuck Strahl. The commission will be chaired by Manitoba Queen's Bench Justice Murray Sinclair. He was the co-commissioner of the Aboriginal Justice Inquiry[73] established by the government of Manitoba in 1988. The commissioners are Alberta lawyer and former MP Chief Wilton Littlechild, and Marie Wilson, a former CBC journalist and manager with the government of the Northwest Territories and Nunavut.[74]

---

71 Norma Greenaway, "Iacobucci to Help Get Commission Back on Track" *National Post* (6 November 2008).

72 Bill Curry, "Two Remaining Truth and Reconciliation Commissioners Resign" *Globe and Mail* (9 April 2009).

73 Public Inquiry into the Administration of Justice and Aboriginal People.

74 Indian Residential Schools Truth and Reconciliation Commission, News Release, "Appointment of New Chairperson and Commissioners of the Indian Residential Schools Truth and Reconciliation Commission" (10 June 2009).

# *Table of Cases*

# Index

# *About the Author*

**Ed Ratushny**, Q.C., B.A., LL.B. (Sask.), LL.M. (Lond.), S.J.D. (Mich.), is a professor emeritus of the Faculty of Law, University of Ottawa. His career as a law professor and legal author has been complemented by extensive professional experience in the field of public law. He served as the first special advisor on judicial affairs to the Canadian minister of justice and is frequently retained by the Canadian Judicial Council on judicial conduct matters. He has acted often as an arbitrator and has served as an advisor and as counsel to government ministers, departments, tribunals, and agencies in diverse fields such as human rights, labour, environmental, transportation, competition, immigration, refugee, military, and criminal law.

Professor Ratushny's contributions to law and to Canadian society have been recognized by his appointments to the Order of Canada and the Order of Ontario, as well as through his Honorary Doctor of Laws from the Law Society of Upper Canada. He received the Justice Award from the Canadian Institute for the Administration of Justice "as a mark of distinction and exceptional achievement," and the first annual CCAT Medal presented by the Council of Canadian Administrative Tribunals for his "outstanding contribution to the Canadian Administrative Justice System."

He continues to be a low-scoring left winger and a student of jazz saxophone.